BELIEF AND ETHICS

BELIEF AND ETHICS

Essays in Ethics, the Human Sciences, and Ministry in Honor of W. Alvin Pitcher

edited by

W. Widick Schroeder and Gibson Winter

C
S
S
R

Center for the Scientific Study of Religion

Chicago, Illinois

STUDIES IN RELIGION AND SOCIETY

Center for the Scientific Study of Religion

For a complete list of the publications in the
series, see the back of the book.

Center for the Scientific Study of Religion
5757 University Avenue
Chicago, Illinois 60637

I S B N: 0-913348-15-5

Library of Congress Catalog Card Number: 77-002057

PREFACE

The essays in this volume, written to honor Alvin Pitcher upon his retirement from the Divinity School of the University of Chicago, reflect the broad development of the field of Ethics and Society during the past quarter of a century. The Ethics and Society field emerged as an element of a 1949 Curriculum Revision of the Federation of Theological Schools and continued through the various institutional and curricular changes of the next decades.

In the American experience, "Applied Christianity" emerged in many theological schools during the twentieth century, and the Ethics and Society field was a part of this larger tradition. However, from the outset, work in this discipline at the Divinity School was particularly concerned with the place of empirical studies and the developing human sciences in theological, ethical, and social institutional research.

In a very broad sense, this work has been influenced both by a persistent interest in structural issues inherent in alternative understandings of the relation of theology and the social sciences and by a desire to respond to and to shape the crucial events affecting the broader society. Although Alvin Pitcher himself never lost sight of these dual interests, one or the other received greater emphasis at various times during his career at the Divinity School. These concerns were expressed in different ways over the years and are reflected in the work represented in this volume.

In the fifties and early sixties doctoral candidates in Ethics and Society were required to undertake an empirical field study. In this process, they were challenged to deal with major methodological problems and to seek to integrate empirical and ethical research. Some students based their theses on their field studies, but many sought to articulate the relations between empirical and theological dimensions in their dissertations. At times the field study outran other elements of the doctoral program. In such instances, students found themselves deeply enmeshed in the problems of sophisticated empirical research. For the most part, however, some attempt was made to maintain a balance of empirical, ethical, and theological aspects of the research.

If we set this period of inquiry in the fuller context of American social and cultural life, we realize that the field of Ethics and Society was emerging in the era of the "exploding metropolis" and of growing awareness of the manifold problems of metropolitan organization. The optimism with which America emerged from the Second World War -- the belief that its technical and organizational problems were open to rational solution -- was being challenged on many fronts, and there was increasing consciousness of the racial and social class problems of the inner cities.

The ethical and practical problems of American society and
its urban form burst on the scene in the sixties. Needless to say,
these problems had been developing over many decades and even centuries, but a new consciousness of their character and a new urgency
to resolve them released an explosive dynamic on the American scene.
     The racial question, placed on new ground by the Supreme
Court school desegregation decision of 1954, now came center stage.
By the mid-sixties the Viet Nam involvement was spreading, and soon
the peace movement, the civil rights movement, and the student rebellion coalesced in a confrontation with the policies of the government and much of the "establishment." Many people became conscious
of America's social and cultural problems in this period, but most
felt the problems could be resolved by a combination of economic
expansion and a proper redistribution of wealth and/or political
power.
     A very substantial majority of the faculty and students
in Ethics and Society in the Divinity School shared the mood and
spirit of the challengers of the "establishment," but some were more
radical in their critiques than others. This consciousness and mood
found its expression in the Divinity School and the field of Ethics
and Society in two ways. First, many faculty and students expressed
an increasing concern for praxis and specifically for cultivation
of a professional ministry in which theological vision and an understanding of social forces could be integrated in ministerial practice.
In this instance, local factors also contributed to these interests,
for in the aftermath of the highly regrettable dissolution of the
Federation of Theological Schools (the University of Chicago Divinity
School, the Chicago Theological Seminary, Disciples Divinity House,
and Meadville Theological School) which had constituted the community of theological inquiry on the South Side of Chicago, the
Divinity School was developing an independent program of professional
theological education.
     Second, many faculty and students in Ethics and Society
became practically involved in the Freedom Movement, the Urban
Training Center (an ecumenically sponsored Chicago-based training
center designed to equip clergy to deal more adequately with urban
problems), and various other voluntary movements for social transformation. During this period much of Alvin Pitcher's energies were
expended in the movement for racial justice, and much of the field's
research was concentrated on problems of social change.
     Thus, during the sixties the Ethics and Society faculty
and students were deeply involved in an emerging Doctor of Ministry
program, an experiment in professional ministry which was to have
broad implications for American theological education, and in practical efforts to transform American social and political life. The
concerns of this period are reflected in some of the contributions
to this volume.
     It is a commonplace that the seventies reflect a reassertion
of more conservative values and a waning of social activism among
the new generation and the churches. Many reasons have been given
for this situation, not the least being the end of the Viet Nam War,
the traumatic shock of some of the confrontations which took place
in the late sixties and early seventies, and the shifting age

structure of the American population. Furthermore, the residual
costs of the Viet Nam struggle and the OPEC oil cartel have contributed to inflationary forces in the economy and to a reduction
in funds in the voluntary sector. Institutions of higher learning,
particularly private ones, are feeling the dual impact of inflation
and the anticipation of the effects of a forthcoming decrease in
college age population. Finally, many are questioning the guiding
visions informing social activists. Whatever the weights of these
various factors, diminution of social action concerns in institutions
in the private sector is indisputable.
     The confrontations of the sixties had an important impact
on most faculty and many students in Ethics and Society. These
experiences persuaded many of the field's members that the social,
economic, and political problems facing both Western society and
the entire planet were deeper and more serious than they had previously thought. Many of them felt the spread of ecological problems illustrated this complexity, for they felt each step to promote
economic development was threatening the environment, and each
attempt to curtail development seemed to threaten employment and
productivity.
     The new mood of the seventies has been reflected in at
least two principal ways in the recent work in Ethics and Society.
First, institutional retrenchment was reflected in a turn by the
Divinity School away from a predominant interest in the integration
of theological, ethical, and professional ministerial concerns and
toward a much closer relation with humanistic and historical studies
in other parts of the University. (This trend is a national phenomenon, occurring in other university-based divinity schools.)
     Second, faculty and students in Ethics and Society be-
came increasingly concerned with theological interpretations of the
cultural problems precipitated by high technology and with practical
issues related to ecology, energy, and economic organization.
     In general, this recent period has seen an attempt to in-
tegrate concerns for distribution of power and goods in the society
with concerns for transformation of the character and content of
American society. As Alvin Pitcher sometimes expressed it, the
concern was not only for how things were distributed but also for
what was to be distributed.
     In one sense, this new era has been a more radical and
difficult period for research in Ethics and Society, for many members
of the field have felt the basic issue was the content of Western
life and its impact on the world. Moreover, because of institutional
retrenchment, this new inquiry was being pursued with little focus
on practical involvement. Nevertheless, as can be seen from some of
the essays emerging from this period and from others published in a
previous monograph, *Belonging and Alienation*, in many ways this has
been a most creative period in the Ethics and Society field.
     Alvin Pitcher's retirement marks the end of a long era of
work in Ethics and Society. It would be difficult, if not impossible,
at such close quarters to evaluate the significance of the research
that has marked its different phases. Inquiries focused on religious institutions, voluntary associations, urban questions, methodological problems, and the broader questions of culture have evolved

in the context of the ongoing life of American society. In the background of these inquiries has been a continuing concern with philosophical and theological interests, a concern which Alvin Pitcher encouraged throughout his career. Here lie many of the most promising and most difficult tasks confronting the field, for integrative work in theology, ethics, and the human sciences will continue to be a major focus and a major contribution of the field to religious social ethics.

Whether such work can be pursued significantly in relative isolation from the praxis of the churches and other institutions in the voluntary sector remains to be seen. For many in Ethics and Society one of the obvious dangers of institutional retrenchment is that theological work may too readily become a means for educational and other institutions to legitimate the *status quo* at the very time when some -- including many participants in the Ethics and Society field -- believe a critical appraisal is most needed. The presence of the Ethics and Society field in the Divinity School and the presence of comparable fields in the Chicago Cluster of Theological Schools will assure that the issues will be kept alive in this community of theological inquiry.

W. Widick Schroeder
Gibson Winter

IN APPRECIATION

We want to thank especially four persons whose careful work on this volume went far beyond the call of duty: Jean Block, whose skillful editing brought a measure of stylistic commonality and consistency to the several essays; Carol Eck, whose careful proof reading and attention to the endless details involved in co-ordinating communication between the editors and the contributors greatly facilitated the editorial process; Josephine Hawkins, whose meticulous preparation of camera-ready copy minimized errors and enhanced the appearance of the volume; and Corrine Niedenthal, whose artistic sensitivity enabled her to create the dust jacket design.

W.W.S.
G.W.

TABLE OF CONTENTS

BELIEF AND ETHICS

INTRODUCTION

SEARCH FOR *KOINONIA* AND SOCIAL JUSTICE
— A GLIMPSE OF W. ALVIN PITCHER:
ALUMNUS, COLLEAGUE AND FRIEND —

by
Joseph M. Kitagawa

The retirement of William Alvin Pitcher from the University of Chicago in 1978 provides a fitting occasion for friends, colleagues, students and alumni to consider and celebrate the many dimensions of his life and work in our company. There have been many turning points in the professional life of this man, yet each one has redounded to the good of those institutions and concerns which have been foremost in his attention and affection throughout the years--the church, the university and those voluntary associations which involve their members with questions of the quality of human community and the structures of justice in the social order. We trust that retirement is one more such significant turning point for Alvin Pitcher, and we can anticipate with good hope the benefits of a redirection of his energies now to be freed from some of the burdens of professional academic life.

My welcome task in this volume is to review from a perspective of colleagueship and friendship, which now approaches thirty years, a few of the events and contributions of this man's professional life. I find throughout a remarkable consistency of interest and of purpose, which I propose to characterize as a search for *koinonia* and social justice.

I first met Al Pitcher when we were both engaged in graduate studies in Swift Hall in the late 1940's. It was the immediate postwar period, when a large number of older married students, many of whom were veterans, were enrolled at the University of Chicago. On the whole, they were an unusually serious group of students. Some of the theological students and their families lived in the 5800 Maryland Avenue student apartments, while others occupied the so-called GI barracks across from Rockefeller Chapel, where Woodward Court now stands. Swift Hall was then the academic center of the Federated Theological Schools of the University of Chicago, whose faculty included such distinguished mentors as Ernest Cadman "Pomp" Cadwell, who served as President of the University of Chicago, Amos Wilder, J. Coert Rylaarsdam, Wilhelm Pauck, Charles Hartshorne, Bernard Meland, Daniel Day Williams, Bernard Loomer, Sidney Mead, James Hastings Nichols and Joachim Wach. In addition, the newly created field of Ethics and Society was led by James Luther Adams, Samuel Kincheloe, Victor Obenhaus and John B. Thompson, and it was to this area of interest that Pitcher's talents were drawn.

In those days all students were enrolled in the common curriculum of the Federated Theological Faculty. While various

degree programs were offered, the foundation of the curriculum was clearly the "common core courses" which were completed only by passing a battery of seven three-hour comprehensive examinations. We students studied madly to prove ourselves competent for further advanced studies by obtaining at least a "B" on the fateful "comps." Occasionally, some of the profs asked the more mature graduate students among us to make classroom presentations, and the students were soon aware and impressed by the fact that James Luther Adams often called upon Mr. Pitcher to take over his classes whenever he was out of town. By that time Mr. Pitcher had already taught for several years at Denison University before returning to Chicago for his doctoral studies. I had heard of him from several students who were impressed by his orderly and methodical classroom presentations; a few credited him for having helped them pass the ES comp.
        In 1952, I welcomed him as a neighbor when he joined the faculty and was assigned to an office next to mine on the fourth floor of Swift Hall. From that year until I moved out of the fourth floor in 1970, I had many opportunities to get to know him better, often sharing sandwiches either in his office or mine. Mr. Pitcher was not inclined to engage in irrelevant chit chat; he was eager to talk about serious scholarly subjects or discuss social issues which concerned him deeply. I learned that he had written his D.B. thesis on "The Religious Problem of Community in Contemporary Thought," and that he was in the midst of working on his Ph.D. thesis entitled "Ethics in the Theology of Paul Tillich and Emil Brunner: A Study in the Nature of Protestant Ethics." From our conversation, I learned a great deal about the thought patterns of Tillich, Brunner, and Richard McKeon. At his urging I bought a copy of Brunner's *Justice and Social Order* so I could understand Al Pitcher's theological concern. He also helped me organize my course on "Ethics of World Religions," and even gave introductory lectures in my classes on how to study ethical systems. I was impressed by his singlemindedness and his commitment to whatever issues he believed to be important, however large or small. He had a pastoral sense in dealing with students. I also remember his thoughtful consideration for the first black faculty secretary in making her feel at home in Swift Hall.
        Through our casual conversations I came to know various phases of his academic and religious pilgrimage. Of his childhood he talked very little except that he was born in Downers Grove and had spent uneventful early years as a Midwestern youth. He spoke more animatedly about his student days (B.S., 1934 and D.B., 1939) at the University of Chicago in the 1930's. It was the heyday of Robert Maynard Hutchins and the Great Books, and the University had a gallaxy of inspiring, though controversial figures on its faculty, including Rex Tugwell, Charles Merriam, Mortimer Adler, W.I. Thomas, Paul Douglas, and a then young philosopher, Richard P. McKeon, who exercised a decisive influence upon Alvin Pitcher. The Divinity School also had an exciting atmosphere with John T. McNeill, William Warren Sweet, Edward Scribner Ames, Shailer Matthews, Shirley Jackson Case, Edgar Goodspeed, Henry Nelson Wieman, and Ralph Marcus as members of its faculty. Understandably, Mr. Pitcher and his contemporaries, including Bernard M. Loomer, Sidney E. Mead, Massey

Shepherd, and William N. Hawley, were greatly stimulated by the
faculty as well as by their fellow students. I gathered also that
Mr. Pitcher's experience in the 1930's was greatly enriched by his
association with Dean Charles Gilkey of Rockefeller Memorial Chapel
where he served as Assistant to the Dean from 1935 to 1940.   In
fact, one of Mr. Pitcher's sons was named after Charles Gilkey.
          After spending the summer of 1940 as Associate Director
of the Quaker Work Camp, Mr. Pitcher became the Assistant Minister
at Amherst Community Church, Snyder, New York, where he was ordained.
He also served as Instructor in Science and Head of Park School in
Buffalo, 1942-44.   In 1944, he accepted the position as Associate
Professor of Religion and Director of the Christian Emphasis Program
at Denison University, historically a Baptist institution, which
was the alma mater of William Rainey Harper, the first President of
the University of Chicago.   Mr. Pitcher's years at Denison were re-
warding despite difficulties and problems caused by World War II.
Later, and quite accidentally, I learned from a Japanese-American
friend, who during the war had found a refuge at Denison from one
of the "relocation camps," that she owed much to Mr. Pitcher for
making her feel like a human being after her experience in the camp.
While at Denison he joined the Baptist Church and his ordination
was officially accepted by the Ohio Baptist Convention.   Mr. Pitcher
left Denison in 1949.   Since 1935, he had been heavily influenced
by the theology of his mentor, Henry Nelson Wieman.   But while at
Denison, Mr. Pitcher's theological positions were challenged by
students of Reinhold Niebuhr.   In order to systematically reappraise
his theology, he returned to Chicago to carefully study the works
of Paul Tillich and Reinhold Niebuhr.   Tillich's theological formulations and Niebuhr's convictions with regard to social action made
a lasting impact,and Mr. Pitcher was asked to join the Federated
Theological Faculty after three years of graduate work.
          As a junior faculty member living in Hyde Park with wife
and four young children, Hugh, Betsy, Charles, and Catherine, life
was not easy for the Pitchers.   He quickly gained a reputation as
a hard worker and an effective teacher.   He was also active in the
Hyde Park Baptist Church.   For example, he served as the chairman
of the Call Committee, and in that capacity he was instrumental in
bringing the Reverend E. Spencer Parsons to serve as the Senior
Minister.   He also served as chairman of the Church's special committee on Community Outreach.   I remember once I was asked by Mr.
Pitcher to speak to an adult group of the Church on Christian World
Mission.   He was as embarrassed as I was frustrated during the
following discussion period when a leading layman vocally insisted
that being a Christian need make no difference in attitude or behavior if one is a businessman trying to make profit out of business
deals in foreign countries!   Besides his participation in the local
congregation, Mr. Pitcher took active part in the affairs of the
Chicago Church Federation, first as chairman of the Research Unit,
and then as chairman of the Department of Christian Citizenship.
He was also involved in the Preparatory Study Commission on "Theological and Moral Considerations in International Affairs" for the
Fifth World Order Study Conference.   In the Baptist circles, he was
asked to chair the study commission on "The Gospel and the Social

and Political Order" of the American Baptist Theological Conference
(1954), the Midwest Theological Conference of American Baptists
(1956), and the Committee on Social Concern of the Chicago Baptist
Association (1960-62). The National Council of Churches also involved him as Chairman of the Commission of Concentrations and Aggre-
gations in Industry--Department of Church and Economic Life.
      The early 1950's were not easy times for junior members
of the Federated Theological Faculty. We did not know what was
going on in high places, but we sensed that there were serious disagreements among the administrators as well as among boards of
trustees of member institutions--Chicago Theological Seminary,
Meadville Theological School, Disciples Divinity House, and the
Divinity School of the University--concerning policies, curriculum,
and the overall leadership. Bernard M. Loomer, Dean of the Divinity
School and Acting Dean of the Federated Theological Faculty, sensing
a lack of support within the Federation and in the University leadership, resigned, and Seward Hiltner became the Acting Dean. After
Hiltner, Thomas Filbey, then Assistant to the Chancellor, stepped
in as the Acting Dean until the appointment of Jerald C. Brauer as
the first Dean of the Federated Theological Faculty in 1955. Meanwhile numerous meetings of the Faculty were held, but very little
was accomplished. During all of this, junior members of the Faculty
were kept in the dark. The whole atmosphere was unsettling even
before the appointment of the new Dean of the Federated Theological
Faculty. The departure of senior professors--Wilhelm Pauck for
Union Theological Seminary in 1953, followed by Daniel Day Williams
also for Union in 1954, Amos Wilder and James Luther Adams for
Harvard in 1954 and 1956, respectively--added more uncertainty to
the future of the Federated Theological Faculty. Mr. Adams' resignation was especially hard on the Ethics program, and few understood or appreciated the heavy burden Mr. Pitcher carried during
those difficult years.[1] Parenthetically, I also lost my senior
colleague, Joachim Wach, by his untimely death in 1955. Mr. Pitcher
and I were saddled with heavy responsibilities for teaching, ad-
vising, and fulfilling committee assignments.[2] Fortunately, Gibson
Winter joined the Faculty in 1956, followed by Mircea Eliade in
1957.
      In spite of the dedicated efforts of the new Dean, Jerald
C. Brauer, by the year 1958 the seams of the Federated Theological
Faculty were beginning to come apart. With the departure of three
of the four deans of the member schools by 1960, we sensed that the
Federation was in real trouble. The departures of Seward Hiltner
and James Hastings Nichols to Princeton Theological Seminary and
Jaroslav Pelikan to Yale did not help the cause. Mr. Pitcher himself was absent for one year, 1962-63, in Tübingen, Germany, but
upon his return was immediately caught up in the tortuous process
of rebuilding the faculty and the curriculum after de-federation.
Needless to say, all of this had demoralizing effects on many faculty and students in the Divinity School, and Mr. Pitcher's pastoral
instincts and steady purposefulness were appreciated highly. The
Ethics and Society field was immediately strengthened with the
appointment of Clark Kucheman as a junior colleague, replacing

Widick Schroeder who joined the faculty of Chicago Theological Seminary.

Even as the Divinity School was much occupied with its internal problems, the early 1960's were marked by a new mood in American society. In this situation, Mr. Pitcher was persuaded that certain social ethical issues were so crucial that practical action should take primacy over isolated "academic" work. Thus, he began to give more of his time and energy to the "freedom movement" as it was then emerging in the northern cities of the land. He asked for and received one-half time leave of absence from the University in 1968-69 to assume directorship of a new program at the Urban Training Center in Chicago, involving a study of white racism and the relations to that problem. Before this time he served as Administrative Assistant to the Director of the Coordinating Council of Community Organizations in Chicago (CCCO), in which position he was instrumental in bringing to Chicago the forces of the Southern Christian Leadership Conference to work under the umbrella of CCCO. He thus became the colleague of the late Dr. Martin Luther King, Jr., the Reverend Andrew Young (now United States Ambassador to the United Nations), and a new young leader in the "movement," Jesse Jackson. His efforts in this activity were immeasurably assisted, and his responsibilities at the Divinity School were shared, by the appointment of another young colleague, Alan Anderson, as Instructor in Ethics and Society in 1965. Mr. Pitcher's association with the leadership of a new organization, Operation Breadbasket, included his being appointed to its Steering Committee and Executive Committee, a post in which he has shifted his emphasis from active participation in social action to further reflection on the religious substance in our culture and the type of knowledge required to achieve the social good.

* * * *

In retrospect, one is struck by an amazing consistency with which Mr. Pitcher has lived, worked, and thought. Characteristically, he has never viewed his own life in career terms. If he had done so, he would have been better off personally. No doubt his multi-dimensional activities are such that his life may be viewed from various perspectives. From my limited standpoint, I am inclined to believe that he has been motivated by a lifelong search for "koinonia" and "social justice," both of which have interpenetrated in his mind. Thus, he states:

> We are at the end of the Protestant era. This proposition underlies my thought and action. Ever since I read Paul Tillich's profound analysis in "The World Situation" . . . , I have found events and theories fit together when viewed from this perspective. The encounter of an end of course is a beginning. A second proposition that we must formulate the law for our day, therefore, provides a positive thrust.[3]

He goes on to explain that in Western culture the Protestant era rejected the absolutizing of wisdom, goodness, and power in church, state, economic life, and education. This rejection—the "no"—was embodied in freedom of conscience, democratic political institutions,

laissez-faire economics, etc. The "no" in turn became absolutized
without due recognition of the "yes" (the catholic substance) which
had informed culture. The basic problem for Mr. Pitcher was the
issue of the religious (catholic) substance of the culture of our
common life--the question of the "what." His starting point was
Tillich's analysis of our religious and cultural situation.
        According to Mr. Pitcher's theological position, the
whole is the most real and not the parts. To him, the real is a
whole apprehended in and through the phenomena of experience either
through reason or through revelation. The whole may be static or
dynamic, however. In dealing with this issue, most Protestant
theologians accept a "dynamic ontology" in which form and dynamics
are held in some tension. Mr. Pitcher himself assumes a dynamic
ontology à la Tillich as the basis for social and ethical prescriptions. Unlike those who posit the situational character of Christian ethics and who find it difficult to apprehend something beyond a certain disposition as the bench mark of Christian ethics,
Mr. Pitcher approached the "something beyond" in two ways. In his
own words:

> First, if God acts in history in his freedom to bring about fulfill-
> ment, one should be able to find guiding images both in the events
> responded to especially as his action, and in the resulting promul-
> gated law or imperatives for action set forth repeatedly in the life
> of the church. Secondly, I have been trying to determine which
> kinds of analyses of the situation (social science) are appropriate
> and therefore useful in the decision-making process.[4]

Understandably, his lifelong struggle has been how to relate the
first and the second--ecclesiology and the social scientific anal-
ysis--beyond the level of generalities.
        Probably the most helpful way to understand Mr. Pitcher's
thought, at least for me, is to view the various phases of his
work as a spiral. That is to say, while his thought appears circular in that he touches on the same issues over and over again,
each time his thought reaches a higher plane. For instance, he has
maintained his early concern for the religious problems of community, but his later reflections on the subject indicate that he
has made several advances since the time when he wrote his D.B. dissertation.[5] Similarly, what he thought was the nature of Protestant
ethics, derived from the study of the works of Tillich and Brunner
(his Ph.D. thesis), has remained central to his thought, although
here again Mr. Pitcher has made several spiral turns upward since
the early 1950's.
        In this connection, I have always believed (rightly or
wrongly) that when Mr. Pitcher talks about social sciences he really
means the philosophy of social sciences. And, following Richard
McKeon, Mr. Pitcher operates with the assumption that there are
definite numbers of modes of fundamental thought underlying social
scientific descriptions of the situation. On this issue, Mr.
Pitcher's approach, according to J. Ronald Engel,

is consistently to move from different specific modes of social
analysis of a particular social problem to different modes of
thought generally, to different modes of prescriptions implied,
which in turn imply different presuppositions about the nature of
the world and man, which in turn imply different modes of thinking
about *what* is the ultimate good.6

It should be noted that Mr. Pitcher is primarily interested in
finding out what social sciences may contribute to our understanding of the situation in which "good action" can occur, and to that
extent he acknowledges that social sciences can legitimately contribute to defining the character of good action itself. When the
social sciences attempt to prescribe fundamental action, however,
he believes that social sciences are developing their own normative
presuppositions. Such presuppositions should be argued at the explicit normative level.

His concern for careful analysis of the presuppositions
of social sciences is motivated by his effort to articulate the
normative positions implicit in social policy--or its lack thereof.
He is alarmed by the lack of awareness of this question as well as
the lack of substance in the social policies of churches and church-
related organizations and by American society and government. Thus,
it is his mission to advocate the necessity of examining, articulating, or developing a new "catholic" substance inherent in social
issues which confront the church, society, and the state. Let us
see how he has dealt with issues, particularly those of the American
business ethics, U.S. foreign policy, racial issues in America, and
the energy crisis.

* * * *

In his article on "The American Business Creed,"7 Mr.
Pitcher sets forth his own presupposition as well as analysis of
the main thrusts of the problem. At the outset, he states that in
many of its elements the American business creed is in conflict
with economic fact and logic as well as with some rather widely
accepted imperatives of the Christian faith. This leads to the
next observation that the business executive, who invariably becomes subject to stresses and strains, is inclined either to reject
the faith or to develop the kind of Christian faith that will conform to the business creed.

In order to support his analysis, Mr. Pitcher first summarizes the content of the business creed and then depicts "the
values of good society" according to this creed: freedom, honesty,
sobriety, prudence, productivity without much concern for the nature
of the product, progress defined as an increase in the standard of
living, competition, equal opportunity, rewards distributed to
everybody (American) on the basis of his contribution, etc. Secondly,
by interpreting the business creed as "ideology," Mr. Pitcher anal-
yzes the creed's correspondence or lack of correspondence to economic
reality. In this enterprise, he contrasts the ideological stances
of the creed and the social scientific analyses regarding such items
as the functions and rewards of ownership, the role and the motivations of the business executive, the relations between business
and labor, the relations between the businessman and his customers,
the functioning of the competitive system, the place of government

in a business economy, and the problem of economic fluctuations.
He points out that there are logical problems involved in the
creed's attempt to combine (1) the correspondence of the system to
the fundamental laws of human nature and (2) the historical uniqueness of the American system. Thirdly, he describes how the American business creed when understood as a set of beliefs, doctrines,
and symbols, is expected to help the businessman do what he is required to do to fulfill his role as a businessman. The fact that
the creed displays unswerving loyalty to the American business
system and to free enterprise is explained by Mr. Pitcher in terms
of the need for solidarity among businessmen. Fourthly, in discussing the significance of the business creed for the churches,
he advocates that it is necessary to deal with fundamental Christian doctrines and with the implications of the Christian faith for
economic life. He believes that a Christian should achieve (1) a
facing of the reality of the businessman's situation by both himself and his minister and (2) a sophistication in the presentation
of the Gospel that takes into account the depth of the demonic
forces in a culture and the impossibility of any easy, simple
Christian answer. Lastly, Mr. Pitcher examines the so-called
"Christian" interpretation of economic life, as exemplified by
Howard Kershner's *God, Gold and Government*, and finds its thrust
very similar to that of the business creed.
        Mr. Pitcher demonstrated his analytical sense, sorting
out issues and examining the presuppositions that are uncritically
accepted by the American business creed as much as by the "Christian" interpreters of American economic life. He is interested in
the problem of the American business creed, because it provides an
illustration of the way in which an understanding of the social
situation helps us to understand the problems of anyone who performs the role. Assuming that the American business creed is in
part a response to personality needs, created by a particular
social situation, Mr. Pitcher raises a series of pertinent questions without attempting to answer them. He asks:

> Do we not have to explore the extent to which Christian symbols are
> appropriated more because of their function in relieving strain than
> because of their truth? Do we not have to ask further than we have
> how ideas meaning one thing to the minister mean something else to
> the man in the pew? . . . Is it not possible that many of those to
> whom we minister are almost required by the pressures of their situ-
> ations to refuse to accept the "truth of the faith?" Can we minister
> to them effectively as long as their situation remains unchanged?[8]

Obviously, Mr. Pitcher was determined to resolve some of these and
other questions as we shall see presently.
                          * * * *
        Another issue that has always concerned Mr. Pitcher is
ethics and foreign policy. Thus a brief examination of one of his
review articles on the subject is in order, partly because he tends
to reveal his views more succinctly in responding to other scholars' works. In this article, he is reviewing Ernest Lefever's
Ethics and United States Foreign Policy (1958).[9] Mr. Pitcher points

out that there are two kinds of "realistic" approaches to foreign
policy: in one, that which is desirable is *determined* by what is
possible, in the other, that which is desirable is *limited* by what
is possible.   His basic criticism of Lefever's position is due to
the latter's basic misunderstanding of the differences in these two
approaches.   Mr. Pitcher proceeds to show how Mr. Lefever is able
to unite a Christian foundation of ethics with Hans Morgenthau's
views on ethics and foreign policy only because his position lacks
consistency.   According to Mr. Morgenthau's own statement: "Man
cannot help sinning when he acts in relation to his fellow-men. . . .
For man's aspiration for power over other men, which is the very
essence of politics, implies the denial of what is the very core
of Judaeo-Christian morality--respect for man as an end in himself.
The power relation is the very denial of that respect. . ."   On
this point, while recognizing the necessity of the power relations,
Mr. Lefever holds to "government by consent" as the content of our
"national interest."   In his own words:

> American national purpose, it can be said, is to preserve and im-
> prove a society based upon consent and mutual respect and to help
> to create an international climate in which government by consent
> can take root and flourish.

Mr. Pitcher rightly criticizes the presupposition implicit in Mr.
Lefever's position that "what is desirable can be determined objectively, but that it is so subject to distortion and manipulation
that government is required in which each person's consent serves
as a protection against such perversions."   Inevitably, however,
says Mr. Pitcher, "'government by consent' is subject to qualification and curtailment in favor of institutions that provide an
opportunity for 'wisdom' to influence national and international
political processes."
        Mr. Pitcher refutes Mr. Lefever's position that the good
is a matter of individual interest or desire as well as his view of
ethics "as a discipline of means, not ends."   Furthermore, Mr.
Pitcher believes that Mr. Lefever's notion of consent and mutual
respect suggests that there is some value in respecting the other
simply because he is other.   Moreover Mr. Lefever fails to show how
national interests are more than a balance of subnational interests.
In reference to international policy decisions: "National power
can be used to support policies which contribute to greater justice,
peace and security; or it can be the instrument of injustice,
aggression and exploitation."   In this respect, Mr. Pitcher questions the adequacy of Mr. Lefever's understanding of ethics as a
discipline of means, not of ends, because a qualitative difference
in purposes is involved in foreign policy decisions.
        Clearly, Mr. Lefever's book provides an occasion for Mr.
Pitcher to raise the following issues regarding the relation between ethics and foreign policy.   In the first case, Mr. Pitcher
raises the question regarding the relationship between Biblical insights and ethics *vis à vis* foreign policy and international relations.   Contrary to many authors (including Mr. Lefever) who look
for a scriptural basis for a "realistic" ethics in foreign policy,

Mr. Pitcher is persuaded that, for the Bible, history neither reveals its meaning nor contains its own fulfillment. It is an unceasing ambiguous struggle between the forces of relative justice and those of injustice. In short, there is no one Christian, or Christian realist, approach to ethics or foreign policy. Secondly, there is the question that pertains to such concepts and phrases as justice, freedom, and mutual helpfulness, all of which have equivocal meanings. Mr. Pitcher feels strongly that some delineation of the meaning of these concepts is needed. The third is the relationship between love and justice. What is it that disinterested love seeks for the neighbor? Is it justice as the form of love? And, if justice is not the form of love, what does love seek for the neighbor? etc. Mr. Pitcher comments: "The relationship between love as motive or impulse and love as the form of the act are as much a question as is usual in those who borrow Reinhold Niebuhr's distinction without analyzing it." Finally, according to Mr. Pitcher, all who distinguish love and justice and appeal to man's misuse of his freedom in pride and self-seeking must say something more about God's grace.

Mr. Pitcher's assessment of the present situation is not very optimistic, for while there is a group of people who happen to be Christians discussing facts, there is not enough recognition that for the Christian, facts may differ, new possibilities may arise, and a different significance may be attached to historical possibilities. His concluding statements are important: "If we are serious about the relationship of ethics, the Christian faith, and foreign policy, far better for us in the present stage of our thinking to take one problem and to try to indicate at what point different views of ethics and of the Christian faith influence our apprehension of the facts, of the possibilities, and of the meaning of Christian responsibility."

* * * *

As we turn to Mr. Pitcher's concern for the racial issue in America, we are reminded of the fact that for him this is not just one of the major problems that confront American society and churches; it is *the* most important issue. It consumed his thought for many years even at the expense of his scholarly activities. As Mr. Engel comments:

> . . . it is not for the sake of personal witness alone that Mr. Pitcher has become involved in the Chicago Freedom Movement but for purpose of "understanding" also. His assumption is that "those who do not know, write; those who do know, do not." This kind of knowledge about good action gained from participation in an issue of religious substance in the culture is the kind of knowledge about what must or ought to be done to achieve the social good which the social sciences do not give.[10]

It goes without saying that the race problem cannot be isolated from other social, economic, political, and cultural problems in America. The interrelatedness of these issues was dramatically portrayed in one of Mr. Pitcher's early public talks. He said in part:

Where there is no vision the people perish. Where there is no
action the people languish. From beginning to end the Bible calls
for vision. From Abraham's first steps toward the promised land to
the vision of a new heaven and a new earth in the Apocalypse of
John, men of vision cry out for justice and for righteousness. And,
when in the course of human events powers that controlled the temporal destiny of men flaunted justice, God spoke. In his love and
mercy he raised up new leaders. In his love and judgment he destroyed cities and peoples. Yea, in the darkest hours he has called
upon religious leaders to move beyond the call of ordinary duties.

Today the future of mankind and of our metropolis depends upon our
capacity for vision and for action. . . .

First, most of us have been content with a shortage of houses. We
have rested easy while thousands of families live in constant fear
of the collapse of their buildings and of destruction by fire. . . .

Second, we have been building a city for its buildings rather than
for its peoples. . . .

Third, we have made no master plan for the metropolitan area. . . .
We have rested easy with a city government in which government by
the people is all too often not government for all of the people. . . .

Fourth, we have created a "white curtain" to sustain the conditions
that make Chicago the most segregated city in America. In our treatment of the non-white we have violated every standard of human de-
cency and of human morals that exists. Mildly stated, in the words
of James C. Downs in 1957, "If this practice or human relationship
system continues to operate to the end of the perpetuation and
strengthening of the completely segregated community let me say that
this city is in trouble. It is in trouble politically; it is in
trouble economically; it is in trouble socially; it is in trouble
culturally." More dramatically, we have permitted a situation to
drift without leadership until we sit on a keg of dynamite. There
are many non-colored people whose religious faith so speaks to their
consciences that they are no longer willing to be silent and inactive. There are many others whose patience has been sorely tried.
There is a restlessness about. There is a growing recognition of
the fact that there is no solution unless the white curtain be
pulled down everywhere. The only question is whether it will be
lowered with order and dignity or with disorder, bitterness, and
increasing conflict.[11]

A similar sense of urgency was voiced in a statement prepared by the members of the Ethics and Society Field of the F.T.F.,
i.e., Messrs. Alvin Pitcher, Victor Obenhaus, Widick Schroeder, and
Gibson Winter, asking the churchmen of Chicagoland to help prevent
the continued destruction of property, of community life due to
rapid transitions, and of human dignity. Inasmuch as segregation
cannot be tolerated, Mr. Pitcher and his colleagues are persuaded
that a new image of the desirable neighborhood must be effected

through the encouragement of neighbors to work and to plan together
for the maintenance of standards, the improvement of education, and
the development of respect among all persons regardless of race,
color, religion, ancestry, or national origin.[12] What is stressed
in that statement is not only the practical measures to be taken
in order to bring about an integrated community, but also the need
for a basic reorientation of the goals and motivations of society.
Mr. Pitcher tries to articulate this concern for reorientation in
terms of the church's attempts to fill the forms of culture, the
social and political institutions, with new meaning and content.
He is concerned as to whether we are to continue to emphasize social
process or to subordinate the process to some view of the ends of
society. For Mr. Pitcher the choice is clear. He says: *"Everything points to the fact that we are at the end of an era.* How much
longer will our parochialism prevent us from recognizing that new
occasions demand new models for human action?"[13] It was this conviction that compelled him to plunge into the Freedom Movement,
which in turn further intensified his conviction concerning the
reality of the social and religious crisis of our time.

Undoubtedly, events in 1965 at Selma disturbed the consciences of thoughtful citizens. What is more tragic, in Mr.
Pitcher's opinion, is our inability to perceive the reality of the
civil rights movement. The reality of crisis, however, does not
mean despair; because Selma, having again exposed rampant racism,
called forth the best of the American spirit--a spontaneous identification with the victims of injustice. More basically, according
to Mr. Pitcher, the civil rights movement "redefines" our political
situation by raising the fundamental question of our political
identity:

> It places in obvious jeopardy the unity of America which is rooted
> more in a sense of vocation than in organic ties of blood and soil.
> It shows that the consensus on the basis of which our stable insti-
> tutions have rested lacks the universality. . . . By the same token,
> the civil rights movement raises questions about the moral integrity
> and psychological health which are the cardinal prepolitical requi-
> sites for the functioning of our political institutions. Finally
> . . . our leadership in the free world is being undermined.[14]

In so stating, Mr. Pitcher pleads not only for a redefinition of
our responsibility *vis à vis* practical measures, but also for religious, ethical reflection; for the issue of race must be seen in
the context of the community of all men. Community is dependent
upon individuals with capacities to relate in an environment of
freedom from many forms of idolatry. Such a freedom is given
ultimately through faith, through which one man is released to
accept other persons as human beings.

Indeed, Mr. Pitcher's involvement in the civil rights
movement and other causes of social justice is derived from his
vision of the *koinonia* without which the renewal of the church and
society is impossible.

* * * *

In more recent years Mr. Pitcher, realizing that he is approaching retirement, has given much of his time to the guidance of the students in the Ethics and Society program, especially since some of them had lost their advisors due to the resignation of Messrs. Alan B. Anderson and Gibson Winter. At the same time Mr. Pitcher has an ambitious agenda for his further study and reflection. Thus he writes:

> What interests me now is the religious situation in the United States, and by implication in the West. This has involved a study of Marcuse, Roszak, Arendt, and Skinner with preliminary analyses of their interpretations of the situation. It remains to locate the sense in which these authors see the issue as religious and the sense in which they use the category of the religious. I expect to look at Etzioni and Parsons in similar ways. This is one side of the inquiry. On the other side I am looking at H. Richard Niebuhr, Tillich, Buber, Eliade, Bellah, and Dewey for explicit views of religion in order to develop a generic view of religion, a view which can be used to understand and assess the various interpretations of our situation. The assessment would involve the attempt to illumine the relation between views of religion, explicit or implicit, and the interpretations of our situation. The study focuses upon the culture and not upon the religious institutions. It assumes that religion can be understood as a dimension of culture as well as what characterizes religious institutions.[15]

Mr. Pitcher's concern with the religious situation, understood in the broadest terms as stated above, in the United States as well as in the West in general can be illustrated by his attention to the current energy crisis that confronts the Western world, especially in the United States. He argues that if the rest of the world should use as much oil as we do in the United States today, the world would consume 100 billion barrels of oil per year. That implies that by the year 2000, with a population of 6 to 8 billion people, the world would use 150-200 billion barrels of oil per year. Similar observations can be made regarding the use of other resources such as natural gas, aluminum, copper, mercury, lead, silver, tin, zinc, tungsten, manganese, molybdenum, nickel, cobalt, and gold. He is persuaded that the energy crisis is basically not the problem of scientific knowledge and technology; it is a religious problem in the sense that we are compelled to ask what we as a nation are about. He cites Detroit as a concrete example of the kind of crisis that concerns him. Detroit, the home of automobile industries and gigantic labor unions, does not represent a viable way of life. Other metropolitan cities are facing a similar plight today. For Mr. Pitcher, the energy crisis in America signifies that we as a nation have adopted a wrong way of life, just as the Hebrews during their captivity had forgotten their ancestral heritage and adopted the Babylonian way of life. "For my thoughts are not your thoughts; Neither are your ways, my ways, says the Lord."[16] In light of such an overwhelming national crisis, which is basically cultural and religious in nature, Mr. Pitcher urges us to think of remedies and solutions that must be found for the

sake of sheer survival. Thus, in a recent luncheon talk at the
Divinity School he shared his views and concerns as follows:

> In the next 200 years our society will move from a focus on freedom
> and equality to a focus on community and quality, from a focus upon
> our independence to a focus upon our dependence upon forces and
> powers beyond our control. Our churches will shift from being places
> where we meet for a few minutes each week . . . to being centers
> where more and more of our lives are involved and where we are more
> and more entangled with each other and our common world.[17]

Implicit in that line of thought is that the new eccle-
siology which is yet to emerge will move from eschatology to history;
it will be based on the interdependence of religion and the political
and economic world. It implies a radical shift from a narrow sense
of spirituality to spirituality as the meaning of everything,
from the transcendent to the immanent, from celebrating the community which does or should exist among members outside of the
church to becoming the community that is being celebrated.
His reading of the contemporary energy crisis, which is
nothing but a symptom of religious and cultural crisis in America
and the West, leads Mr. Pitcher to propose the following nine
guiding principles for the *koinonia* that must be actualized simultaneously both in the church and community life. (1) Congregational
life will involve more of its members' concern, time, and being.
(2) There will be cooperation in developing a much simpler style
of life--there will be less consumption, less travel, more meaning,
more excitement at home--less need to escape. (3) The church will
function as an extended family--with fewer people, perhaps, but more
deeply related, certainly. (4) In this new way of life economic
life will be secondary, it will be instrumental--it will not be the
focus for meaning--hopefully economic life, in many cases, will
absorb less time. (5) Education will be the ultimate responsibility
of the congregation. (6) There will be much more of a common discipline involving worship, economic sharing, mission projects, and
communal consideration of career decisions, etc. (7) The congregation will take some responsibility for the income of its members.
(8) The mission projects will involve political activity as well
as educational and social service activities. (9) Somehow the community will transcend the race, class, and sexist barriers of our
society.[18]
Mr. Pitcher's recent public statements may sound like
visionary utterances to some people. But to those who have known
various stages of his spiritual pilgrimage, these statements appear
to be consistent with his lifelong search for meaning in life. As
stated earlier, Alvin Pitcher's primary concern has always been
with the question of the religious substance of the culture of our
common life. That concern led him to appropriate Paul Tillich's
analysis of the world situation in terms of the "end of the Protestant era." The end, however, implies a beginning--the "reformulation of the law for our day," which involves a rethinking of the
form of justice, or principles of self-initiation, countervailing
power, democratic participation, dissent, etc. Mr. Pitcher's own

analysis of the assumptions behind the descriptions of the social
sciences has convinced him that American social thought is more concerned with the *how* of decision-making than with the results. In
that situation his own search for the alternative of substance or
goal-dominated orientation had driven him to stress the all-
important role of the community as a whole. Here, Mr. Pitcher tries
simultaneously to uphold the role of the state as the virtue-
informing and creating agency and the role of the church as a
bearer of authentic catholic substance. Opinions no doubt vary as
to how successfully he has resolved the inevitable tension between
the role of the state, in his case the United States, and the role
of the church; but few would deny that he has made serious efforts
to reconcile the two. His effort was not simply an intellectual one;
it led him to dedicate years of his life for the cause of social justice.

It would be misleading to attempt fitting Alvin Pitcher
into pigeon holes. To be sure, he is, by virtue of his upbringing,
a Midwesterner, an American, and a Protestant; one can readily see
in him all of these qualities with their strength and limitations.
But he also defies usual categorizations. He is an unusual Midwesterner, an unusual American, and an unusual Protestant. He is
an intellectual who can participate fully in various kinds of social
action. He is a professor who believes in the Socratic method of
teaching on the one hand and urges students to worry about the
future of America and humanity on the other. He is a patriot, believer, and a rebel. In his recent years, with increasing disen-
chantment with the present substance of American culture, Mr.
Pitcher has stressed the role of the church both as the bearer of
the catholic substance and that of Hebrew prophetic tradition.
Ironically, in his opinion the church has abdicated its proper
function and thus has lost channels for discovering new content for
the law or a new style of life for the Christian. Hence the urgency
for the transformation of the church.

Knowing Alvin Pitcher, his temperament and his sense of
commitment, I doubt whether retirement will make any difference in
his continued search for *koinonia* and social justice. Throughout
his academic career, he has been critical of the university in
spite of the fact that he has spent most of his adult life in it.
He has also been critical of the church, because he feels that the
church has become captive in another way of life--the culture of
the Babylonians. Yet he remains hopeful that institutions like the
university and community organizations have the potential for providing opportunities for dialogue and responsible action. He remains hopeful that the church will rediscover its faith in the
source of creative power that alone can bring about human fulfillment.

> Keep justice and do righteousness,
> for soon my salvation will come,
> and my deliverance be revealed. (Isaiah 56:1)

> . . . they who wait for the Lord shall renew their strength,
> they shall mount up with wings like eagles,
> they shall run and not be weary . . . (Isaiah 40:31)

NOTES AND REFERENCES

1. *The Divinity School News,* Vol. XXVI, No. 4 (November, 1959), 33-34.

2. *Ibid.*, XXVII, No. 2 (May, 1960), 21.

3. "How can one maintain relevance without succumbing to relativity?" in *Criterion*, Vol. 6, No. 1 (Winter, 1967), 13.

4. *Ibid.*, 14.

5. See his "'The Politics of Mass Society:' Significance for the Churches," in D.B. Robertson (ed.), *Voluntary Associations: A Study of Groups in Free Societies--Essays in Honor of James Luther Adams* (Richmond: John Knox Press, 1966), pp. 233-59.

6. Quoted from Mr. Engel's letter to the writer, dated October 14, 1976.

7. W. Alvin Pitcher, "The Significance of *The American Business Creed* for the Churches: A Summary and Interpretation," *The Journal of Religion*, Vol. XXXIX, No. 1 (January, 1959), 1-24.

8. *Ibid.*, p. 18.

9. W. Alvin Pitcher, *"Ethics and United States Foreign Policy:* A Review Article," *The Chicago Theological Seminary Register,* Vol. XLIX, No. 3 (March, 1959), 18-21.

10. Quoted from Mr. Engel's letter, dated October 14, 1976.

11. W. Alvin Pitcher, "Where There is No Vision the People Perish," given at Joint Meeting of the Clergy and Rabbis in Metropolitan Chicago, sponsored by the Archdiocesan Conservation Council, the Church Federation of Greater Chicago, and the Chicago Board of Rabbis.

12. This statement is entitled, "The Churches and Community Organizations," dated December 29, 1959.

13. W. Alvin Pitcher, "Darwinism and Christian Ethics," *The Journal of Religion*, Vol. XL, No. 4 (October, 1960), 256-66.   (Italics mine.)

14. W. Alvin Pitcher, "An American Crisis," *Criterion*, Vol. 4, No. 1 (Spring, 1965), 7.

15. Mentioned in Mr. Pitcher's letter to the writer, dated October, 1973.

16. Isaiah 55:8 (RSV).

17. Taken from Mr. Pitcher's talk in 1977 under the title, "Faith and the Next 200 Years."

18. *Ibid.*

Part One
Philosophical and Theological Ethics

Part One

Philosophical and Theological Ethics

JOHN DEWEY'S PHILOSOPHY OF THE COMMON WORLD

by
J. Ronald Engel

The New Ecological Consciousness

One notable change in the mode of apprehending the common world of ordinary human experience that has taken place in recent years is associated with the new ecological consciousness. This change has had the salutary effect of underscoring the fragility of the natural landscape and contributing to an appreciation of the destructive impact of human society upon the sustaining physical matrix of its existence. But the root ideas and principles of ecology are variously defined and interpreted. While there is general agreement that the science of ecology has to do with the ways in which organisms interact with their physical environments and with each other as parts of interdependent wholes, there is ambiguity when its principles are applied to the landscape inclusive of humanity and the rest of nature, the common world. Such concepts as "homeostasis," "ecosystem," "equilibrium," "web of life," "balance of nature," and "holism," are now frequently used both to describe the material conditions under which all life exists, and to develop the more normative notion of a natural order tending towards harmony, stability, and beauty. There are various extrapolations from these principles to notions of an ecological attitude or ethic. There are also claims that ecology entails a basic religious perspective analogous to primitive and Eastern apprehensions of the divinity immanent in the landscape. Precisely what will be the outcome of the new ecological consciousness for the normative meaning of the world that humanity shares with the rest of nature, the common world of ordinary human experience inclusive of both the native landscape and human civilization, is presently unclear.

Holmes Rolston, III distinguishes two primary concepts of ecology currently offered as sources for a new ecological social ethic: the concept of *homeostasis* and the concept of *holism*. In his analysis, recognition of the first entails an ethic which is only secondarily ecological because it merely describes the conditions or medium in which the presumed ethical maxim "promoting human life" must operate. The holistic principle, however, claims more than this. It is ecological in substance, not merely in accident:

> The claim seems to be that following ecological nature is not merely
> a prudential means to moral and valuational ends independent of
> nature but is an end in itself; or more accurately, it is within
> man's relatedness to his environment that all man's values are

21

> grounded and supported. In that construction of values, man doubt-
> less exceeds any environmental prescription, but nevertheless his
> values remain environmental reciprocals. . . His valuations, like his
> other perceptions and knowings, are interactionary, drawn from en-
> vironmental transactions, not merely brought to it.

Rolston finds a primary ecological ethic to be grounded in this
simultaneous discovery of both "ought" and "is" in the ecosystemic
community.

> Ecological description finds unity, harmony, interdependence, sta-
> bility and these are valuationally endorsed, yet they are found, to
> some extent, because we search with a disposition to value order,
> harmony, stability.

The moral maxim which emerges from holism is that one ought to preserve and promote the beauty, stability, and integrity of the total
ecosystem which is inclusive of human and other natural communities.
In obeying such a prescription, humanity acts to affirm its own integrity and diversity by preserving the integrity and diversity in
the rest of nature. There is a coincidence of human and ecosystemic
interests.[1]
      Rolston seeks to understand the claims of holism in terms
of the evolution of a new human conscience which circumscribes the
whole. Placed in the context of the categories of religious social
ethics, the interpretation of the new ecological consciousness to
which he is pointing is one which perceives the inclusive integrity
and variety of the common world as itself the locus of humanity's
ultimate belonging. There is a religious dimension inherent in the
holistic character of the total ecosystem in which humanity and the
native landscape share. All communities of nature belong together
as parts of one ultimate community of value.
      The purpose of the following essay is to contribute to
the definition of this particular religious form of the new ecological consciousness, and its correlative ethical principles, by means
of a constructive interpretation of the meaning of the common world
as found in the philosophy of John Dewey. The general proposal to
be advanced is that the philosophical perspective of naturalistic
humanism has heretofore unexplored resources for understanding the
religious and ethical implications of holism in the new ecological
consciousness.
      By virtue of a common historical genesis and underlying
first principle the science of ecology and the philosophy of
naturalistic humanism are closely related. Each appeared as a
rather direct outcome of the Darwinian revolution in scientific
worldview and each emerged as a distinct influence in American
thought through the common impetus of the "Chicago School" at the
turn of the century.[2] Most important, each assumes a "transactional"
understanding of the way in which diverse organisms adapt to a given
environment which is constantly changing and which is in turn modified by their activities. Thomas B. Colwell, among others, has recognized that the "Dewey-Bentley sense of 'transaction' . . . lends
itself especially well to ecological thinking."

When the ecosystem approach is translated into philosophical terms, the importance which modern philosophy has attached to the problem of knowledge--i.e., to the possibility of its attainment--comes to be replaced by theories and techniques which enable us to make the requisite distinctions and identifications among interacting processes and gross, integrating systems of relationships. Knowing would become a matter of finding ways of reporting and formulating reciprocal transactions between natural entities, man being one of these.[3]

In Colwell's view, Dewey's instrumental method of scientific inquiry, as the means to the greater integration of human individuals with one another and with their natural environment, finds exemplification in the principles and purposes of contemporary ecology.
However, Dewey's importance for understanding the religious and ethical implications of the idea of holism in the new ecological consciousness goes far beyond his contributions to the notion of a transactional process of evolution common to all organisms and their environments and a scientific methodology for discriminating its various manifestations. Dewey's chief importance lies in the *particular combination of analogies* with which he sought to understand the norm intrinsic to the interactive evolutionary process, and the integrative principles or criteria which these analogies yield. His choice of the value-laden traits which most significantly link human activities with the rest of nature--the pivotal speculative concepts by which he sought to re-connect the new natural sciences with the inherited humanistic tradition of Western civilization--places his philosophy in a unique intellectual position in any effort to define the normative unity of the common world. In this respect, naturalistic humanism exceeds the assumptions of scientific ecology and leads inquiry into the most complex and qualitatively immediate aspects of ordinary human experience.
The analogies which Dewey used to illuminate the meaning of the common world were drawn from the most specialized forms of historical experience in keeping with his methodological principle that consummations, the most complex and qualitatively rich wholes of human experience, are best able to reveal the generic traits of the whole of existence. The two primary analogies between human and natural activities with which Dewey worked were "art" and the "social." These were the two highest actualizations of the common world accessible to human observation and the proper point of departure for an imaginative re-construction of the normative relations of humanity and nature. It is in the fertile inter-penetration of these two aspects of experience within the framework of the transactional paradigm that the creativity of Dewey's philosophy for the formulation of the religious and ethical content of the new ecological consciousness is to be found.[4]
The following three sections present a constructive interpretation of Dewey's philosophical starting point, which grounds the principle of transaction, and the overlap of esthetic and social categories by which he defines the normative content of the common world. Discussion focuses upon the three constitutive principles through which the potentiality of the common world for holistic or

transactional integration may be best actualized--reciprocity, variety, and scope, and the distinctive characteristics of the esthetic and ethical qualities in such integration. The concluding section is a summary sketch of the religious social ethic which this study proposes as the definitive content of the ecological idea of holism in light of the philosophy of naturalistic humanism.

The Continuity of Experience and Nature

Dewey never tired of contrasting his own perspective on the common world--"the common life . . . we share with all living creatures"[5]--with those positions which, in his opinion, made a sharp separation between humanity and nature, whether in the guise of spirit versus matter, values versus facts, ends versus means, ideal versus real, or subject versus object. He struggled throughout his life to give philosophical precision and scope to the first principle that the *continuity* of experience and nature is the primary fact of human life, and that the question for humanity is how to use its specialized capacities to make that continuity a more unified, stable, and fulfilling one. In his first chapter on philosophic method in *Experience and Nature* Dewey gives the following as his epistemological starting point:

> Thus the value of the notion of experience for philosophic reflection is that it denotes both the field, the sun and clouds and rain, seeds, and harvest, and the man who labors, who plans, invents, uses, suffers, and enjoys. Experience denotes what is experienced, the world of events and persons; and it denotes that world caught up into experiencing, the career and destiny of mankind. . . . The value of experience for philosophy is that it serves as a constant reminder of something which is neither exclusive and isolated subject or object, matter or mind, nor yet one plus the other. The fact of integration in life is a basic fact.[6]

In particular, Dewey sought to distinguish his view from two extremes: a subjectivist instrumentalism which assigns to nature the status of mechanical "means" to be known by scientific analysis, and to humanity the superior status of "ends" to be treated uniquely in terms of ethical and esthetic values; and an objectivist organicism which assigns to nature the status of an internally unified Being to whose completeness and permanence humanity must submit. He considered these views as the obverse of one another--the inheritance of the erroneous split between subject and object which had established the epistemological quandary of modern thought. The consequence of this split for philosophy was to confirm the Western dualism of theory and practice, belief and knowledge, quality and quantity. The consequence for religious thought was to confirm the supernaturalistic separation of humanity from its home in the universe: "The self becomes not merely a pilgrim but an unnaturalized and unnaturalizable alien in the world."[7] The consequence for social thought was to confirm the hegemony of scientifically induced technology in humanity's practical dealings with the physical world, and to reduce the realm of choice and value to matters of inter- and intra-personal existence. Dewey's philosophy was a protest against the technological fragmentation of the common world in which humanity exists in continuity with all of nature.

Epistemologically considered, the first principle of continuity means that all modes of experiencing are ways in which "genuine traits of nature" come to manifest themselves in interaction with the human organism.

> If experience actually presents esthetic and moral traits, then these traits may also be supposed to reach down into nature, and to testify to something that belongs to nature as truly as does the mechanical structure attributed to it in physical science.[8]

Whatever is "in" human experience is also in some fashion "in" nature. Access can be gained therefore to metaphysical traits--to the generic traits of existence--through ordinary human experience of the common world. When experience is analyzed from this perspective, it is discovered that both nature and humanity are characterized by harmonies and disharmonies, qualities and relations, goods and evils, the precarious and the stable, necessities and freedoms.

Of all the traits found in the common world the most fundamental is the structure of fulfilled experience itself. This is the *transaction* between an organism and its environment by which both are modified and a more harmonious equilibrium achieved. By employing the term "transaction" instead of "interaction" in his later works, Dewey sought to emphasize the meaning of experience as a process in which subject and object, organism and environment, can only be separated by abstraction. Dewey used examples such as that of "breathing" to explain the meaning of transaction. Breathing is an act more integrative and complex than either the lungs or the air which compose it. "Transaction" so defined is the generic trait which most fundamentally defines the evolutionary continuity between humanity and the farthest reaches of organic and inorganic existence.

The unique distinction which falls to humanity in the evolutionary continuum is its peculiar ability by means of symbolization to augment and "liberate" the tendencies found in nature's transactions, and consequently to contribute to the greater integration of human existence both within itself and with nature. In 1898, in a public lecture at the University of Chicago entitled "Evolution and Ethics," Dewey sketched the evolutionary faith that guided his philosophical enterprise from its earliest neo-Hegelian period to its culmination in a naturalistic metaphysics half a century later:

> Man is an organ of the cosmic process in effecting its own progress. This progress consists essentially in making over a part of the environment by relating it more intimately to the environment as a whole; not, once more, in man setting himself against that environment.[9]

In this same lecture Dewey defined the "ethical" as the "fittest with respect to the whole of conditions" with the understanding that now humanity and nature together constitute the "whole" whose "integrity is to be so sustained and more intensely unified."

Art and Nature

The first analogy by means of which Dewey sought to define the content of transformative transactions between organisms and their environments, and the norm of unification which such transactions when successful embodied, is that between "art" and "nature." Dewey opens his two most substantive works with declarations of the centrality of this analogy. In *Experience and Nature* he writes:

> The highest because most complete incorporation of natural forces and operations in experience is found in art . . . Art thus represents the culminating event of nature as well as the climax of experience.[10]

And the opening chapter of *Art as Experience* is devoted to showing how certain "biological commonplaces . . . reach to the roots of the esthetic in experience."[11]

Art is defined by Dewey in *Experience and Nature* as a kind of transaction between the agent and environment which achieves full reciprocity of subject and object. Any activity that is simultaneously "means and consequence, process and product, the instrumental and consummatory" is "art."[12] Later, in *Art as Experience*, Dewey employs the term "esthetic/artistic" to characterize the reciprocal integration of the passive and appreciative with the active and formative aspects of the transactional process. The esthetic side of the process initiates action by the perception of the given pervasive qualitative unity of the common world. All "artistic" endeavor begins with the attempt to "clarify, enhance, complete" those harmonious transactions of the organism and the environment which may be considered to be "an" experience:

> An object is peculiarly and dominantly esthetic, yielding the enjoyment characteristic of esthetic perception, when the factors that determine anything which can be called an experience are lifted high above the threshold of perception and are made manifest for their own sake.[13]

The esthetic perception of achieved harmony also defines the conclusion of the successful esthetic/artistic event. The creation of a good art-product enhances the integration of the agent with the world. The artistic side of the process is the intervening step. It emphasizes the plurality of factors which are in tension and conflict and which must be actively brought into new rhythms of interaction for a new unity to be achieved. The esthetic/artistic transaction is thus envisaged by Dewey as a rhythm of doing/undergoing, suffering and response, passivity and making, contemplation and action. Appreciative enjoyment both begins and concludes the process.

The formal norm of the esthetic/artistic process is the unification of the many parts of the transactional whole in such a way that the individuality of each is promoted; it is therefore a "unity-in-variety," or as Dewey once phrased it, "repose in stimulation."[14] Only by the retention and enhancement of *all* the unique individual parts in the final art work can there be an increased harmony of experience which is qualitatively intense and vivid. Dewey had a number of ways of speaking about the formal structure of unity-in-variety and the interactive rhythms which achieve it. Two of the most concise are these:

> The objective measure of greatness (of the work of art) is precisely the *variety* and *scope* of factors which, in being rhythmic each to each, still cumulatively conserve and promote one another in building up the actual experience.[15]

> There is an old formula for beauty in nature and art: Unity in variety. . . The formula has meaning only when its terms are understood to concern a relation of energies. There is no fullness, no many parts, without distinctive differentiations. But they have esthetic quality, as in the richness of a musical phrase, only when distinctions depend upon reciprocal resistances. There is unity only when the resistances create a suspense that is resolved through cooperative interaction of opposed energies. The "one" of the formula is the realization through interacting parts of their respective energies. The "many" is the manifestation of the defined individualizations due to opposed forces that finally sustain a balance.[16]

The three formative principles of art are *reciprocity*, *variety*, and *scope* (or universality). Together they compose the qualitative unity of the transactional whole when it is successfully achieved. These principles are inherent in the definition of the esthetic/artistic process as the creation of a "cooperative unity" through the reciprocal relations of all the diverse parts of an indeterminate situation. As the generic traits of fulfilled experience in humanity and nature they are normatively constitutive of what Dewey means by the common world.

By employing the analogy of art and nature as the conceptual key to the evolutionary continuity of human action with the processes of nature, Dewey translates into modern naturalistic terms one of the oldest of Western ideas about the good of the cosmos, and one which has been peculiarly influential in the emergence of modern ecology. According to Clarence Glacken, the holistic notion of the "ecosystem" is ultimately derived from the long preoccupation of Western thinkers with trying to see earthly environments as manifestations of cosmic order. This idea was present in classical philosophy as well as in *Genesis*, was subsequently developed by Christian scholastic theology, and reached its most influential pre-evolutionary development in the so-called "physio-theologies" of the seventeenth and eighteenth centuries. Glacken writes:

I am convinced that modern ecological theory, so important in our attitudes toward nature and man's interferences with it, owes its origin to the design argument: the wisdom of the Creator is self-evident, everything in the creation is inter-related, no living thing is useless, and all are related to the others.[17]

By characterizing a "work of art" as the "mutual adaptation of parts to one another in constituting a whole" Dewey in effect brings the historically generative notion behind the new ecological conscious-ness back into prominence as the normative content for ecological theory in its modern scientific dress.[18]

Society and Nature

There is a second analogy which is required in addition to that between art and nature in order to understand the full meaning of the common world which Dewey envisaged. This is the analogy of "society" and "nature." Without this comparison, the analogy of art and nature tends to take an organicist turn and to focus upon the similarities of the individual organism with the work of art. In consequence the transactional structure of the esthetic/ artistic process is lost from view. The common ground which lies between delight in well-executed works of art and delight in a virgin wilderness area is substantially influenced by the perception of both as composed of the reciprocal transactions of many distinct and well-defined individual parts which exist as organic wholes in their own right. In the ordinary experience of the common world, trees are not perceived as diverse cells in the "body" of the forest, but as diverse individual organisms with integrities matched by other integrities. This implies reciprocal resistances and conflicts as well as mutual forms of support within a *society of equals*.[19]
Dewey was concerned with the category of the "social" from the time of his earliest writings, and his subsequent philosophical development may be read in part as a struggle to achieve a more adequate view of the social--one which would maintain the organic ideal of the integrity of the whole but without sacrifice of the uniqueness and freedom of the individuals that compose it. Dewey's early evolutionary organicism led gradually towards a more open contextualistic viewpoint. Throughout this development, however, he held to the basic position that the social is the content for the ethical and, when actualized as "community," the norm as well.[20]
By 1930 Dewey had developed his thought to the point at which he could propose that the social constituted not only the in-clusive category for understanding human existence, but was the "inclusive philosophic idea" itself. By this he meant that social phenomena were "an exemplification upon the widest and most intricate scale of the generic trait of associated behavior or interaction" which ran through all physical, organic, and mental behavior.[21] Like the analogy of art, therefore, where in order to understand what the less complex and more remote esthetic forms and processes in nature are like it is first necessary to examine the esthetic forms and processes of human creation, Dewey argued that in order to understand

the meaning of associated behavior as manifested in other realms of
existence it is necessary to begin with human society.

That "associated or conjoint behavior is a universal characteristic of all existences" and that "the qualities of things
associated are displayed only in association" Dewey took as axiom-
atic.[22] The question was with the unifying norm of association as
given in that complex whole called human society. Dewey made several answers to this question--in his political philosophy, in his
ethics, and in his explicit statements on religion--and they all revolved about the meaning of "community."

In *The Public and Its Problems*, Dewey defined the ethical
ideal of human community in the following terms:

> Wherever there is a *conjoint* activity whose consequences are appre-
> ciated as good by *all singular persons* who take part in it, and
> where the realization of the good is such as to effect an energetic
> desire and effort to sustain it in being just because it is a *good
> shared by all*, there is in so far a community.[23]

In his *Ethics* Dewey equates the supreme ethical ideal of the "social"
with the realization of "community" defined by the answer to the
question:

> How to *harmonize* the development of *each individual* with the main-
> tenance of a social state in which the activities of one will con-
> tribute to the *good of all the others*?[24]

What is remarkable about these and other definitions of
the ethical norm of the "social," or "community," which Dewey proposes throughout his work is their sharp parallelism with the three
esthetic principles identified in the previous discussion of art.
The good of the whole is a shared unitary good which is both the
result of a variety of individuals' conjoint relationships and the
source of their unique realizations. The integration of the collec-
tivity which occurs when *all* the *unique individualities* which compose it participate in *reciprocal inter-relationships* with one
another is simultaneously esthetic and social! This unity is manifested with peculiar richness in human experience but is continuous
with unifications found throughout nature. It is not simply that
art is a socializing influence, or that art is an expression of
society. Rather, the ethical principles of the social when fulfilled in community *are* inherently esthetic/artistic, and conversely,
the principles of a work of art are inherently social-ethical. To
Dewey, "acts of social intercourse are works of art."[25] The quality
and structure of society is at best the conjoint composition of a
community of artists. This analysis concurs with that of Van Meter
Ames:

> In the last analysis, the esthetic is taken up into if not identified
> with the social. The esthetic is the finest and the social is the
> most real and comprehensive of Dewey's categories. The finest must
> involve the real and the comprehensive, almost as the idea of God was
> thought to include his existence.[26]

It is one of the incomplete aspects of Dewey's philosophy
that this convergence is variously touched upon and acknowledged
but nowhere explicitly developed. In the *Ethics* the parallelism
finds such expression as this:

> The positive import of "common good" is suggested by the idea of
> sharing, participating--an idea involved in the very idea of com-
> munity. . .   To partake is to *take* part, to *play* a role. . .   Its
> proper analogue is not physical division but taking part in a game,
> in conversation, in a drama. . . [27]

It is also one of the pervasive themes of *Art as Experience*:

> When it is a matter of technology, domestic economy, or social
> polity, we do not have to be told that rationality, intelligibility,
> is measured by orderly co-adaptation of means moving towards a common
> end...What we perhaps are less cognizant of is that this organiza-
> tion of energies that move cumulatively to a terminal whole in which
> the values of all means and media are incorporated is the essence of
> fine art.

Or:

> In art, as in nature and in life, relations are modes of interaction
> . . . A social relation is an affair of affections and obligations,
> of intercourse, of generation, influence and mutual modification.
> It is in *this sense* that "relation" is to be understood when used to
> define form in art.[28]

Repeatedly, Dewey draws analogies between the normative
principles of a work of art and the normative principles of the
social. Perhaps the most important identification is that of reciprocity, or coincidence of ends and means. It will be recalled that
Dewey's definition of art was a perfect interpenetration of ends and
means, the instrumental and the consummatory. The same definition
is given in the *Theory of Valuation* for the norm of ethical value:
what he there calls the "continuum of ends-means."
    At the conclusion of *Art as Experience* Dewey makes his
most explicit statement on the inter-relationship of art and ethics
and the two are given an identical referent:

> Were art an acknowledged power in human association and not treated
> as the pleasuring of an idle moment or as a means of ostentatious
> display, and were morals understood to be identical with every as-
> pect of value that is shared in experience, the "problem" of the re-
> lation of art and morals would not exist.[29]

Dewey is suggesting that were both art and ethics to be reconceived
in terms of one primary transactional or associational activity,
then they would be recognized as two aspects of the same thing--the
one pointing to the creative process or "power" of association, the
other to that process or power as a deliberately "shared" end.

The lack of development by Dewey of the intersection of the analogies of art and the social has led to various interpretations of his meaning. As Stephen Pepper observes: "One is at a loss to say of Dewey's *Art as Experience*, which has proven quite justifiably the most influential work in contextualistic literature, whether it is mainly a book in esthetics or in ethics."[30] The meaning taken here is that the only valid distinction between the two in his thought is that between an esthetic emphasis upon a commonly shared *unifying quality* and an ethical emphasis upon the *obligation* or deliberate effort to achieve such quality. Both are aspects of the evolutionary holistic transactions of existence which now may be defined as "social-esthetic" or "collective works of art."

There is little question that in Dewey's view the esthetic is prior as the content of the good which it is the purpose of the ethical to achieve. The good carries its own warrant of value; it is "had." The end of evolution is the preservation and enhancement of the good--the qualitative unification of the many. The ethical question is to what degree nature and humanity achieve vivid and harmonizing unions or consummations, which in turn is a question of how well the many individuals which compose the common world conjointly "intend" common esthetic goals and artistic activities. Ugliness, or the absence of the esthetic, is a moral failure. The communal fulfillment of the wholes of existence is found in the qualitative enjoyments and activities of art; the purposeful fabric of human intentionality required to achieve and maintain such fulfillments constitutes the content of social ethics, or politics. The highest actualization of art and ethics is the art of politics itself.

This interpretation is close to, but not identical with, that proposed by Sidney Zink as a legitimate distinction of the esthetic and the ethical in Dewey's philosophy:

> An acceptable view might be that in the esthetic orientation means-end designates the elements of the individual, unique, esthetic experience, whereas in the ethical context the means and end involved are capable of symbolic representation and thus comparable with similar elements in other experiences; the function of intelligence in esthetic experience being to concentrate the elements of this particular experience in self-contained wholes, the function of intelligence in the ethical experience to make the end of the particular situation harmonious with the ends of other experiences.[31]

Like Zink, the interpretation offered here stresses the intermediate status of the ethical and the more direct emphasis of the esthetic. But rather than make the distinction revolve on symbolic representation, the present proposal is that the essential distinction lies between two qualities expressive of two particular moments in the complete transactional process: that of mutual purpose, intentionality, obligation, and that of mutual consummation, fulfillment, harmony. Dewey's concept of "qualitative thought" suggests that he would argue that the role of intelligence in integrating the ends of particular situations with the ends of all other

experiences is as esthetic as ethical. Zink acknowledges that Dewey
probably would disallow his distinction in this regard.

The interpretation made here has a unique advantage. It
opens the way for the ethical, like the esthetic, to be continuous
with the rest of nature. But this implication of the principle of
continuity requires a new consideration of the ultimate meaning of
the common world which is distinctly religious in quality.

The **The Common World as a Covenantal Work of Art**

The preceding three sections have sought to define the
meaning of the holistic character of the common world of humanity
and nature which is both explicit and implicit in Dewey's worldview.
It was first noted that the transactional integration of organism
and environment is the inherent structure of the evolutionary process as it moves towards increasing complexity and order in nature.
This is the basic structure of the ecological principle of holism
in Dewey's empirical metaphysics. It was then observed that the
normative content of organism-environmental transactions is esthetic/
artistic and that their success may be measured by three constitutive principles: *reciprocity*, *variety*, and *scope*. Finally, it was
shown that these esthetic principles are identical with the ethical
principles of the social so that community as a work of art is the
fullest exemplification of the common world available to human experience. The question with which inquiry was left was the distinct
meaning of the "ethical" within the social-esthetic whole and the
kind of continuity which links the ethical as exemplified in the
human sphere with the rest of nature and hence the common world.
The proposal made was that "obligation" was the distinctive trait
of the ethical and that it was continuous throughout nature.

At this point of exposition the present inquiry is working
at the creative edge of Dewey's own thought. To speak of mutual
obligation or purpose uniting humanity and nature smacks of a philosophical idealism which Dewey rejected. Yet, at the same time, Dewey
affirmed the view that those esthetic and ethical qualities discovered in human experience are also "in" nature.

Now it is clear that Dewey affirmed "reciprocity" as the
dynamic principle of art and of ethics and the principal norm for
the fulfillment of the transactional processes of exchange between
the human organism and the natural environment. Reciprocity means
equivalence of value; it does not require *identity* of value (or intentionality). Artistically considered, this means that the human
organism in interaction with the environment is esthetically fulfilled when it is both means (instrument) and end (consummation) for
that environment, and the environment is in turn means and end for
it. But what can this mean ethically? It can only mean that humanity and nature have a reciprocal obligation to one another to fulfill
that esthetic relationship! This is the distinctly ethical meaning
of what is involved in the view that humanity works within nature to
the end of liberating its potentialities for harmony.

This is not an easy doctrine to attribute to Dewey's philosophy. Indeed, in the context of Western thought generally, it is a

thoroughly radical notion.[32] For its part, nature makes available
certain capacities and resources which serve the harmonious development of human civilization. In return, humanity has an obligation
to use its capacities for the harmonious fulfillment of nature. The
common world of humanity and nature is one in which the potentialities of both for esthetic harmony *should be* realized in purposeful
conjunction with one another. This means, in keeping with the previous analysis of the three constitutive principles of social-
esthetic fulfillment, that the reciprocal relationships between all
of nature's and humanity's diverse entities *ought to be* perfected
in order for the qualitative unity of the common world to be realized.
But what can such a transcendent unifying purpose be but the ultimate
purpose of the universe? And what can the consequent qualitative
unity be but the ultimate religious quality--the immediately intuited
divinity of an esthetically perfected common world?

    Dewey suggests precisely this on a number of occasions,
sometimes stressing the esthetic harmony or wholeness of the unification of the common world, at other times stressing the sense in
which humanity and nature share in the common ethical purpose of
evolution.

    Basic to Dewey's religious thought, for example, is the
notion of humanity and nature as equal members of a cosmic community.
While prone to emphasize the importance of the human community, Dewey
never stops with it when he moves to describe the full and complete
object of religious feeling and obligation. Thus, at the conclusion
of *A Common Faith* he dramatically shifts from the human social abode
of the religious function to suggest that "The community of causes
and consequences in which we, together with those not born, are enmeshed is the widest and deepest symbol of the mysterious totality
of being the imagination calls the universe." That what Dewey has
in mind is far more than human community alone is confirmed by his
previous insistence that any religious ideal which omits "natural
piety" is simply human egotism:

> The essentially unreligious attitude is that which attributes human
> achievement and purpose to man in isolation from the world of physical
> nature and his fellows. . . *Our successes are dependent upon the co-*
> *operation of nature.* The sense of the dignity of human nature is as
> religious as is the sense of awe and reverence when it rests upon a
> sense of human nature as a cooperating part of a larger whole.[33]

Similarly, at the conclusion to *Human Nature and Conduct*, Dewey expands the notion of community to mean the "infinite relationships
of man with his fellows and with nature. . . set in a whole to which
they belong and which belongs to them."[34]

    In one remarkable passage in *Art as Experience* Dewey com-
bines allusions to the esthetic and the political as religious
qualities of the universe:

> A work of art elicits and accentuates this quality of being a whole
> and of belonging to the larger, all-inclusive, whole which is the
> universe in which we live. This fact, I think, is the explanation
> of that feeling of exquisite intelligibility and clarity we have in

> the presence of an object that is experienced with esthetic intensity. It explains also the *religious feeling that accompanies intense esthetic perception.* We are, as it were, introduced into a world beyond this world which is nevertheless the deeper reality of the world in which we live in our ordinary experiences. . . We are carried out beyond ourselves to find ourselves. . . Where egotism is not the measure of reality and value, we are *citizens of this vast world* beyond ourselves and any intense realization of its presence with and in us brings a peculiarly satisfying sense of unity in itself and with ourselves.[35]

What can it mean to be a "citizen of this vast world beyond ourselves"--the "universe"--but to be in *covenant* with that world to the end of its common good? The ultimate religious ground of human ethical obligation is located within the common world which humanity and nature share as the imperative of that world for community. John F.A. Taylor has defined the concept of "covenant" as "a community of persons mutually allied by virtue of the obligations they are committed to preserving with respect to each . . . obligation *is* the political reality."[36] Dewey has analogized the notion of covenantal community as it is employed to describe inter-personal relationships (and Biblically, divine-human relationships) with the basic moral meaning of humanity's relationship with the rest of nature and identified it as the purpose of existence itself. In a sense, "nature" has replaced "God," not as an object of worship--*that* is the process of community creation itself, the "active relation between the ideal and actual"[37]--but as humanity's chief *partner* in the cosmic evolutionary process.

This is the meaning intended by Dewey in his 1898 address on "Evolution and Ethics."

> But I question whether the spiritual life does not get its surest and most ample guarantees when it is learned that the laws and conditions of righteousness are implicated in the working processes of the universe; when it is found that man in his conscious struggles, in his doubts, temptations, and defeats, in his aspirations and successes, is moved on and buoyed up by the forces which have developed nature; and that in this moral struggle he acts not as a mere individual but as an organ in maintaining and carrying forward the universal process.[38]

It is also the ethical meaning of the principle of continuity which Dewey thirty years later explicates in *Experience and Nature*. There he holds that the "community of causes and consequences. . . in which we, together with those not born, are enmeshed" is objectively prior to any individual experiencing of it, and the individual only has the real choice of deliberately affirming that community and sharing in responsibility for its outcomes and in enjoyment of its benefits, or withdrawing into an illusory isolation. Hence the very *act* of human self-affirmation is simultaneously an act of covenant: "To say '*I* think, hope, and love', is to say in effect that genesis is not the last word; instead of throwing the blame or the credit

for the belief, affection and expectation upon nature, one's family, church, or state, one declares one's self to be henceforth a *partner*."39
    The conclusion to which these considerations lead is that the religious meaning of the first principle of continuity is summed up in the notion of the common world as a "covenantal work of art."
    On the basis of Dewey's philosophical perspective it is possible to project an esthetically grounded religious social ethic to inform the new ecological consciousness. Such an ethic would propose that the principles of reciprocity, variety, and scope, which define the unified actualizations of human works of art, and which are continuous with processes throughout all of nature, should also define the common world which humanity and nature share. Such an ethic would be preservationist-oriented. To lose the inter-dependencies, diversity, and universality of the native landscape is to lose both a major repository of achieved esthetic value and a foundational experience for new artistic creation in human civilization. According to this ethic, the community of value which humanity and nature share is a landscape in which both nature and human society are esthetically harmonized, and in which their transactions with each other have the character of a shared work of art; in which, in other words, they serve as reciprocal means and ends for one another.
    From the perspective of naturalistic humanism, the pledge of human beings to work for the esthetic/artistic perfection of the whole of being (and faithfulness to that pledge even under the most difficult of circumstances) is the essence of the religiosity implicit in the new ecological consciousness. In this interpretation of human experience, humanity's place of ultimate belonging, humanity's true home, is in the common world which it shares with the rest of nature--on this earth, and in this universe. The "good news" which it proclaims is that in those ordinary, and particular, "places" in which persons have found an esthetic harmony of civilization and nature, and to which they have been faithful in covenant, they will be "introduced into a world beyond this world. . . carried out beyond ourselves to find ourselves."

NOTES AND REFERENCES

1. Holmes Rolston, III, "Is There an Ecological Ethic?" *Ethics* 85 (January, 1975), p. 99, 100.
2. The contributions of the Chicago pragmatists to the growth of naturalistic humanism are well recognized. Less well known is the simultaneous development at the University of Chicago of the new science of ecology under the leadership of Henry C. Cowles. In 1899, one year after Dewey wrote: "The unwritten chapter in natural selection is that of the evolution of environments," Cowles published the first of his pioneering ecological studies on the evolution of the environment of the dunes of Lake Michigan. See John Dewey, "Evolution and Ethics," in *The Early Works: 1882-1898*, ed. Jo Anne Boydston, vol. 5 (Carbondale: Southern Illinois University Press, 1969), p. 52; and Henry C.

36   BELIEF AND ETHICS

Cowles, "The Ecological Relations of the Vegetation on the Sand Dunes of Lake Michigan," *Botanical Gazette* 27 (1899), p. 95.
3. Thomas B. Colwell, Jr., "The Balance of Nature: A Ground for Human Values," *Main Currents in Modern Thought* 26 (1969), p. 51. Eugene P. Odum defines the "holistic" approach of ecology in these terms:

> Living organisms and their nonliving environment are inseparably inter-related and interact upon each other. Any unit that includes all of the organisms (i.e., the "community") in a given area inter-acting with the physical environment so that a flow of energy leads to clearly defined trophic structure, biotic diversity, and material cycles (i.e., exchange of materials between living and non-living parts) within the system is an ecological system or *ecosystem*.

Fundamentals of Ecology, 3rd ed. (Philadelphia: W.B. Saunders Co., 1971), p. 8.
4. In order to appreciate the significance of these two metaphors for the new ecological consciousness, it is only necessary to refer to the now classic formulation of the notion of a land ethic by Aldo Leopold in 1949: "A thing is right when it tends to preserve the integrity, stability, and beauty of the biotic community." The two principles involved in this definition are esthetic harmony ("integrity," "stability," "beauty,") and social ethical intentionality ("right," "community"). See *A Sand County Almanac* (New York: Oxford University Press, 1949), p. 262.
5. John Dewey, *Art as Experience* (New York: G.P. Putnam's Sons, 1934), p. 20.
6. John Dewey, *Experience and Nature*, 1st ed. (London: George Allen & Unwin, 1925), p. 28. The postulate of "continuity" may be considered the one *a priori* principle of Dewey's empirical philosophy. He wrote in his essay, "The Inclusive Philosophic Idea:" "Upon the hypothesis of continuity--if that is to be termed a hypothesis which cannot be denied without self-contradiction . . . " *Philosophy and Civilization* (New York: G.P. Putnam's Sons, 1931; reprint ed., Gloucester, Mass.: Peter Smith, 1968), p. 81. As H.S. Thayer comments:

> One does not often find Dewey philosophizing with hypotheses that cannot be denied without contradiction, i.e., with analytic or a priori principles for, presumably, empirical purposes. And one suspects that this is as close as a duly chastised and disillusioned Hegelian can come to maintaining a belief in an absolute . . . The idea of continuity, surely, is the inclusive category of John Dewey's philosophy.

See *Meaning and Action* (New York: Bobbs-Merrill Co., 1968), p. 461.
7. John Dewey, *Experience and Nature*, 2nd ed. (London: George Allen & Unwin, 1929; Dover Publications, Inc., 1958), p. 24.
8. *Ibid.*, p. 2.
9. John Dewey, "Evolution and Ethics," in *The Early Works: 1882-1898*, ed. Jo Anne Boydston, vol. 5 (Carbondale: Southern Illinois University Press, 1969), p. 38.
10. Dewey, *Experience and Nature*, 2nd ed., p. vi.
11. Dewey, *Art as Experience*, p. 18.
12. Dewey, *Experience and Nature*, 2nd ed., p. 361.
13. Dewey, *Art as Experience*, p. 57.

14. Dewey, *Experience and Nature*, 2nd ed., p. 359.

15. Dewey, *Art as Experience*, p. 171.

16. *Ibid.*, p. 161.

17. Clarence Glacken, *Traces on the Rhodian Shore* (Berkeley: University of California Press, 1967), p. 523.

18. Dewey, *Art as Experience*, p. 134. Recent use of the analogy of art and nature has been made by both biologists and estheticians. See, for example, Paul Weiss, "Beauty and the Beast: Life and the Rule of Order," *Scientific Monthly* vol. 81, no. 6 (1955); Susanne Langer, *Feeling and Form* (New York: Charles Scribner's Sons, 1953); Reuben Wheeler, *Man, Nature, and Art* (New York: Pergamon Press, 1968).

19. The attempt to analogize the model of the individual organism with the ecosystem or ecological whole has received both scientific and esthetic critiques. Recently, for example, world-systems theorists using the organic analogy have had to recognize the need for differentiation of relatively self-sufficient regional systems. See Mihajlo Mesarovic and Eduard Pestel, *Mankind at the Turning Point* (New York: Dutton & Co., 1974). The esthetic limitations of organicism constitute an object of Stephen Pepper's critique in *The Basis of Criticism in the Arts* (Cambridge: Harvard University Press, 1946).

20. For example,

The very problem of morals is to form an original body of impulse tendencies into a voluntary self in which desires and affections center in the values which are common; in which interest focuses in objects that contribute to the enrichment of the lives of all.

John Dewey and James H. Tufts, *Ethics*, rev. ed. (New York: Henry Holt and Co., 1932), p. 336.

21. John Dewey, *Philosophy and Civilization* (New York: G.P. Putnam's Sons, 1931; reprinted ed., Goucester, Mass.: Peter Smith, 1968), pp. 78-79.

22. *Ibid.*, p. 77.

23. John Dewey, *The Public and Its Problems* (New York: Henry Holt & Co., 1927), p. 149. Italics added.

24. John Dewey and James H. Tufts, *Ethics,* rev. ed. (New York: Henry Holt and Co., 1932), p. 389. Italics added.

25. Dewey, *Art as Experience*, p. 63.

26. Van Meter Ames, "John Dewey as Aesthetician," *The Journal of Aesthetics and Art Criticism* 12 (December, 1953), p. 145.

27. Dewey and Tufts, *Ethics*, p. 383.

28. Dewey, *Art as Experience*, pp. 171-172, p. 134. Italics added.

29. *Ibid.*, p. 348.

30. Stephen Pepper, *The Basis of Criticism in the Arts* (Cambridge: Harvard University Press, 1946), p. 59.

31. Sidney Zink, "The Concept of Continuity in Dewey's Theory of Esthetics," *The Philosophical Review* 52 (1943), p. 400.

32. Scott Buchanan seeks to extend the third formulation of Kant's categorical imperative in order to express a new "metaphysical teleology" as follows:

Each natural thing, whether rational, or non-rational, must be treated as an end in itself, not merely as a means . . . Furthermore, they all belong to a community of reciprocal means and ends in which the condition for the human use of nature is always men's service to nature.

38   BELIEF AND ETHICS

See his "Natural Law and Teleology" in *Natural Law and Modern Society* (Cleveland: World Publishing Co., 1961), p. 141.

33. John Dewey, *A Common Faith* (New Haven: Yale University Press, 1934), p. 85. Italics added.

34. John Dewey, *Human Nature and Conduct* (New York: Henry Holt, 1922), p. 301.

35. Dewey, *Art as Experience*, p. 195. Italics added.

36. John F.A. Taylor, *Masks of Society* (New York: Appleton-Century-Crofts, 1966), p. 254.

37. Dewey, *A Common Faith*, p. 51.

38. Dewey, "Evolution and Ethics," p. 53.

39. Dewey, *Experience and Nature*, 2nd ed., p. 233. Italics added.

ETHICS, METAPHYSICS, AND THE NATURALISTIC FALLACY

by
Franklin I. Gamwell

I.

When he assumed the chair of Professor of Philosophical Theology at Union Theological Seminary, Paul Tillich said that this name "suits me better than any other, since the boundary line between philosophy and theology is the center of my thought and work."[1] Paul Tillich has been one of the principal mentors of Alvin Pitcher -- and, with his mentor, Pitcher has always believed that theology should be pursued in conversation with contemporary philosophy and formulated with philosophical precision and sophistication. For him, as for Tillich, the Christian theologian must also be a philosophical theologian. More broadly, Pitcher's belief places him within a distinguished tradition of theologians and philosophers who have forged over the centuries a friendship, if not always a marriage, between Christian thought and metaphysics. Because metaphysics is understood, with Aristotle, as the study of "being qua being"[2] or, with Tillich, as the study "in which reality as such is the object,"[3] it has long been thought to provide terms within which the meaning and truth of Christian claims about the Creator and Redeemer of all things may be explicated. Pitcher's own constructive thought in theological ethics, then, has illustrated this tradition. It has sought to formulate an ethic which is essentially related to a view of reality as such.

I have just said that Pitcher and Tillich stand within a long tradition of Western thought. It is well-known, however, that another tradition in Christian theology has eschewed a friendship with metaphysics. Moreover, theologians like Tillich and Pitcher probably represent a minority of their theological contemporaries because this latter tradition, in its most recent form, has occupied the throne for much of the last fifty years. This most recent form is, of course, the general theological persuasion known as "neo-orthodoxy" which holds, roughly speaking, that truths of the Christian faith so transcend the power of rational (and, therefore, metaphysical) discernment that the friendship in question is a kind of idolatry. More recently, there has been movement within the theological enterprise back toward the metaphysical tradition and a renewed interest in seeking a metaphysical basis for theological claims. This has meant not only continued constructive attention to Tillich's work but also efforts to appropriate Thomistic, existentialist, and Whiteheadian thought. During my tenure as a student at the Divinity School of the University of Chicago I became convinced, in considerable measure because of Pitcher's

39

influence, that theology requires a metaphysical basis; consequently, I applaud this recent movement. In agreement with many who have studied at that Divinity School, however, I found the general perspective of process philosophy more persuasive than Tillich's ontological analysis -- and this all the more so insofar as the Whiteheadian perspective has been restated and refined by Charles Hartshorne.[4] Among other things, this choice set the terms for an interesting -- and, for me, always educational -- conversation with Alvin Pitcher.

If the movement beyond neo-orthodoxy has opened new metaphysical discussions among theologians, however, it has also raised into prominence a philosophical antagonist which, like neo-orthodox theology but for very different reasons, is unfriendly to metaphysics. Throughout most of the twentieth century, a prominent circle of philosophy has argued that metaphysics is a futile enterprise. Roughly speaking, I refer to the work that has fallen under the rubrics of logical positivism and linguistic analysis and which I will call the tradition of analytical philosophy. Whatever new philosophical thought has been generated within the theological community, it is probably fair to say that discussion with this branch of philosophy has been minimal. This essay hopes to forward that discussion, at least with regard to the question of ethics.

In no area has the general perspective of analytical philosophy been more decidedly anti-metaphysical than in philosophical ethics.[5] In 1903, G. E. Moore published *Principia Ethica*.[6] No other single work has had a greater influence upon Anglo-American philosophical ethics in this century, and one of the basic tenets for which this circle of thought is indebted to Moore is the claim that metaphysical theories of ethics are false. Moore held that the term "good" is the fundamental concept of ethical discourse, such that possible actions are right or obligatory because they will or probably will produce the greatest good (that is, intrinsic good or good-as-an-end). But the meaning of good is, he continued, simple and indefinable. "If I am asked 'what is good?' my answer is that good is good and that is the end of the matter."[7] Consequently, a statement of the form "X is good" cannot be defended by argument or by appeal to evidence beyond itself; it is "incapable of proof or disproof;"[8] rather, something is known to be good solely through direct inspection or direct awareness. In this sense, Moore's understanding of intrinsic good is intuitionist and his ethical theory has been called an example of intuitionism. Consequently, Moore held that all metaphysical theories of ethics are misguided, because they attempt to define in terms of some "supersensible" existence what can never be defined -- namely, the meaning of good.[9] Although they differed from Moore at significant points, H. A. Prichard and Sir David Ross may also be mentioned as ethical philosophers who rejected metaphysical ethics for intuitionist reasons.[10]

After the first third of the century, intuitionism was rapidly replaced on center stage by the emotivist or non-cognitivist perspective in ethics. This position, which is still current today in some quarters, was at one with Moore in claiming that good is indefinable and that utterances of the form "X is good" cannot be

defended -- but the grounds for this conclusion shifted. No longer
was it said that the meaning of good is simple; rather, emotivists
held that ethical terms have no cognitive meaning, so that ethical
utterances do not constitute claims or assertions at all. Ethical
discourse, in other words, is simply a way of expressing or attempting to evoke emotion, such that ethical utterances are never
properly called true or false. Judgments of the form "X is good"
or "X is right," one might say, are solely matters of preference.
Clearly, the most widely-read statement of this position was Alfred
Jules Ayers's *Language, Truth and Logic* -- although, partly because that volume was principally devoted to other questions, the
perspective received more extensive and competent treatment in the
work of C. L. Stevenson.[11] In any case, as G. J. Warnock summarizes,
this position "was thought for some years, by very many, to have
brought great illumination to the study of ethics."[12]
          More recently, there has been a turn away from emotivism
as well as intuitionism and a return to the belief that ethical
assertions are defensible by argument. Among other reasons for
this turn was the realization, especially telling within the tradition of analytical philosophy, that emotivism simply misrepresents
the way in which ethical terms actually function in ordinary language -- i.e., emotivism could be true only if ordinary language
were massively deceptive. Perhaps Kurt Baier and R. M. Hare are
examples of this new interest; Marcus G. Singer, Stephen Toulmin,
and John Rawls clearly are.[13] Those who have moved in this direction,however, have not simultaneously returned to metaphysics --
i.e., their exploration of ethical philosophy which is defensible
is not meant to give comfort to those who persist in a fancy for
metaphysical ethics. On the contrary, in their attitude toward
metaphysics, the more recent efforts show considerable continuity
with the intuitionist and emotivist positions that they otherwise
reject.
          It is noteworthy that both intuitionism and emotivism
ruled out metaphysical ethics *in principle*. For Moore, metaphysical
ethics (as naturalistic ethics) assume that good is definable,
while in truth it is not; for Ayer, metaphysical ethics (as all
normative ethics) assume that ethical evaluations are cognitive,
while in truth they are not. From these perspectives, in other
words, it was not necessary to examine each proposed metaphysical
ethic on its merits; on the contrary, the very nature of ethics
made all such proposals invalid. But if, with more recent ethical
philosophy, ethical evaluations are now assumed to be defensible,
can metaphysical ethics still be rejected in principle? This essay
will argue for a negative answer to that question -- i.e., will
seek to show that the premise of defensibility precludes a whole-
sale dismissal of metaphysical ethics. Given this conclusion, recent philosophical ethics, because it accepts the premise, and recent theological ethics, because it seeks a metaphysical backing,
will have some common ground to explore -- for both will have reasc
to entertain proposed metaphysical theories of ethics. This essay,
then, seeks to establish that common ground.
          It is a well-known dictum that one counter example dis-
proves a universal claim. The relevant universal claim is that the

premise of defensibility rules out metaphysical ethics as such. I will seek to refute this claim by showing that it does not hold with at least one understanding of metaphysics -- namely, that of Charles Hartshorne. Assuming that metaphysics is what Hartshorne says it is, in other words, this paper will argue that a defensible ethic must be metaphysically based. The thesis may be stated more concisely: given Hartshorne's view of metaphysics, a defensible ethic must be metaphysical.

II.

The scope of the argument to be attempted requires a few comments toward greater precision. I will postpone until a later section a clarification of Hartshorne's definition of metaphysics and discuss in this section what is meant and what is implied in speaking of defensible ethical theory. It is well-known that many philosophers in this century, again through a debt to G. E. Moore, have distinguished between two different senses of the term "ethical theory." It is one thing, they explain, to ask for an *analysis* of ethical terms -- i.e., for an understanding of the nature of these concepts or how they function in discourse or by what method, if any, claims using them may be validated. It is something else to ask for the *moral content* of these terms -- i.e., for an understanding by virtue of which good or right decisions may be distinguished from bad or wrong ones. The first set of questions, we are told, belong to the realm of meta-ethical theory; the second to the theory of normative ethics. Some who advance this distinction have insisted that answers to meta-ethical questions are devoid of normative implications, a claim which I am inclined to think can be true only if emotivism is true -- i.e., only if normative ethical theory is impossible. But one need not posit a complete independence of the two realms in order to believe that the distinction is important. Indeed, I would call this paper a meta-ethical discussion, although I do not think that it is entirely neutral with respect to normative questions. Be that as it may, however, the point I wish to stress is that the discussion is *about* normative ethical theory -- i.e., the thesis asserts that a theory which distinguishes good and bad choices must, given the stated qualifications, be metaphysical. Since it is normative ethical theory that I presume to be defensible, I am ruling out by hypothesis both the emotivism exemplified by Ayer and Stevenson and the intuitionism exemplified by Moore, Prichard and Ross. If ethical evaluations are defensible by argument, they are necessarily cognitive and the fundamental concepts of ethical discourse cannot be indefinable.

Some attention should be given to the notion that the defensible foundations of ethics can be defined. I take this to mean simply that there is some general principle or principles to which all ethical evaluations should conform. In putting the matter so, I may be charged by some with covert dismissal of the view that what one ought to do depends solely upon the particularities of the agent's context -- i.e., the view that the definable basis of ethics

is always "situational" or "contextual" or "relative." Such a view
has found expression in some versions of existentialist theory and,
alternatively, in the claim that the criteria of obligation are
always relative to one's culture or society. The issue, however,
is whether evaluations consistent with such a theory could be defended by argument. Contextualists may contend that they can be --
if by none other, at least by the argument that a given evaluation
was made without attention to anything beyond the relevant particularities of the situation. But just insofar as this is said to be
an argument, appeal is made to a general principle -- namely, the
principle that choices should always be made solely on the basis of
the relevant particularities. Moreover, only a general principle
could specify what constitutes a *relevant* particularity. But since
appeal is made to a general principle, choice is *not* made solely on
the basis of particularities. In short, I hold that if contextual-
ism or relativism can be defended, it is not relativism any more --
and, therefore, I conclude that defensible ethics involves a general principle or principles.

   I have just used the phrase "general principle *or principles*." But can there be more than one general principle in defensible normative ethics? Some philosophers say yes, that there are
at least two fundamental principles, neither of which can be rede-
fined as a special case of some other. William Frankena, for instance, has argued that "there are at least two basic and independent principles of morality, that of beneficence..., and that of
justice."[14] According to this view, there are conceivable situations of ethical choice in which the alternative in conformity with
one principle is not the alternative in conformity with the other.
Presumably, the agent is then left with no ethical criterion to
which he might appeal in choosing between the two alternatives --
and in order to act, must arbitrarily choose. I hold, however,
that such a theory cannot be true if ethical evaluation is defensible. Ethically speaking, arbitrary choice is permitted when two
or more choices are equally good or best or right. If this is not
the case, and if one is presented with no criterion to which choice
might appeal, ethical theory has insofar returned to non-cognitivism.
If, on the other hand, two or more alternative choices are equally
worthwhile, there must be a single definition or principle which
both exemplify. To argue in this way is not necessarily to deny
that ethics involves in some sense both beneficence and justice.
The argument does require, however, that beneficence and justice
can in some way be compared to each other, so that alternative
choices can, in principle at least, be called equally good. Consequently, there must be some common coin of the ethical realm,
some common measure -- and, in this sense, one fundamental principle
of ethics.

   I will call this fundamental principle of ethics the definition of good, so that defensible normative theory requires a defensible definition of good. In choosing the term "good" as the
fundamental concept of ethics, however, I do not mean to take sides
in the debate between "deontologists" and "teleologists" in ethical
theory. Alan Gewirth has summarized the considerable discussion of
this distinction as follows: deontological criteria are those

whereby "one ought to do that which is inherently fair or just or right, as determined either by direct consideration of the action and its situation of itself, or by reference to some general formal principle;" teleological criteria are those whereby "one ought to do that which will have the best consequences, do the most good, maximize utility."[15] It might be argued, as Gewirth does, that this distinction is something less than completely clear. There seem to be several issues involved -- e.g., whether the fundamental principle of ethical discourse identifies a form to be simply exemplified or a content to be maximized; whether action is ethical by virtue of its own character or the character of its consequences or probable consequences. In any case, all such questions are left open in the way "good" is intended here -- which is simply to identify whatever most general principle justifies ethical choice. If one wishes, the term "positive value" in its ethically relevant sense can without loss of meaning be substituted.[16]

The remainder of this essay, then, is concerned with the belief that ethics requires a definition of good which is defensible by argument. The price of that premise is the issue to be addressed, and I will argue that a defensible definition of good must be metaphysical. In the next section, I will try to show that this definition must be constituted by some existential feature or aspect. In the following section, I will try to show that the existential feature in question must be, in Hartshorne's sense of the term, metaphysical.

III.

One of the claims most widely used to sustain the putative independence of ethics from metaphysics is the claim that metaphysical ethics always commits the naturalistic fallacy. My discussion of what is implied by a defensible definition of good will proceed through an examination of this claim. The term "naturalistic fallacy," as is well-known, is another part of the legacy of G. E. Moore.[17] For reasons that are not completely clear, and which, in any case, we do not need to discuss here, Moore held that the simple and indefinable property that "good" denotes is a "non-natural" property. Further, he held that most, if not all, proposed definitions of good identify intrinsic value with some "natural" property. Consequently, his central claim that good is indefinable could be restated as the fallacy of every attempt to define a non-natural property in terms of a natural one. "This method [the fallacious naturalistic method] consists in substituting for 'good' some one property of a natural object or collection of natural objects."[18]

Subsequent philosophers who did not share Moore's ethical intuitionism have nonetheless believed that his discussion of the naturalistic fallacy contains an insight that transcends his particular ethical theory. They have, then, sought greater clarity of statement. "The question," writes William Frankena, "is whether our most basic ethical and value premises can be derived logically from factual ones alone."[19] With much the same meaning, G. J.

Warnock says that the issue is whether we are "logically obliged
to adopt any particular facts or features as standards or criteria
of evaluation."[20] Many, including Frankena and Warnock, have
argued that naturalism is fallacious because, as Moore saw in his
own way, description and evaluation, statements of fact and statements of value, are logically independent.[21] Thus, for instance,
to describe the character of Ghandi never commits one logically to
calling Ghandi a good (or bad) man -- however true that judgment
about Ghandi may be. The term "fact," however, may also be misleading, since it is often understood to mean "empirical state of
affairs" -- i.e., some existential situation or aspect thereof that
might have been otherwise. To the contrary, Moore and most subsequent anti-naturalists have explicitly included metaphysical and
theological descriptions in the ban. In this regard, the character
of God and the character of Ghandi are said to be on equal footing.
Consequently, "statements of fact" is perhaps best replaced with
"existential statements" -- where, for our purposes, an existential
statement is one that denotes some feature or features of actual
and/or possible states of affairs. Anti-naturalists hold, then,
that our basic ethical and value premise or principle cannot be
derived from an existential feature alone -- metaphysical or otherwise. In relation to the concern of this essay, the import is
clear: if naturalism is a fallacy, the definition of good cannot
be metaphysical.

But why is naturalism always fallacious? Anti-naturalism
has frequently been defended through what has been called the "open
question argument." Were it the case, this argument runs, that an
existential statement constitutes the definition of good, then to
affirm the statement and deny the definition would be self-contradictory. But take any existential statement you please (e.g., a
description of the character of Ghandi); it remains an "open question" (i.e., a meaningful question) whether the existential feature
there denoted is good. Consequently, there is no contradiction involved in accepting the statement and denying the definition -- and,
to say the same, some criterion or principle independent of the
proposed definition is required to settle the evaluative issue. So
stated, however, the open question argument is unconvincing. Indeed, as William Frankena (among others) has pointed out, this argument merely begs the question of naturalism. Any given naturalist
might reply that the existential statement or feature upon which
his ethical theory is based does *not* permit a meaningful question
about evaluation. For the anti-naturalist to say that every such
statement does is simply to restate, but not to demonstrate, his
thesis -- and, with this, the discussion returns to its beginning.[22]

Having made this point, Frankena goes on to advance a
further argument for *why* any given existential statement leaves open
the question of evaluation. He invites us to propose any naturalist
definition of good we please. The naturalist, Frankena continues,
must claim either that this definition of good currently informs
common discourse or that we *should* use the term "good" as proposed;
the naturalist, in other words, is either "reportive" or "reforming"
regarding our use of ethical terms.[23] In either case, he implies
that it is *good* to use the term "good" in this way, and *that*

evaluation of our actual or possible discourse wants justification.
If "the character of God" is proposed as the definition of good,
the proposer implicitly asserts that it is good for us in our
ethical deliberations to use the term "good" with this meaning.
But this last judgment -- which implies an ethical principle something like: so act as to be insofar as possible similar to God --
has not been justified by the proposed definition. Naturalist
theory, in other words, includes a suppressed premise or disguised
principle without which the move from existential statement to
ethical evaluation is illicit.

> In other words, to advocate the adoption of or continued adherence
> to a definition of an ethical or value term seems to be tantamount
> to trying to justify the corresponding moral principle. Appealing
> to a definition in support of a principle is not a solution to the
> problem of justification, for the definition needs to be justified,
> and justifying it involves the same problems that justifying a
> principle does.[24]

The naturalist, to say the same, falsely implies that his definition
of good is true by definition. The naturalist proposal, and this
is simply a way of summarizing Frankena's point, is a persuasive
definition.
    Let us examine Frankena's defense. Why does it seem
plausible to argue that every naturalist definition is persuasive
because it suppresses a premise to the effect that "good" should
be used in the way proposed? Surely the answer is that "good"
seemingly could be defined differently than proposed.[25] Should a
given naturalist suggest that good is defined by the character of
Ghandi (or God), someone else might propose that good is defined
by the character of Hitler (or in any one of a number of ways different from the original proposal). However repugnant the counter-
proposal may be, Frankena's point is that at least one alternative
definition is meaningful, i.e., logically speaking, could be true
-- and it is the presence of a meaningful alternative to any given
naturalist definition that makes the latter a persuasive definition.
In other words, a given definition of good cannot be true by definition if alternatives are possibly true.
    This last point is indisputable, but it suggests a ques-
tion. Suppose it could be shown that a particular naturalist definition of good has no meaningful alternative -- i.e., that every
supposed alternative is sheerly verbal or meaningless. In that
case, there would be no suppressed premise. Given that ethical
theory is defensible, the implication that it is good to use "good"
in the way proposed would be justified by the unavoidable assumption that it is good to use the term meaningfully. The definition
of good would be, in the case now in question, true by definition.
The anti-naturalist might concede this point, but only with the
comment that it is hollow. Surely, he might claim, a meaningful
alternative is available for every proposed naturalist definition
of good. However plausible this claim may seem, let us not take
the concession lightly. In making it, the anti-naturalist admits
that Frankena's argument also begs the question of whether naturalis

is always fallacious until it is demonstrated that every possible naturalist definition of good has a meaningful alternative.

But, some will argue, this is easily demonstrated, for the definition of good does not have to be naturalistic, i.e., may not be constituted by an existential statement. Let us, for want of another term, call theories which hold to a non-naturalist definition of good "formal" in character.[26] Of course, if a formal definition is offered, it like any other proposal faces the problem of getting itself proved. But that problem need not be solved here. If it can be shown that a formal understanding of good is so much as meaningful, Frankena's argument against naturalism will be upheld -- for that argument merely requires that every naturalist proposal have a meaningful alternative.

We may use the term "formal" to characterize supposedly non-naturalist definitions of good because this position holds that the definition of good identifies simply the proper form of moral reasoning or moral logic -- "the moral point of view." Some insist that such a definition is "purely formal" -- i.e., has no determinate moral content or, more generally, says nothing about what is good or bad -- and for this reason is non-naturalist. R. M. Hare, for instance, argues that moral reasoning must be prescriptive and universalizing, but that these "rules of the moral 'game'," this "framework within which moral reasoning takes place,"[27] is entirely neutral regarding what one ought to do or what constitutes good action. "Ethics is morally neutral,"[28] as Hare puts it. We need not examine the intricacies of Hare's carefully reasoned discussion to discover a dilemma in the attempt to distinguish absolutely between the form of moral reasoning and the content of the moral life. Consider the following question: Is the agent whose reasoning about his actions follows the proper form insofar a morally better person than one whose reasoning does not? If the answer is "yes," then clearly some determinate moral content is embodied in Hare's theory; actions are always better insofar as they are taken on the basis of moral reasoning, worse insofar as they are not. If the answer is "no" (i.e., that such a judgment is a matter of moral content regarding which the theory is neutral), then this theory is, at least at the fundamental level, a form of emotivism; moral reasoning and all that follows from it is better only if one prefers to take action on that basis. The dilemma arises because reasoning about one's actions is itself a human activity -- indeed, an activity which is (or at least may be) a part of all human action. Consequently, the claim that good has a purely formal (i.e., devoid of determinate content) definition (i.e., the theory is non-emotivist) is incoherent.[29]

Other formalists may concede that "the moral point of view" is not morally neutral but still insist that it provides a non-naturalist definition of good. Frankena himself seems to take this position. We need not pause to seek precisely what for him constitutes the moral point of view. Suffice it to say that, following Kurt Baier, he includes in it such characteristics as being free, informed, impartial, and willing to universalize one's judgments -- and the claim is that the very meaning of "moral" requires this perspective.

If one considers an item in this reflective way and comes out in
favor of it, one is rationally justified in judging it to be intrinsically good, even if one cannot prove one's judgment. In doing
so, one claims that everyone else who does likewise will concur; and
one's judgment is really justified if this claim is correct, which,
however, one can never know for certain.

The fact that ethical and value judgments claim a consensus on the
part of others does not mean that the individual thinker must bow
to the judgment of the majority in his society. He is not claiming
an actual consensus,...He is claiming an *ideal* consensus which transcends majorities and actual societies.[30]

But how can it be said that this definition of good is
non-naturalist? A point of view which is free, informed, impartial,
willing to universalize, etc., is clearly something that does or
might exist, is a feature of human consciousness -- and for some
thing or some action to be favored by such a point of view is a
relation that does or might exist. Again, the point is that human
reasoning about action is itself an activity, i.e., something that
exists. Frankena's apparent attempt to suggest that this theory is
non-naturalist because it appeals to an ideal rather than actual
consensus merely confirms the point being made here. For an ideal
society no less than an actual one could only be described by
existential statements.
I conclude that the notion of a formal alternative to
naturalist definitions of good, whether "purely formal" or not, is
meaningless. Recall, then, Frankena's implied claim that naturalism
is fallacious because every proposed naturalistic definition of good
has a meaningful alternative. Since non-naturalist definitions of
good are not meaningful, Frankena's claim can be true only if *all*
definitions of good have a meaningful alternative, i.e., if *no* definition of good is true by definition. But if all definitions of
good are persuasive, no one is defensible. Hence, if naturalism
is a fallacy so too is the premise that ethical evaluations admit
of reasoned defense. Since we have presumed the latter, the conclusion to be drawn for the purposes of this paper is that naturalism is not always fallacious. In the context of this discussion,
in other words, Frankena's argument serves only to show that some
definition of good constituted by an existential statement (i.e.,
some naturalistic definition of good) is true by definition.

IV.

If the argument of the last section is correct, we are
now in search of the existential statement or existential feature
which constitutes the non-persuasive definition of good. But our
thesis includes the claim that this definition is metaphysical, and
we are a far cry from giving decent reason to think that. Nothing
has been said, in other words, to show that ethical naturalism must
be metaphysical naturalism, simply because all existential statements are not metaphysical statements.

The full thesis under discussion is: given Hartshorne's definition of metaphysics, the defensible definition of good is metaphysical. At this point, then, I turn to the thought of Charles Hartshorne and draw upon the distinction he develops between two kinds of existential variables.[31] The term "existential variable" means a recurring feature or form of existence -- and, therefore, a feature in terms of which some or all existential possibilities might be compared. Clearly, some such variables, in the nature of the case, can be illustrated by some but *not* all states of affairs. Hartshorne calls these "local variables." Self-consciousness is, for instance, something that varies from human individual to human individual in, say, clarity and breadth; but it is not something in terms of which one kind of plant may be compared to another. Presuming that only humans are self-conscious, this is, in Hartshorne's terms, a variable local to or restricted to human existence.

But, Hartshorne continues, every local variable is a specific form of some wider variable. Thus, if plants are not self-conscious, there is some more inclusive existential feature that is illustrated in both human and plant life and of which self-consciousness is an example. Life itself might be such a wider variable -- self-conscious life differing from plant life in, say, its complexity. Hartshorne suggests sentience as another common form. But some of the variables in terms of which plants and people are compared, e.g., life, are still local, even though less provincial than self-consciousness. For they do not characterize inorganic existence. In conceiving of ever wider variables, then, one comes, sooner or later, to the notion of cosmic variables -- i.e., existential features illustrated by all possible states of affairs, forms universal throughout all existential possibility. "Thus the breadth of the [cosmic] variables is that of the whole universe of what is and what might be."[32] As it happens, Hartshorne believes that sentience, properly understood, is such a variable. Indeed, he wishes to argue that, properly generalized, psychic categories (e.g., feeling, purpose) apply to all existence; hence he has called his thought "panpsychism."[33] But we need not pause to judge the merits of his particular candidates. The point is that these cosmic variables, whatever they are, occupy the metaphysical throne -- i.e., the understanding of metaphysics which will inform this discussion holds that metaphysical features are cosmic variables.[34]

Of course, this view of existential features and, especially, of metaphysical features may itself be challenged. At the least, however, I hold that it is not obviously false -- and, therefore, that only an extended discussion can convincingly weigh its merits. Consequently, it will be significant for ethical discussion if we can show that with this understanding a defensible ethic must be metaphysically based. Having said that, a comment is still in order regarding the necessity for cosmic variables in Hartshorne's view -- for this is probably the question which most readily comes to mind. Why must we acknowledge the presence of cosmic forms of existence? Presume, Hartshorne replies, that there are only local variables. In that case, there are differing features of existence

(e.g., human and plant existence) which are not specific forms of
some more general feature. Moreover, the difference between them
must be definite; sheerly indefinite difference leaves no two things
to be different. But definite difference requires a common variable
in terms of which the difference may be specified. Hence, the
denial of cosmic variables is untenable; local variables presuppose
them.

> The...local variable differs from other local variables, and not
> anyhow but in a determinate way. Now something must measure the
> difference between the...local variable and other variables, must
> indicate the extent of likeness and difference involved. Only a
> more inclusive, ultimately a cosmic, variable can furnish such a
> measure.[35]

Given that the definition of good is constituted by some
existential feature, we may now, for the sake of linguistic economy,
speak of local definitions of good and cosmic or metaphysical definitions of good. The question, then, is whether any local definition will suffice -- i.e., could be true by definition. Examination
of this question may be approached by way of an example. That the
definition of good is local is the inescapable claim of ethical
humanism -- i.e., some character specific to human action or to
human experience is said to be the defining feature. Thus, it
might be said that human happiness or human welfare, understood in
some specific way, constitutes the good, such that choices are
ethically approved insofar as they promote or intend to promote the
greatest human happiness. Alternatively, some humanists might argue
that human action which is just, given some understanding of justice,
is the ethically relevant definition of good. In either case, and
in all humanist cases, some existential form restricted to human
existence provides the criterion or definition of good.
Many have levelled against ethical humanism the charge
of imperialism toward non-human existence. If "nature" is taken to
mean non-human or at least sub-human existence, it is said, then
ethical humanism implies that the natural environment within which
human existence is set is without intrinsic worth. As a consequence,
the indictment reads, humanism has aided and abetted an exploitative
orientation toward nature, the destructive consequences of which
have only recently become apparent on a widespread scale. Whether
ethical humanism is necessarily committed to such exploitation is
an issue demanding at least an essay of its own -- and, therefore,
one I will not try to settle here. I make reference to the discussion solely in order to suggest that humanism excludes the
applicability of "good" to some forms of existence. If good is defined by some form of human action or experience, then non-human
forms of existence can never be good. So much follows strictly
from the fact that forms of specifically human existence are local
variables. But, then, it follows that no statement about human
existence can provide a definition of good which is true by definition. For to every definition of good constituted by a specifically
human variable, there is a meaningful alternative -- namely, a definition by virtue of which the applicability of good is wider.

Consequently, for reasons which Frankena presents, every humanistic understanding of good is a persuasive definition.

Consider the proposal that some given form of human action defines the good. To this proposal a meaningful alternative may be found by so defining good that it applies not only to this form of human action but also to some forms of non-human existence. Some have argued, to specify the example further, that human action that respects the purposiveness of other humans is not only good but undeniably so. Briefly stated, the argument runs as follows: every human action involves an inescapable affirmation that the purposiveness of the agent is good; consequently, the agent is always caught in contradiction if he or she does not affirm (respect) the purposiveness of those who are recipients of the action; hence, human action respectful of purposiveness is good, or at least better, and action disrespectful of purposiveness is bad, or at least worse.[36] This argument deserves a far more precise and extended statement than I have granted before one judges its merits. For our purposes, let us presume its validity and call the good human action in question "just" action. To do so does not commit one to the view that just human action is the *definition* of good. That something is undeniably good does not entail that it *alone* is good. On the contrary, as a definition of good, the kind of action we have been discussing has a meaningful alternative -- e.g., a criterion of good by virtue of which the term applies also to some forms of nature, a definition constituted by some wider variable of which just human action is a specific form. Such a criterion might be found in the suggestion that anything (human or otherwise) is good insofar as its existence promotes harmony among all things. Since respect for the purposiveness of others may be understood as an attempt to maintain harmony among human beings, just human action becomes a specific form of this wider definition. But if there is a meaningful alternative, just human action is a persuasive definition of good.[37]

The argument may be generalized to show that the definition of good cannot be constituted by any local variable or existential form. Take any proposed definition so constituted; there is always a meaningful alternative -- namely, a definition constituted by a wider existential form. Consequently, the first definition proposed is persuasive. The same considerations may now be applied to the wider variable if it too, its width notwithstanding, is local. Thus, no local definition of good can be true by definition. If the definition of good is defensible, it must be constituted by some other kind of existential feature. But there is only one other kind -- namely, a cosmic or metaphysical existential variable. Hence, the defensible definition of good must be metaphysical.

Antagonists are likely to claim that this conclusion has been reached much too quickly. We should, therefore, consider at least the more obvious objections -- and, in the process, perhaps clarify the argument. Granted that no local definition of good is true by definition, some may say, it has not been shown that some metaphysical definition is. Indeed, the argument may be stood on its head. If a cosmic definition of good is a meaningful alternative to a local one, then the reverse is also true -- and, at best, the argument shows that good *might* be metaphysical. But this objection has missed the point. If a cosmic application of the term is so much as meaningful, a narrower application of good cannot constitute the definition. For the definition of good must be true by definition -- and if a proposed local definition were, the cosmic application would not be so much as meaningful. The reverse, however, is not the case. The fact that applying good to some local forms of existence is meaningful does not rule out a metaphysical definition. For the metaphysical definition is entirely consistent with, indeed demands, the narrower application. In short, if a metaphysical definition of good is meaningful, a local definition cannot be meaningful *as a definition* -- or, if good might be metaphysical, it must be, and the argument cannot be stood on its head.

A second objection, then, may question whether a metaphysical definition of good is meaningful. The definition of good under discussion, we are reminded, is to be the basis for a defensible *ethical* theory -- and, whatever else ethical deliberation involves, it provides grounds upon which to choose one alternative or course of action rather than another. But, this objection contends, a metaphysical definition of good implies that everything, actual or possible, is good -- so that it cannot provide grounds for choice. This objection assumes, however, that to call everything good is to call everything *equally* good, and that assumption is gratuitous. We saw earlier that, for Hartshorne, the differences between local variables must be measurable in terms of cosmic variables. The same point may be turned slightly: because there are differences between local variables, the cosmic forms of existence must be variables. Different exemplifications of the variable good, in other words, may be good in different measure, even though each is good in some measure. Hartshorne, following Alfred North Whitehead, has argued that the metaphysical definition of good is aesthetic in character, such that realization of unity-in-diversity is good. "The basic value is the intrinsic value of experiencing, as a unity of feeling inclusive of whatever volition or thought the experience contains, and exhibiting harmony or beauty."[38] Or, as Whitehead says it, "the teleology of the universe is directed to the production of beauty."[39] Although all existence exhibits beauty or unity-in-diversity in some way, any particular example will do so in greater or lesser measure. Just because cosmic variables provide a measure by which differing forms of existence can be compared, in other words, a metaphysical definition of good provides grounds upon which to weigh alternative choices or courses of action -- and thus a basis for ethics.

The mention again of comparison provides a term with which the argument in this section may be summarized. Take any proposed definition of good that is local. That proposal implies that some forms of existence are not good (whether "not good" means "bad" or "neither good nor bad"). But the comparison between things good and things not good is an *evaluative* comparison -- so that the variable in terms of which this difference is measured must be a definition of good. Hence, the proposed local definition of good cannot be true and the evaluative variable (definition of good) must be cosmic or metaphysical. In short, just because good things must, in regard to their goodness, be compared to other things, the criterion of their goodness must be something common to all -- and if ethical evaluations are defensible, they can appeal only to a principle established in the nature of all things.

V.

This essay began with a comment regarding Alvin Pitcher's commitments in theology -- and, whatever has been accomplished since, we are still some distance from demonstrating the viability of *theological* ethics. The discussion has concerned itself with *metaphysical* ethics -- and, in this, has only sought to show that the quest for a defensible ethic must consider each metaphysical proposal on its peculiar merits. The conclusion is reached by demonstrating that one view of metaphysics entails that defensible ethics are metaphysically based. If successful, the defense of this modest thesis does no more -- and no less -- than open the door for ethical discussion between some recent analytical philosophers and some recent theological ethicists. It may come as no surprise, however, that I chose Hartshorne's view of metaphysics as the basis for the argument because Hartshorne himself is a theist, and because I wish to recommend attention by both philosophers and theologians to his thought. In saying this, I certainly do not imply that his understanding of metaphysics is dictated by a prior commitment to theism. On the contrary, what recommends Hartshorne's thought to me is that he is a theist for philosophical reasons.

The line of thought which leads from the present essay to theistic ethics may be briefly suggested. Given Hartshorne's view, I have argued that good must be a cosmic variable because the comparison of good things to others is an evaluative comparison. I may now suggest that in some sense there can be, finally, only *one* cosmic variable; for all difference implies comparison, and two different cosmic variables would leave the problem of comparing that difference. Hartshorne surely would say that this one universal form may be analytically divided into aspects, but these must be aspects which imply each other, so that any one in its full implications embraces all the others. According to the argument of this essay, good is one of the aspects of this inclusive principle in terms of which all things are to be measured, the variable in terms of which all things are to be understood. Finally, if, as Hartshorne goes on to argue, the metaphysical measure of all things requires a metaphysical individual, so that one may speak of a being in relation to which all things are understood, and whose very essence defines the good, one is at least very close to saying that good is defined by the character of God.[40] To be sure, these comments provide no more than the roughest outline of an argument -- and, therefore, call for extensive further discussion. It is equally clear that the discussion is one which Alvin Pitcher would find expressive of interests and commitments which have long informed his academic and religious life.

NOTES AND REFERENCES

1. Paul Tillich, *The Protestant Era* (Chicago: The University of Chicago Press, 1948; Abridged Edition, Phoenix Books, 1957), p. 83.
2. See Aristotle, *Metaphysics*, 1003a 21-32.
3. Paul Tillich, *Systematic Theology* (3 vols.; Chicago: University of Chicago Press, 1951), I, 18.
4. Indeed, I am inclined to think that Hartshorne has, through several decades devoted to the task, fulfilled the charge which he gave to himself in the preface of an early work:

> To the mountainous -- I had almost said monstrous -- mass of writings devoted to "philosophical theology," what can there be to add? I answer simply, if without apparent modesty, there is exactitude, logical rigor.

Man's Vision of God and the Logic of Theism (New York: Harper and Row, 1941; Hamden, Conn.:   Archon Books, 1964), p. vii.
5. A reading of any of the competent reviews of twentieth century ethics in Anglo-American philosophy is sufficient to convince one of this point. See, e.g., Mary Warnock, *Ethics Since 1900* (London: Oxford University Press, 1966); G. J. Warnock, *Contemporary Moral Philosophy* (New York: St. Martin's Press, 1967); Brand Blanshard, *Reason and Goodness* (New York: Macmillan Company, 1961).
6. G. E. Moore, *Principia Ethica* (Cambridge: Cambridge University Press, 1903).
7. *Ibid.*, p. 6.
8. *Ibid.*, p. x.
9. See *ibid.*, chapter 4.
10. See Mary Warnock, *Ethics Since 1900,* chapter 3.
11. Alfred Jules Ayer, *Language, Truth and Logic* (London: Victor Gollancz Ltd., 1936); C. L. Stevenson, *Ethics and Language* (New Haven: Yale University Press, 1945).
12. G. J. Warnock, *Contemporary Moral Philosophy*, p. 18.
13. Kurt Baier, *The Moral Point of View* (Ithaca, New York: Cornell University Press, 1958); R. M. Hare, *Freedom and Reason* (New York: Oxford University Press, 1963); Marcus G. Singer, *Generalization in Ethics* (New York: Alfred A. Knopf, 1961); Stephen Toulmin, *The Place of Reason in Ethics* (Cambridge: Cambridge University Press, 1964); John Rawls, *A Theory of Justice* (Cambridge, Mass.:   Harvard University Press, 1971).
14. William K. Frankena, *Ethics* (Englewood Cliffs, New Jersey: Prentice-Hall, 1963), p. 35.
15. Alan Gewirth, *Political Philosophy* (New York: Macmillan Company, 1965), p. 5.
16. Some philosophers have distinguished between purely formal and substantive principles of good, such that those of the first class are devoid of determinate implications regarding what choices or things in particular are good. In what has been said, I have not meant to rule out the possibility of a purely formal definition of good. That question will be considered below in the context of whether the definition of good must be constituted by an existential statement.

17. However, as G. J. Warnock points out, "the idea is certainly older than that, and has commonly been supposed to originate with Hume." *Contemporary Moral Philosophy*, p. 62.

18. Moore, *Principia Ethica*, p. 40. I think Mary Warnock is correct when she says of Moore's thought,.

> It is clear, then, that first and foremost it is supposed to be fallacious to define "good" and secondly it is fallacious to define a non-natural in terms of a natural object.

Ethics Since 1900, p. 13.

19. Frankena, *Ethics*, p. 80.

20. G. J. Warnock, *Contemporary Moral Philosophy*, p. 65.

21. See, e.g., *ibid.*, pp. 64-65.

22. Frankena, *Ethics*, pp. 82-83.

23. *Ibid.*, p. 81.

24. *Ibid.*, p. 84.

25. More precisely, the answer is that good seemingly could be defined differently than proposed *or not defined at all*. But this additional alternative identifies either intuitionism or non-cognitivism, both of which we have ruled out by hypothesis.

26. Some who take what I call the formal position in ethical theory may object to the suggestion that they are proposing a *definition* of good. Frankena, who uses "definism" as synonymous with naturalism, clearly would be one. See *ibid.*, p. 80. The issue, however, is purely verbal. The point, however named, is that these theories defend a non-naturalist principle for ethical evaluation.

27. R. M. Hare, *Freedom and Reason* (New York: Oxford University Press, 1965), p. 89.

28. *Ibid.*, p. 88.

29. Another way to put the same point is to say that a purely formal definition of good could only be a meta-ethical, not a normative, definition. And the fact that Hare's understanding of moral reasoning could be purely formal only if his theory is fundamentally emotivist lends credence to what I suggested above -- namely, that a complete independence between meta-ethical and normative ethical questions is consistent only with emotivism.

30. Frankena, *Ethics*, pp. 94, 96. See Kurt Baier, *The Moral Point of View* (Ithaca, New York: Cornell University Press, 1958; Abridged Edition, New York: Random House, 1965).

31. See Charles Hartshorne, "The Cosmic Variables" in *Beyond Humanism* (Chicago: Willett, Clark and Company, 1937; Bison Book Edition, Lincoln: University of Nebraska Press, 1968), pp. 111-124. Hartshorne's view of metaphysics is developed in many of his articles and books. I recommend especially *Creative Synthesis and Philosophic Method* (LaSalle, Illinois: Open Court, 1970).

32. *Ibid.*, p. 114.

33. See *ibid.*, pp. 115f.

34. This understanding seems a plausible example of the Aristotelian and Tillichian definition of metaphysics mentioned at the outset of this paper -- i.e., the study of "being qua being" or "reality as such."

35. Hartshorne, "The Cosmic Variables," p. 113.

36. I first encountered this kind of argument in a paper by Alan Gewirth, "Categorical Consistency in Ethics," presented at the University of Chicago in 1966. To my knowledge, it is unpublished.

37. It will not do to say that the argument is illicit because "just human action" is a deontological criterion while "promoting harmony" is a teleological one. Whether the definition of good is deontological or teleo-logical (presuming this distinction to be sensible) is one of the questions at issue -- and if deontological criteria are necessarily local to human existence, then the argument serves to show that the definition of good cannot be deonto-logical.

38. Charles Hartshorne, *Creative Synthesis and Philosophic Method*, p. 303.

39. Alfred North Whitehead, *Adventures of Ideas* (New York: Macmillan Company, 1933; New York: Free Press, 1967), p. 265.

40. For one statement of this argument, see Charles Hartshorne, *A Natural Theology for Our Time* (LaSalle, Illinois: Open Court, 1967).

PURPOSE, BELONGING, AND EVIL:
PIVOTS OF MEANING

Philip Hefner

In this essay, I intend to focus on an aspect of the
question of meaning. At the outset, let me say what I am dealing
with when I use the word "meaning," and what it is that I consider
to be the "problem of meaning." One of the most fundamental ways
of describing the human adventure pictures the human creature immersed in, overwhelmed by, waves of raw or very particularistically
interpreted experience that cries out for interpretation. The
vividness of the experience and its local significance are very
real, but the segments of experience are largely disconnected; they
do not hang together; they have no ordering principle or organized
coherence. It is this putting together of experiencing, this ordering and organizing of events that I call "meaning." The problem
of meaning is, in the focus that I have chosen for consideration,
the problem of putting our experiencing together in a coherent
shape. When this coherence is found, there is meaning; without it,
there is no meaning.

What is it that provides meaning? Symbols, images, models,
hypotheses that are able to order our experiencing. A symbol that
is large enough and persuasive enough to put our world together is
the key to meaning. This symbol may be vivid and pictorial or abstract and cerebral. Eugene Gendlin has put this as forcefully as
anyone I know. In his own way, he puts it:[1]

> Meaning is *formed* in the interaction of experiencing and something
> that functions symbolically. Feeling without symbolization is
> blind; symbolization is empty. . . . Meaning is formed in the inter-
> action of experiencing and something that functions as a symbol.
> This fact . . . (is) the basic source of order in human experience.

What is the "something" that functions as a symbol? Anything may
so function -- a verbal symbol, a thing, situation, person, act.[2]
Although Gendlin's analysis is directed more at the micro-level
which concentrates upon meaning at an individual level, I believe
that what I am suggesting parallels his effort at a macro-level.
Gendlin is concerned to explain how uninterpreted raw experiencing
is brought to meaning. My intention focuses on this level also,
but even more on the process in which smaller bits of meaning are
brought into conjunction with larger meanings, thus enabling us to
say that "our world has meaning."

A few examples may clarify the formation of meaning and
its problems, as I assess it. A verbal symbol or concept may order

experiencing. The material dialectic of history as elaborated by
the Marxist philosophy functions as symbol for millions of people.
These people have experienced and do experience serfdom, revolution,
hardship, poverty, inefficiency, scarcity, comradeship, victory,
defeat, a whole range of feelings and events, and all of it is put
together and given coherence by the symbol of the dialectic of history which unfolds in class conflict, the overturning of bourgeois
institutions, and the imposition of collectivist structures that
constitute a proletarian society. So gripping is this symbol and
the coherence which it brings that fantastic flips of the mind and
will are undertaken in order to make it square with experiences
that seem to the outsider to be outright contradictions of what the
symbol affirms. The symbol is flexible enough, however, to endure
through a variety of events and experiences. The Marxist symbol
itself, however, is verbal, highly, and at times monotonously, abstract.
          A person and his experience may function as a symbol. I
may be permitted to observe how the person of Martin Luther has
served to give coherence to many. Werner Elert has written that
for most Lutherans, to be Lutheran has been to recapitulate Luther's
own so-called "tower experience."[3] In that experience (and whether
it was a single experience or the amalgamation in Luther's recol-
lection of a whole series of events is still disputed), Luther moved
from the fear and terror that struck him because he believed that
he was in the hands of a wrathful God who demanded righteousness to
the letter, to the position of acknowledgment that God was gracious,
a God who accepted Luther as he was, without one plea, so to speak.
This is the movement from Law to Gospel. For millions of Lutherans,
this transition functions to bestow coherence on the myriad experiences they know. It is their hope that they may know this transition in their own lives, and many believe that they have known it,
and they can interpret the most intimate personal experiences as
well as the most sweeping historical, social, or economic and political events under the categories of Law and Gospel. Time and time
again, they have affirmed that to be authentically Lutheran is to
accept this experience of Luther's as normative, although they have
often dressed that affirmation in layers and layers of dogmatic
garments.
          I take it that the chief characteristic of the problem of
meaning for us today, for us who are moderns and post-moderns, is
that we either cannot unearth symbols that give coherence to our
experiences or, if we do find such symbols, we find such a pluralism
in the systems of coherence which we embrace that we must question
whether there is meaning. All we can affirm, at best, is that there
are meanings, and at the macro-level at which I am speaking, to say
that there is only a plurality of meanings is to deny that there
is any single meaning. If it is true, as Gendlin says, that meaning
is formed in the interaction of experiencing and something that
functions symbolically, our problem is clear. Particularistic
meanings there are, because private and micro-level symbols do exist, but meaning in broad terms, the meaning that can bind a society
or an entire species together is difficult, if not impossible, since
at the macro-level the symbols do not grasp the human community.

The search for meaning, then, is a search for symbols of a larger
sort that can provide meaning.
    In these reflections, we give our attention to three
grand proposals that do claim to be symbols that can bring coherence to our experiencing. As a result of a scrutiny of these symbols, we will conclude that there are certain very clear requirements which any symbol of meaning must fulfill if it is to be adequate.
    The question of meaning, as I have sketched its outlines,
has fundamentally to do with how humans interpret their encounter
with their physical and social world. The search for symbols that
can give coherence to our experiencing is a search for a coherence
that makes sense of the entire world and ourselves in that world.
The absence of meaning implies that we do not understand our "fit"
with the world about us.
    One of the most impressive attempts at meaning has sym-
bolized this encounter between us and our world with an image that
insists that there is ultimately no proper fit. This is the absurdist symbol. The symbol has been set forth by many, perhaps by
none so eloquently as by Albert Camus. The symbol is the figure
of the mythic Sisyphus,[4] exemplified in Meursault, The Stranger,
or Dr. Rieux, who battles the plague.[5]
    Sisyphus was condemned by the gods to devote his days to
pushing a boulder up the hill, only to let it roll down again and
perpetually repeat the process. The absurdity of Sisyphus, and of
all human existence, lies in the fact that there is a divorce between us and our world. We live in a world "suddenly divested of
illusions and lights" in which we feel ourselves strangers. Man's
"exile is without remedy since he is deprived of the memory of a
lost home or the hope of a promised land. This divorce between man
and his life, the actor and his setting, is properly the feeling of
absurdity."
    The fundamental cause for this divorce is that we bring
a set of assumptions to the world, only to find that those assumptions are not really in force. Or, we bring with us certain desires and expectations which the world about us simply refuses to
fulfill. Camus writes:[6]

I said that the world is absurd, but I was too hasty. This world
in itself is not reasonable, that is all that can be said. . . .
Universal reason, practical or ethical, those categories that explain everything, are enough to make a decent man laugh. . . .What
is absurd is the confrontation of this irrational and the wild longing
for clarity whose call echoes in the human heart.

Man stands face to face with the irrational. He feels within him
his longing for happiness and for reason. The absurd is born of
this confrontation between the human need and the unreasonable silence of the world. This must not be forgotten. This must be clung
to because the whole consequence of a life can depend upon it. The
irrational, the human nostalgia, and the absurd that is born of
their encounter--these are the three characters in the drama that
must necessarily end with all the logic of which an existence is

capable. . . .I am thus justified in saying that the feeling of absurdity does not spring from the mere scrutiny of a fact or an impression, but that it bursts from the comparison between a bare fact
and a certain reality. It lies in neither of the elements compared;
it is born of their confrontation. . . .the absurd is not in man nor
in the world, but in their presence together. For the moment it is
the only bond uniting them.

        In his novels, the characters live out this absurdity,
but they have obligations laid upon them--to struggle against evil
in the world in an attempt to use their finite freedom to fill their
earthly lives to the fullest that is possible. Sisyphus is interesting to Camus, because each time he turns to descend the hill,
in that moment he is aware of his fate, and he accepts it. His
further efforts to push the boulder thus are efforts of defiance
and efforts to make that life as rich as it can be.
        Disjunction, out of synchronization, out of kilter--this
is the message of the absurdist symbol. It makes sense of our
experiencing and thus bestows meaning, in an ironic fashion, because it tells us that we should expect no fit between ourselves
and the world. It seems strange to say that the absurdist Sisyphus
is a symbol of meaning, but we can say this, because the Sisyphean
figure does organize our experiencing and thus makes sense of it--
at least to a large degree, on the surface. It may be a coherence
of noncoherence, but it does provide the security of meaning, the
lucidity of knowing that absurdity is all there is. This lucidity,
Camus tells us, was Sisyphus' victory over his fate

        There is no fate that cannot be surmounted by scorn. . . .There is
        no sun without shadow, and it is essential to know the night. The
        absurd man says yes and his effort will henceforth be unceasing. . .
        he knows himself to be the master of his days.[7]

        Contrasted with the absurdist symbol, which makes its own
peculiar contribution to the equation that includes experiencing
and meaning are the symbols that come from the sciences--the natural
and the socio-cultural sciences. One of the most important symbols
from these sciences is that of evolution, if we understand that
evolution is not a simplistic image of the steady progress of life
under the popular rubric of survival of the strongest. Evolution,
as I refer to it, asserts that homo sapiens and the culture that
homo sapiens has developed are an intrinsic part of the world ecosystem. The human community is in the world of nature, but nature
is also in the human being. Homo sapiens has created culture, but
in turn is created by culture. Homo sapiens and his culture evolve
according to principles of selection that are commonly observed
throughout the world ecosystem, the principles that set forth the
law that survival proceeds by way of adaptation, just as extinction
awaits the maladaptive. In this context we may even say that within
limits there is purpose in the process of evolution, since the
environment selects for that which is consistent with the order
which is already present in the world.

This symbol from the sciences stands in a curious opposition to the vision of the absurdist, because it speaks of no alienation or out-of-kilteredness between us and our world. Such a gulf is genuinely inconceivable, because the lines of relatedness between ecosystem and homo sapiens, between human culture and physico-natural world are so obvious and discernible. The scientific view is one of belongingness to the world, just as the absurdist vision was one that made non-belonging the basic premise.

Our whole picture of the world, as shaped by the sciences, speaks to us of our belonging within it. From the cosmic singularity which brought the cosmos into being, through the formation of our sun and its planetary system, followed by the evolution of our own planet Earth, with the emergence of life from the inorganic elements and the appearance of human beings who have evolved biologically and culturally up to the present global species community --all this is a picture of the most intimate belonging relationship between us and our world. The human sciences, which chart our dependence upon the social network of language, symbols, values, and survival needs, also testify to the interrelatedness between us and the social world. Language and symbols shape us before we are even aware of being individuals in our own right. Through upbringing, values from our culture form us inwardly without our even knowing it, almost until we reach adulthood. Those values, together with the social needs that are related to the survival of the society, influence mightily our vocational preparation and the careers and occupations we follow. Even the rebel is hardly separable from the environment in which protest is carried out and against which it is directed.

For millions of people, and the number is increasing steadily, some such model or symbol of evolution is highly influential for the way in which they understand themselves and for the way in which they put their experiences together. This symbol puts us and our experience into a vast, complex living system, a system whose stuff is the matter of which we are made, and whose inexorable processes carry us along. This symbol may be a deterministic one, but it is not necessarily such, since we know that we have the freedom to contribute to the system and even to alter it, if ever so slightly. We can even understand how the system in some sense depends upon us. Nevertheless, the organizing power of the symbol lies in its assertion that we are integral to the living system and its workings.

Any number of experiences seem to underscore the power of this symbol. What we have glimpsed about ourselves in relation to our world in the crises of ecology and energy makes sense, because the dislocations are clearly linked to our denial or misunderstanding of our belongingness to the world. Some of the appeal of the Eastern religions, of the American Indians, and of the "back to nature movement" seems to lie in their strong statement about being part of the family of Brother Earth and Sister Nature. Such movements are often considered to be counter to science, but they in fact are one way of affirming the interrelatedness which Evolution as symbol affirms. I include the Marxist vision here, because it claims also to be a scientific view of history, and it has its own way of stating the

principle of selection; it insists in its own way that affirming
our belonging to the process and conforming to it in its evolutionary development is the only viable option for the human community. Whether it is in fact scientific and whether it has discerned accurately the process of historical selection are questions
of dispute, but formally, it shows characteristics of the scientific
style of symbolizing experience.
      Now each of these two powerful symbols of meaning, the
absurdist Sisyphus and the science-based theory of evolution, imposes very great burdens of incrediblity upon us, even though they
do make sense of much of our experience. The absurdist symbol takes
its rise no doubt from the experience of evil which continually
thwarts human intentions, even the very best. It does not, however,
ask simply that we accept a world that is deaf to our cries and
out of synchronization with our desires and enterprises. Nor does
it urge us to consider that we are simply victims of the evils that
absurdity brings with it. On the contrary, it presses us to rebel
against absurdity. For Camus, the absurd man will never accept
the world as it presents its meaningless face to him, even though
he has no reasonable hope that world will become meaningful. He
is resigned to his fate, yet continually dissatisfied with it, re-
volting against it. There is no finer sight, he says,[8]

> than that of the intelligence at grips with a reality that transcends
> it. The sight of human pride is unequaled. No disparagment is of
> any use. That discipline that the mind imposes on itself, that will
> conjured up out of things, that face-to-face struggle have something
> exceptional about them.

The demand, therefore, is to revolt against the absurd world, even
though it is an item of belief that this revolt is itself absurd,
bearing no correlation to the world and thus bearing no promise of
effectiveness.
      In addition to revolt, or perhaps as an elaboration of
it, the absurdist asks us to be scornful of the absurdity. "There
is no fate that cannot be surmounted by scorn. The absurd man says
yes and his effort will henceforth be unceasing. . .he knows himself to be the master of his days."[9] This is Meursault at the end
of the novel, The Stranger, scoffing at his fate, spitting in its
faceless countenance.
      The injunction to revolt against absurdity, even while
the revolt itself is absurd, together with the scorn that is also
enjoined, constitutes, I have said, a burden of incredibility, because it requires a courage in the face of evil and defeat that has
no credible ground. It asks for courage against all hope with an
intrinsic denial of vindication. Why? Simply because it is human.
If we take this injunction to courage seriously, we are on the verge
of having to conclude that humanity is not absurd, that its tenacious insistence on heroism is rooted in the nature of things, but
that would be to contradict the absurdist symbol. It is more likely
that we will not take the challenge up and rather carry out our
Sisyphean tasks in a zombie-like manner, grasping what pleasure we

can on those walks down the hillside after the boulder has rolled
again to the valley.

The symbol of evolution provides us with a ground for
participating in the world around us, a very powerful one. We participate in the world for the same reasons that we share in the
activity of our own body: it is us and we are it. It is precisely
the intimate belongingness with the world, the interpretation between ourselves and the world, that becomes excruciating for us if
we allow this symbol to guide us. Such intimate belonging is in-
tolerable when we reflect on the evil that is in this world and on
the question of whether the world is purposive. Our belongingness
to the world becomes sheer terror if the world is both lacking in
purpose and also full of evil. We find ourselves in the position
of a parasite who depends on the host for its life and yet sees that
host dying a senseless death before his eyes. We have no other host
except the ecosystem of which we are a part. If the celebrated
words of Sir James Jeans, for example, ring true, that this world
and life in it is like a match struck in the night that burns without purpose and for a very brief time before it goes out, then it
is cold comfort for us to know that we belong irrevocably to this
world. Our symbiosis with this ecosystem becomes a symbiosis of
mutual death and purposelessness.

Evolution falters as a symbol of meaning, I believe, to
the extent that it deals inadequately with evil. Evil often goes
unacknowledged, in an emphasis on continuities within the evolutionary process. Evolution does, however, at times take note of evil.
Evolutionary movement from one phase to another is not an easy one;
dislocation is frequent, and the unfit do not ordinarily survive.
Death is intrinsic to evolution. Yet this view tends to look at
evil as something simply to be endured. Death is not just the
termination of one life, it also makes possible the ascendancy of
the new. Without death, life could not continue, because the places
which new life could occupy would be fully taken. Or, evil is something to be endured, because survival will be served in the end,
even if the extinction of one or other of the species, including
our own, is demanded. The evolutionary machine lumbers along,
leaving pain and suffering in its wake. Yet this must be endured,
because it is part of evolving. The encounter with evil itself and
rebellion against it plays no decisive role in the nature of things.

The absurdist rebels against the world system because he
knows that he is not part of it; it is alien to him and he is a
stranger to it. His revolt makes no sense, because out of kiltered-
ness is the name of the game. The person who sees himself in the
evolutionary symbol must simply absorb the twists and turns, the
evil and injustice, of this world. His revolt would make no sense
because he is so fully interpenetrating with the world that revolt
is not even an intelligible category. Rebellion for the person in
the evolutionary scheme would be comparable to my rebelling against
the fact that I have eyes or legs. In each case, it is an inadequate response to evil that raises the question of credibility.
The absurdist symbol takes evil very seriously, in fact evil seems
to be the mainspring of the symbol's emergence. But in its response, it makes any grappling with evil senseless. The evolutionary

symbol tends either to overlook evil or else to say very simply
that evil must be endured for the sake of the process.

It is at this point that I introduce the third symbol for
discussion, since it is a symbol which seeks to take both evil and
belonging into account.

A third symbol which aims at providing meaning by organizing our experience is the Christian symbol of Jesus dying on the
Cross. The content of this symbol is that the power to overcome
evil is unleashed in actions that are directed to building up the
world and our fellow human beings. Like the symbol of Sisyphus and
unlike the symbol of Evolution, the symbol of Jesus Christ takes
evil seriously as a primary datum of this world and life within it.
Unlike Absurdism and like the symbol of Evolution, it images this
world as a larger system of which humanity is an integral part.
Like the symbol of Evolution, it images this world as an ordered
world, but it carries this image even further to the assertion that
this world is part of a larger purpose.

The similarities and differences between the symbol of
Jesus Christ on the Cross and the symbols of Sisyphus and Evolution
are clear if we probe for a moment into the layers of interpretation
that are implicit in the Christ symbol. Jesus' dying on the Cross
is interpreted as a sacrifice, which means that it is a saving
death. If we strip away some of the stereotypes which incline us
to think of sacrifice as a primitive sort of attempt to barter with
the gods and manipulate them, the concept of sacrifice becomes a
very illuminating one. The act of sacrifice is the giving of a
gift--at least on the surface and initially. This giving, however,
was conceived as the triggering of a process that transcends initial
gift-giving and which has little to do with barter and manipulations.
In the giving of the sacrifice, a relationship with the ultimate
power of the world, with God, is renewed or perhaps initiated, in
which God responds and thus His power flows out to encompass the
giver and the world in a peace which overcomes evil. Sacrifice
consequently was looked upon not as an autonomous action of human
beings, but rather as an institution of God's, whereby humans could
approach God and share in His power. Sacrifices were appropriate
in ancient times on the occasion of success (which was to be celebrated), of estrangement from one's fellow humans (which was to be
reconciled), and of outright transgression against the laws of God
(which was to be forgiven). In every case, the literature of the
Jewish Scriptures, and of some other religions as well, testifies
that the sacrificers had no sense that they were manipulating the
gods or bartering with them. Rather they had the sense that they
were enacting a ritual which God Himself had ordained and in which
God, not the human giver, was the chief actor, doing his work of
reconciliation.

Jesus' death on the Cross is set in a sacrificial context
by the Biblical writers, reflecting the normative interpretation of
the first generations of his followers. His death is at the Passover time; it is the offering of his body and blood for the world.
The conclusions follow directly--his death was intended as an
occasion for God to work His reconciliation and peace in the world.

The Jesus symbol, therefore, organizes our experiencing of the world by acknowledging that we are indeed part of a larger system, to which we do belong in an intimate and irrevocable manner, since that system has created us and given us the circumstances in which we are to carry out our lives. The symbol, furthermore, understands that evil is an inescapable concomitant to life in the world, but it believes that the power of the world system can overcome this evil through the instrumentality of what we call sacrifice or living in behalf of the world and our fellow humans. The symbol intensifies the sense of belonging which the symbol of Evolution suggests, since it asserts that the system to which we belong is our Friend, that it is ultimately benevolent in its purposes. The world system of which we are a part is therefore not only something to which we do by nature belong, but to which we are attracted, to which we wish to belong, because its processes ultimately aim at our fulfillment, not our negation. The courageous struggle with evil which the symbol of the Absurd stresses is also intensified, inasmuch as this struggle is the instrumentality by which the power of the system overcomes evil and works its benevolent purposes. The encounter with Evil, we may say, plays a constitutive role in the world process, since in that encounter courageous self-giving becomes an occasion for fulfillment.

These three symbols certainly do not exhaust the types of symbols that are relevant and pressing for our allegiance as we search for meaning today. They may serve, however, to illumine some of the fundamental issues that are neuralgic, which stretch symbols of meaning to their very limits and perhaps even beyond. It is not even appropriate to term these "issues," because they are existential realities that emerge from the wrestling of humans with their world, as Jacob grappled with the angel. These realities are rooted in the empirical life of humans as they grapple with meaning, even though they are not resolved in the empirical realm.

The significant realities with which our symbols must deal are the question of purpose in the world, the question of belonging to the world, and the presence of evil in the world. We may set it down as an axiom that any symbol or set of symbols that offers meaning must respond significantly to these three realities if it is to succeed in granting meaning. Each of these realities is so existentially demanding and exhausting that we despair even of taking up the challenge to deal with it. The power of the Absurdist symbol lies in its relative narrowness. It does, for all practical purposes, focus on the reality of evil and withdraws from any attempt to encompass the world's purposiveness and our belongingness in that world within its symbolic structure. It is precisely because Sisyphus and Meursault and Rieux are able to render the questions of purpose and belonging inoperative for their own lives that they can explore courage and rebellion so deeply. The power of the Evolution symbol resides in its forceful description of our belonging to the world. Indeed its description is so forceful that it is nearly impossible to disregard it. Evolution as symbol also speaks to us of penultimate purposes, the purposes of selection processes in the various sectors of the ecosystem and the requirements for survival within those processes of selection.

While this penultimate set of purposes is of deep importance for
this symbol, to speak of *a* purpose, a single intentionality of the
world system or the cosmic system is not allowed in the grammar of
this symbol. Evil, as we have suggested, is integral to evolution,
but as a process to be endured, rather than as an existential reality to be wrestled with.

     The Jesus symbol is more pretentious, I would argue, in
that it takes on the challenge to respond with equal force to each
of the three realities. Consequently, its promise is greater,
since it places each of these realities which are rooted in human
experience on center stage. At the same time, the doubts concerning its cogency are also greater, since in grappling with each
of the three realities it has taken on a burden which for many persons today is three times impossible. It places a burden of incredibility on us also, since it forces us to accept purpose in the
world and asks us to give our lives in behalf of the world as a
mode of overcoming evil. Its attempt, however, is a reminder that
human beings ought not settle for anything less than full meaning,
even if it is unattainable. The Jesus symbol is a testimony to the
grandeur of the human spirit, that it dare not settle for too little
meaning.

     Our belongingness to the world system is hardly to be
challenged. The Jesus symbol reveals that that belonging is scarcely bearable if the system itself is not purposive and benevolent.
Evil is existentially central to the human enterprise and courage
in the face of evil seems to be very near to the center of what it
means to be human. The Jesus symbol asserts that without purpose,
there is no hope for courage, and unless the struggle with evil be
part of that purpose, courage makes no sense. Even if the Jesus
symbol be rejected, it has set forth the issues in a way that
measures the adequacy of all other symbols.

     If this be the case, then perhaps we ought to look more
closely at the Jesus symbol, particularly in its response to the
reality of evil. Both the symbol of Sisyphus and that of Evolution
testify to the presence of evil in an important way, the former
urging revolt, the latter acceptance and endurance. The Absurdist
perceives clearly that evil is a threat, but since he rejects belongingness, revolt against evil is doomed ultimately to be a de-
pressing defeat, in which humanity demonstrates its absurd nobility.
In Evolution, evil plays a very significant function, since death
and extinction are significant lubricants in the selection process.
Inevitably, the symbol of Evolution tends to emphasize acceptance
of evil to the point that it shades into endurance of the inexorable
movement of the selection process. For Evolution, the appearance
of evil is not absurd; it has a place in the wisdom of the process
of natural selection, but the threat, which elicits the courage
and nobility of the human self, seems underplayed. The Absurdist
view of evil is epitomized in the line from *The Plague*: "We must
become accustomed to wars without armistices," whereas the Evolutionary view is summed up in the judgment that "the poor you will
always have with you."

     The Jesus symbol can content itself with neither of these
views of evil. Evil seems to be intrinsic to the process of life,

but it is to be overcome, and in the struggle to overcome, the forces of transformation and redemption are set free. Its view of evil is summarized in the words ascribed to Jesus at the Last Supper, the bread and wine are explicitly referred to his own impending death on the Cross, where his body would be broken and his blood poured out. The words are: "This cup is the New Covenant in my blood." The covenant was the covenant which God had made with his people, the covenant which gave them life and which bound them in the shalom peace with their fellow human beings and with the land to which they belonged. Jesus' death is a symbol that suffering and dying in behalf of others may be the occasion for the renewal of life and belonging through the unleashing of a power that is not our own.

The Jesus symbol, or its equivalent, has been powerfully represented in our time by persons like Martin Luther King, Jr. and, I would argue, by Gandhi, as well as by innumerable others. These persons were willing to sacrifice in the situations in which they lived, but they looked upon that sacrifice as the calculated and intentional giving of themselves in a way that would contribute to the healing of all those in the situation, and which would ultimately bring the best out of the situation. They made it clear, as did Jesus, that sacrifice is shrewd, not naive, a show of strength, not weakness, a strategy of health and healing, not a response of masochism or sadism.

Interestingly, there are other witnesses to the credibility of the notion that the encounter with evil may be the source of freedom and healing. One of the strongest, in my opinion, is that of Hegel's philosophy of the dialectic of negation. Hegel believed that in our encounter with the world, we are compelled to undergo a negation as we confront a reality which is genuinely other than we are--whether that reality be another person, the physical world itself, the challenge to understand and master something that is outside us. In all such relations, Hegel believed that a negation takes place which is both a death and a new life, both an annihilation and a fulfillment. The negativity is not extrinsic to life, for Hegel, but intrinsic. Without negativity and transition through it, in strength, growth and life are impossible. Hegel's dialectic of negation has had many adherents, even though his philosophy has generally been under a cloud. I believe that he was correct in his interpretation of what life is about.

Another significant development, which we can only touch upon here, is the work of sociobiologists and psychologists on the subject of altruism. Professor Donald Campbell of Northwestern is perhaps the most noteworthy name to be mentioned here. In an important Presidential Address to the American Psychological Association in 1975, Campbell laid out his thesis in chaste, understated scientific terms.[10] His thinking runs like this: the *genetic* component in human evolution continually selects for selfishness and hedonism, even though in our increasingly complex social situation, selfishness and hedonism are being shown to be highly maladaptive. Biological evolution, however, is accompanied by cultural evolution, in fact overshadowed by it. Within cultural evolutionary processes, there are strong inputs or quantities of information that select for

altruism and counter-hedonic behavior. These inputs of altruistic
information are chiefly the religious traditions and, in the West,
chiefly Christianity, centered in the symbol of Jesus. On scientific grounds, Campbell argues, the cultural traditions of altruism
are to be trusted and encouraged over the traditions of hedonism
and selfishness, and they are crucial for the redirection of biological evolution, for making up a dangerous deficiency in the
human genetic makeup.

        The purpose of these reflections is not to attempt a con-
clusive answer to the question of meaning today, nor is it an attempt
to show that Christian symbols are demonstrably superior to other
symbols. Rather I want to probe just what is required if meaning
is to be granted to us in these days, and from this probing the conviction emerges that the realities of evil, purpose, and belonging
are the pivots on which such meaning is hinged. In this context,
the symbol of sacrificial living, of giving one's life for the
benefit of the world takes on, I believe, renewed relevance.

NOTES AND REFERENCES

        1. Eugene Gendlin, *Experiencing and the Creation of Meaning* (Glencoe, Ill.:
The Free Press, 1962), pp. 5, 8.
        2. *Ibid.*, p. 134.
        3. Werner Elert, *The Structure of Lutheranism* (St. Louis: Concordia Pub-
lishing House, 1962).
        4. Albert Camus, *The Myth of Sisyphus and Other Essays* (New York: Alfred
Knopf, 1955), especially the first essay.
        5. See especially Albert Camus, *The Plague* (New York: The Modern Library,
1948).
        6. Camus, *The Myth of Sisyphus*, pp. 21, 28ff.
        7. *Ibid.*, pp. 121ff.
        8. *Ibid.*, p. 55.
        9. See note 7.
        10. Donald T. Campbell, "On the Conflicts Between Biological and Social
Evolution and Between Psychology and Moral Tradition," *American Psychologist*
30 (1975): 1103-26. Reprinted with commentaries in *Zygon: Journal of Religion
and Science* 11 (1976) 167-208.

THE FREE AND RELATIONAL SELF

by
Bernard M. Loomer

This brief essay on the nature of the self is an attempt to combine understandings operative within process/relational modes of thought and insights derived from our theological tradition, especially the writings of Reinhold Niebuhr.

The paper is characterized in part by what it does not include. It makes no reference, for example, to the unconscious. Except in the most general terms it does not discuss the problem of identity, a topic on which critics of process/relational philosophy have been most insistent. No attempt has been made to do justice to the personal, cultural, or spiritual dimensions of the self. The essay is in fact a bare framework within which to develop these and related topics.

The self is at once communal and individual in its being, at once relational (or dependent) and independent, and at once determined and free. The first terms (communal, relational, and determined) belong together, as do the second terms (individual, independent, and free). The discussion will be developed in the given order of these two sets of concepts.

I. The Self as Communal and Relational

Since the rise and development of the social sciences, it has become somewhat commonplace to say that there are only social or communal individuals. As individuals we exist in a society and the society lives in us. But the full import of this doctrine is not commonly understood. The concept of the communal nature of the self means most fundamentally that the self is a relational self. It means that as individuals we are largely constituted by our relations with the realities of our environing world, both natural and human.[1] These constitutive relations are the means whereby the realities of our world are objectively present within our own lives. They are present in us as parts of our very being.[2] In being present in us, in the process of entering our lives, they create us. This is how the community "lives" in us.

We don't create our world in the first instance. Our world creates us.[3] The qualitative energy of our life, which is the stuff of our being, is derived from the qualitative energy of the given realities of our contextual world. (Energy always comes to us clothed in some quality or other, such as a density, or a color, or a mood, or a purpose.) As fully formed, these given

69

objects transmit their energies beyond themselves and thereby objec-
tify themselves into the present. (These objectifications are perspectives of these objects.) These objectified energies are the
relational impulses from which our present individual existence
originates. These impulses are "relational" because they directly
connect those past actualities (of which they are expressions) to
ourselves as present individuals in an internal or determining fashion.[4] The connections are real and formative. We experience these
relational impulses as causally efficacious in our creation. We
experience them vectorally, that is, as derived from elsewhere, as
derived from the given actualities of our contextual world. We begin our existence as individuals by our vectoral feelings of these
objectified and relational impulses. The notion that we are constituted by our relations with our world embodies these understandings.

The theory of the communal and relational nature of the
self does not mean that there are presupposed and fully formed
individuals who have experiences with their communal world. The
influences derived from the contextual world of an individual's
immediate past are many in number. Also they vary in strength and
relevance for any particular individual. But prior to the appearance of these objectified impulses there is no presently existing
and unified individual self to experience them. There is no actualized self into whose being these impulses enter. The self, and
this of course includes its unity, is not given or presupposed.
The self is to be created. Its unity is to be achieved. This is
accomplished through a process of prehending and synthesizing these
objectified and relational impulses of qualitative energy into some
kind of subjective unity. This process of synthesizing is the
actualization of the self and the achievement of its unity. The
actuality of the self consists in its process of becoming itself,
of becoming something definite. The individual self, as actualized
in this process, is therefore an emergent from these relational impulses. When it has become something definite, when its process
of becoming a unified self is terminated, the qualitative energy of
its being is released from itself and objectified beyond itself.
In this fashion it in turn influences its contextual world.

The process of synthesizing, wherein the actuality of the
self is realized, is an occasion of experience. Each occasion of
experience is relatively momentary in the duration of its actuality.
The length of its life is determined by the duration required to
achieve a synthetic and complex unity from the impulses inherited
from the given world.[5]

In this interpretation of the self, the individual in
his concrete life is to be understood basically as an occasion of
experience. His actual or concrete selfhood is actualized only in
these occasions. In contrast to the traditional notion of the self,
the individual doesn't have experiences. Rather he *is* his experience. His experience consists of his encounter with the world and
his response to it. His response is what he makes of what he has
been given by his world. What he has been given are the relational
impulses. His response consists of his process of unifying these

impulses of qualitative energy.   ("Process is the becoming of experience.")

As an occasion of experience, the concrete selfhood of the individual is momentary in its duration.   It has its "hour" (or minute) on the stage of life, and is then superseded by another concrete occasion of itself.   This is the self as momentary or episodal.   The life of an individual who endures for three score years and ten consists of an incredibly complex historical series of these episodal occasions of experience.

The relational impulses from which the individual is derived are efficient causes.   The individual who emerges in the process of synthesizing these impulses will largely conform to them. It is the nature of efficient causes to reproduce themselves or to create effects which basically resemble or conform to the originating causes.   In this fashion the emergent individual is for the most part shaped and determined by his contextual communal world. By and large he is what he has been given.   To this extent the communal individual is not free.

The phrase "to this extent" must be emphasized.   The foregoing analysis is not the complete description of the self.   The individual in his concrete selfhood is not to be understood as being wholly a function of the relational impulses from which he is derived and which enter into the inner constitution of his being.   As a process of synthesizing, the individual makes his own contribution to his concrete actuality.   This is his "free" nature, a topic to be discussed shortly.   But for the moment the focus is on what he derives from the others who compose his communal world.

The concept of the communal and relational self means, in short, that we are what and who we are largely because of what we have been given by others, including our past selves, and because of what we have absorbed from others.   It means that we create each other, that we are quite literally derived from each other.[6] Within this organismic process of mutual creation we feed upon each other psychologically, intellectually, and spiritually, much as we feed upon other organisms for our physical food.

The concept of the relational nature of the self, as analyzed up to this point, stands in vivid contrast to the traditional understanding of the self.   In this latter interpretation, which is shared by many or most contemporary theologians (e.g., Tillich), the self has no relational character.   It lives in a context, to be sure.   This is unavoidable, even for hermits.   But this context is not part of the very warp and woof of its being.   It has relationships with others.   This also is unavoidable.   But its inner being is not constituted by these relationships.   They are not a causal context from which the being of the self emerges.   The self has experiences, but it is not identified with them.   It transcends them, much as an artist transcends his painting.   The self is not to be identified with its actions, or its behavior, or its relationships, or its experiences.   It transcends all of these functions that are necessary aspects of its life.   The self is not only more than any one of these functions, or all of them together. It is basically different in kind from all of them.

In this classical interpretation the self derives neither its being nor its self-identity from others. Its being is derived from God and from God alone. This is the only basic or constitutive relation of dependence the self has. Apart from this, the self is what it is by itself and in itself. Its self-identity is synonymous with its being. Its identity can be said to be either self-derived or, since the endurance of the self is due to the sustained creativity of God, derived from God. Its self-identity may be ascertained but not determined by its relations to others. This understanding of the self conforms to the Cartesian definition of a substance as that which requires nothing but itself (and God) in order to exist.

But while the individual, in the traditional view, does not derive his existence from others, he does have a dependence on others. He requires a community because he cannot fulfill himself by himself. He is a social individual only in the sense that he needs other people in order to exercise his various talents and to realize his potentialities. Society is the arena for his fulfillment. It has the status of being a means to his own ends. His possibilities are inherent or latent within himself, analogous to the way in which an acorn contains all the possibilities that are to flower later into the adult oak tree. His experiences with others are occasions in which these potentialities are actualized.

In this view the status of an individual's freedom is analogous to the status of his possibilities. In fact, in some respects freedom is one side of the coin whose other side carries the imprint of an individual's possibilities. Freedom has many dimensions. But in most of its facets freedom, in the traditional view, is a quality of the individual's spirit in itself. It is his possession. It derives from himself alone. It is not an emergent from his relations. Others can neither give it nor take it away. They can be the occasions for the exercise of his freedom. They can restrict the expression of his freedom, practically as well as theoretically. They can limit or further his accomplishments. But the dimensions of freedom that involve creativity, responsibility, motivation, self-transcendence, and commitment, are his alone to control and exemplify.

This interpretation of the self and its freedom seems to imply that a society is a cooperative organization made up of essentially independent and self-reliant people. It is a voluntary creation of free men. To state the point most abstractly and with greater generality, relationality is derived from freedom (rather than the other way round as it is in process modes of thought). But the relationality that is the product of self-derived freedom is essentially external in character.

For some Christian interpreters of this traditional view, another dimension is added. They indicate that, because man is to be viewed in the light of Jesus Christ, love is of his essence (however flawed) and love is the law of his being. The individual needs other people in order to exemplify this law. He needs others in order to love them, even though his relationships of love are not part of the fabric of his soul. He is to love others because they are fellow creatures. He is to love them for themselves and

in terms of what is for their own good. He is to love them because God loves him and all creatures. He is to love others as
God loves us, ideally with no concern for what the other may give
to him in return. From this it follows, as can be seen in the
writings of Reinhold Niebuhr, that all forms of mutual love are incomplete and inferior exemplifications of the love that is required
of us.

The individual needs to love others, and God. But the
flaw in his spirit which manifests itself as sin prevents him from
fulfilling the requirements of his true nature. The overcoming
of this condition requires the help and the love of God in one form
or another. (The sense in which the sinful individual needs the
help of his fellows in order to gain his redemption is not clear in
this interpretation.) But except for his relation of dependence on
God, the author of his being and the gracious source of his salvation, any substantial dependence on others is understood as a weakness, an inadequacy, a regrettable instance of a lack of self-
sufficiency. Basically the individual is to act toward others out
of his strength and not out of dependency on them.

I suggest that there is one Biblical strand of tradition
that interpreted Jesus essentially in these terms. He is pictured
as one who derived his power from God alone. He owed nothing to
his fellow human beings. He came to minister and not to be ministered unto. He ministered to other people in their need out of his
strength. The only thing they gave him was his crucifixion. His
resurrection was due solely to the power of God.

In the relational view of the self an individual's possibilities do not simply inhere within the energies of the self. Like
the being of the self they are creations or emergents from constitutive relationships. To state the point in words I have used
elsewhere:

> A wife is not the occasion whereby a man actualizes husbandly pos-
> sibilities that reside or subsist wholly within the confines of his
> enclosed selfhood. The husbandly and wifely possibilities of the
> respective partners are peculiar to and are created out of that
> particular marital relationship in which each helps to create the
> other. The more deeply mutual and creative the relationship, the
> wider the range of emergent possibilities for those participating
> in the relationship. The wealth of possibilities is not simply
> there as a present and completed fact, subsisting as a latent con-
> dition that is in some sense independent of the world of actual
> events. Possibilities are created or emerge as possibilities along
> with the advances that occur within the natural and historical en-
> vironments.[7]

Freedom, in the relational view, is a quality that belongs to the individual in his uniqueness and solitariness as it
does in the traditional interpretation. But, as will be discussed
later, his freedom like his selfhood is an emergent from his relationships. It is peculiarly his, but it is not simply self-
derived. It is a quality of his inner being, but it also reflects
the world from which he emerged.

In the relational view nothing belongs to an individual
simply and wholly in himself. Nor does the individual have by himself whatever he possesses. Everything he has is to be viewed as
derived in part and/or as an emergent from his communal constitutive relations. His language is a social gift, his name is a
social (or at least a familial) identification, and his mind (his
ability to see connections and perceive meanings) is at least in
part a social achievement. His very uniqueness, solitude, freedom,
and mystery (qualities deeply constitutive of his inner subjective
life) are emergents from his relationships. He has them as uniquely
his own only because of and in the contextual presence of others.
Even his ability to transcend his society, in sensitivity, in
vision, in accomplishment, and in stature, is derived in the first
instance as an ironic gift of his society which called him forth.
It is ironic because it is this very society which is often strongly
critical when he reaches beyond its limits.
        Sin ultimately is always a betrayal of God. But there is
no sin against God that is not at the same time and in the same act
a failure to advance the cause of our fellows, whether or not they
welcome the advance. There is no redemption that does not involve
either the gracious help of our human companions or the healing
power of natural creatures and forces. It isn't the case that as
individuals we just happen to have relationships with others. It
isn't the case that others exist in a society which functions simply
as a necessary means to our fulfillment as individuals. It isn't
the case that the members of a society just happen to exhibit a
common and identifying characteristic. This defining trait is
causally inherited one from another. Without this causal and relational sharing there would be no limitation which grounds the
actuality of the society. A society is a given unity, but it is
an achieved given. A society is itself a social accomplishment.

II. The Self as Free and Individual

        The self as individualized is an emergent from its re-
lationships. It is a process of synthesizing the objectified energies from its contextual world. This is its subjective life. This
is its quantified moment of immediacy. Its process of synthesizing
its inherited data is its emergence. Or, alternatively, its emergence is its process of synthesizing.
        In the previous section it was maintained that the world
largely creates the self. But this is only half of the truth. The
other half is that the self, in its emergence from its relationships, also creates itself. In its emergence it becomes its own
cause. Its creativity in the first instance is its self-creativity.[8]
Its self-creation is its process of synthesizing the objectified
qualitative energies out of which it emerges. In creating itself
it makes a decision about what and who it is to be. This decision
is its own reason for being what it is.
        In the discussion of the relational character of the self
it was emphasized that the self doesn't have experiences. Rather
it is its experiences. A similar point can be stressed with respect

to the relation between the self and its decision. The self is not a completed subject who makes a decision about what it will do. The self as subject does not ontologically transcend its decision. The self is its decision. The process of becoming a self is the same process by which a decision is reached. The process of arriving at a decision is a process of resolving all indeterminations. The result is the unity of the self. The self as a completed actuality is the decision as attained. The decision, like the process of self-creation itself, is an emergent.

Again, in discussing the relational nature of the self, the point was made that the self largely conforms to the efficient causes that create it. But the self in the immediacy of the process of its actualization is not completely determined by its world. It is not simply and wholly a function of its causal relationships. Its self-creativity is its freedom to become what in fact it becomes. Its decision is the option that it freely chooses. Its freedom is conditioned by its contextual world. Yet its freedom, which is an emergent from its relations, includes not only its self-creativity; it also has the quality of transcendence which emergence provides.

The self creates itself out of what has been given to it. It is not responsible for what it has been given, as the child is not responsible for the parents who gave it birth. But the self is accountable for what it makes out of what has been given to it. Regardless of its past, its emergent self-creativity means that it must bear the onus of shaping itself. To the extent of its freedom it is responsible for being who and what it is. Its guilt is not transferable. In becoming what it in fact becomes it either adds or detracts from the qualitative richness of life.

Since the self is its decision, the decision can be neither reduced to its conditioning causes, nor analyzed nor explained. The self as a synthetic unity of relational causes cannot be reduced to its causes. Its decision cannot be reduced to its motives. In trying to "explain" a specific decision of the self, one can only say that the self is the individual who is *that* decision (or, more loosely, who made *that* decision). The attempt to explain a decision of the self presupposes that the self is a collection of its conditioning causes or motives. But the self is a unique unity. It is a "one" which is an emergent unity from its many relations. The elements that enter into a decision can be enumerated and characterized. But the emergent unity or decision transcends the elements which enter into its content. Once the unity or decision has emerged, it cannot be dissolved into its elements. The emergence and the unity are not parts of the included elements. The elements are factors in the emergence. The self cannot "explain" itself.

The same considerations apply to the freedom of the self. The self in its freedom cannot be explained or fathomed or rationalized. Freedom "explains" itself. And this is no explanation. If explanation is "an analysis of coordination" (Whitehead), then only the structures of concrete events or individuals can be analyzed and thereby explained. The individuals and events in their concrete actuality cannot be explained. Freedom, like the actuality

of the self, obeys no laws of logic, Hegelian or otherwise. To over-
state the matter, perhaps, freedom is a quality that is not definable
in terms of whatever structural characteristics, if any, it may
possess.

In saying that the self is its decision, and that the
self in its freedom cannot be explained, and that freedom "explains"
itself, perhaps a very obvious point should be stressed. Freedom
is not an entity or a substance to which the self is attached.
Grammatically, it is not a noun. It is not best understood as an
adjective, as in "the free self." It is basically an adverb. As
a quality, freedom is not an adjectival quality, such as blueness.
It is rather an adverbial quality that refers to a manner in which
the self functions.

It is not freedom that makes a decision. It is the self
that freely comes to a decision. The quality of freedom does not
determine what the decision will be. It is not a direction or a
what. It is not freedom that creates the self. Freedom is the
self freely creating itself. It is not freedom that is transcending.
It is the self that freely transcends itself. It is not freedom
that is over-reaching. It is the self that freely over-reaches itself. The mystery of freedom is the mystery of the self.[9]

The emerging self is its own unique center of subjectivity.
It exists for itself. It is a value to itself. "Value is the self-
enjoyment of being actual" (Whitehead).[10]

This is the ontological solitariness of the self. Solitariness is the price for the achievement of unique individuality.
It exists only in the context of relationships, and not apart from
them. Yet it is a transcendence of relationships that occurs within relationships. Solitariness is not loneliness. Loneliness is
a condition that can be overcome by means of relationships. The
sense of solitariness is deepened by means of more meaningful relationships. Solitariness can only be borne. Even God must respect the solitariness of the self.

Solitariness is an ultimate fact. For some individuals
it is also an awful and at times an almost unbearable state. Some
vainly attempt to overcome the chill of solitariness by becoming
absorbed in another individual (or group), as in marriage. The un-
ending attempt to communicate one's solitariness to another creature
is profound evidence of the relational character of the self. The
frustration that attends such an effort is equally profound evidence
of the self's irreducible individual nature. Perspectives of one's
unique solitariness can be communicated, but not the concrete
solitariness itself. Yet the longing to be known and understood
fully by another is one of the deepest bases for the life of prayer
and the outreach of religious trust. No human community or relationship can provide an adequate response to such a longing.

III. The Self as Spirit

It is to be observed that the notions of synthesizing,
self-creativity, decision, freedom, and emergence are tied together.
They are all internally related. The terms are almost but not

quite synonymous. They refer to different aspects of the process
of becoming a definite self. It could be maintained that synthesizing, self-creativity, decision, and freedom are all dimensions
of the mystery of emergence. On this basis emergence would be the
key to the individual nature of the self. In this sense emergence
would also be one of the keys to the understanding of process itself.
But, apart from the point that the concept of emergence is not
usually conceived of in such fashion, this usage would lead to
various types of cumbersome and misleading analyses.

It seems preferable to maintain that synthesizing, self-
creativity, decision, and emergence are dimensions of the mystery
of freedom. Freedom has several dimensions,[11] but its two major
expressions are freedom as self-creativity and freedom as self-
transcendence. In the above analysis, the four factors are reduc-
ible to these two dimensions of freedom. Synthesizing and decision
are collapsable into self-creativity, and emergence is another name
for freedom as transcendence. This means that freedom is a basic
key to understanding process, where process is the becoming of
occasions of experience or the becoming of actual selves. The
mystery of the self is the mystery of freedom. Freedom then plays
its role within the mystery of the unanswerable and age-old question as to why there is something rather than nothing.

In terms of this analysis, freedom is the key to the
individual nature of the self, as relationality is the key to the
communal nature of the self. But this does not mean that there are
two "natures" to the self (any more than Whitehead's God has two
"natures"). There is no dualism within the self, although there
is a tension between freedom and relationality (as will be discussed
shortly). There is only one self with its unity. There is only one
concrete self-creating individual in whom perspectives of other individuals exist as constitutive relational factors. In this sense,
to put the matter abstractly, relationality exists within freedom.

But relationality is not derived from freedom. Ontologically, relationships are prior to freedom. In terms of the processive character of reality, freedom is an emergent from relationships with respect to their qualitative richness, but it does not
create them. The freedom exemplified in a present occasion of experience could be said to create the future through its self-
transcending projections. But these projections are relational
objectifications which are the carriers of energy from which self-
creative and transcending selves emerge.

Relationality and freedom can be viewed as distinguishable
but not separable aspects of the process of becoming.[12] Beyond the
subjective process of unification wherein the self creates itself,
freedom "creates" the future only indirectly through the medium of
relationships.

Instead of always referring to the self in its freedom,
we may use a term with a long history. We can speak of the individual as spirit, where spirit means the unity of the self in its
freedom. But in using the term "spirit" in connection with this
interpretation of the self, two reminders need to be stressed in
order that this usage of the term is not confused with many other
interpretations. First, spirit as freedom has its being only as a

quality of the process of becoming. The becomingness of things
does not derive from spirit as a self-existing source of the energy
of the world. In this sense spirit is a quality within the process
of creation. Becomingness rather than spirit is the more inclusive
category. Second, spirit does not have its being apart from relationships. It is an emergent from them. But as an emergent from
them it bears within itself the marks of its rootage. Spirit is
the unity of the self in its freedom, but the unity of the self is
a unity of elements derived from the relationships of the self. In
this respect the unity of the self is not simple, that is, without
parts. The unity is complex or composite, that is, it is a "one"
that includes "many." Freedom bears within itself the scars of the
struggles of its originating community.[13]
         The concept of spirit, loosely defined as the unity of
the self in its freedom, where freedom has special reference to
self-creativity and transcendence, does not lend itself to precise
description. (It follows, of course, that the notion of the self
as freedom is not amenable to exact specifications either.) A
person's spirit is his fundamental stance or posture. It's the way
he goes at the business of living. It is his manner of creating
himself, his way of becoming. It has to do with his essential
passions, their strength and direction. It refers to his basic
dynamics. It is the aura of his "presence."
         An individual may be described as a unified complex of
"whats" (or nouns and adjectives). But, to borrow a term from
Whitehead, a person's spirit may be more adequately understood as
a complex set of qualitative valuations or "hows" (or adverbs).[14]
The "hows" come closer to describing both the processive and the
deeply formative emotional aspects of the self. They are more
adapted to indicating the dynamics of the self. They are more expressive of the manner in which the self uses its freedom either to
enhance or weaken the creative energies of its life. It's the contrast between "how are you?" and "who or what are you?"
         A person's spirit is conveyed by how he responds to life,
how he relates to his world, how he deals with his relationships,
how he creates himself, how he uses his freedom to transcend
(or not transcend) his past, how he faces the problems and challenges that confront him, how he handles defeat and victory, and
how he attempts to grow in size. In short, *how* the individual becomes determines *what* he becomes.
         The concept of spirit as the unity of the self in its
freedom means that freedom is a quality of the whole self, and not
of a specific dimension of the self, such as its rational capacities or its will (unless "will" is used to refer to the self in
its unity). To whatever extent it is free, it is the self in its
unity that is free, just as it is the total self that is its decision. It is the self in its wholeness that is self-creative. We
may be enabled to be free, or freer, because of our ability to think.
But our intellect is not the source (or the sole source) of our
freedom, where freedom means either self-creativity or transcendence.
         Our capacity to think is our ability to see connections
between things, to analyze the priorities of value, to discern forms
and structures within events, to abstract these forms and structures

from their embeddedness in concrete events, and to conceive of alternatives and novel forms. Without the capacity to think we would
lose our moral conscience and our sense of religious discrimination.
We would not be self-conscious. Our sensitivities would lack a
source of critical judgment. We would not be able to "know" what
we are doing or to organize our individual and social lives
effectively. These are obviously essential functions in the achievement of human freedom.

Our capacities to abstract and to conceive of alternative
forms or structures, for example, greatly enlarge the self-creative
and self-transcending dimensions of our freedom. Because we are
able to abstract, we are able to escape the full force of the inertial causality of the past. By virtue of our ability to envisage
alternative ideas, we are able to enjoy the refreshment that novelty
adds. With this refreshment our physical energy may be recreated
and the self may be enlarged.

So reason is an indispensable condition for human freedom.
Yet reason is an agency within freedom. The impulse of freedom derives from freedom itself, that is, from the self as an organic
whole. The impulse for the refreshment of life that novelty may
bring is an organic passion. It is the spirit of man that is re-
freshed and recreated, not just his mind.

Each factor or dimension within the self is what it is
because of its relations with the other elements. The intellect is
not a self-sufficient and self-sustaining function within our spirit.
A free mind requires a free self, particularly a self that is emo-
tionally free and secure.

We may be attracted to some purpose or ideal. We may be
"moved" toward it. This is the persuasive power of final causes
(Whitehead's "eros of the universe"). The fact of being attracted
is a real element in the constitution of the self and its freedom.
But unless we thoroughly intellectualize the self, this is not a
full explanation of any genuine movement toward the ideal. Commitment may occur because of the persuasiveness of the ideal. But commitment that is simply intellectual is partial. If the ideal is to
be striven for, the commitment must be organic. The whole self
needs to be persuaded. We may be lured or "led" toward a desirable
goal. But whether we will "follow" depends on whether we are im-
pelled to do so from within.

In Whitehead's system, a physical feeling is a prehension
of an actual entity in our world. A conceptual feeling is a prehension of an abstract form or an "idea." "How" we feel physically is
conformal to "what" we feel. That is, how we physically prehend
our world is determined by what we physically prehend. We are
shaped by what we physically feel. This is one of the basic en-
tailments of efficient causality.

Now in keeping with a basic empirical principle, most of
our ideas are conceptual reflections of what we have physically experienced. But, for Whitehead, "how" we think about something is
not determined by "what" we are thinking about. The "how" of our
conceptual functioning is autonomous. We can think about what we
have experienced in such a way that we are led to think about something other than what we have previously experienced. We can con-

ceptually envisage alternative and novel ways of doing things, something beyond anything seen on land or sea. So novelty is derived from the manner of our thinking. Since freedom is correlative with novelty, for Whitehead, freedom is therefore derived from reason.

This is freedom both as self-transcendence and self-creativity. But even here the restiveness that impels us toward the creative use of the autonomy of reason is an organic restlessness, a passion, large or small, of the spirit.[15]

There is a characteristic of freedom, or the self in its freedom, which is decisive for the full understanding of man's spirit. This quality manifests itself in the phenomenon of self-transcendence.[16] Self-transcendence is an outreach of the self for an alternative other, a movement that aims to go beyond any achieved state or given condition. It is a discontent of the self, a restlessness to move beyond present levels of satisfactions, whether they be high or low. This surge may be a desire to escape boredom, to find new meanings, or to accept larger challenges. It may also take the form of a commitment to a great cause, or an openness toward greater size. This discontent is strikingly evident in the modern evolution of our expectations.

This outreach develops a momentum of its own. It becomes a passion for the "more." This "more" is expansive. The desire for the more may become, for some people at least, an appetite for the indefinite more, an unquenchable yearning for what the tradition called the infinite. This outreach may take the form of a dedication to be the best in some dimension of life, to do what no one else has ever done, to conquer what has been regarded as unconquerable. This drive may manifest itself in the most trivial of pursuits as well as in the most significant of social endeavors.

The point is that no preestablished limits can be set which exhaust the restless passion of the spirit. The spirit can transcend in fact or in imagination any socially determined boundaries which purport to define the range of possibility concerning our outreach toward the more, the beyond. The distinction between what is factually and imaginatively realizable is important. What is not, as yet, historically possible, is yet possible in our imaginations, our speculations, our ideals, and our dreams. What is only theoretically or imaginatively possible now may in time become historically actualizable. In the interim, our dreams help us to maintain the sense of alternatives which is a characteristic of the open and creative spirit. The modern world is a period in which pre-modern limitations have in fact been transcended historically.

There are limitations to this expansiveness, of course, as we moderns are slowly discovering. These limiting factors are both external and internal to the human spirit. The upward spiral of self-transcendence has some inherent and ironic qualities that confound the unwary or the naive.

The expansive quality of or within freedom sometimes results in a condition that continues to upset liberal theories in the areas of ethics, politics, and psychology. Since freedom is a quality of the total self, the self-transcending outreach toward the indefinite "more" means that any major impulse or interest of

the self may become inflated to an obsessive degree. The desire
for power, wealth, security, prestige, status, or knowledge may
transcend any "reasonable" point of satiety. When the expansiveness
of our desires is combined with the fact of our inequalities, we
have the grounds for radical injustices and demonic tyrannies.
Given this propensity, any claim of an individual or group may become inordinate and presumptuous. The writings of Reinhold Niebuhr
have brilliantly documented this proposition.

IV Conclusion

It is time to try to bring together the free and relational
dimensions of the self. Ideally, there is a harmony between freedom
and relatedness. Ideally, each functions to enhance and enlarge the
reality of the other. As we saw under the relational conception of
the self, possibilities are emergents from relationships. These
emergent possibilities are possibilities for the members of the
relationship. The greatest possibilities emerge from those most
deeply internal and creative relationships wherein the members are
most fully committed to the relationship. Our largest individual
stature is possible in terms of such relationships.
Thus we are related so that our freedom as self-creative
agents may assume larger dimensions whereby we become more complex
selves. We are free in order to make the greatest possible contribution to those relationships wherein all the members are enabled
to become larger-sized individuals. Great societies produce great
individuals, and great individuals advance the common cause. We
are freest when we are most deeply and creatively relational and
when others behave in a like fashion. The "more" of freedom thereby
becomes both an individual and a relational "more."
But this ideal of the mutual enhancement of freedom and
relatedness is seldom if ever exemplified. In actual fact there
is a tension between the two dimensions, and this tension is often
broken on the side of freedom. Freedom is ambiguous in its functioning. We can exercise our freedom either to affirm and enhance
our relatedness to others, or to attenuate and even deny our relatedness. We can use our freedom to enhance our ego-centricity
and use others as means to our ever-expanding egoistic ends. Or we
can use our self-transcending freedom to commit ourselves more
fully to those relationships whereby we as well as others attain
a "more" in the form of greater size.
The fact of sin is always a denial of the most creative
of relationships. And sin is an orientation of the total self toward itself. The freedom of the sinner is an expression of this
kind of orientation. And the "more" of the expansive freedom of
the sinner is a furthering and a deepening of this orientation.
The tenacious and inertial quality of sin can be broken only by
means of the enabling grace inherent within those kinds of relationships that free the individual from his self-absorption. In these
relationships he is enabled to be freer of the destructive use of
his freedom. Yet even here, enabled or not, the individual is yet

free to accept or reject this enabling and emergent grace. This is
the mystery of his freedom.
        This account of the tension between freedom and related-
ness is of course oversimplified. The exercise of freedom in its
uttermost depths and outreaches cannot be nicely geared to immediate relational considerations. The relations between freedom and
relatedness are not perfectly symmetrical or coordinated.
        There is sometimes a wildness to the spirit and its free-
dom. It is the nature of freedom not to be domesticated or tamed.
The domestication of freedom is a self-contradiction. The excesses
of freedom cannot be exorcised without decimating the strength of
the spirit. Great strength always involves the risk of great misuse
of its power. The evil of great power cannot be overcome by the
surgical removal of the sources of its strength. Sometimes there
seems to be no alternative, especially if the evil is overwhelming
in its destructiveness. But this method is surely tragic. The
most creative solution involves the transformation of the self that
has great power such that this power is used to achieve other goals.
The strength of great passion is too rare to murder.
        Sometimes freedom must transcend available relationships
in the interests of a creative advance. Sometimes freedom must
move without relational support or the means of societal expression.
There is the solitary explorer of unknown spaces. There is the
solitary thinker whose thoughts move beyond the limits of all known
horizons. (Ultimately, the concern for understanding for its own
sake is the most creative form of knowledge.) There is the solitary
explorer of the heights and depths of spiritual passion. And if
the adventurer of the spirit is of sufficient stature, and if the
time is ripe, a religious tradition and community may emerge. Sometimes freedom must dream of things to come, and hope for the relational actualization of the dream in its season.
        The theological tradition has defined man as created in
the image of God. The attribute of God that has been the basis for
the images has been, usually, that of His freedom, which is derived
from His sovereignty and His transcendence of the world. God's
freedom, in this view, means that He has His being on His own terms.
It means that He has His own purposes and that He is not bound by
our expectations, hopes, or desires. It means that any relationship
between Him and His creatures is not a social contract that is derived from a joint decision. The terms of the contract (or covenant)
are essentially His terms.
        But beyond this, as one can see in an extreme form in Karl
Barth, for example, God's freedom has been interpreted to mean that
God freely chose to be related to His creatures. This would seem
to imply that God in His love could have freely chosen not to be
so related and involved. That is, God's relatedness is (or was)
optional. A negative decision ostensibly would not have compromised
either His love or His divinity.
        It is important, in this traditional viewpoint, to stress
the point that God's love is freely given. It is not coerced. (In
this tradition God's act of relating Himself to His creatures through
the person of Jesus is spoken of in terms of "condescension" or of
an "emptying" of Himself.) His love as a relational presence and

concern is a free gift. His love is an act of free grace wherein
He responds to us out of His mercy rather than in terms of His
justice. Because His love is a free grace, His response to us
transcends what our poor goodness deserves. Divine love is a concern for the good of the creatures that involves no concern for
itself.

In short, God's relationships to His creatures (as expressions of His love) are derived from His freedom.

Traditionally, the image that defines man, therefore, is
not love but freedom. Man's freedom includes responsibility for
his thoughts, decisions, and actions (which are aspects of self-
creativity), his self-transcendence, and his transcendence over
nature.17 As mentioned before, he has his being in himself. He
has no relational dimension internal to his being. In his freedom
and independence (although with the help of God's grace) he is to
love as God loves, freely and with no thought of self.

I am not concerned with what appear to me to be speculative
and unwarranted aspects of this concept of God. For me, there is
much more metaphysical and theological machinery than the job requires. But I am concerned with a conception of love wherein the
relatedness of love is optional. Relationships are what love is
all about. They are where love has its being. Love conceived of
apart from relationships is either an emptiness or a self-absorption.

In terms of an extension of the relational principle, God
has no choice about whether or not to love. He has no choice about
whether or not to be related. Love means relationships (even though
of certain kinds). The choice of freedom for God is a choice within relationships. It is a choice as to how God will relate or how
His love will be expressed. He gives of His love, or of Himself,
for the sake of the relationship between Himself and His creatures.
God has a relational as well as an individual nature. In short,
God's freedom is indigenous to his relationships.18

More generally, there is no giving of a gift without a
relationship. If one is to give, someone else must receive. The
importance of the giving is partly dependent on the importance of
the receiving. If one gives of oneself out of love, then it is
important to the giver whether or how the gift is accepted. The
one who loves cannot be indifferent as to whether or how the gift
is received. If he is indifferent, then the gift is not one of
love for the other. If the one who gives is not different in his
being from what he was prior to the giving, then he has not really
given--at least of himself. In this case his giving is external
to his concrete life. If in his giving one is not prepared to receive from the other, and if his receiving from the other is a
matter of indifference to him, then his love is truncated. He does
not truly love the other.

At the human level we are free to love or not, that is,
we are free to be fulfilled or not. But if we choose life in its
fullest, if we opt for larger size, then we have no choice but to
love. If we choose to love, we have no option but to be related to
others in deeply internal ways. Because of our limitations we cannot be deeply related to all others. But we must be internally related to some others.

The point was just made that in the theological tradition it was important to accent the notion that love is freely given. For some people the inescapability of relatedness seems to compromise the freedom of the giving of one's love. The freedom of love seems to mean for them that the establishment of a specific relationship is a free giving of love. And so it is. Since one must have some specific relationships, freedom involves a selection from among many possible relationships. But beyond this obvious aspect of freedom, all other choices of love occur within relationships. Love is always free. A coerced love is a contradiction. Freedom within relationships means that one cannot demand love from the other or determine the limits of the other's love. The freedom of love may well mean that the other may give of his love beyond our expectations or beyond our feelings of worth. The other's love, freely given, may involve the self-transcendence that the quality of freedom possesses. The other's love may transcend in range and depth anything that we could ask or demand of the other. In respecting the freedom of the other, in love, the other may give a gift of love that both surprises and humbles us.

This freedom of love within relationships is a choice concerning the quality of the relationships. It is an option for larger or smaller size--for all who participate in the relationships. Freedom exists, finally, as a handmaid of relational qualities and size.

Thus the final reflection. The tradition, in defining the essence of man either in terms of his reason or his freedom, indicated man's superiority to and transcendence over nature. Biblically, man's status was ranked just below that of the angels. In emphasizing spirit as man's distinctive characteristic, Niebuhr pointed to the greatness of man in his capacity for indefinite transcendence. This stress on man's transcendence by means of his freedom or his reason or his spirit was of a piece with the tradition's insistence on the transcendence of God. But the analogy between God and man involved a fundamental contrast. This contrast was derived, in part, from the assumption that potentiality is a characteristic of man but not of God. Man's transcendence meant that he not only transcends nature but he also transcends himself. His self-transcendence implied that he has the potentiality for growth, that in actuality he is unfinished and incomplete. God's transcendence meant that He is finished and complete. In His actuality He transcends the world but not Himself.

This transcendent God was also a God of love. Yet seldom does the theological tradition define the image of God in man in terms of love. This alternative is not adopted in part because of man's propensity to sin, and in part because while love is of God, love is not God. But it may also be the case that this alternative was rejected because neither God nor man was defined relationally. And love, whatever else it is, is a relational activity.

From the standpoint of this paper the image of God in man is neither his reason, his freedom, nor his spirit. The greatness and the tragedy of man require another factor in addition to his reason and his freedom. This other dimension is his love, or his capacity to sustain deeply creative relationships. Man's reason is both a function and a source of his self-transcending freedom. But both his reason and his freedom as spirit are emergents from his relationships. The elements of freedom, reason, and love can be fused so as to form a more relational image.

I suggest that the singular and distinctive characteristic of man is his capacity to develop in stature, and to refuse to be so transformed. His growth in size and his sinful refusal to the great invitation are possible because he is at once a communal and an individual self. He is both relational and free.

NOTES AND REFERENCES

1. Technically, this is the contextual world of our immediate past, including our own past selves.

2. More precisely, aspects or perspectives of these realities are present in us, not these actualities in their concrete fullness.

3. Epistemologically, the object creates the subject, the known gives rise to the knower, the thinker emerges from the thought or feelings.

4. We don't determine these past actualities. They determine us. As past actualities they are already fully determined. The relationship is external to them and internal to us.

5. The concept of an occasion of experience as "momentary" is not synonymous with Whitehead's concept of occasions of experience as ultimate units of reality, the building blocks of the universe which are sub-atomic in spatial and temporal extension. In his view all units of greater extensiveness are either nexūs of occasions or societies. For Whitehead an occasion of experience, or an individual, cannot be further divided into other individuals or occasions. If this view is held to strictly, it becomes difficult and awkward (and quite incorrect!) to speak of human beings in the large as individuals. For the purposes of these pages human organisms in the large are treated as individuals, even though from the Whiteheadian viewpoint we as human individuals are incredibly complex societies within societies. But even as human individual complex occasions of experience we are relatively "momentary" in our duration and quite episodal.

6. The mutuality involved here does not mean that we create each other simultaneously. The mutuality is of the crisscross variety. Your past self influences my present self. My present self will influence your later self. Mutually contemporaneous selves do not influence each other. The notion of mutuality presupposes the existence of enduring individuals whose histories as selves are composed of a series of concrete occasions of experience.

7. *Criterion*, Winter, 1976, p. 22.

8. Later, as a completed actuality, it can help to create other selves or occasions of experience which supersede it. But it cannot create others until it has created itself.

9. In the following pages whenever characteristics of freedom are mentioned, it is to be understood that this is a form of shorthand to speak of characteristics of the self.

10. After it has become a definite and actualized self, its energy is released to create another occasion of experience which supersedes itself. It then becomes a value for others. But it cannot be a value for others until it has become a value to itself.

11. I have discussed the notion of freedom at greater length elsewhere. See "The Dimensions of Freedom" in Bernard Lee and Henry James Cargas, eds., *Religious Experience and Process Theology* (New York: Paulist Press, 1976).

12. Technically, and in Whiteheadian language, relationality could be said to refer to process as transition, while freedom would refer to process as concrescence.

13. It might be maintained that in the theological tradition the Holy Spirit was both the source or the agent for the transformation of man's freedom and the creator of human community.

14. These "hows" are Whitehead's "subjective forms"--an unfortunate term. These qualitative "hows" are not wholly describable in terms of his "eternal objects." These latter elements are ingredients or "qualifications" of these subjective reactions.

15. Whitehead's "subjective aim" may be conceptual in nature. But the choice of an aim and the impulse to achieve it are not only conceptual operations.

16. My great indebtedness to Reinhold Niebuhr at this point will be obvious.

17. In the tradition, his rational capacity is either an agent or the source of his freedom.

18. From this point of view, God's freedom would also be an emergent from his relationships. It would be an aspect of His self-creativity which in turn would be reflected back into His relationships.

Part Two

Theology and the Human Sciences

GOD AND ECONOMICS

by
James Luther Adams

G. K. Chesterton once said that the most important question
to ask about a new landlady is, What is her world view? In effect,
he was saying that economics raises the question regarding world
view. Economics cannot be confined to the study of the production
and interchange of goods and services; it must also take into
account the world view that informs these activities and which gives
integrity and direction to human community. In short, the topic
"God and Economics" brings us sooner than later to the question regarding the meaning of life and the resources for its fulfillment --
macroeconomics in an even broader sense than usually attaches to
that term. It leads to a discussion not only of the meaning of
meaning but also of the symbols that are pertinent for considering
our topic. Indeed, it brings us to the question regarding the myths
(and therefore also the root metaphors) which generally come into
play in any treatment of religion and economics. We must briefly
explain this conception of meaning and myth here at the outset in
very broad strokes; and then we must indicate the limitations we
aim to place upon the present discussion.

Being religious means asking the question of the meaning
of our human existence. And what is the meaning of meaning in this
context? It is the concern for significant relatedness. Wilhelm
Dilthey long ago suggested that meaning or significance has to do
with the relationship between the parts and the whole, a relatedness
that holds past and present together in some continuity.1 This conception of meaning may or may not include a conception of God, depending upon one's definition of the whole. Apart from that question we may close in on our topic by referring to two quite different
conceptions of the relationship between the parts and the whole.

In ancient Israel, meaning, or significant relatedness,
was immanently "located" within the arena of nature, society and
history in contrast to the type of religion which envisages meaning
primarily in interpersonal relatedness and which looks toward essential fulfillment outside or above history. For these ends symbols are created in society and history. They define and promote
some sense of relatedness and continuity in human life.

An elaborated symbolization achieves what may be called a
mythological articulation -- an imaginative, integrating, metaphorical
conception of Whence and Whither within a temporal sequence. In a
broad sense this sort of articulation may be spoken of as religious
insofar as it provides, or aims to provide, a sense of identity and
responsible vocation for the individual and the group. Some such
mythological conception generally informs any economic philosophy.

89

We shall see presently that the outlook of Adam Smith and of
laissez-faire economic theory lives from such a myth. Previously
the world had been viewed as a machine, and before that, in ancient
Greece and the Middle Ages, as an organism. Such a myth appears
also in nineteenth-century conceptions of progressive evolution.
J. B. Bury, a non-theological historian of ideas, detected in the
idea of progress a residue, a secularization, of the idea of divine
Providence. Here we see myths that depend upon root metaphors
drawn from mechanics, biology and theology. These metaphors are
not only the consequence of experience; they are often its pre-
requisite. They create and order experience.[2]

Strictly speaking, however, a myth is a story about the
gods. In Western tradition symbolic behavior is explicitly and
overtly religious when it presupposes activity of the divine in relation to the human -- a relationship between the whole and the
parts. In its Old Testament prophetic form, for example, it involves not only persons in their immediate interpersonal relations
or in the individual's relation to God but also in institutional
behavior. To be sure, this comprehensive, integrated view attaches
to a largely pre-pluralistic society.

From this Old Testament prophetic perspective the confinement of religious meaning to interpersonal relations is a grossly
truncated sense of meaning or significant relatedness. In modern
terms we may say that this confinement represents an attempt, a
spurious attempt, to understand the human enterprise only psychologically and not also sociologically and politically. In contemporary individualistic existentialism the confinement assumes itself
to be concrete, but in actuality it is highly abstract; it is a misplaced concreteness that ignores the institutional framework and
support. It therefore ignores institutional behavior and responsibilities. It imprisons the flower within the crannied wall. In
the poem *Peter Bell* Wordsworth uttered protest against the failure
to recognize a broader relatedness.

> A primrose by a river's brim
> A yellow primrose was to him,
> And it was nothing more.

In the Old Testament tradition the sense of authentic ecology is an
ecology of grace. It is present in society and history -- in institutions as well as in personal experience -- though it may be interpreted in distorted, even magical, fashion.

The present discussion of our theme will be limited to considering two major ingredients or models of tradition, the one from
the Old Testament and the other from the seventeenth century Radical
Reformation deriving its sanction from the New Testament. Both of
these models are versions of a great mythological invention, a
doctrine of covenant, one of the most influential metaphorical creations of the Jewish and Christian tradition. In important respects
these two models represent contrasting perspectives, even though
they are rooted in the same symbol. It is precisely because they
are contrasting perspectives regarding the divine-human relationship
that they are selected here for discussion. As we shall see, the

one perspective interprets meaning in terms of the integrity of relationships and responsibility in the total territorial community --
a broadly collective orientation; the other interprets meaning in
terms of the integrity and responsibility of the small group, the
gathered congregation -- a more narrowly collective orientation.   In
both types of perspective institutions play a crucial, indispensable
role in the relatedness between the parts and the whole.

***

          In its initial religious form the shaping of the concept
of covenant was primarily the work of the Old Testament prophets,
though its origin and development are not confined to their influence.   This covenant involves a deeper kind of personal relationship
than a contract and should not be confused with any form of bargained
pact.   In general, covenant is a means whereby a transnatural,
transcendent deity is represented as binding his worshippers to himself by a sovereign act of grace eliciting a moral agreement and
calling them to obedient allegiance and faithfulness.   It is an
agreement ostensibly entered into in voluntary consent (a historical
fiction).   It forms a bond of loyalty for the sake of fellowship
with God and of harmonious living -- righteousness and peace.   From
the human side this covenant is a commitment to what is deemed to
be an ultimate reality, a reliable though mysterious basis of confidence.
          There are various covenants, for example, with Abraham,
David and Moses as representatives.   Thus the concept is a composite
one including the election of a people, a promise of land, a justification of possession of the land, a binding obligation upon the
king, a relating of the people as a whole to a divine purpose and
imperative, a divine sanction also for law and cultus.   It may be
seen as an aspect of the development of the identity, unity and
vocation of a people, a harbinger of national survival but also a
humanitarian commitment looking toward eventual universality.   A
dominant idea was the conviction that the covenant gives the promise
of God's power to liberate from enslavement, a promise already
initially manifest in the liberation from Egyptian bondage.   This
identity and commitment includes the individual as well as the collective, the deprived as well as the privileged.
          In these developments there were various tributaries re-
flecting differing motifs and different social structures.   In recent
scholarship much has been made of the invention of the metaphor of
covenant as a construct reminiscent of a suzerainty treaty between
a superior political power and a vassal.   Insofar as this aspect of
the metaphor is emphasized, however, it can mislead one into assuming that the religious covenant is only a legal one between God
and Israel and that it is only for the collective.   The basis of
the covenant is not so much law as it is affectionate response to
liberation from bondage arousing trust and faithfulness on the part
of the individual as well as of the collective.
          Violation of the covenant is not so much a breaking of
law as it is betrayal of trust -- a violation of a relatedness.   The
violation brings judgment upon the people.   George Foot Moore used

to sum up this aspect of covenant by defining a prophet as one who proclaims doom -- God's execution of judgment upon the faithlessness of the people. This "doom" threatens the entire people as a corporate personality. Yet, renewal of covenant is possible, for the divine purpose is to be fulfilled in the endtime.

Now, there are three features of this relatedness which are especially significant in our constructed model.

(1) The metaphor of covenant is a form of political rhetoric. Like the metaphors, the kingship of God, the kingdom of God, and the Messiah, it is drawn from the political realm -- an example of what Shailer Matthews called "transcendentalized politics."[3] As a political metaphor it embraces the whole of society in history. Nothing individual or collective, naturistic or human, inner or outer, personal or institutional, is excluded from meaning, from potential relatedness, before the Divine Majesty. No spatialization into a segment of relatedness is approved. This feature is characteristic of the exclusive monotheism of Israel, ("Thou shalt have no other gods before me").

This comprehensive conception lies behind the prophet's claim that God is the Lord of history, and also behind the warning of doom ("The Lord hath a controversy with his people"). The covenanted people are responsible for the character of the society as a whole, for institutional as well as individual behavior.

Martin Buber calls this idea of covenant "a special kind of politics, theopolitics." Meaning, significant relatedness, points to a holy ground, to an ultimate source and resource.

(2) The covenant belongs to all the people, and therefore it includes the deprived and the poor as well as the privileged, the weak as well as the strong. Righteousness and peace require concern and care for the poor and even the stranger at the gate. The nerve of a responsible society is the divine compassion engendering respect for persons regardless of status. There remains here a reminiscence of the pre-urban, more egalitarian, less corrupting, nomadic life when, it was thought, Israel was faithful to the covenant.

Ernst Troeltsch, considering this aspect of the ethos, asserted that the prophets were anti-urbanites representing the simple ethics of small agricultural business and common farmers, and that since the city and world politics (with the money economy) are here to stay the message of the prophets even in their own day was "impossible." Yet, their neighborly ethic "by leaping over all complicated cultural relationships to a humanely personal brotherliness achieved an immense world-historical significance."[4] It remains as a perennial antidote to the depersonalizing forces of "civilization."

(3) The meaning of life is grateful, affectional, inward response to the divine, gracious, creative, sustaining, liberating, transforming power, the ultimate source and resource of righteousness and peace. Accordingly, the covenant as a gift of this power is the basis for confidence, identity and vocation for the individual and the society before the unapproachable holiness of the divine.

Now, this conception of covenant is an "ideal type" -- in two senses of the term -- in the Weberian sense of being a descrip-

tive synthetic model accentuating selected features, and also in
the sense of providing a religious-ethical norm. The question remains, What were the ethical implications of the covenant for
economic behavior and institutions?

It is of course difficult to arrive at satisfactory,
comprehensive generalizations to cover the long history of Israel,
beyond asserting that the earlier rural, neighborly, tribal egalitarianism recurrently served as a challenge to the self-serving
economic and political power that came on the scene long after the
emancipation from Egypt. The criterion of impartiality finds expression again and again. Respect for the person was combined with
the view that there is no respect of persons with God. This combination of ideas is repeatedly evident in paradigmatic stories
reaching from the story about the prophet Nathan on through the
history.

The covenant provides sanction for the prophetic denun-
ciation of the indulgence of the elite in luxury, the pomp and
politics of the court, the callousness of the king and the palace
guard, international alliances, the conduct of war with horse and
chariot, and an enlisted army (in imitation of the great powers).
The egalitarianism is to be observed in practice in kinship obligations with respect to the possession and retention of property
by the owners and their kin, in laws regarding loans and security,
in the rejection of the *lex talionis*, in laws requiring humane
treatment and regulated manumission of slaves, in privileges for
the poor to glean in the fields, in the relief of the sabbatical
year with its care for the tender land, and also in the Utopian
ideal of the Jubilee every fifty years. To be sure, the contention
with powerful neighboring states and the necessity of maintaining
armaments, the need for a balance of trade, the crushing taxation,
gave advantages to the elites in their aggrandizement of power.
Economic and political powers, domestic and foreign, largely controlled the enterprise (partly for this reason the prophets proposed the need for a "Remnant").

We shall see something similar to this whole development
when we view an outcome of the second model of covenant. But nowhere in antiquity can one find outside Israel such a complex of
values or the theological sanction for these values, and also for
prophetic dissent, as one encounters in the doctrine of covenant
and covenant renewal.

***

The second and contrasting model of meaning or relatedness
is congregational polity. It comes to birth in the seventeenth
century in the gathered, covenanted churches of England and New
England, though it is rooted in earlier sectarian movements and
finds its sanction in the New Testament church. The term was also
familiar in secular usage. I once asked Dr. Geoffrey Nuttall, the
eminent British Congregationalist historian, to name the principal
sources of the term at this time. He replied by quoting a line from
the American musical, *Oklahoma*: "It was," he said, "bustin' out
all over."

A typical congregational covenant contained such phrases as a free community, a particular church, a communion of "visible saints" engaging to walk together by a voluntary consent in holy fellowship, to worship God according to His Word and under the headship of the living Christ. The believer was brought into the visible fellowship through confession of faith and adult baptism (the latter being a cause of dissension among the churches), "to make no difference of persons" and "bearing each other's burthens." The written covenant contained what might be called an abbreviated confession of faith, brief in order to avoid imposing upon the individual conscience an elaborate set of articles.

The Christians of congregational polity were Puritans who wished to purify the church and the society through recovering authentically Christian faith and fellowship and through finding the earthly center of religious life in the local congregation of believers. We may speak of this movement as being in the direction of localism. In place of a national covenant of Geneva or Edinburgh vintage -- or of Old Testament type -- these congregationalists (some of them being called "Independents") formed a covenant for each congregation.

Generally, however, each congregation recognized the living Christ in other congregations, and through "connectionalism" these congregations entered into cooperation with each other. These congregations protested against the centralized powers in the established church. They wished to be liberated from the hierarchical authority of bishops or clergy and from the association of the church hierarchy with the state and the monarch. They therefore promoted the separation of church and state, in order to place institutional authority in the self-governing congregation. Instead of a church for the masses they wanted a voluntary church only for believers. Here explicit faith, close interpersonal relations, and moral discipline were possible.

This self-governing congregation was to be self-supporting, thus rejecting financial support or control coming from non-believers or from coercive taxation at the hands of the political authority. Consequently, the passing of the collection plate (as well as the reading of the Bible) became a kind of sacrament. In this congregation every member in principle would have the right and responsibility of joining in the determination of policies (radical laicism).

What with the emphasis given to the reading of the Bible, a high premium was placed on literacy. These people wished to substitute participative coarchy for hierarchy. Not that the congregation considered itself to be autonomous. The principle of the consent of the governed was closely related to a doctrine and discipline of the Holy Spirit in accord with Scripture. In some degree, then, congregational polity was a pneumatocracy. The proponents of the polity appealed to the New Testament as sanction for the demand that the minister possess charismatic "gifts and graces." The congregation for its part was expected "to tast [sic] as it were the savour of his spirit."[5]

The principle of local autonomy entailed the struggle for freedom to form independent religious associations, a struggle that aroused persecution. This struggle was somewhat similar to that

of the primitive Christian churches in face of the establishment
in ancient Rome which also demanded a civil religion for the sake
of territorial unity and stability; indeed, according to Roman law
the churches were considered to be "illicit."

This demand for freedom of religious association gradually
became the stimulus for the demand for freedom to form voluntary
secular associations. In this fashion the principle of freedom of
association was eventually applied to spheres beyond the church to
intermediate organizations -- to philanthropic enterprise, to education and the founding of Nonconformist academies, and to economic
enterprise (and later on to political dissent).

It has been argued that the self-governing congregation
with its radical laicism and its emphasis on literacy became the
model for democratic political theory, that the idea of the democratic state was born by analogy from the conception of the self-
governing congregation. The self-governing congregations became
also the seed of a pluralistic, a multi-group, society (to be seen
in contrast with medieval traditionalist society).

This whole development represents a radical dispersion of
power and responsibility, the dispersion of the capacity and freedom
to participate in the making of social, institutional decisions. An
analogous way in which this process was promoted was through the
encouragement to work (toward the end of overcoming the under-
employment of the time). Max Weber has amply demonstrated that a
new this-worldly asceticism and sense of vocation were developing
among the Puritans.

The Separatists made a special appeal to "small men in
town and country." Among them diligence in a worldly calling was
viewed as an indispensable service to God. They were to be monks
in the world. Already in 1588 Robert Browne, a leader among the
Elizabethan Separatists, had even asserted that an idle person
should cease to be a member of the church of God. Here we see the
beginning of "the achieving society," of the rejection of ascribed
status in favor of acquired status. The appeal was not to the
propertyless or to the privileged classes. It was to the emerging
middle class, to the economically independent, to householders, to
small employers and the self-employed.6

These economically independent people in search of greater
freedom protested against the chartered monopolies. The special
privileges of these monopolies licensed by the monarch were set
forth blatantly in the commercial, royal charters (fascinating documents, by the way). The protests against these privileges sound
very much like the protests against the royally appointed prelates
of the established church.

There is reason to believe that many members of the small
convenanted congregations were these independent folk and small
employers. (In my recent conversation at Oxford with Christopher
Hill, the British historian of the radical Puritans, he confirmed
this view, asserting that we need further research in this area.)
Of primary significance was the claim that the government should
not interfere with the free church or with free business enterprise.
Like the self-governing congregation, economic enterprise was becoming independent in a burgeoning, pluralistic society. The

congregations were strictly parallel in their voluntary organization to trading corporations, as defenders of religious toleration (like Roger Williams) pointed out. These defenders as "Dissenting Brethren" claimed for their churches the freedoms "such as corporations enjoy."[7]

Dispersion of power was taking place in both the small church and the small business enterprise. In both spheres, then, we see the emergence of a "congregational" localism. Positive relatedness was to the parts, not to the whole.

It is a striking thing that the pattern of meaning adopted later in laissez-faire economic theory (depending upon free market and contract and not upon status) was analogous to that of congregationalist convenant theory. In both spheres the assumption apparently was that if the parts are authentic (or efficient), the whole will take care of itself by virtue of "providential" automatic harmony -- in economic theory this harmony was to be effected by "an invisible hand" in the operation of the free market. The parts are not, as in earlier prophetic theory of covenant, responsible for the character of the society as a whole. They are responsible, rather, for promoting the kind of society which protects freedom for the parts. With these views the mind and conscience could be set at rest regarding the broader social and political consequences of this localistic freedom.

We should now consider an impressive formulation of the ethos of congregational localism, as it appears in the theory and practice of one of the great eighteenth century representatives of covenant theory, the New England Baptist Isaac Backus (1724-1806), a tireless itinerant preacher in addition to being pastor of a congregation. A renewed sense of his significance in the American scene is largely a consequence of the editorial and interpretative work of the American historian, William G. McLoughlin.[8]

Backus started out as a Congregationalist, and later under the influence of the Great Awakening became a Baptist in his protest against persecution promoted in the name of the establishment. His protest was against birthright membership and in favor of membership based upon voluntary adult baptism following upon regeneration. His protest was also against the coercive taxation supporting the parish system, a protest that brought numerous Baptists into prison. He rejected the sanction for a national covenant which the theocratic Puritans appealed to under the rubric of the Abraamic covenant. He denied the continuity of the Old Testament covenant with that of the New Testament. The authentic congregation of believers must rely upon an individualistic, voluntary church in which God was producing conversions and engendering a "new reformation."

Although Backus for most of his career retained adherence to the predestinarian Calvinism of the Old Lights, he adopted the view of the New Lights that new enlightenment was to come through the working of the Holy Spirit, though he resisted perfectionism and Universalism. In the church of this "new reformation" the members (under the guidance of the Holy Spirit) and not the ministers alone were to make the decisions regarding admission of new members and regarding eligibility for ordination. The right of the majority to rule in the congregation was essential. Backus held that this

right had been usurped by the clergy of the establishment. The
Great Awakening was radically opposed to all ecclesiastical bureau-
crats.

         With regard to broader public policy Backus gradually
moved in some measure away from the radical localism of the majority
of Baptist pietists. This change is to be observed especially in
his decision to support ratification of the new federal Constitution. He was the first Baptist of prominence to take this position,
and he did so to the disappointment of most other Baptists, both
clergy and lay. These Baptists were fearful of any substantial
federal authority, retaining their adherence to radical localism
and their distrust of democracy on any large scale. The reasons
for his support of the ratification were the Constitution's exclusion of "all titles of nobility or hereditary succession of
power" (ascribed status) as well as of religious tests, and also
later the protection of freedom of religion and the prohibition of
establishment afforded by the First Amendment. Equally important
was his view that "the American revolution was built upon the principle, that all men are born with an equal right to liberty and
property, and that officers have no right to any power but what is
fairly given them by the consent of the people"; but he did not
favor Jeffersonian Enlightenment formulations with regard to
natural rights. His desire to protect freedom of religion was so
strong that he approved of civil disobedience in face of even
"legal" suppression of this freedom.

         Backus believed that the health of the society depended
upon freedom of individual conscience and upon the Christian
character of the citizens. In this matter he was very optimistic.
Jefferson thought the majority of citizens would become Unitarians;
Backus believed the nation was destined to become Baptist. The
bulk of his writings, however, were devoted to the definition of
authentic Scriptural doctrine (as adumbrated in the Westminster
Confession). Accordingly, he admonished obedience to the powers
that be. But he apparently did not assert that the individual
Christian in democratic society (in contrast to living in the society in which St. Paul found himself) is a part of these powers and
is under obligation to attempt by institutional means to affect
them. As a pietist he was perhaps too much of an anti-institution-
alist, too much of an individualist, to sense that obligation.

         This pietistic ethos did not, according to Dr. McLoughlin,
prevent Backus from criticizing merchants, lawyers and the oppressors of the poor. But he did not view the economic establishment
as requiring institutional remedies. He was too successful as an
evangelist in converting prominent people, and perhaps he had been
sufficiently successful as a farmer on his inherited land, to
transcend his primary interest in the parts and to concern himself
with the character of the whole economic structure. For this institutional criticism one would have to wait until the appearance
of more prophetically oriented Baptists such as Francis Wayland
(1796-1865), the fourth President of Brown University, and Walter
Rauschenbusch (1861-1918), the proponent of the Social Gospel.
(Congregationalists were also leaders in the Social Gospel Movement.)

Yet, with his congregational principle of separation of church and state, and the principle of the consent of the governed, also with his support for ratification of the federal Constitution and with his evangelistic appeal to the common man, Backus helped materially to shape the American ethos of the future. In these respects he maintained the heritage of the Radical Reformation stemming from the seventeenth century in England and New England. On the other hand, his pietistic lack of an institutional philosophy and his insensitivity to the prophetic conception of covenant did not help to prepare for combat with the new economic establishment that was the wave of the future.

***

Adam Smith observed that the isolated individual was persuaded by the evangelistic sect to believe that he has an eternal soul, thus gaining a new sense of his dignity and worth and of his freedom to accept the Gospel, but that after entering the sect he found himself in a tight vise of external discipline. Something analogous to this process of reversal was to be the fate of congregational localism -- and that in both the church and the business enterprise. At the outset this localism, as we have seen, promoted a dispersion of power and responsibility. Eventually, however, it found itself surrounded by powers, especially economic powers, which like a vise constricted freedom in the corporate community.

Adam Smith had identified the constrictor of freedom in the landed estates. (It is often overlooked that Smith was as much opposed to the unaccountable power of the owners of these estates as he was to commercial monopoly.) But his reliance upon free market and open competition was connected with his assumption that business enterprise would be small enterprise. He did not, could not, foresee the emergence of the mammoth corporation.

It is noteworthy that already in the 1830's President Andrew Jackson made vigorous attack on the special privileges of chartered corporations. Between the American revolution and 1801 state governments had created more than 300 corporations. Jackson's attacks on their special privileges under charters (attacks demanding competition) remind one of the attacks made upon chartered monopolies in the first half of the seventeenth century.

We cannot in the present discussion trace the development of corporate economic behavior in the first half of the nineteenth century. It will suffice if we indicate the emergence of the prophetic model with its concern for the character of the society as a whole in opposition to mere "localism." In our previous section we have centered attention upon the Baptists; now we may consider an opposing trend right within the churches of congregational polity, this time among the Unitarians.[9]

Radical criticism of the social system begins to appear in this group in the 1830's, the "age of Jackson." In 1832 the Rev. William Ellery Channing (Boston), a grandson of a signer of the Declaration of Independence, wrote "that the old principles of property are to undergo a fiery trial, that the monstrous inequalities of condition must be redressed, and that greater revolutions

than the majority have dreamed of -- whether for good or evil --
are to be anticipated." In the following year he renewed his
attack upon the accumulation of great wealth.

In 1841 Brook Farm (not exclusively Unitarian) was established with the purpose of substituting a system of brotherly
cooperation for one of selfish competition. It operated on a joint
stock proprietorship, and each member had free choice of occupation.
(Adam Smith half a century earlier had said that division of labor
was producing "dolts.") The Associationist Movement advocated a
plan for the democratic organization of industry.

In 1843 William Henry Channing, Ellery Channing's nephew
and biographer, attacked what he called "the degradations of our
present social state."

> The charity we need is justice -- justice in production, justice in
> distribution, the rallying cry today is social organization ....
> The error of the modern doctrine of liberty has been its tone of
> selfish independence; its idol has been individualism; its sin, law-
> lessness, its tendencies to anarchy.

Less than a decade later he wrote that liberalism "cannot stop
short of socialism. Mere modifications in government will in no
wise secure this integral development of human nature in all classes
which the conscience of the age demands."

In 1844 the Rev. James Freeman Clarke (in the latter part
of his career a Professor of natural religion and Christian doctrine
at Harvard) called for radical change in the system.

> The evils arising from want of organization appear most evidently
> when we consider this other great principle of modern society --
> freedom in the direction of industry. We have adopted the free
> trade principle in its fullest extent. We say, leave trade and in-
> dustry to regulate themselves. We say to Government -- 'laissez
> faire, let me alone' .... On the let-alone principle capital will
> always be able to take advantage of labor, and for the simple
> reason, the capital can *wait*, labor cannot.

John S. Dwight, the music critic who had been a member of
Brook Farm and an Associationist, emphasized the importance of the
social sciences for the battle against injustice. He spoke of
social science as "the second babe in the manger," the first being
Jesus.

Horace Mann, the principal education reformer of the
nineteenth century, called for "a laborious process of renovation
sustained by the power and resources of the government." "Wealth,"
he said, "wealth, by force of unjust laws and institutions, is
filched from the producer and gathered in vast masses, to give
power and luxury and aggrandizement to a few. Of production, there
is no end; of distribution, there is no beginning."

These Unitarians and Transcendentalists do not speak of
the congregational covenant, probably because the polity up to that
time had been supported by the state establishment and also because
of the regnant economic individualism in the denomination. They

speak rather of "Divine Love" and "Laws of Divine Justice." "Liberalism is of God, and ... its heaven-appointed end is social organization," said the younger Channing.

***

        We have now come full circle, from the holistic pre-
industrial society of the Middle Ages through the period when congregational, covenanted polity and capitalist free enterprise appear, to the beginning of the demand for socialism, a concern again
for the whole in its relation to the parts. Viewing the longer
historical development of the meaning of life as it has been surveyed in the present essay, we may say in simplified formulation
that the Old Testament prophetic covenant was moral, religious and
political, and that the historic congregational covenant was moral
and religious but not (positively) political; religious socialism
in opposition to capitalism is again moral, religious and political.[10]
        The terms *capitalism* and *socialism* are weasel words. The
same may be said,of course,regarding any key words that have per-
sisted through a protracted period, for example, words like *God* and
liberalism. During the past century and a half the terms *capitalism*
and *socialism* have been undergoing considerable change. In the
earlier part of this period capitalism was connected with the theory
of the negative state which gives to the political order the economic function only of creating or maintaining conditions necessary
for economic freedom and competition, necessary (that is) for the
encouragement of the initiatives that release new energies and
elicit capital investment.
        Toward the end of the nineteenth century, however, new
conceptions of economic responsibility began to emerge. The change
is evident in the sphere of law. This change in legal thought has
been described as a shift from emphasis on the rights of the individual will to the older "common-law idea of relation." (It is
noteworthy that the term "relation" which is crucial for our definition of meaning appears here.) The individual with his "free
contract" has been brought more and more (not without dust and heat)
to recognize duties as well as rights, in terms of "social justice"
instead of merely individualistic "legal justice." Thus the concept of meaning as mutually responsible relatedness within a
societal framework was coming to the fore.
        Roscoe Pound years ago characterized the change as a
movement in the direction of a "feudal principle."[11] This restoration of a feudal principle was in part the gateway to the development of the welfare state where capitalism reluctantly became a
mixed economy.
        Meanwhile, great changes came in the technology of trans-
portation and communication; also, the managerial revolution, with
its hierarchy of salaried executives replacing the direction by the
owners, evolved. In short, capitalism has passed through a number
of phases, requiring differing definitions.
        The definition of socialism likewise has assumed differing
definitions extending all the way from anarchism to centralism.

Under its name have been such varied configurations as are suggested
by the Social-Democratic Welfare states of Western Europe, the
Leninist-Stalinist regimes of Russia and Eastern Europe to the
various Third World regimes, not to speak of new African forms of
socialism and the *Kibbutzim* of Israel. Moreover, within the past
century in the United States socialist theory has borrowed from
laissez-faire theory (particularly as skepticism developed regarding
the adequacy of centralist socialism) and laissez-faire theory has
borrowed from socialism (with the advent of the welfare state).
     The old dictionary definition of socialism reads, "A
political and economic theory of social organization based on
government ownership." This definition is now in many quarters an
anachronism, especially in face of current conceptions of democratic socialism.
     In this connection we should look briefly at the devel-
opment of religious socialism. Within the same decade as the
Unitarian socialists were demanding social reorganization the movement calling itself "Christian Socialism" was initiated in the
Church of England by F. D. Maurice and Charles Kingsley. Its purpose was to "Christianize socialism" and to "socialize Christianity." In practical terms it was mainly a cooperative movement and
an experiment in adult education, but it became a stimulus for the
criticism of the current capitalist economics. A similar movement
was beginning in the German Lutheran churches. Roman Catholic neo-
medieval socialist theory antedated these movements, for early in
the century they were making radical attacks on capitalism as a
form of modern chaos dissolving community and societal responsibility.
     It is not surprising that these movements should appear
in territorial churches accustomed to a national establishment
rather than in churches that began by rejecting establishment. To
be sure, the prophetic demands had been previously at a vanishing
point. The quotations from the Unitarian socialists we have cited
could be interpreted in part as the reappearance of the holistic
perspectives of earlier Calvinist territorial covenant. (Troeltsch
was wont to speak of primitive Calvinism as Christian Socialism.)
Calvin, being a lawyer, was saturated with Old Testament law and
covenantal lore. From the point of view of the congregational
"Independents," however, the Genevan covenant was the inspiration
for the non-Separatist Puritan attempt to replace the Anglican
establishment with their own theocratic and coercive covenant.
     For their part the religious socialists of the nineteenth
century in England and the U.S.A. were coming to recognize that they
faced a new, an economic, establishment, indeed that "automatic
harmony" and "the invisible hand" had been frustrated by the cres-
cent corporate, economic powers.
     The emergence of the oligopoly of mammoth business cor-
porations produces the paradox of the society of free enterprise:
on the one hand it opened the way for a new freedom, a freedom that
has produced an impressive array of goods and services and a rise
in the standard of living for many, but on the other it has produced a system that provides new compulsion[12] at the hands of corporate and centralized powers largely unaccountable because in the

market they define the needs through advertising, and the markets
have not always remained free. In some respects these powers are
stronger than the government as well as stronger than the market.
Moreover, since economic congregational localism did not assume responsibility for consequences in the commonwealth, its conscience
could remain clear regarding the millions who have been left out,
millions now become billions in the Third World where the poor are
becoming ever poorer. A contemporary unconventional economist has
called this outcome "socialism for the rich" by reason of its advantages for the profits of the affluent.
      Ellery Channing a century and a half ago had asserted
that the social system should be judged by its effects on the human
person. A major effect even upon those who contentedly live within
and from the corporate enterprise is to make them "kept" men and
women -- dissent is practically unknown among them, so much so that
Ralph Nader has suggested that we need a new Bill of Rights for
dissenters within the corporations.
      Troeltsch long ago predicted that the enthusiasm for
political rights could not be maintained if the economic powers
could not meet the needs of body and mind in the general populace.
The present system has engendered or tolerated massive inequalities, inequalities in the forms of racism and sexism and also of
poverty at the gate of the affluent society. The richest 10 percent of our households receive 25.1 percent of our income while the
poorest 10 percent receive only 1.7 percent. Blacks earn 69 percent as much as whites; women who work full time earn only 56 percent as much as men. Some 80 percent of female workers labor in
"pink-collar" jobs. These jobs are segregated by race and sex.
      Now, these inequalities are not to be remedied by govern-
ment ownership of basic industries. Few people believe that government employees can be more efficient on the whole than employees
of private corporations. One can see, however, the possible advantage of government ownership of military production to remove
this segment from its inordinate political influence and from sub-
sidies that syphon off profits to the private sector instead of
assigning them to the people as a whole.
      If we add to the problems mentioned the issues raised by
the tax structure, by the multinational corporations with their
use of cheap labor abroad and their stripping of natural resources
to the profit of the developed nations, also by the ecological and
the energy crises, and by massive unemployment, we encounter areas
in which the wealthy and the middle class resist control. The
problem, as Dean Pound asserted, is that of injecting morals into
the law.
      We have a national covenant called the Constitution. But
the working constitution includes all of the patterns or customs
that define our relatedness to each other. And these patterns in
appalling ways add up to "restrictive covenants" (actually, this is
the use of the term *covenant* most widely familiar).
      Democratic socialism aims to break through these restric-
tive covenants. It urges that the democratic principles that have
obtained in politics should be applied to the economic sphere. In
the context of our present discussion the aim is that of combining

the prophetic sense of responsibility for the character of the society at large with the social ideals that came to birth in congregational polity -- the consent of the governed, participation in the process of making social-institutional decisions, the "bearing of each other's burthens," the dispersion of power and responsibility, the achievement of a just relation between the parts.

These values are now shared by people whose rootage is not in the explicit tradition of congregational polity, and they require application not only in the sphere of industry but also in education, in health services, and in the control of natural resources. The participation of the governed here would be calculated to re-personalize the individual participants in a pluralistic society which is now threatened by the giantism endemic in the culture.[13] The ways proposed (and in some places already attempted) include the introduction of worker participation in the determination of policies of the factory and the office, so that, for example, the workers may begin to own or participate in the control of the means of production and distribution. This strategy has already been adopted in Germany and Scandinavian countries. In Germany it is called *Mitbestimmung* (co-determination), and in order to make it effective labor representatives are being given training in special topics (investment, marketing, management) so they may serve with some competence on boards of trustees of corporations. Prime Minister Helmut Schmidt has asserted that this whole development is the major contribution of Germany since World War II to modern democracy.

Viewing the sluggishness of American concern for the inequalities in the society, Julian Bond has compared it to climbing a molasses mountain in snowshoes. We remain in what the prophet called the Valley of Decision, whether to worship the false gods of restrictive covenants and respectable hardness of heart or to "turn" in costing gratitude to the creative, sustaining, judging, forgiving, transforming Power that brings forth treasures old and new. This is the relatedness that gives meaning, identity and vocation to our pilgrimage. The alternative is affluent callousness and emptiness.

NOTES AND REFERENCES

1. W. Dilthey, *Selected Writings*. Edited, translated and introduced H.P. Rickman (New York: Cambridge University Press, 1976), pp. 215, 235.
2. Robert N. Nisbet, *Social Change and History* (New York: Oxford University Press, 1969), p. 5.
3. Speaking of "transcendentalized politics" Matthews says,

Our theology is not a system of philosophy, but an extension of the forms of social experience to religious belief. It is a sort of parable in whose plot can be read the history of the social experience of centuries. Its purpose is to make religious experience consistent with other experience and so reasonable.

The Atonement and the Social Process (New York: Macmillan, 1930), pp. 22, 25.

4. Ernst Troeltsch, *Gesammelte Schriften* (Tübingen: J.C.B. Mohr [Paul Siebeck], 1925) IV, pp. 57-58. The essay, "Galube und Ethos der Hebräischen Propheten," was first published in 1916.

5. Geoffrey F. Nuttall, *Visible Saints: The Congregational Way, 1640-1660* (Oxford: Basil Blackwell, 1957), p. 85.

6. Christopher Hill, *Society and Puritanism in Pre-Revolutionary England* (London: Secker and Warburg, 1964), ch. 14.

7. Nuttall, *op. cit.*, p. 142.

8. William G. McLoughlin, *Isaac Backus and the American Pietistic Tradition* (Boston: Little, Brown & Co., 1967); *Isaac Backus on Church, State, and Calvinism.* Ed. with an Introduction by William G. McLoughlin (Cambridge: Harvard University Press, 1968).

9. John MacNab, *Unitarian and Socialistic Ideas in the United States Prior to 1860* (Boston, 1953). A paper prepared originally for a Seminar in Intellectual and Social History of the Modern World, under Professor Crane Brinton at Harvard University, 1951. Privately printed.

10. Another way of describing the differences typologically is to say that although all of these perspectives have a cosmic or theological orientation, the prophetic covenant is microcosmic, mesocosmic and macrocosmic in scope -- it interprets meaning in terms of the individual, of the middle, infrastructural institutions, and also of the broader societal structures. The congregational covenant in the period we have surveyed gives no emphasis to the macrocosmic. This concern re-appears in religious and secular socialism.

The covenant conception in the Gospels has not been presented here, for the members of the primitive Christian churches had no opportunity to participate in the shaping of policies in imperialistic Rome.

11. Cf. Roscoe Pound, *The Spirit of the Common Law* (Boston: Marshall Jones Co.), chs. 1, 2, 7. A major thesis of this book is that modern legal history can be charted as a transition from "a feudal principle" (mutual relatedness of parties in obligations) to a "Puritan principle" (emphasis on individual rights) to a return to "feudal principles" (the restraint or limitation of individual and property rights).

12. This view was already set forth by Thomas Hobbes, summarized by C.B. Macpherson:

> The market makes men free; it requires for its effective operation
> that all men be free and rational; yet the independent rational de-
> cisions of each man produce at every moment a configuration of forces
> which confronts each man compulsively. All men's choices determine,
> and each man's choice is determined by, the market. Hobbes caught
> both the freedom and the compulsion of possessive market society.

The Political Theory of Possessive Individualism (Oxford: Clarendon Press, 1962), p. 106.

13. W. Alvin Pitcher discusses these problems of participation and also strategies available to the churches, in his essay on "The Politics of Mass Society," appearing in D.B. Robertson, ed., *Voluntary Associations. A Study of Groups in a Free Society* (Richmond: John Knox Press, 1966).

Al Pitcher for years has been a creative and dedicated leader in race relations projects in Chicago. Paradoxically, the human-relations approach had to be combined with a law-and-order approach. Speaking of the situation in Hyde Park (adjacent to the University of Chicago) an old-timer once said, "From 1952 on it was a schizophrenic experience to live here. There was Jesus Christ walking down one side of the street, and Julius Caesar marching along the other." Al Pitcher as leader walked with faith and fortitude on both sides.

THE SEARCH FOR METHOD IN SOCIAL ETHICS

by
Alan B. Anderson

For a number of years, George W. Pickering and I have been engaged in a study of the civil rights movement in Chicago. In retrospect, much of our endeavor has been a search for method.

Our search for method was not just because we were students of Professor Pitcher -- though we were that, and his own concerns with method form a central theme of his academic life. Nor were we concerned with method simply because we were members of the Ethics and Society Field of The University of Chicago -- though we were that too, and Pitcher had institutionalized his concerns there.

For the most part, our search for method in Social Ethics arose out of our subject matter, the civil rights movement, and each proposed method had to be tested for its empirical adequacy and interpretive fruitfulness in terms of that subject matter. Since we share with Pitcher and others the notion that the standing of Social Ethics as a discipline depends upon the specification of its method and subject matter, our own search may be of interest here.

Our inquiry began with a subject matter -- the Coordinating Council of Community Organizations (CCCO). This civil rights coalition existed in Chicago from 1961 to about 1968, during which time it grew from about a dozen organizations to over fifty. It is best known for sponsoring school boycotts in 1963-64, undertaking daily protest marches in the summer of 1965, and joining with Dr. Martin Luther King, Jr.'s Southern Christian Leadership Conference (SCLC) to form the Chicago Freedom Movement during King's Chicago campaign in 1965-66.[1]

It was the second boycott of the Chicago schools in 1964 that started us thinking about the Coordinating Council of Community Organizations as the subject of a study. We began with questions about the effectiveness of that boycott. To be sure, as an isolated occasion, the second school boycott might have been considered effective: 175,000 students were absent the day of the boycott, and, while that number was 50,000 less than in the first boycott, it had been achieved in the face of anti-boycott activity by the Daley machine. Yet the second boycott seemed to strain the patience of even the supporters of CCCO; it left the Coordinating Council internally divided; and it produced no more change in the policies of the school board than had the first boycott.

Our initial focus, therefore, was on the problems of public interpretation and understanding of civil rights goals.[2] Our thinking turned to something like market research. We decided to have one of us in CCCO to take note of the kinds of considerations

107

which seemed to count there in decision-making. The other of us
was to take a sample of churches and try to devise a questionnaire
to get at the kinds of considerations by which people evaluated the
Chicago drive for civil rights. Our intent was practical. In the
end, we planned to have two contrasting sets of factors which, we
hoped, might be helpful as CCCO set out to plan its future actions.
Given the information which we had from the newspapers, this appeared to be a likely line of inquiry.
          However, once we began to learn some of the internal
workings of CCCO, we found a much more complex phenomenon than
we had been led to suppose. It was by no means clear what considerations might appropriately enter into the decisions of CCCO; that
was the question which seemed to recur in the discussion of the
delegates, though without being settled thereby. In addition, it
became clear that the idea of a questionnaire involved enormous
problems of sampling. A good study of CCCO itself seemed to be the
first order of study if there was to be any base from which to study
other things.
          We shifted, then, to a study which was to focus on the
problem of conflict and consensus within CCCO.[3] Our thought was
that we would have a study in the unsuccessful attempt at conflict
management within the constellation of Chicago civil rights organizations. We thought so for two reasons. In the first place, CCCO
was at a low ebb when we began our study. In the second place, the
organizations which comprised CCCO seemed to have such different
purposes and maintenance needs that CCCO appeared to be an arena
of finally unmanageable conflict. When this was our aim, we prepared to administer a series of scheduled interviews, first to the
delegates of CCCO and then to the executives of the organizations
which they represented. The point was to locate and identify, as
well as possible, the strains between individual organizational
needs and purposes and the attempt to formulate a common policy and
program in CCCO. Still, our intent remained practical; for we hoped
by identifying the factors which were driving this coalition apart
to contribute to the development of a more effective organizational
vehicle for the pursuit of civil rights aims.
          The plan to establish the sequence of events in which
these strains had been experienced seemed like a minor and an easy
thing to do. We intended to research the minutes of CCCO meetings
for exchanges that would illustrate these strains and document
their growing importance. But we very quickly learned two things
about CCCO. In testing our interview schedule, we learned that the
sequence of events and the roster of actors were quickly and easily
forgotten. In studying the minutes of CCCO meetings, we learned
that organizational strains were far from the most important data
which they contained. In addition, as we researched the newspaper
coverage and compared it with what we knew from the minutes and
other documents of CCCO, we came to see that very little hard reporting had taken place. Interpretations were offered in stories
and advice was offered editorially, but very few data were put forward in substantiation of either.
          Finally, in view of the partial memories of the actors
and the partial and somewhat speculative reporting in the newspapers,

it became our overriding purpose then to recover as much as we could of the story of CCCO. Recover, of course, is hardly the word for a story which has never been told and which, in one sense, has never been known. Parts of it are in the newspapers, parts of it are in the minutes, and still other parts of it are in the memories of the actors. We took as our problem getting these parts back together as once they were in events. By using each source as a check on the others, we found that the actors, when reminded of the sequence of events, tended to remember much better their own roles and the roles of their friends. Fortunately, the minutes record in lively detail many of the exchanges that took place in the formal meetings. Our interviews became much more open-ended, consisting mostly of questions about events in which we already knew the interviewee to have been deeply involved.

In such manner, our method of research came to be modified to suit the purpose of the study and the nature of the subject matter. These modifications, however, were not yet at an end; for conceiving the study as a story did not by any means settle the terms in which the story was to be told.

Our search for a more adequate interpretative context was, at this point, decisively influenced by the publication of the *Festschrift* for James Luther Adams in 1966.[4] We had long had difficulty conceiving the organizational form of CCCO. Most of the current theories of organization seemed to us most suited to social, economic, or governmental affairs--but not very helpful in understanding CCCO. Certainly we had never considered CCCO a "voluntary association," for in the literature with which we were familiar, voluntary associations were presented as ineffective and somewhat fraudulent enterprises. According to one interpretation, for example, the very "voluntary" character of this form of association means that it is "constantly under the necessity of convincing its members that they are accomplishing something worthwhile through it" in order to gain their support. "But it must do this without touching anything controversial," lest it lose some support in the process. As a result, a voluntary association "usually . . . deals with this dilemma in one or both of two ways: it gives the members prestige, publicity, and other such satisfactions in lieu of a sense of accomplishment, and it substitutes evidence of accomplishment of means for evidence of accomplishment of ends."[5]

Against this background, the appearance of *Voluntary Associations: A Study of Groups in Free Societies* provided a fresh perspective. In focusing upon the groups that stand between the individual and the state, and in interpreting them as an essential locus of democratic freedom, Adams and his students represented a tradition which appeared to articulate much of the best political and religious thought of the West--a tradition which was agreed by observers from de Tocqueville through Weber to be of unusual relevance to the American scene, and which offered exciting possibilities for both historical and philosophical interpretations.[6] "In this view of man and his associations," Adams recently wrote,

we have the rudiments of a doctrine of man and also the framework for a philosophy of history. Man is an associational being, and his history is the history of his associations. The history of any open society is the history of the changing character of the associations, and of the changing relations between the individual and the associations, and of the changing relations between the various associations.[7]

In this context, we began to think that CCCO could be understood as an episode in the history of association--as an attempt to address an associational problem (segregation) through associations (the constituent organizations of CCCO) by changing the relations among them (CCCO itself). And, as voluntary associations, CCCO and its constituents might be thought to embody a number of important values, functions, and problems not otherwise represented in a mass society. As the convenient summary of Adam's thought by James D. Hunt put it,

> Voluntary associations serve as a principal means in modern society for the articulation and protection of differences, as did the nonconforming congregation. They provide an instrumentality for the freedom of the individual to associate with others in the promotion of forms of consensus which are not shared by the total community. At least in principle, they resist a monolithic social order: they stand between the individual and the state and provide a means for dispersing power and opportunities for participation. They protect the freedom to criticize, the freedom to express newly felt needs, the freedom to define the situation in a new way, and the freedom to instigate or to implement social change. Thus they become, in a mass society, an indispensable means for dealing with injustice, with strain and conflict, and for shaping public opinion. By engendering the habit of discussion and participation, and training leadership, and providing opportunities for the definition and expression of concerns, they help prevent the appearance of splits that could create revolutionary situations. We may say that voluntary associations institutionalized and gradualized revolution. Mass man may be defined sociologically as the man who is not a participant in the process of decision-making with respect to public policy. Such participation for the citizen and churchman can only be effective through associations, and accordingly any realistic ethical program must include the requirement of participation in the groups which seek to affect policy for the general welfare.[8]

As we explored the phenomena and literature of voluntary associations further, however, it became apparent that not all voluntary associations possessed these characteristics or exercised these functions equally well. We were disturbed, for example, by Grant McConnell's critique of voluntary associations. Working out of the Progressive tradition in American politics and its distrust of private power, McConnell argues that "far from providing guarantees of liberty, equality, and concern for the public interest, organization of political life by small constituencies tends to enforce conformity, to discriminate in favor of elites, and to eliminate public values from effective political consideration."[9] But we were equally disturbed by those affirmations of voluntary

associations which led to what were, from our point of view, un-
acceptably conservative conclusions.10
     It seems, in fact, that any number of conclusions may be
drawn concerning the role of voluntary associations in public life
--depending on which voluntary associations one is talking about.
Thus, the essential problem becomes identifying a principle by which
the public contributions of these various associations may be evaluated, and some of them affirmed--others qualified or denied.11
     It might be thought that what Adams has called "the vol-
untary principle" might itself serve this function. Adams, however,
does not think so because he writes, "unfortunately, the voluntary
principle can serve as a sleeping pill as well as stimulant," and
"the voluntary principle, *insofar as it pursues worthy ends*, requires
sharp critical judgment of the actualities and vigorous, though
serene, commitments that can make of freedom of association, religious or secular, the salt that has not lost its savor."12 In
saying this, Adams apparently considers the voluntary principle
more a descriptive principle of social organization than a normative
principle for social organization. This point is emphasized by
Pitcher, who writes,

> No process as such or no kind of participation in intermediate organ-
> izations guarantees the good (order, stability, freedom, etc.). With-
> out a consideration of the ends sought and served, no process can be
> judged. Hence, no process is absolute. Every process or form has
> its day.13

     Yet, these considerations may not dispose of the matter.
Alan Gewirth, for example, finds something like the voluntary principle morally defensible. According to him, the "voluntary" and
the "purposive" are the two characteristics of human action

> that constitute the categorial rules of human action. Whenever an
> agent acts, he necessarily applies to himself these two categorial
> rules. Hence, by the principle of reciprocal consistency, he ought
> to apply these same two rules to his recipient insofar as the latter
> is a potential or prospective agent. We thereby obtain, by combining
> the general principles of reciprocal consistency with the categorial
> rules of action, what I shall call the *Principle of Categorial Con-
> sistency: Apply to your recipient the same categorial rules of
> action that you apply to yourself*. This principle . . . is, I sug-
> gest, the supreme principle of morality.14

If this argument be even close to true, we should not pass over
the "voluntary principle" too quickly. To be sure, Gewirth's formulation is abstract, but this seems more due to his pursuit of
principle than some deficiency in his statement. It is, after all,
the nature of principles to illumine a variety of situations. As
a result, they settle nothing in particular; only some serious examination of the context of their intended application could lead
to that. But they are, just for that reason, capable of being developed with increasing specificity for a given cultural situation
or, even, the needs of individual actors. Indeed, both Adams and

Pitcher might be best understood not as rejecting the voluntary principle but as calling for some further specification of it in terms of Gewirth's other, "purposive" characteristic of human action.
In order to deal with this problem, we began exploring the capacity of the concept of "democratic social change" to serve as a specification of our critical principle. In emphasizing non-violent and democratic means to a structural reorganization of society, democratic social change seemed roughly compatible with the voluntary principle it was to specify. There was the problem, however, that while the democratic left has been quite productive politically of voluntary associations, they have not received much intellectual attention within this tradition--except as represen-tatives of the "social forces" and classes in terms of which the democratic left tends to cast its analyses. Further, in approaching democratic social change as a specification of a more general prin-ciple, we were clearly taking it up on quite different grounds than its major exponents had proposed. They thought democratic social change was a principle in its own right.
Still, we thought this concept might be fruitful for a variety of reasons. In the first place, it corresponded to changes taking place in the civil rights movement itself as it, in the words of that most astute strategist, Bayard Rustin, turned "from protest to politics."[15] In the second place, as developed by Michael Harrington, it seemed a specification capable of application to the broad spectrum of issues in American political life.[16] In the third place, our use of the principle of democratic social change placed us in indirect continuity with the tradition of democratic socialism in America--a tradition which, as represented by W.E.B. DuBois, A. Philip Randolph, and Rustin himself, we had come to ad-mire through our study of civil rights. Finally, and this was cru-cial for our purposes, democratic social change could be operation-alized--and operationalized for voluntary associations. Indeed, that was the major focus of the principle. As used by Rustin and Harrington, it meant locating that majority of citizens who did (or, more often, might) affirm the need for fundamental (or, at least, significant) social change, and then working to create a coalition of the voluntary associations in which such citizens might be found. There was even rough agreement on which associations these would be: civil rights organizations, labor unions, churches, and uni-versities. Thus, through a combination of the associational and socialist traditions of social thought, we seemed at last to have an adequate interpretative context in which to cast the story of CCCO--as an organization (a voluntary association) in pursuit of a principle (democratic social change) through a strategy (creating a coalition among the groups of the democratic left).
But how was such democratic social change to be measured? As a principle, democratic social change seemed to turn very quickly into a strategy--the creation of a coalition; and in emphasizing this strategy, the danger is increased of "substitut(ing) the evi-dence of accomplishment of means for evidence of accomplishment of ends."[17] Why is it that this transition takes place, turning prin-ciple into strategy, ends into means, substance into context? And,

since this phenomenon is by no means peculiar to the democratic
left, how may it be avoided?

We contend that this transformation of principle takes
place not because the principle is a bad one but because it is un-
hinged from any actual situation in terms of which its meanings may
be clarified. Thus, democratic social change, like the voluntary
principle before it, requires some further specification. And since
the pre-eminent fact in any actual situation, practically considered,
is the issue at stake in it, we suggest that these principles must
finally be specified in terms of some issue. This can be seen in
the case of CCCO where, however relevant and important the notions
of voluntary association and democratic social change were to the
issues it pursued, it was not contention over *their* meaning which
characterized CCCO debates; it was, rather, the question of what
to do about the *schools*--their inequality and their *de facto* segregation.

Now, it has been held by some that such public issues are
created by "the maintenance and enhancement needs of large formal
organizations."[18] In this view, the agenda for our public life is
set by constituencies in search of issues that will serve their own
needs. This seems far from descriptive of the situation as we find
it in CCCO, however. Indeed, our research suggests that the converse is true--that *de facto* segregation in the Chicago public
schools has a long history; and that the issue has been pursued by
constituencies which changed in their personnel, in their organizational locus, and in their definition of the issue. In this
case, at least, we find an issue in search of a constituency.
Rather than seeing our public life, then, as a heap of issues to
be picked up or put down by various groups according to their interests, we have come to see the public realm as specified by some
enduring problems which stand in judgment upon various attempts to
turn them into organizational programs. Therefore, in our view,
issues are absolutely crucial in both inquiry and action, giving
specified meanings to principles and providing operational standards for action. Issues, as it were, establish the "cash values"
in practical situations. If we add this pragmatic emphasis to our
previous formulation, then the story of CCCO is that of a coalition
of voluntary associations in pursuit of effective forms of action
by which to embody the principle of democratic social change in relation to an issue. This brings us, finally, to what now appears
to be the most fundamental question: what was that issue in search
of a constituency which came to be located in CCCO?

During most of the story narrated here, the issue was
said to be segregation and, since our story is set in the North,
it was specifically *de facto* segregation which was said to be at
stake. This definition of the issue has not stood the test of time
very well, however. In the time since the events under inquiry
transpired, the public statement of the issue has undergone some
fairly radical changes which have complicated the task of arriving
at our own statement of the issue. It may help, therefore, to note
those transitions by way of indicating our sense of how the issue
might be more adequately defined--both for the understanding of

American society and for the understanding of the civil rights movement in it.

Since the Report of the National Advisory Commission on Civil Disorders, popularly known as the Kerner Report, appeared in 1968, "racism" has replaced "segregation" in our public rhetoric. Unfortunately, this shift in our language has not been accompanied by any major developments in our understanding. To be sure, the Commission concluded, in a famous afterthought, "our nation is moving toward two societies, one black, one white--separate and unequal."[19] But the evidence cited for this conclusion was largely the inequalities between the races which have been regularly documented by a flood of statistics flowing from the Government Printing Office; and the recommendations of the Commission were of the same sort-- having noticed that blacks get less of everything, the Commission suggested a variety of programs by which they might get more of everything. It was as though a person, on discovering bankruptcy, claimed the only problem was insufficient funds! This was not the operational understanding of the issue which was needed if the search for effective forms of action in relation to it was to have any prospect of success.

What was this "racism?" Where was it located? How did it operate? If, as the Commission suggested, "white society is deeply implicated in the ghetto," if "white institutions created it, white institutions maintain it, and white society condones it,"[20] just how does all that take place? And if, indeed, "Our nation is moving toward two societies, one black, one white,"[21] how would we recognize that movement *in concreto* and, most important, how might we reverse that process?

In the years immediately following the Kerner Report, a number of attempts were made to identify the things for which the Report had given us the name. They all suggest the importance of locating racism and the problematic character of that endeavor--for these studies concerned "institutional racism," "white racism," and "urban racism," and these specifications of the issue have now entered our popular vocabulary. Unfortunately, these studies also suggest the difficulties of achieving an operational understanding of the issue, for they conclude by calling for a small group approach to what by all accounts is a massive problem or conclude with the somewhat pious hope that black health might heal white sickness.[22]

For ourselves, as we pondered these questions in the context of our study of CCCO, it became increasingly apparent that the primary locus of racism was in that commonly inherited form of interaction which we call the social order. In saying this, we mean to affirm the recent discussions of "white racism," "institutional racism," and "urban racism," in that all are concerned to reach beyond identifying racism with the specific actions of identifiable groups in society operating with conscious intent. While earlier understandings may have worked well enough as long as we were dealing with slavery and Jim Crow, they seem quite inadequate in our present situation where the normal workings of our socially structured situations, institutions, and understandings appear quite capable of producing racist outcomes without the support of attitudinal bias or legal sanctions.

In this, we understand ourselves to be developing the insights of some CCCO delegates. To be sure, CCCO delegates were all familiar with the effects of racism in their private existence and, for some, it may have even been this widely shared personal experience which led them into association with each other. But, the delegates found, segregated and unequal education in the Chicago public schools was not simply an experience which large numbers of persons happened to have. It was, rather, part of a massive social pattern which was working itself out in and through a variety of institutions. And while the delegates never doubted that there were some bigots around or that this pattern of segregation and inequality raised some fundamental questions about our cultural understandings, they became increasingly clear that the societal pattern they confronted was quite able to proceed without benefit of legal sanction or attitudinal bias. Now there is more than a little hindsight involved in putting the issue this way.[23] In any case, we took the social as distinct from the existential, cultural, and religious modalities of our common humanity as the primary locus of racism, and, within the social, we took the social order itself, rather than specific actions, attitudes, or groups within it, as the major vehicle for racism in its contemporary form.

As we examined the relevant literature, we discovered that segregation, subordination, and violence were all said to be involved in the issue. There was no agreement, however, on the relationship among and relative importance of these phenomena. "Liberals" of various sorts usually emphasized segregation as the problem which, if overcome, would eliminate the subordination as well. "Radicals" of various sorts frequently focused on subordination-- be it economic or political--which, if overcome, would make segregation irrelevant. Both groups agreed that violence was related to whichever phenomenon they took as basic but disagreed as to whether that violence was unfortunate or merely necessary.

It is tempting, at this point, to enter into the discussion of what we have come to call the "metaphysics of racism"--those apparently endless discussions of what the *real* issue is: education or housing, politics or economics, segregation or subordination, etc., *ad infinitum et nauseam*.[24] There is, however, an urgent practical problem involved in these debates, i.e., how to understand racism in such a way as to guide action opposing it. But *that* is a practical problem which must be taken up in relationship to some actual occasions--and is only obscured by being discussed in generalities.

Once again our empirical materials suggested the way to proceed. In the discussions by CCCO delegates, there is almost universal agreement that all these dimensions are, in fact, part of the issue, and all must be dealt with, sooner or later. When, from time to time, a discussion was initiated of "metaphysical" priorities among various aspects of the issue, this had to be argued through to some analysis of current political realities, tactical opportunities and organizational capacities--and choices were made in those terms. Thus, the practical wisdom of this association led us to seek a definition of racism which made the various dimensions of it internally related and cumulative--though in just what way they were so was to remain a function of the empirical situation and was not to be settled by the definition.

The resolution of this problem came as we considered what segregation, subordination, and violence might be internal to, and what they might be cumulative of. We came to see that racism, in all these respects, constituted a major fact in our common humanity --where "common humanity" is simply that part of ourselves and that portion of our history that all human beings have in common in any given civilization.[25] In fact, racism was a particularly patholog- ical fact of our common humanity since it constituted a massive denial of our common humanity.[26] Thus, we suggest, segregation, subordination, and violence are in, and are a cumulative denial of, our common humanity.[27]

Segregation, however, has always meant more than it seemed to say. A variety of phenomena had been related and given an appar- ent unity by their common implication in the Jim Crow form of racism. If we now separate these aspects of racism, and distinguish within segregation the elements of separation, discrimination, and abase- ment, then the final formulation of racism involves six dimensions:

1. Continued or increasing separation of the "races" geograph- ically, socially, and institutionally.

2. Continued or increasing subordination of black people, American Indians, Puerto Ricans, Mexican-Americans, and pos- sibly others as well, in terms of their access to basic life needs, to high quality public institutions and to structures for political freedom and power.

3. Continued or increasing denial to these groups of ordinary status within the social order.

4. Continued or increasing abasement of non-white life by the dominant white society.

5. Continued or increasing legitimacy for and recourse to violence toward non-white populations in general, blacks in particular.

6. Continued or increasing capacity to rationalize any of the above.[28]

At the risk of some repetition, several observations must be made about this formulation if it is to be properly understood. First, these six dimensions are cumulative in the sense that, where any one of them is actual, all the others are probable. Thus, when any aspect of racism occurs, what needs explaining is not the pres- ence of violence but its absence. Second, and this is the basis of the first comment, these six dimensions are all dimensions of the same thing. Each involves a denial of our common humanity--a denial that increases as one dimension is compounded with another. But if our common humanity is not, finally, a quantitative notion subject to utilitarian calculations but is, instead, a qualitative

reality--the full sense of which may be subverted in a single vio-
lation--then the denial of our common humanity becomes progressively
easier as its forms become progressively virulent. It is this internal dynamic of racism which makes violence an inherent, if not
necessary, outcome of it. Third, discovering precisely how these
six dimensions are related will always involve some reference to
an empirical situation. We can think of occasions, for example,
when separation has led to violence; but, conversely, we can think
of occasions when violence has led to separation. The only generalization about racism in the American social order implied in
our formulation is that, in the absence of massive efforts and overwhelming evidence to the contrary, it is continuing or increasing.
But this is an empirical generalization.
        It is just at this point that so many analyses lose their
empirical bearings; for, seeing the dynamics of racism at work in
our midst, the mind turns almost naturally to search for the oper-
ator which stands behind these operations. They have, in fact,
been variously attributed to the white psyche, to Western imperialism, to monopoly capital, etc. The result is to confuse racism
with some other processes with which, to be sure, it is frequently
associated. In our opinion, however, these associations are best
left to be explored by further inquiry rather than being settled
by definition. Thus, we consider it both possible and desirable
to define racism in its own right, as precisely these six dynamic
dimensions and nothing else--whatever other issues may, occasionally
or frequently, be associated with it.
        It should be noted in this connection that we do not con-
sider racism as some sort of "issue of issues," such that if we
dealt with it we would have achieved some final solution to the
problems of the social order. Apart from the tragic history of the
clutch after final solutions, we readily acknowledge that there are
many problems of our social order other than racism, some of which
(sexism, for example) are equally as radical and absurd in that they
also constitute a denial of common humanity on an arbitrary basis.
Our main point is not that racism is an issue of issues but that
it is *an issue*, deadly in its effects and ultimately serious in its
claims, and worthy of thought and action in its own right--without
eliminating other issues, or reducing them to functions of it, or
conversely.
        The problem remains, however, of stating the unity of the
six dimensions of racism and adding to their specificity without,
as it were, changing the subject. If we ask ourselves what might
it be which has this strange capacity to separate us, to subordinate
some, to give some of us extraordinary status, to abase our common
humanity, to render us subject to the continual threat and frequent
fact of violence, and to make all of this appear reasonable, then
the answer lies as close as any American metropolitan area or map
thereof--for the striking characteristic of all our urban life is
the color line drawn through it.
        The appeal to a map here, however, may be misleading for
it is not just metropolitan demography we have in mind--as our six
dimensions make clear. Indeed, even calling this fundamental reality the "color line" may lead to misunderstanding. While the term,

the color line, has a longer history, it apparently came into popular use with W.E.B. DuBois' brilliant analysis and rhetoric at the
turn of the century.[29] It has continued to find favor with such
reporters as Roy Stannard Baker[30] and social scientists such as
Drake and Cayton. Three of the chapters of their *Black Metropolis*
are titled in relation to this term ("Along the Color Line," "Crossing the Color Line," and "The Shifting Line of Color"), and the two
volumes of their study are distinguished by whether they are looking
at the color line as it was created, maintained, and developed in
Chicago (in their terms, "Black Metropolis" in relation to "Midwest Metropolis") or whether they are examining patterns of life
within the confines of the color line ("Black Metropolis" as
"Bronzeville"). In the first case, we see the dynamics of the
color line between the races; in the second,the life it makes possible for one. Thus, for Drake and Cayton, the concept of the color
line functions primarily to establish the external and internal
dimensions of "Black Sociology."
        Our own use of the term "color line" differs from these
in several respects. First, while we acknowledge the effects of
the color line upon our common humanity, we also find it an ultimate
denial of that common humanity and, therefore, except for its effects and its practical significance, we give it no ultimate standing as anything except a socially institutionalized lie. Second,
and as a consequence of the first, because we take the consequences
of the color line seriously without accepting the lie about our
common humanity which it is, we are in a position to treat actors,
institutions, and social processes in relation to that lie without
presupposing it as organizing their relations to it, i.e., "black"
and "white" persons, institutions, and social processes may alike
be found perpetuating the color line, exploiting the color line,
consenting to it, or opposing it. Which, is an empirical matter
because it cannot be settled by reference to which side of the line
they are on but only by their relationship to it. Finally, at least
as compared with most observers of the color line, we find it not
a social atavism to be overcome, "some day," but an active and
dynamic social force at the center of our social order, such that
not opposing the color line not only means accepting it but allowing
it to continue its process of expansion and consolidation. In this
sense, at least, "if you are not part of the solution, you are part
of the problem."
        In any case, it is for these reasons of denial of common
humanity on the basis of color that we have chosen the terms "color
line" and "racism" rather than, say, the "Negro problem" or "race
relations." The former limits the "problem" to a social minority
while we are more inclined to view the problem as more like a
rapidly metastasizing cancer of the body politic; and the latter
not only subordinates the substance of the issue to the relations
we might have in spite of that substance but appears, at least, to
take the color line that separates us more seriously than it does
our life together in our common humanity.
        Still, there is massive evidence that this line allocates
differing quantities and qualities of life according to which side
of it we are on. That is its main claim to fame. In any case, if,

as we suggested, each of the dimensions of racism can be understood as denials of our common humanity, what more basic denial might lie at the heart of them all than the denial of humanity on the basis of color? From our perspective, the issue of the color line is that specific--and that ultimate. On these grounds, then, of empirical adequacy and interpretative fruitfulness we find the color line crucial for our inquiry. Thus, racism is the dynamics of the color line, and the color line is the theme of the history of the civil rights movement.

With this statement, we have reached a turning point in the argument.[31] Until now, we have been unable to proceed constructively because the principle of inquiry was not yet in place. From our present standpoint, however--from which we see the color line as a problem in, and denial of, our common humanity--some of our earlier problems are resolved. We now have grounds to specify at least one meaning of democratic social change--breaking the color line--and to evaluate the various strategies proposed for democratic social change by their effectiveness in doing so. We may now examine critically the public contributions of the various voluntary associations to which the voluntary principle directs us --by their relationship to the color line, both in their own organization and in American society generally. We may now tell the story of CCCO--with its theme as the color line, and with its plot as the dialogue in search of effective forms of action by which to oppose the color line. We can now see what the conflict and consensus in CCCO was about--what was, from time to time, to constitute such effective forms. And we can even now see why civil rights goals were so exceptionally difficult to interpret and understand publicly--for nothing is a greater threat to rational discourse and humane commitment than this denial of common humanity on the basis of color. All this is now possible because the color line is now in focus as the central issue. Indeed, the history of our study, which we have just recapitulated, now appears in retrospect to have been an extended search for just this issue, and for operational forms of understanding in relationship to it. Thus, our thesis, empirically stated, concerns what kind of problem was at stake in the civil rights activity--namely, the color line in the social order.

Since our search for operational forms of understanding in relationship to the color line is remarkably parallel to what we interpret as CCCO's own search for effective forms of action concerning the same issue, the question arises about the relationship of this inquiry to that action. For example, we have already said that although CCCO usually understood the issue as segregation and inequality, we have, in subsequent reflection on the history of CCCO, come to accept racism as a more adequate statement of the problem. Some have even used this later statement of the issue to impugn the accomplishments of the civil rights movement generally. In our definition of racism, however, we have sought to build on those meanings which were present in the civil rights movement--and not to deny them. Though we now call it "racism," that separation and subordination which was called "segregation" in the sixties was very real; it was very wrong; and it was opposed by the civil rights

movement. It is, in fact, still very real; it is still very wrong;
and it is still a practical problem. In any case, it was only the
efforts and final failure of the civil rights movement which revealed the limitations of their definition of the issue; and those
who have the wisdom of hindsight should also have the grace to affirm their dependence on the experiences by which it was purchased
at so great a price. Retrospective privilege is historical depen-
dence--not moral superiority.

     The fact remains, however, that the civil rights movement
died in the process of making its discoveries. It might be thought,
therefore, that any inquiry--especially a practical inquiry--which
affirmed its basis in the dead past was perverse or, at least, archaic. If anything, however, the end of the movement quickened our
efforts to tell the story of CCCO, and to do so from a practical
point of view. As the high hopes of the movement passed into what,
at best, were modest outcomes; as, in recent years, even those
limited accomplishments became increasingly tenuous; and as the
whole episode became sicklied o'er with the pale cast of futility,
we became increasingly concerned to give some enduring form to the
questions raised and the interpretations suggested by the civil
rights movement--in the hope that the passing of that movement
would not mean the loss of the understandings it made possible, as,
indeed, it did not mean the end of the issue which made those understandings necessary. The movement is dead; the issue remains. And
in pursuing intellectually that issue which the movement pursued
politically, we find ourselves at one with them.

     This is because practical relationships, as understood
here, are primarily relationships in terms of the issue addressed.
Such other relationships as are involved in practical situations--
for example, affinity in action and compatibility in perspective--
are, in this view, indeterminable except as functions of some continuity in the issue. This point may be emphasized by restating
our thesis in a slightly different context. Empirically, we have
said that the issue is the color line in the social order. Method-
ologically, our thesis is that the issue has priority as the ordering principle in social inquiries. In this case, that issue is the
color line.

     Much of the ground for this thesis was laid earlier. We
have asserted that the case of CCCO is best understood as an issue
in search of a constituency. We have suggested that such issues
establish the "cash values" in terms of which the meaning of principles may be specified and the standards of action developed. We
have already found that, in the absence of these cash values, social
inquiries tend to slide from the issue into organizational strategies,
associational capacities, decision-making processes, societal functions, pious hopes, etc. And we have continually found it fruitful
to take up "scholars" and "activists" together. The reason for
this now becomes clear: under the criterion of the issue, standing
in judgment upon the meaning and effectiveness of both understanding
and action, "scholars" and "activists" appear as equals--as those
citizens who, for better or for worse, are finally responsible for
the issue.

These comments bear upon the question of the relationship between social science and social action or, more generally put, between theory and practice--in which form the problem is coterminous with the entire Western intellectual tradition where it has perennially troubled scientists and activists alike.[32] Without pretending, therefore, to do justice to this very complicated and fundamental matter, it may still be helpful if we state our position concerning it.

In many current discussions, what appears to disturb social scientists is the way in which the values that inform action become involved in inquiry. One recent text in the field of race relations, for example, tells us that,

> Ironically, one of the major barriers to a better comprehension of these phenomena is the indignation of the investigators. Social scientists are human beings, and their emotional reactions to the injustices they see make difficult the cultivation of a detached stand-point. Men who are angry often look for a responsible agent to blame, and this search for culprits often vitiates research. There was a time when other obnoxious phenomena were explained in terms of malevolence; earthquakes and diseases have been attributed to the machinations of personal enemies. Other scientists seem to have overcome the animistic approach, but still it persists in the social sciences. When difficulties are perceived in moral terms, there is a tendency to explain events by imputing vicious motives to those who are held responsible. Furthermore, moral indignation often blinds the student to many facts that would otherwise be obvious. All too often deeds regarded as reprehensible are assumed to be fundamentally different from those that are approved, and the moral dichotomy often prevents one from recognizing that both may be manifestations of the same social process. John Dewey once wrote that the greatest single obstacle to the development of the social sciences was the tendency to approach human problems in terms of moral blame and approbation, and in no field is this more true than in the study of inter-ethnic contacts.[33]

Thus we see that for these authors the tendency toward moral evaluation inherent in action is subversive of social science and not apparently capable of being disciplined itself.

Conversely, however, those engaged in action have equally good reason to be disturbed about the way in which the values and practitioners of science enter the realm of practice. In the case of the history of the civil rights movement in Chicago, two world-renowned social scientists from The University of Chicago each headed panels of distinguished scholars that prepared official reports concerning segregation and inequality in the Chicago public schools. The creation and composition of these panels, however, was the subject of extended political controversy; both panel chairmen came, in time, to call for the resignation of the then General Superintendent of Schools, Benjamin C. Willis (this was almost two years after CCCO had first called for Willis's dismissal); and both men ended politically discredited--in one instance, unable even to get appointed to the school board. In any case, these reports--prepared by large staffs at great cost under the supervision of

distinguished scholars--add much less than might be thought to the
studies conducted by a handful of CCCO volunteers or to those produced by the quite modest research department of the Chicago Urban
League. Given this history of politics in scholarship and scholars
in politics, the distinction between social science and social action seems analytical at best--if it should be drawn at all.

We doubt that it should, at least in the usual manner in
which it too frequently involves some invidious difference in kind
or status in the human community--as, for example, between "experts"
and "amateurs," the "objective" and the "biased," or the "wise" and
the "foolish." To be sure, differences of all these sorts exist,
but they are not necessarily institutionalized roles.

We have come to doubt the usual distinctions because we
have seen that scholars of a variety of sorts are ready, if not
eager, to draw lessons from the civil rights movement or, even, to
become its pedagogues--leading it, by word or deed, safely through
difficult straits. Talcott Parsons, for example, takes it upon
himself to suggest that "the Negro community has the opportunity
to define itself as the spearhead of one of the most important im-
provements in the quality of American society in its history--and
to do so not only in pursuit of its own obvious self-interest, but
in fulfillment of a *moral* imperative."[34] Pierre van den Berghe observes that "many well-meaning American 'liberals' mistakenly regard racism as the underlying cause of most evils in their society,
instead of viewing it as but a fairly superficial symptom of much
more widespread and basic problems."[35] How is it that both are
willing to make judgments about the real meaning and the actual or
possible effectiveness of that movement without undertaking a
serious study of it? Why not admit that when it comes to the civil
rights movement these men are not experts but lay persons?

Actually, of course, such evaluations and recommendations
are quite frequently made by scientists and scholars. The important
question becomes, therefore, not whether such conclusions are appropriate in the science but whether they are responsible to the action.
What is involved in making some reasoned judgment about a phenomenon
like, say, the civil rights movement? What is required of those
who would praise or blame its past and enter into deliberation about
its future? Most self-interpretations of the civil rights movement
--and many observers as well--agree that it was, in some sense, a
struggle for justice, perhaps heroic, perhaps pathetic, misguided
or revelatory--but a struggle for justice it was, and most evaluations concern its effectiveness in achieving some justice. But
knowing whether it did or not would require giving some adequate
and operational meaning to the concept of justice--what it is and
how we might go about getting it in some actual situations.[36] And
this task, difficult to be sure, does not seem different in principle from the struggle of the civil rights movement with the same
questions. This does seem to require the explicit introduction of
moral and practical considerations into social science, with all
the attendant dangers of which Shibutani and Kwan are wary. But
at least we will have gained this much: that we can search for
some common principle under which to bring both social science and
social action. Here, both are seen in terms of their contribution

to the struggle for justice in relation to the color line. And in seeing them together in this way, we have fulfilled the ancient maxim, "The rule of many is not good; one ruler let there be."[37]
      Thus, the methodological statement of our thesis--the priority of the issue as an ordering principle in social inquiries --has important implications in coming to grips with the contention we find inherent in our subject matter. In our study, contention about civil rights is ordered in terms of the issue which we find empirically to have been at stake in the civil rights movement, i.e., the color line. In this context, various scholarly interpretations of that movement, including our own, appear among the contenders struggling for effective forms of understanding and action in re- lationship to that issue. Rather than considering other perspec- tives from the standpoint of our own, then, or distinguishing per- spectives by the variety of meanings they attach to common terms, all points of view--again including our own--are examined here pri- marily in terms of the action they make possible concerning a com- mon problem.
      Thus, it is a primary contention of this essay that the search for method in Social Ethics is finally a problem in what Richard McKeon calls the "non-systematic relations of ideas," "the relation among ideas apart from their organization in the systems of philosophy, and therefore the relations among ideas brought into relation in the contacts of heterogeneous systems."[38] It is for this reason that we call our method pragmatic *pluralism*, because other positions are viewed, not from our own position, but in terms of the issue to which they are addressed--in this case, the color line.
      This is pluralism, but it is also pragmatism; the diver- sity is ordered in terms of the issue. Thus such pluralism is com- pletely at odds with any sort of permissiveness in morals, laissez- faire doctrines in politics, or anarchism in philosophy. We find pluralism to be a fact, and an ineluctable one at that. Therefore, we take account of it--but we do so from the standpoint of the color line. From that standpoint, we find that human beings have various roles in relationship to the color line which they exercise in various ways--and, hence, the pluralism. But from this same stand- point, these various roles must be understood as divided among those who are victimized by the color line, those who consent to the color line, those who exploit the color line, those who oppose the color line, etc. And since we have already suggested that this color line is a massive denial of our common humanity, those roles must be interpreted as occupied by those who are victimized by, consent to, exploit, or oppose this denial. Again, this is a direct implication of the methodological statement of our thesis; the priority of the issue as an ordering principle in social inquiries means that the characters of our study are cast in terms of the color line. And if heroes there be in this story, they will appear among the opponents of the color line.
      This emphasis on pragmatic pluralism serves to distinguish our search for method from that of our colleagues in two respects.
      In the first place, the search for method in Social Ethics is usually cast in terms of the contention among proponents of

Tillich and Niebuhr, Aristotle and Whitehead, Arendt and Heidigger, etc. This use of some fundamental system of thought in Social Ethics is, of course, an enormous advance over reliance upon special revelation, a specific historic tradition, the given values of a particular culture, or any such arbitrary grounds which can only give rise to ad hoc methodological procedures. But no position, however systematic, is sufficient to resolve the search for method. Any given position is, at best, a systematic statement of the relations among some ideas. In attempting to describe and interpret social ethical phenomena, however, any position encounters other actors and other interpreters--frequently enough, each with his or her own such systematic statement. And such a buzzing, booming pluralistic world is simply too rich and too diverse to yield to a single point of view.

The proponents of such a single point of view are left with a series of equally unsatisfactory methodological alternatives: to interpret the world as a series of illustrations of their own favored doctrines, to convince their opponents of the truth of the chosen position, or to understand other points of view as converging toward their own. Politically, these alternatives are known as ideology, conversion, and imperialism, respectively--and bad politics is not improved by calling it method. For these reasons, we have said that the search for method is finally a problem in the "non-systematic relations of ideas."

The second distinguishing mark of our search for method is that it is *pragmatic* pluralism. The meaning of this is best seen in McKeon's distinction among three problems in the non-systematic relations of ideas--the "political" or pragmatic, the "semantic," and the "philosophical."

> The problem of political debate and opposition is a problem of relating divergent ideas to possible courses of common action, whereas the semantic problem is a problem of understanding divergent meanings attached to common terms as their definitions are determined by divergent principles, and the philosophical problem is a problem of reconciling divergent ideas and their implications to the requirements of one set of principles and a single method.[39]

In these terms, Pitcher might be understood to have undertaken semantic analyses of different approaches to both foreign policy and American political process, while W. Widick Schroeder and Gibson Winter used semantic devices to open arguments concerned with the philosophical problem.[40]

While it is clear, therefore, that the search for method in Social Ethics has mostly addressed philosophical and semantic problems, it is not clear that a focus on the non-systematic relations of ideas has been maintained. Even among Pitcher, Schroeder, and Winter, who are likewise indebted to McKeon, it is not always easy to tell whether they are addressing a systematic or a non-systematic problem. McKeon has discussed this issue in relation to Winter.[41]

Be that as it may, this essay has attempted to argue that Social Ethics might best address the non-systematic political problem, "relating divergent ideas to possible common courses of action," and do so by means of what McKeon calls "problematic history."

> Problematic history, or history conceived according to the method of inquiry, is based on an evolution in the recognition and statement of problems, in the solutions found for them, and in the human activities made possible by the successive solutions of problems.42

It is for this reason that this essay has recounted the evolution in our recognition and statement of problems in our study of the civil rights movement, coming finally to focus on the problem or issue of the color line.

It is for this reason that we have conceived our history of the civil rights movement as one in which citizens, having undertaken action in relation to the issue of the color line, find new understandings open to them, and, having appropriated new understandings of the color line, find new forms of action available to them.

And it is for this reason that this essay ends as it began, with Professor Pitcher--who has done so much to recognize and state the problems of Social Ethics, to find solutions for them, and, as a result, to make Social Ethics possible as a human activity.

NOTES AND REFERENCES

1. For a detailed narrative of the history of CCCO, see Alan B. Anderson and George W. Pickering, "The Issue of the Color Line: A View from Chicago," which appears as a joint appendix to our separate dissertations: Alan B. Anderson, "The Issue of the Color Line: Some Methodological Considerations," and George W. Pickering, "The Issue of the Color Line: Some Interpretative Considerations" (both Ph.D. dissertations, University of Chicago, 1975). The present essay is based upon pp. 17-50 of my dissertation which, under the title "Methodological Considerations in the Study of Religious Movements," was presented at the 1973 Annual Meeting of the Society for the Scientific Study of Religion in San Francisco.

2. As examples of this kind of research, see Gary T. Marx, *Protest and Prejudice: A Study of Belief in the Black Community* (New York: Harper & Row, Publishers, 1967) and Jeffrey K. Hadden, *The Gathering Storm in the Churches*, Anchor Books (Garden City, New York: Doubleday & Company, 1970).

3. For examples of this kind of research, see John H. Bracey, Jr., August Meier, and Elliott Rudwick, eds., *Conflict and Competition: Studies in the Recent Black Protest Movement*, Explorations in the Black Experience (Belmont, Calif.: Wadsworth Publishing Co., 1971); and Gary T. Marx, ed., *Racial Conflict: Tension and Change in American Society* (Boston: Little, Brown & Co., 1971).

4. D.B. Robertson, ed., *Voluntary Associations: A Study of Groups in Free Societies*, Essays in Honor of James Luther Adams (Richmond, Va.: John Knox Press, 1966).

5. Edward C. Banfield and James Q. Wilson, *City Politics* (Cambridge: Harvard University Press and M.I.T. Press, 1963), p. 251. Banfield and Wilson's brief discussion of voluntary associations (pp. 250-256) is largely devoted to

their ineffectiveness and to the way in which their professional staffs subvert the purposes of their boards.

6. As an example of our initial appropriation of this tradition, see (Stanley J. Hallett and Alan B. Anderson) "Rationale," *The Commons: An Institute of the Independent Sector*, A Report of the Organizing Committee (Chicago: Planning and Strategy Committee of the Division of Christian Life and Mission of the National Council of Churches of Christ, U.S.A.; and Joint Strategy and Action Committee of the American Baptist Convention, the Episcopal Church, the United Church of Christ, the United Methodist Church, and the United Presbyterian Church, U.S.A., (*sic*) 1968), pp. 9-15.

7. James Luther Adams, "The Voluntary Principle in the Forming of American Religion," *Religion of the Republic*, ed. Elwyn Smith (Philadelphia: Fortress Press, 1971), p. 225.

8. James D. Hunt, "Voluntary Associations as a Key to History," in D.B. Robertson, *Voluntary Associations*, pp. 370-71.

9. Grant McConnell, *Private Power and American Democracy* (New York: Alfred A. Knopf, 1966), p. 6. For a similar argument, see Theodore J. Lowi, *The End of Liberalism: Ideology, Policy, and the Crisis of Public Authority* (New York: W.W. Norton & Co., 1969).

10. See for example, Richard C. Cornuelle, *Reclaiming the American Dream* (New York: Random House, 1965, and Toronto: Random House of Canada Limited, 1965), and Richard M. Nixon, "The Voluntary Way," ABC Radio, October 6, 1968. For a critique of this conservative view, see George W. Pickering, "Voluntarism and the 'American Way'," *Journal of Current Social Issues* 9 (Summer, 1970), pp. 4-9.

11. The first systematic treatise on voluntary associations by an American, William Ellery Channing's "Remarks on Association," published in 1830, was devoted to just this question. Channing's answer was, "The value of associations is to be measured by the energy, the freedom, the moral power, which they encourage and diffuse." William Ellery Channing, *The Works of William E. Channing*, 8th ed., 6 vols. (Boston: James Munroe & Co., 1848), 1:302, quoted in James L. Adams, "The Voluntary Principle," p. 236.

12. *Op. cit.*, Adams, pp. 245 and 246. Emphasis mine.

13. W. Alvin Pitcher, "'The Politics of Mass Society': Significance for the Churches," in D.B. Robertson, *Voluntary Associations*, p. 259.

14. Alan Gewirth, "Categorial Consistency in Ethics," *Philosophical Quarterly*, 17 (October, 1967): 292. Incidentally, Gewirth illustrates his argument in terms of racism.

15. Bayard Rustin, "From Protest to Politics: The Future of the Civil Rights Movement," *Commentary*, 39 (February, 1965): 25-31.

16. Michael Harrington, *Toward a Democratic Left: A Radical Program for a New Majority* (Baltimore: Penguin Books, 1969).

17. *Op. cit.*, Banfield and Wilson, p. 251.

18. Edward C. Banfield, *Political Influence* (Glencoe, Illinois: Free Press, 1961), p. 308.

19. National Advisory Commission on Civil Disorders, *Report* (New York: Bantam Books, 1968), p. 1.

20. *Ibid.*, p. 2.

21. *Ibid.*, p. 1.

22. See for example, Louis L. Knowles and Kenneth Prewitt, eds., *Institutional Racism in America*, Spectrum Books (Englewood Cliffs, N.J.: Prentice-Hall, 1969); Robert W. Terry, *For Whites Only* (Grand Rapids, Mich.: William B. Eerdmans Publishing Co., 1970); and Harold M. Baron, "The Web of Urban Racism,"

in Knowles and Prewitt, *Institutional Racism*, pp. 134-76. For their recommendations for action, see Knowles and Prewitt, pp. 126-33; Terry, pp. 93-97; and Baron, pp. 173-76.

23. In particular, it is likely that the combination of court decisions attacking deliberate segregation in Northern public schools, on the one hand, and the increasing conviction that school segregation in Chicago was created, maintained, and extended by the conscious intent of public officials, on the other, prevented the delegates from exploring the full implications of their own insights.

24. A brief, but excellent treatment of this subject is Ralph J. Bunche, "The Programs of Organizations Devoted to the Improvement of the Status of the American Negro," *Journal of Negro Education* 8 (July 1939): 539-50.

25. This definition is a paraphrase of that given for the related phenomenon of "common sense" by Hannah Arendt, "Understanding and Politics," *Partisan Review* 20 (July-August 1953): 386. It is important to note, however, that we do not mean "common" in the sense of universal distribution of identical characteristics, as in John Dewey's "common faith," but rather "common" in the sense of "belonging or pertaining to the community at large; public." *Webster's New International Dictionary* (Springfield, Mass.: G.C. Merriam Company, 1945).

26. The contradiction between being a *fact in* our common humanity and being a *denial of* our common humanity is only apparent. Both denials of and affirmations of our common humanity presuppose the common humanity out of which they emerge and into which they enter--for better or for worse. See Alfred North Whitehead, *Adventures of Ideas* (New York: Macmillan Company, 1933) especially the discussion of appearance and reality in Part 4, "Civilization."

27. Thus, "common humanity" plays a crucial role in our argument, for it provides the grounds for seeing as one thing, "racism," what most observers have taken to be several--separation, subordination, denial of ordinary status, abasement, violence, and rationalization.

28. Pickering, "Color Line: Interpretative Considerations," p. 3. We consider these six dimensions empirically adequate in the double sense of adequate to the dimensions of the issue in the story of the civil rights movement, and adequate to the interpretations of racism in the scholarly literature which we have examined. For example, in *Black Metropolis* (New York: Harcourt, Brace & Co., 1945), St. Clair Drake and Horace R. Cayton take up the major parameters of racism under three headings: the "Black Ghetto," the "Job Ceiling," and the "specter of social equality." Each of these, according to their account, involves (in varying proportions) elements of separation, subordination, denial of ordinary status, and abasement. And Drake and Cayton are quite aware of the history of violence along the color line, and of what they call the "moral problem"--the tendency of American culture to avoid the issues by rationalizing the racism. In relation to such ground-breaking scholarship as that of Drake and Cayton, we understand ourselves merely to have given equal attention to some sometimes neglected dimensions of the issue, and to have generalized and operationalized the processes involved (the six dimensions) in such a manner that they are no longer so closely identified with the institutional mechanisms (employment, housing, sexual relations, education, etc.) through which the processes work.

29. W.E.B. DuBois, *Souls of Black Folk* (Chicago: A.C. McClurg & Co., 1903).

30. Roy Stannard Baker, *Following the Color Line* (Garden City, N.Y.: Doubleday, Page & Co., 1908).

31. Aristotle, *Nichomachean Ethics* 1.4. 1095a 29-35.

32. For a historical treatment, see Nicholas Lobkowicz, *Theory and Practice: History of a Concept from Aristotle to Marx*, International Studies of the Committee on International Relations of the University of Notre Dame (Notre Dame, Ind.: University of Notre Dame Press, 1967); for a systematic treatment, see Richard McKeon, "Philosophy and Action," *Ethics* 62 (January 1952): 79-100; for a treatment in relationship to race, see Gunnar Myrdal, *An American Dilemma: The Negro Problem and Modern Democracy* (New York: Harper & Bros., 1944), "Appendix 2. A Methodological Note on Facts and Valuations in Social Science," pp. 1035-1064. See also (Alan B. Anderson), "Basic Studies," *The Commons*, pp. 29-33.

33. Tamotsu Shibutani and Kian W. Kwan, *Ethnic Stratification* (New York: Macmillan Co., 1965), pp. 14-15. Quoted in Peter I. Rose, *The Subject is Race: Traditional Ideologies and the Teaching of Race Relations* (New York: Oxford University Press, 1968), p. 79.

34. Talcott Parsons, "Full Citizenship for the Negro American? A Sociological Problem," *Daedalus* 94 (Fall 1965): 1048.

35. Pierre L. van den Berghe, *Race and Racism: A Comparative Perspective* (New York: John Wiley & Sons, 1967), p. 93.

36. See Pickering, "Color Line: Interpretative Considerations," Chapter 4, "The Problem of Democratic Social Change," pp. 136-98.

37. Aristotle, *Metaphysics* 12.10. 1076a5. *cf.* Homer, *Iliad* 2.204.

38. Richard McKeon, *Freedom and History: The Semantics of Philosophical Controversies and Ideological Conflicts* (New York: Noonday Press, 1952), p. 23.

39. *Ibid.*, p. 24.

40. W. Alvin Pitcher, "Radically Different Approaches to Foreign Policy," *Chicago Theological Seminary Register* 50 (April 1960): 22-26, and "Theology and Political Science," 1971 (Mimeographed); W. Widick Schroeder, *Cognitive Structures and Religious Research* (East Lansing: Michigan State University Press, 1970); Gibson Winter, *Elements for a Social Ethic* (New York: Macmillan, 1966).

41. See his review of *Elements for a Social Ethic, Journal of Religion* 49 (January 1969): 77-84.

42. *Op. cit.*, McKeon, *Freedom and History*, p. 32.

SEARCHING FOR THE SWITCHMAN

by
Robert Benne

In the long and on-going debate touched off by Max Weber's *The Protestant Ethic and the Spirit of Capitalism*,[1] some exceedingly provocative ideas have emerged concerning the relation of religious ideas and values to historical change. Classical Marxists argued vigorously against Weber's thesis because it gave too much influence to the role of religion and morality in shaping history. In addition, many non-Marxists such as H.M. Robertson and Kurt Samuelsson, have argued that capitalism arose from the material conditions of civilization rather than from religious impulses. Indeed, for this whole group of theorists, religious notions are more a reflection of economic change than a shaper of it.[2]

Weber, however, has not been left without defenders. R. Stephen Warner and Niles M. Hansen, among others, have shown that Weber's interpretation of the role of ideas in affecting the flow of history are much more sophisticated and subtle than the critics allege.[3] It is their view that Weber's notion of ideas as "switchmen" is crucial in understanding the perspective he proposed. In this essay we shall examine in some detail the concept of "switchman," outline the shape of the switchman that has been formative for important segments of Western society, and speculate about the search for an emerging switchman as those segments struggle for renewed public meaning.

The Concept of Switchman

Contrary to the more simple-minded criticisms brought against him, Weber did not believe that ideas *caused* historical change. He in fact rejected any one factor as the ultimate historical cause. Rather, he believed that "material and ideal interests" were the motor of human action. Ideas do not directly shape individual or corporate pursuits. The "material and ideal interests" that motivate humans consist of "the need for material security, status acceptance and social honor, power over others, assurance of his salvation (certitudo salutis), and a sense of order in the cosmos."[4] This mixture of material and spiritual needs is expressed through and interacts with the economic and social changes that happen mysteriously in history. Thus, according to Weber, material conditions for the development of capitalism ripened with the discovery of new and rich lands in the sixteenth and seventeenth centuries, technological innovation, accumulation of capital by the

129

wealthy, and the breaking down of traditional society.[5] The con-
catenation of these events and surging human interests produced new
experiments that were the forerunners of capitalist organization
and division of labor. Weber tells a charming story about how such
organization could have emerged in the weaving industry.[6]

But new experiments arising from shifting material conditions must be legitimated. Even more, they must be enveloped
with and guided by value orientations that give them meaning. While
the underlying material and ideal interests move forward ceaselessly
within these mysterious new events, the whole emergent has little
world-historical impact if it is not refracted through meaningful
world-images. These ideas of the world *define* what security *is*,
what honor *is*; define the nature of salvation, and a moral order
for personal life. Although material and ideal interests provide
the engine of historical movement, they do not provide the tracks
of meaning upon which the movement must ride.

Compelling religious or quasi-religious ideas and values,
then, play the role of switchmen in history. They stand at a junc-
tion in which perennial human interests are expressed within new
material conditions and switch those interests onto a specific set
of tracks. Let Weber himself articulate this intriguing notion.

> Not ideas, but material and ideal interest, directly govern men's
> conduct. Yet very frequently the 'world-images' that have been
> created by 'ideas' have, like switchmen, determined the tracks along
> which action has been pushed by the dynamic of interest. 'From what'
> and 'for what' one wished to be redeemed and, let us not forget,
> 'could be' redeemed, depended upon one's image of the world.[7]

Specifically, Weber argues that the ethos of left-wing
Calvinism became the condition for the development of capitalism
as a world-historical force. The Protestant ethos became a switchman that set incipient but chaotic energies onto an orderly path of
meaning. Put another way, Protestantism had an "elective affinity"
with newly rising middle classes. The ideas and values of Protestantism were created and chosen by the middle classes (elective)
even as those ideas and values fit in with their material interests
(affinity).[8]

In each critical stage in world history, switchmen come
into play. The old order of public meaning gives way before the on-
slaughts of dynamic new factors that cannot be dealt with by the old
order. Such critical moments can be identified in the seventh century B.C., the centuries surrounding the birth of the Christian
movement, and the sixteenth and seventeenth centuries. In each case
a new switchman gave burgeoning interests and movements enough
focused coherence so that they were able to penetrate and shape
whole cultures. Roman Catholicism was able to construct the archi-
tectonic whole of medieval culture. The Protestant Reformation--
with the aid of the Enlightenment--became the switchman for the last
great Christian synthesis of culture. It is appropriate at this
moment to look more closely at this last switchman.

Our Inherited Switchman

It is the highly unoriginal contention of this section that the regnant switchman since the sixteenth century was shaped by the Protestant Reformation and the Enlightenment. Protestantism --especially Calvinism and its off-shoot Puritanism--provided legitimation and guidance for the inner motivations of the cutting edge of Western civilization. The Enlightenment, in a complementary fashion, provided a comprehensive, over-arching canopy of meaning for the new world that was a-borning in those crucial centuries. These two historical movements combined most effectively in England and the Calvinist areas of the European mainland. Later, they penetrated the United States and Canada. Lutheran areas of Northern and Middle Europe followed even later, with varying degrees of struggle and reaction. As the North Atlantic community became increasingly dominant economically, politically, and culturally, the ideas and values it bore began to penetrate other parts of the world.

Without duplicating Weber's argument concerning the Calvinist part of the equation, we can lift up the salient points he made. He asserted that a specific religious ethos, that of left-wing Calvinism in its Quaker and Puritan forms, had certain unintended social and economic effects that were necessary for the full development of capitalism. Two features of that ethos--inner-worldly asceticism and the impulse to organize life rationally--were the critical elements that legitimated and guided the aspirations of the rising entrepreneurial class. The Reformation doctrine of the calling--particularly in its more dynamic Calvinist form--unleashed tremendous amounts of energy into the world. One glorified God in one's calling; energetic work in the world thereby took on religious significance. Doing well in business, for example, was a means of glorifying God. This motivation toward hard work in the world was coupled with a thorough-going austerity in religious and worldly affairs. The Calvinist emphasis on the prohibition of idolatry and graven images--as measured by the fact that that prohibition commands status as a separate commandment in the Calvinist ordering--created a sharp animus against sensual enjoyment and frivolity.

Moreover, the Calvinist tradition lifts up the doctrine of predestination in which one is elect or damned from all eternity. Nothing--neither priest, church, nor means of grace--can make any difference in this situation. The Protestant is cut off from reliance on the age-old channels of grace. But he is also doubtful about whether he is elect or not; he searches for more certainty about his status. He strives toward the signs of election--prosperity, seriousness, discipline. Coping constructively with uncertainty, the Calvinist grasps for success in his vocation.

If these elements sum up the "inner-worldly asceticism" in the Protestant ethic, then its commitment to a Third Use of the Law accounts at least in great part for its rationality. The Calvinist tradition has maintained that God's Law, which is orderly and rational, not only governs and sustains the secular structures of the world and condemns the sinner; it also provides a discernible

structure for the individual and corporate life of the redeemed.
Because of this commitment, Calvinism has always had more potential
for and interest in rationally organizing all facets of life than
Lutheranism. The faithful individual and community ought to organize their lives according to God's prescriptions for them. Politics, economics, and church-organizational life ought to be shaped
according to a rational pattern. Thus, the Calvinist was free to
apply rational calculations to his work in the world. He was liberated from the bonds of tradition.

Now this ethos was not *intended* to enable the emergence
of capitalism. But its religious ethos had social and economic
effects. Glorification of God through one's calling led to disciplined, successful hard work in the world and the concomitant accumulation of capital. The animus against sensuality and frivolity
led to saving and re-investment of capital. Predestination stimulated individualism and its attendant social and geographical mobility. The drive for certainty of salvation moved toward acquisition as a sign of election. Conversely, poverty and failure demonstrated a lack of moral and religious rectitude. Finally, the
commitment to organize life according to God's Law enhanced the
level of applied rationality in economic life.

These religious ideas set the new impulses of the middle
classes onto a track that was soon to penetrate the most dynamic
areas of the Western world. There is little doubt that Weber has
described a powerful set of ideas in history. But the Calvinist
vision was directed primarily to the life of Protestant Christians
and their organizations. What would hold together all these liberated persons and groups that were glorifying God in their business
and organizational life? What would make sense of this new world
in a comprehensive way? What would give orderly, coherent, public
meaning to the broader worlds of politics, economics, education,
and society? What would fill the vacuum left by the erosion of
Catholic authority and tradition, which for so long had been the
glue that held it all together?

To answer these questions we must turn to the Enlightenment, the comprehensive dimension of the last great switchman. The
guiding principle of the Enlightenment was belief in reason. Reason
was the common rule and measure that God had given man; through it
man could discover the natural order of things in the world. The
natural laws so discovered would "furnish a reliable and immutable
standard for testing the ideas, the conduct, and the institutions
of men."[9]

Reason did not mean simply the process of reasoning, but
was rather the very principle of humanity which gave humans dignity
and liberated them from the repressions of religious, political,
and economic control. The acknowledgment of every person as a
rational being, capable of autonomy in all facets of life, was a
basis of the winning struggle by "bourgeois society" against author-
itarianism and tyranny. Thus, we have, in Weber's words, another
case of "elective affinity." As the ethos of Calvinism was setting
the energies of the rising middle classes onto the tracks of disciplined acquisition through economic rationality, the Enlightenment
was offering assurance that that liberated energy had an internal

guidance system, reason, which would lead it to conformity with the natural order of things. One element of the switchman gave religious guidance and significance to act into the world, while the other element assured the actors that their play would end well provided they followed their rational pursuits.

Perhaps Tillich describes this latter element most clearly:

> In the struggle out of which the modern world was born, one presupposition was always present, sometimes avowed, sometimes tacit. It was the belief that the liberation of reason in every person would lead to the realization of a universal humanity and to a system of harmony between individuals and society. Reason in each individual would be discovered to be in harmony with reason in every other individual. This principle of automatic harmony found expression in every realm of life.[10]

Tillich goes on to analyze the way in which the principle of rational harmony was applied:

> In the economic realm, it was believed that the welfare of all would best be served by the unrestrained pursuit by each individual of his own economic interests; the common good would be safeguarded by the 'laws of the market' and their automatic functioning; this was the root principle of the economy of *laissez-faire*. In the *political* realm, it was supposed that the political judgment of each citizen would lead automatically to right political decisions by a majority of citizens; community of interest would assure sound democratic procedures. In the *international* realm, the play of interest among the nations would result in a comparatively stable balance of power between sovereign states. In the sphere of *education*, the essential rationality of human nature would produce, through free self-expression by each individual, a harmonious community.... Finally, this all-controlling idea found *philosophic* expression in various doctrines of pre-established harmony, those of Leibnitz, Descartes, and their schools. The individual monad is a microcosm of the world. Ripening according to its own inner laws of logic, it develops in pre-established harmony with the whole of being.[11]

It is not difficult to see how the switchman of the sixteenth to eighteenth centuries, a composite of Calvinist Protestantism and Enlightenment, provided legitimation and guidance to the dominating industrial nations of Holland, Switzerland, Great Britain, and later, and pre-eminently, the United States and Canada. It is particularly revealing to notice the lively admixture of Puritan and Enlightenment thought in the definitive self-understanding of America. In the writings of Sydney Ahlstrom and Sidney Mead, we glimpse the cross-fertilization and amalgamation of those traditions, as well as their tensions and incompatibilities.[12] While one author may emphasize Puritanism and the other Enlightenment, it is clear from their studies that the switchman has found his latest and greatest incarnation in the American ethos, which has in turn set the vast American colossus onto tracks that still determine its direction.

While many of the ideas and values of the switchman have been shorn of their religious roots and are now sustained by a kind of civic piety, they still hold sway over our world of discourse. It is questionable how firmly, or how long, they will be dominant. Many significant commentators have long since announced their demise. Spengler saw the organic cycle of birth, maturity, and death encompassing the West. Marx saw bourgeois society collapsing under the weight of its own contradictions. Conservative and aristocratic theorists, usually of European background, have foreseen its collapse from the mediocrity, superficiality and conformity of the mass society it has spawned. Tillich saw the period of the 1930's as a time of *kairos* for the emergence of "religious socialism" from the disintegrating hulk of bourgeois liberalism. Contemporary thinkers from Heilbroner through Bell to Ferkiss toll the switchman's death knell. Third-World writers predict that the dialectic that failed to occur on the national level will occur on a world-wide basis as the rural periphery rebels against the oppressions of the metropolitan center.

What to make of all this? One thing is certain: the obituaries have been decidedly premature. Western liberal societies limp on into the future. In fact, sometimes the limp turns into a rather sprightly gait. And the fascism that is always descending upon the liberal West as it enters its death throes seems always to land elsewhere. It is not clear that the values brought forth by the last switchman are dead. Indeed, they live on and some small portion of the folk are willing to defend them. If there will be a new switchman, which there must be, it will be one that we might hope would incorporate the best values of the old.

One thing is clear, however, the religious meaning and commitment that undergirded the old switchman have eroded drastically. The Puritan devotion to calling, frugality and a Christian moral social order has waned along with the theological view of God and world that sustained it. The "virtues" of hard work, restless competitiveness, acquisitiveness, and economic and technological rationality live on as secular verities. The Enlightenment confidence in progress, automatic harmony, and immutable natural law discernible by reason has evaporated with the Enlightenment projection of God and world. Indeed, reason can no longer be spelled with a capital "R." But we do bear forward secular belief in civil liberty, sovereignty of the people, and equality before the law. We are in a time when the values generated by the last Christian synthesis of culture are in competition with newly emergent values of both a destructive and a constructive character. But neither the traditional nor the emerging is being incorporated into a persuasive and vivifying religious vision that can again organize these inchoate aspirations and thereby give them clear definition and intentionality.

We are in a transition time when the old switchman is no longer playing his guiding and legitimating function, and the new one is not yet clear. That does not mean we are collapsing nor does it mean that we have no need of the public meaning the switchman can supply. It does mean that we are in a search for the switchman.

The New Search

This search will consist of at least four phases as it seeks the renewed personal motivation and comprehensive meaning that a switchman can bestow. The search will go on among secular and religious elements of our societies; it is certainly going on already. However, here we will examine these phases from the viewpoint of the Christian tradition, with hope that it yet may have the vitality to shape a new synthesis of religion and culture.

The first phase could be called *interpretative*. This will mean a stage of active listening, of receptivity. Its main goal will be to identify rising interests and necessities that will demand an alteration of the present order. Taking a hint from Weber, we will be called to point to modern and changed forms of perennial "material and ideal interests." And we should look for them among those persons and groups directly immersed in the dynamics of modern life. We should be attentive to the business communities when they request indicative planning, to the working classes when they demand cohesive neighborhoods, to the middle classes when they call for decentralization, to the "conservatives" who caution about the dark side of liberation in relation to issues like abortion and pornography, to economists who warn us that our appetite for consumption is outstripping our capacity for increased productivity, to persons from the developing world who rail at unequal distribution of wealth and power. Our listening should not be limited to the voices of those whose intellectual filters allow them only to hear the voice of the "oppressed," particularly their choice of the "oppressed."

Somewhere in the welter of these impinging "material and ideal interests" will appear some that will have broad and long-range importance. It seems that burgeoning ecological consciousness may be one such interest. The shift in the business world from the manufacture of goods to the providing of services may augur a change in interest that will have powerful repercussions in our lifestyle. The persisting rise in expectations among the relatively and absolutely poor everywhere in the world cannot be discounted.

However, while these underlying interests move forward ceaselessly within the course of events, the whole emergent will have little world-historical impact if it is not refracted through meaningful world-images. Thus, the second phase in the search is an *intellectual* phase. For Christians, the intellectual task will involve translating the Christian religious tradition into new world-images that can gather up the disorganized, inchoate "material and ideal interests," shape them into a coherent pattern, and prescribe models for pressing interest into action. In short, the Christian intellectual task is to reconstruct a public theology that can help to set those interests on appropriate tracks.

The secular intellectual world is already busy at such a task. Heilbroner prescribes the austere myth of enduring Atlas to us as we enter a world of stringent limits, instead of the more extravagant myth of soaring Prometheus.[13] Daniel Bell offers the image of the "public household" to overcome cultural contradictions inherent in capitalism.[14] Victor Ferkiss suggests "ecological

humanism" as the new structure of public meaning that will replace
outworn liberalism.[15]
     What these attempts have in common is the search for a
convincing world-image that can set us on new and different tracks.
But while the authors intend these images to have compelling symbolic
power, they exhibit little existential punch. One should not expect
that of them, for they appear only briefly in isolated books. In
order for the contours of the switchman to appear with gripping
power, they will have to take shape out of the traditions of living
religion.
     Several Christian efforts at world-image construction
might be mentioned as examples of the intellectual task. A most
obvious one is that of Latin American liberation theology, done out
of both Catholic and Protestant contexts. The Christian revelation
interprets and is interpreted by revolutionary socialism. A new
synthesis of Christ and culture is being attempted. Instead of
Christian revealed wisdom integrating with Aristotelian philosophy,
it is Marxism this time around. There is no doubt that this translation of the Christian tradition meshes with irresistible historical interests. The theological symbols have a cogent "elective
affinity" with the aspirations of the poor. Without going into an
extended critique, though, it is hard to see how this significant
effort will have relevance for the major industrial powers of
Western society. The Marxist analyses are too simplistic to illuminate the complexity and dynamism of the modern economic and political order in the developed world. Moreover, they have not been
able to account for the reforming and innovating capacities that
thrive in the "free world." Certainly there are legitimate vitalities of world-historical import being expressed in the wealthy,
liberal societies. What will give them public meaning?
     A second attempt at the construction of a public theology
is taking place in the dialogue between theology and the natural
and biological sciences. The change in world-view wrought by
Newtonian science undercut orthodox Christian formulations at the
same time as it paved the way for Enlightenment philosophy and theology. Later, the world-view associated with modern, post-Newtonian
science in turn undercut the Enlightenment formulations. Now the
stage is set for major attempts at relating modern scientific insights into the nature of reality to Christian theology. Certainly
the massive efforts of Teilhard de Chardin are representative of
the battle that must go on if a new switchman is to spring from
Western Christian soil. Process thought also provides a viable possibility. In future projects of that nature the "ecological humanism" proposed by Ferkiss may take on the necessary religious power.
Such projects could again grasp the best minds of the time and
through them begin to penetrate all dimensions of life with meaning.
     At any rate, the intellectual task we are referring to
will be carried off by religious groups who take seriously the first
phase, that of listening to signals from all of reality. They will
not be sectarian in outlook, but will bear the classical marks of
the "church type," i.e., they will be open to learnings from the
created world and they will be committed to permeating that created
world with religious meaning and morality.

The third phase of the search may chronologically precede the first two. Both the listening and the intellectual construction will grow out of religious communities that possess modes of *disciplined spirituality*. No doubt it is true that religious affections and moral patterns precede the theological reflection upon them. Catholic orders, Calvinist churches and cities, and Puritan enclaves all exhibited a disciplined spirituality that could vivify and reinforce the world-images they bore. And, finally, the religious communities that helped shape the switchmen of the past had capacities for *organizing* their radical witness. They created and maintained social organizations that could listen, do theology, express a spirituality, and, above all, aggressively penetrate other sectors of the broader human society.

This speculation about the phases of the search should not be taken to mean that we can *make* the switchman appear. It is not even evident that the time is ripe for his appearance. Perhaps the old one is not as dead as the educated elite think he is. Perhaps he is, but the present system will muddle on for many decades to come; the crisis stage may not be here. Or, perhaps we are already far into the process of bringing forth a new world-image. The transition may be further along than we can grasp. Indeed, maybe the Christian Marxism of Latin America *is* the new switchman. Or its African variant. It is possible that Christian energies in the West have run their course and will reappear in the developing churches and cultures of Africa and Latin America. Perhaps other religious or quasi-religious groups will provide the impetus. History will tell the story. The Lord has his own way of bringing up green shoots from charred stumps or of felling large trees. We make our best attempts and wait on Him.

NOTES AND REFERENCES

1. Max Weber, *The Protestant Ethic and the Spirit of Capitalism*, (New York: Charles Scribner's Sons, 1958).

2. Robert Green ed., *Protestantism, Capitalism and Social Science*, (Lexington, Massachusetts: D.C. Heath and Co., 1973), pp. 53-88, 106-136.

3. *Ibid.*, pp. 32-52, 137-149.

4. *Ibid.*, p. 39.

5. *Op. cit.*, Weber, pp. 19-20.

6. *Ibid.*, pp. 66-69.

7. *Op. cit.*, Green, p. 38.

8. *Ibid.*, p. 138.

9. Earl Becker, *The Declaration of Independence*, (New York: Alfred Knopf, 1942), p. 26.

10. Paul Tillich, *The World Situation*, (Philadelphia: Fortress Press, 1965), p. 3.

11. *Ibid.*, pp. 3-4.

12. Sydney Ahlstrom, *A Religious History of the American People*, (New Haven: Yale University Press, 1972) and Sidney Mead, *The Nation With the Soul of a Church*, (New York: Harper and Row, 1975).

13. Robert Heilbroner, *An Inquiry Into the Human Prospect*, (New York: Norton, 1974), pp. 142-144.

14. Daniel Bell, *The Cultural Contradictions of Capitalism*, (New York: Basic Books, 1976).

15. Victor Ferkiss, *The Future of Technological Civilization*, (New York: George Braziller, 1974), pp. 87-206.

CULTURE, SELFHOOD, AND THE PROCESS OF INTERPRETATION

by
Bernard O. Brown

Introduction

The scientific study of cultures is replete with varying conceptions of what the term *culture* really designates, leaving the impression of a "studied vagueness"[1] that adheres to this the master concept of the discipline of anthropology. In general, we consider the culture of a community to consist of patterns of life ways that have become established among the members of that community as constituting the "normal" or "right" manner in which the common projects of life are pursued. Here the terms "normal" and "right" refer to standards of valuation imputed to the members of the community. They are not the statistical norms of the behaviorists' scales. They are not what the scientist himself regards as valuable in the life ways of others. They are supposedly those valuations that a people's behavior patterns embody, or that their idealizations express -- the genuine moral significance that a people attribute to their own experience.

When a scientist provides a description of the culture of a particular community he is, of course, objectifying what he alleges to be a subjective orientation for the members of the community itself. Cultural science is premised upon the assumption that it is possible to gain a valid understanding of the mental structures by which a people hold their life-world before them as meaningful and valuable. The scientist attempts to penetrate to the very core of meaning and feeling by which the members of a cultural community order and evaluate their experience. It is done by a process in which there is a translation of cultural factors (however identified) from the context of immediacy within the lived experiences of a people, into another setting entirely, into a form of discourse in which the immediate articulation of motive and action is suspended in order that mental experiments can be conducted by which the efficacy, consistency, or moral valence of cultural values can be tested. All of this is done under the assumption that the clearest and most truthful descriptions and analyses of the values by which other people live can be made by one who wills to enter no value judgements of his own upon what he perceives.

The question should be pressed whether or not a pattern of life ways that a people regard as "normal" or "right" becomes something different when translated into the objectified language of cultural science. It may even be asked whether or not the patterns so objectified are actually the creations of the mind that has

139

observed and described the phenomena for the benefit of a scientific community that is far removed in temper and susceptibility of mind from the community of persons who allegedly believe as it is said they do.

The question nags and persists because of the inherent paternalism of a position which claims to have knowledge of how a system of life operates for a people who themselves have no recourse to such objective and helpful knowledge, who merely live out the strategies imputed to their modes of experiencing and evaluating the world. There is a sense in which,

> In claiming to recognize the other in all his conditionedness, in claiming to be objective, the knower is really claiming to be the master.[2]

Such paternalism has not seemed intrusive or obnoxious, perhaps, when the objects of cultural studies were far removed in place and "cultural time" from the milieu in which scientific investigations were reported and their implications considered. But when the peculiarities of the different ways of living under scrutiny belong to a largely subject class of people, with whom the scientific community shares common space, common access to scarce goods, and a future of inevitable interdependence, then the problems become suddenly serious and even inflammatory, as when cultural science has sought to characterize the culture of the urban poor, or that of the people of the black ghettos of this country. Knowledge is, after all, power. At least it is so within the technocracies of Western civilization, a fact not lost upon people who are conscious of living in ways distinctive to themselves, and who wonder at the motives, propriety, and even the possibility of outside observers representing "objectively" the meaning of their existence.

The problem here can be seen as well by asking what we understand to be the nature of the self, and how it is possible to appropriate the meaning of selfhood as experienced by another individual. The primary experience of selfhood is of consciousness in relation to another consciousness bearing its own structure and meaning. It is the experience of the self having a world, of a self-consciousness that is also an other-consciousness. Consciousness of being is consciousness of something being something. In the words of Ernest Hocking,

> "I think" is an incomplete statement. No one is ever "just thinking," he is always thinking something.[3]

This essential condition of conscious life, this point of beginning for all thought about the emergence of the self, posits the reality of communicative structure at the ground of self-awareness. The philosopher Charles Hartshorne, has described this "first level" of experience as,

> .... feeling in confrontation with feeling, feeling with a social structure, not cognition of bare facts or matter (whatever that would be) or mere neutral qualities or forms.[4]

Thus, at the primary level of sentient experience, it is erroneous to conceive of the human mind as an independent agent, an objective "inter-cerebral" process, monitoring stimuli that intrude upon the organism, affecting a discharge of emotional responses in accordance with some latent, innate ordering of "needs" and "interests."[5]   It is an abstraction which falsifies the nature of experience to conceive of the human self as a "mere datum,"[6] an autonomous structure existent somehow prior to its engagement with a society of minds. The mind is itself dependent upon a context of shared meaning for its emergence as an active creative force.[7]   The self is a creation of a social process even as it is creative of meaning within that process.

Nor is this understanding of the self as realized in a context of meaning the same as that which understands the self as a mere reflection of a "social self." Implicit in the various mirror image theories is the notion, again, of an unformed substance, the self, which takes on form in response to public or cultural definitions of the self's reality.[8]   This approach is very powerful and indeed useful for many therapeutic and educational purposes. But the mirror image theories begin from another assumption than that which is, I claim, the starting point for an understanding of man in culture.

The self is a reality created and recreated in a social process of interpretation in which the self attains real identity at the same time as it is subject to reinterpretation within the dynamic process. The point of critical difference between this position and those based upon various concepts of the "social self" is that the reality of the self is not described in relation to a set of culturally formed images which themselves define the limits of meaning. Instead, the meanings, the "content," of the self are transcended in the moment of the self's realization in objective form. So the act of knowing in fact what is true of the self's relation to reality is the act that creates a new context for the known.

We know ourselves as being known, as living within relationships with real entities that make claims upon us to acknowledge their true meaning and value even as we realize our own. The problem is to be able to establish what is real in the being of another without reducing those expressions of being to mere functions of our own understanding. Or the opposite danger must also be avoided, which is to falsify the nature of the self by objectifying its expressions of being as mere data signifying an autonomous structure.

The problem of this paper is to indicate a way beyond the dilemmas created by trying to understand another person, or a cultural group, by reducing the matter to a function of one's own understanding, or by fixing the reality of personal or cultural meanings in a realm of "objectivity" which is in no way affected by the interpretive action of the observer. The way beyond is to understand the process of interpretation itself. As a first step, I propose a consideration of the theory of interpretation developed by Josiah Royce.

The Transcendence of the Social Self

The idea of a "process of interpretation" draws upon the formulation by Josiah Royce of a metaphysic of interpretation in his lectures entitled *The Real World and The Christian Ideas*.[9] Royce addressed his proposals to a philosophic community which he considered stymied in an essentially sterile debate on the primacy of empirical perceptions over rational constructions of reality, on the one hand, as opposed by the argument that empirical observations depend upon rational constructions for the means of leading and shaping perceptions. Royce sought to define a third type of intellectual activity, called by him "interpretation," which he believed was fundamental to any act of knowing. Furthermore, he understood the process of interpretation to be the key to a generalization about the nature of reality in which many moral problems relating to man's being in community would become clear.

Royce chose as evidence for this distinct form of intellectual activity the problem of understanding the reality of mind as we experience it in encounter with other persons. We know that our neighbor engages in conscious intellectual activity, but not because his mind is present to ours as a datum of perception, having immediately recognizable qualities of extension, color, movement, etc., or because we possess a general conception of mindedness, created by analogy with our own mental processes and confirmed through observations of mental behavior in other people. It is rather the case that we become engaged in our own minds by activities of the neighbor that seem to signal the desire to convey meanings that originate outside of our own subjective mental processes. In order for these signals to be received and "understood" by our own minds a transformation must occur whereby the meaning intended by the second mental agent is formulated in a way that both minds can affirm as faithful to a common intention to unite themselves in a true representation. It is an act of creating a third reality, a socially perceivable and acknowledged sign representing a convergence of meaning, that Royce calls the process of interpretation. We know that other beings are possessed with minds because we participate in a process by which mediating ideas, interpretive signs, are created which unify the separate centers of mental activity in a common meaning.

For three reasons, according to Royce, an interpretation is a unique cognitive reality when compared to what we normally understand a percept or concept to be. A percept we understand to be the immediate impression we receive from a particular experience of reality. A concept is a generalization we make that identifies certain common properties of reality. But an interpretation is fundamental to both of these cognitive acts. It is the mediating reality by which an individual mind lays hold of the meaning of that which occurs in immediate experience. It is the means by which generalizable characteristics are brought into a meaningful configuration. An interpretation is distinctive therefore, first, because it is the result of a *social* process rather than an act of an individual mind. Two minds meet with the purpose of reconciling divergent perspectives upon a given event or thing. The goal is not

that of obtaining an individual perception, nor that of creating
an abstraction. It is the social goal of comparing the relative
grounds of an experience for the purpose of creating a unified
understanding of a common world. The unity is achieved in the
reality of a new form in which individual minds are enabled to affirm a common meaning that satisfies both parties. Thus the goal
of achieving a true interpretation is identical with the goal of
creating a social unity.

> ....an interpretation is real only if the appropriate community is
> real and true only if that community reaches its goal.[10]

Second, an interpretation is itself a *mental* construction,
a sign created for the purpose of making possible a unity of *minds*
in reference to a given experience. It is the result of an active
process, the fulfillment of a particular need. The essential requirement of creating a means of convergence for distinct minds
leads to the creation of a sign showing wherein that unity is realized. This means, third, that the sign is itself no more than a
"leading" idea directing us towards another interpretation. The existence of an interpretation depends upon its function in sustaining
the process. The sign is nothing in itself, but only exists in its
power to unite persons in a process of interpretation.

The fundamental experience of reality is trinitarian in
form -- the mind that engages an object, the object engaged, and the
interpretation by which the nature of the object is expressed. This
is not the same as saying that the mind simply forms an idea of the
object, for that will not resolve the conflict, or problem inherent
in the otherness of the object. The idea that resolves the problem
must be conformed to the nature of the *object* in terms of its claim
upon the subject, and to the nature of the *mind* that seeks to know
-- i.e., to the elements of conceptual material, the memories,
associations, feelings, intuitions, etc. with which the mind is
endowed. The interpretation is a "third" reality within the process,
a mediating expression that satisfies the nature of the object confronting the mind, insofar as that nature bears upon the mind in
determinate and unequivocal ways, and the structure of the mind
which reaches a new understanding of itself and the world.

The nature of interpretation is finally the ultimate explanation for what we experience as the real world, according to
Royce. We are conscious of a reality that is outside of and distinct from our own inner thoughts because we are confronted continuously with problems, conflicts, contradictions, and claims which
cannot be resolved unless we, first, submit ourselves to their
influence upon us, their claim to be recognized as distinct from
ourselves, and second, we seek a means by which the nature of those
claims can be interpreted satisfactorily, for which we depend upon
a community of minds that can agree. Thus we affirm the reality
of other entities by means of the interpretations by which they
satisfy their demands to be acknowledged and our need to comprehend.
There is no way to get behind the interpretation itself to a more
elemental or material dimension of reality, for that would involve
the use of a further interpretation achieved through the same process,

i.e., the comparison of separate experiences which are finally unified through the creation of a sign with a common meaning.

By the real world we mean simply the true interpretation of this our problematic situation.[11]

Thus reality is revealed to be an infinite series of mental expressions, interpretations, each one answering an intention of mind to be united with other minds in comprehending that of which both are aware, with each interpretation requiring further acts of interpretation. The ultimate truth which may be stated about the universe is that it contains its own interpretation, which means that reality will yield itself to a search for that meaning by which community is created. It is the nature of universe that it reveals the means by which men may be led to a state of "co-inference" in the awareness of a common past, a real present, and a destiny of interdependence.

Man is completely dependent upon the community of interpretation for any valid experience of the world. The community consists of all men who engage themselves in a process of representing faithfully the reality of which they are aware. Thus there is a universal ethical quality required of all men who seek to join others in common actions based upon truth. It is the quality of loyalty which is expressed as a readiness to make any personal sacrifice necessary to create the means by which a valid unity may be achieved, that is, to dedicate oneself to the goal of representing the nature of things in such a way that the other with whom one is engaged would concur in that representation of reality. By this act, and this act alone, repeated innumerable times, is man enabled to live in contact with the world and his fellow beings. Insofar as there is an achievement of an interpretation, just so are men unified in their understanding of one another and the world, even though that unity may be no more than a true interpretation of the exact terms upon which they differ. But no interpretation, no unification, is ever complete, is ever statically fixed for all of time, rather, it consists of the means by which, through other heroic acts of loyalty, new interpretations and new unities are realized. The point is that Royce has defined an ethical stance that is essential to the possibility of life itself in a world of interpretations. The value of a loyal action in helping to create the terms of a new unity is not relative to the form in which the interpretation is expressed but is intrinsic to the possibility of meaningful form itself. It is a value constitutive of the real world that humans experience, and it implies other values that depend upon loyalty for their justification.

We may now state what Royce understood to be the nature of selfhood given the interpretation of reality as consisting of "signs and their interpretations." The self is never aware of itself in a state of pure receptivity. It is always a participant in a form of consciousness united with some portion of the world. Its experience is that of an act of mind seeking to realize an interpretation of reality. An interpretation, as we have seen, is a mental construction which establishes a unity between two or more

minds experiencing a common object, or event. Such a unity results
from the success of the interpretation in encompassing the perspectives by which both parties experience their common world. Thus
the self which attends in particular to its own role, or situation,
in the self-world relation participates in an interpretive process
that is fundamentally like the social process described above. The
self which reflects upon its own experience must proceed as if there
were another observer of the process whose perspective must coincide
with one's own if there is to be a truthful representation of who
one is in relation to the world. We all participate, of course, in
a private interiorized life of reflection upon our own actions and
experiences. But we impute a public, or societal measure of validity to these reflections, in the sense that we act as if our conclusions would be those shared among two or more competent and
honest observers.

The process of interpretation of the self is the same
triadic act of comparison, contrast, and unification of understanding that has been outlined above. The mind casts about for the
signs of comparison and distinction that will help to create a true
description. Eventually a third idea, which encompasses the objectivity of the event and the mental state in which we make the inquiry, indicates the way toward a unification of perspective in
which we learn, not only about the object of our attention, but
about ourselves in relation to that object.

> .... the new, or third, the interpreting idea, in these elementary
> cases of comparison, shows us, as far as it goes, ourselves, and
> also creates in us a new grade of clearness regarding what we are
> and what we mean.[12]

If the primary motivation for our inquiry is to know more about
"what we are, and what we mean," the focus of attention is directed
to the self and its responses. However, the favorable result of
the process is precisely that of an interpretation, an idea of the
self that satisfies the requirement of a society of minds loyally
devoted to the unity of the self with others in a true representation
of reality.

In this process we are, to be sure, dependent upon interpretive materials available to us in the fund of conscious experience we share with our fellow human beings. Hence it is reasonable
to assume that much can be learned about the way in which persons
understand themselves by examining the content of the interpretive
materials which are held in common by a group of people who share
many of the same conditions of life -- a common language, neighborhood, kinship system, climate, history, etc. But it is never sufficient to assume that the content of selfhood is identical with
the fund of images, concepts, and associated feelings so identified,
since the self is always an active participant in the process of
appropriating what is present for it in the world of interpretations.
An interpretation has no reality except as it is the ingredient by
which a further interpretation is made,except as a sign pointing to
a new unification of the community of minds. This means that the
self is never determined or limited by the content of objectified

meanings available to it. The self is real in the form of a sign
demanding an interpretation within a community, which means that
the objective meaning of the interpretation is transcended in the
very act of objectification.

The concept of the social self, suggesting a configuration
of publicly understood meanings which are appropriated by a finite
entity, the substantial self, distorts the real nature of the self
precisely in the degree to which it ignores the dynamic inherent
in the process of interpretation. The critical factor to be considered in any achievement of identity within the self-world relationship is that the signs by which that identity is interpreted
lead toward the creation of further interpretations which encompass
other dimensions of understanding.

For example, let us suppose a young man understands himself to have been enslaved by a compulsion to destroy his own opportunities of success in a job. His self-awareness at that point is
that of a man who has been "his own worst enemy." It is this interpretation which unites a personal experience of persistent failure
with an analysis made, let us say, with the assistance of a wise
and friendly counselor. The selfhood of that man is not circumscribed by the fixed content of the interpretation. Quite the contrary, the interpretation is a means of appropriating the meaning
of the past as it leads towards a reformulation of meaning in the
present. It conveys the situation in which a person has realized
the full effect of the objective conditions under which he has suffered and toward which he is now in a different situation. The sign
represents an objective fact, real in its independence of an effect
upon it by the subject, but transcended in the subjectivity of one
who suffers the effect of the truth upon himself. The experience
of transcendence is that of a community of interpretation enabling
a man to know as he is known, and to live in some degree beyond the
power of the known.

Creative Subjectivity

There is no doubt that the gentle and hopeful spirit in
which Royce developed his ideas of the real world and the moral
realities is redolent of an optimistic and pacific cultural environment as unlike our own as it is possible to imagine. But this
should not cause us to mistake his fundamental insight for merely
a felicitous restatement of a naive and inconsequential rationalism.
Royce was driving for an understanding of the mental process by
which people formulate a *workable* representation of the real world.
He felt intellectually obligated to extend his speculations to a
metaphysic of reality in which the process of interpretation was
the key. The nature of interpretation had to be the key because
the extension of any other generic idea of reality to the status of
a metaphysical principle could be reduced finally to the single
problem he found to be irreducible, i.e., the question of how human
beings can speak knowingly of a real world. More than this, Royce
felt morally bound to the task of formulating the universal and
irreducible ethical entailment of his speculations, the requirement

upon all persons to represent their experience of reality faithfully, to the fullest extent of their intellectual and imaginative abilities, for the sake, not of some abstract ideal of truth, but of the very possibility of life in communion with a real world.

It is significant that as some of our contemporaries have tried to begin with the same problem Royce accepted as fundamental, they have chosen to offer some remarkably similar explanations, although they have usually eschewed the metaphysical task of extending these speculations to their final implications. Clifford Geertz, for example, has described the process as a cultural one in which symbols that constitute "templates of reality" are projected as problematic representations of experience. The resultant cultural orientation functions as both a "model of and model for" reality, a symbol which unifies a community of people around the solution to particular problems or projects in life.[13] Some social psychologists will accept for the meaning of the concept "reality" only that concretization of meanings which persons in particular communities have realized as the consequences of their projections of expectations and beliefs upon the world, their experiences of acting *as if* reality were of one form or another.

It is difficult, nevertheless, to avoid the conclusion that Royce's position is in constant danger of collapse into subjectivism, into the assertion that all meaning or value is projection by the knower on that which is known. Royce did not engage a challenge to his thought in which the nature of the real would have to be acknowledged as somehow determinate and unequivocal in its influence upon the mind of the interpreter, at the same time as its being in the form of an interpreted sign was established. How is it possible to think of real entities which are clearly independent of the influence of the knower upon them as objects, which are yet intrinsically related within a process of interpretation? We will seem to have reached a point of logical absurdity by contending that an object is at the same time a subject, and that subjectivity provides the final explanation of the real. But we may consult the reasoning of Charles Hartshorne to clarify what appears to be a contradiction of logic and causality.

The notion that an entity is real and objective for the sole reason that it is not relative or subject to another reality is considered necessary only because of an unjustified metaphysical preference for absolute objectivity, a situation that is made plausible logically only by the removal of the dimension of temporality from logical considerations. When a temporal succession is restored to the consideration of how real entities come to exist and have their effects upon the world around them, the logical problem disappears. To use a form of a favored illustration in Hartshorne's argument, we can see easily that to strike the musical tone of *A natural*, and to follow it shortly thereafter with the tone of *B flat*, is to have established, first of all, the prior tone independently of the latter. There is no sense in which the *A natural* can be known to be dependent upon any particular tone which may or may not succeed it. It is not the same for the relationship of the *B flat* to the tone that has preceded it in time. It is heard inevitably as having followed upon *A natural*, and therefore, as bearing some

kind of tonal relationship with the first tone. In some contexts
it will be heard as the tonic tone of the key of *B flat*, strengthened in that impression by hearing *A natural* as a leading tone.
    Now this argument cannot be advanced without dealing with
the challenge that we have spoken only of a relationship that is
heard to exist between two tones. This is not the same thing as to
say that there is a *real* dependence or independence of one tone in
relation to another. But here we must consider Hartshorne's use of
the term "subject" to mean "something that *simpliciter* or by definition is aware of something, something determinate or unequivocal."[14]
Hartshorne uses subjectivity to mean "a state of awareness" rather
than as a subjective substance of some kind, such as an ego.

> Descartes may not have proved that he existed as substance, or per-
> manent ego, but he did prove, if anything can be proved, that there
> are momentary experiences. These experiences, as being of something,
> are the "subjects" of this article.[15]

    Thus there is a sense in which the example of musical
tones presupposes a kind of state of awareness, or state of respon-
siveness, of one tone in relation to another. To be sure, the conventions of musical tradition, the evolution of a musical consciousness, are the means by which tonal relationships are discovered and formed as musical expressions. But the possibility of
tonal relationship is, in fact, real enough to be discovered, and
does not exist only in the imagination of the artist. That is,
the relationship of *B flat* to *A natural* is real in the sense that
an auditor must submit to its effect upon him before the question
of what musical sense can be made of it is considered. The presence
of an auditor to that succession is necessary, of course, to receive the sounds and testify to their relationship. But this only
adds to the conditions for musical relationship the presence of
another subject, and does not qualify the intrinsic pattern of relationships which tones in succession bear with one another, a
pattern which we have described as an awareness of that which is
determinate or unequivocal in what has preceded it in time.
    But it is not contradictory to claim an objectivity for
that which is determinate and unequivocal in its influence upon one
form of subjectivity, and to argue as well that every objective
form is itself subject for and relative to some other determinate
entity. The tonal relationship in the example above is fully objective for that which it influences, but is itself dependent upon
temporal precedents which have influenced the form in which it is
experienced.
    This would seem to lead toward a logical conclusion in
which the ultimate reality is absolute objectivity, that which has
determinate and unequivocal effects upon all the rest of reality,
but is not itself affected. However, this conclusion can be reversed by the contention that causal relationships are explained
finally by a process in which subjectivity *submits itself* to the
effect of objectivity. Since it is the diagnostic quality of objectivity to be independent of that which follows and is dependent
upon it, therefore, the reality of inter-relationships of entities,

that is, our experiences of relatedness among realities connected
in sequences of cause and effect, must be understood as a function
of that which evinces the diagnostic quality of dependence, that
is, subjectivity.

> Modern logic should by this time have cured us of the absurd pre-
> judice that, to explain everything, the great thing is to find the
> nonrelative, or absolute. On the contrary, not nonrelation is our
> main problem, but relation, a world of structured order. And noth-
> ing can constitute this but something that can intrinsically have
> relation, be genuinely relative. A subject, according to realism,
> is just such an intrinsically relative entity, in its very nature
> more or less conformed to something not itself. The subject is
> rich in relations, the mere object has no relations, at least not
> to the particular subject which has it as object.[16]

Thus the position to be affirmed is as follows: (a) there
is no reason to deny the evidence of common sense experience that
real entities exist independent of influence upon them by particular
knowing subjects who are themselves affected by the act of knowing;
(b) the equally common-sense experience of the inter-relationship
among entities is explainable according to the subjectivity or that
which is affected, in successive occasions of becoming, rather than
by the objectivity of that which is unaffected; (c) the experience
of this subjectivity is of a connected series of events in a passage of time; (d) this metaphysical situation is ultimately subjective, so that we may speak of a process of creativity in which
real entities, which bear determinant and unequivocal influence,
are given their actuality by that which is finally influential in
all, even as it is subjectively related and affected by all.[17]
What does this metaphysical position add to our understanding of the self? The experience of the self is that of subjectivity in relation to a world of objects upon which one is dependent which have clear and definite influences upon selfhood.
The metaphysical analogy of a world of subjects is, of course,
drawn on the basis of human subjectivity, a state of awareness of
something being something, experienced as having continuity and
duration in time. But the subjective dependence of the self upon
a world of objects is itself a state subject to a continuous process
of reformulation. That is, human subjectivity reveals the creative
power of that which submits itself to the influence of objective
reality, the power to restructure the forms of relationship so that
there is a transcendence of objective determinants in the precise
moment of realization of the real conditions of determination.
Human subjectivity is evidence of the resourcefulness of subjects
in submitting to determinate objectivity, in engaging the self within an order of intrinsic relativity to the real, in order to transcend the objectivity of the given.
The materials drawn from Royce and Hartshorne indicate
ways of engaging and resolving two aspects of the problem identified
at the outset of this discussion, the problem of interpretation.
The dilemma faced by anyone entering upon the role of the interpreter
is that of representing faithfully the personal and cultural orien-

tation toward reality of another person or community, without reducing the matter to a function of one's own understanding, or on
the other side of the dilemma, without "objectifying" the forms of
personal and cultural expression in a way that effectively destroys
their actual power to convey meaning. The contribution of Royce
has been to identify the elements of the interpretive process, including the essential commitments of those who engage in it, whether
from within a clearly defined "orbit of human association," a cultural group, or across the communicative barriers that define
separate groups. The question of the influence of the interpreter
within the process is thus acknowledged as relative to the real
possibility of achieving the goal of a true interpretation, which
is to create a new community of interpretation in which particularity and distinctness are preserved in a comprehension of the
matter which all share.

Hartshorne's speculations enable the interpreter to with-
stand the challenge that subjectivity acknowledged in relation to
the real is destructive of the human capacity to know the objective,
the particular, the independently real. Because causality is not
ultimately the influence of the fixed and independent upon the
relative and dependent, but is the reverse, i.e., the influence of
the subject suffering in itself the effect of the object, we can
claim for the interpreter his rightful capability of acknowledging
the integrity and intrinsic significance of the cultural object.

We are prepared, therefore, to consider more fully the
ethical vocation of the interpreter among cultural communities as
one for whom the truth of the reality he comprehends and the value
he enacts in the process are never separable.

The Interpretation of Cultural Meaning

The task of providing descriptive analyses of cultural
ways has been largely a project of interpretation with a particular
community of scientific minds, wherein certain values and methods
of procedure are regarded as "normal" and "right." These are the
familiar values of objectivity and freedom, the methods of critical
testing, etc. As noted above, the assumption has been that the
clearest and most truthful description and analysis of the values
by which another people live can be made by one who enters no value
judgements of his own upon what he perceives. In order to unify
the community of scientific minds an interpretation of cultural
phenomena must satisfy the above-mentioned essential conditions of
understanding within the community.

It should come as no surprise that, for a people whose
values are under scrutiny, an interpretation which treats all that
orders, animates, and enriches their life in community, but which
presumes to be unmoved or unaffected by the compelling power such
values wield among the communicants, should seem to be an unworthy
representation indeed, if not a complete distortion. Perhaps some
scientists have felt a similar outrage when, as believers in the
efficacy and humanity of their mode of understanding the world, they
have read the poet's interpretation of their approach to life.

While you and I have lips and voices which are for kissing and to
sing with who cares if some oneeyed son of a bitch invents an instrument to measure Spring with?[18]

To be sure, the scientist of culture intends not to scorn,
but to acknowledge and convey the respect of science for the integrity of life realized in the culture of another people,[19] a goal
which ethnographers have sometimes accomplished, in spite of what
they perhaps considered to be the pure objectivity of their approach.
But let us consider Royce's formulation of the vocation of the interpreter who strives to create the new forms by which the mental
processes of another person, or other people are represented.

His (the interpreter's) office is to conform to the mind which he
interprets, and to the comprehension of the mind to which he addresses his interpretation. And his own ideas can "work" only if
his self-surrender, and his conformity to ideas which are not his
own, is actually a successful conformity; and only if his approach
to a goal, which, as a member of a human community of interpretation
he can never reach, is a real approach.[20]

The first task of the interpreter is to "conform to the
mind he interprets." The interpreter must suffer himself the shaping
and moving objectivity of that to which he wills to be related.   In
texts on methods of ethnographic research something like this principle is enjoined upon the student of an alien culture, but always
under the aegis of the doctrine that what others "praise and endorse"
has moral significance only for them, and what the scientist honors
above all else is the objectivity of his approach to reality.   But
this is quite different from what Royce understood to be the informing spirit of interpretive inquiry.   The validity of the approach is entirely relevent to the goal of the process, which is
envisioned as a unity that constitutes a new reality within the
world -- not a mere description of an entity that has a form of being in its own right.   The real nature (that is to say, the objective and independent character) of a given reality is established
when it is encompassed by a symbol (or set of symbols) which expresses the relativity of those who are joined in an act of knowing.
Interpretation is an act of knowing with its fulfillment in a way
of being.

The question is raised therefore as to what community is
to be envisioned as the goal of an interpretive inquiry into cultural realities? Is cultural science an "objectifying" project intended to be imitative of the more primitive natural science models
in which every effort is made to establish the independent identity
of the object by the exclusion of any reference to the "standing
place" of the minds for whom the interpretation is intended? If
so, the cultural interpretation must exclude from its unifying effect anyone for whom the symbols are supposed to represent their
own cultural orientation, any "communicant" of the beliefs so represented.   That such an intention is even possible of realization
requires a view of the nature of culture in which cultural meaning
is relative entirely to those who live within the boundaries of the

cultural community. The scientist of culture creates an elaborate
but provisional reconstruction of what he sees within that cultural
community. But his interpretation is entirely for those minds that
share the same cultural distance from the object as does his own.
       This kind of stance for a science of human behavior is
as incongruous in its intention as it is incapable of realization,
even though it may have seemed possible when studying the lore of
an illiterate tribe of bushmen. It is incongruous, that is, if the
cultural dimension of human existence is accorded any significance
whatsoever in shaping and determining the actual lives of people.
For it is in the realm of cultural symbols, what Royce has called
"interpretive signs," that we observe the nature of man's interaction
with the world. It is an interaction in which cultural symbols indicate not merely the limits within which human experience is determined, by language, tradition, and other circumstances, but also
the human power to achieve a point of transcendence in relation to
the world. The cultural symbol is the sign of a liberation achieved
from determinisms, for it represents the unification of a community
of minds upon the real world, an idea that has "worked" in providing a solution to problems posed by ignorance of a heretofore
intractable environment.
       An interpreter of cultural symbols is, of course, an in-
terpreter of interpretations. The symbol is not a cognitive abstraction, but a concrete representation of meanings by which a
people acknowledge a common orientation within reality, a common
ground and motive for action within the world. One's aim in cultural science, therefore, cannot be that of destroying the interpretation by aborting the interpretive process itself, by refusing
to extend the scope of the symbol, by failing to create a wider
society of minds that participate in the knowledge of the world
they convey. The aim must be to create another context of meaning
to include those who have lived in one kind of contact with the
world through the symbol that is interpreted, *and* those who seek to
know the alien world as, in fact, part of their own world.
       When one human mind is able to express what another has
"praised and endorsed" within his life-world the interpreter has
encompassed thereby two worlds of meaning, and has created a third.
To have understood the esteem and honor with which an Eskimo regards
an aged parent, whom he has nevertheless left alone to freeze upon
the ice, is to have established a new frame of thinking about the
reality of family fealty. Odd or contrasting patterns of belief
and behavior are found to share a universe that yields to an interpretation which unites persons in the knowledge of a common world.
       The values an interpreter brings to his study of another
culture are precisely those elements with which he is able to exercise the interpretive art, to consider what is different in the
power of a strange symbol to move and shape one's experience of
reality, to realize that difference by knowing the sense in which
it is *not* his way of holding his own experience as meaningful. The
interpreter conforms to the mind which he interprets *and* "to the
mind to which he addresses his interpretation." That conformity
and that comprehension must be real in the sense that the interpreter intends a result which expresses the meaning vital to the

representatives of both cultures, to both participants, in what is an essential dialogue of life.

This does not mean that the task is any less one of being scrupulously faithful to what is given in the original structure of meaning. We must guard against the supposition that the process of interpretation aims toward a unity of understanding which is simply a washing out of particular cultural distinctions. We are not proposing a new synthesis in which the mediating idea is essentially a reductionist strategy. The only way to preserve the integrity of that which is subject to interpretation is to accept the fundamental nature of the process, in which the symbol bears the intrinsic intention of becoming the means to a new social reality, a community of interpretation.

The truth of an interpretation must be stated as the ideal of knowing as we are known, of realizing the unity of understanding which preserves those aspects of reality by which we and others have been brought within the community of interpretation, and which illuminates those aspects for all alike.

Conclusion

The transcendence of the social self, I have argued, is realized not through the attribution of a preformed objective structure to the personal role (the "I") in the dialogue of self and society, but by reflecting upon the creativity of the subject, in bearing the influence upon itself of that which it experiences as objective and past. Turning to the problem of understanding objective realizations of meaning in the common experiences of other peoples, it is again the creative act of interpretation which passes over the gap between inquiring subject and observed object, a fact which prefigures the existence of a wider, and inherently universal community of interpretation.

In the relations of self-understanding and of cultural understanding we reach an appreciation of the creative power in that which is relative to the fullest degree, in that which can sustain in itself the determinate and unequivocal effects of objective reality and bring forth new events and their meanings. The process of interpretation is thereby both an analogy and an exemplification of the Divine Life.

NOTES AND REFERENCES

1. This observation and the phrase in quotation marks are drawn from Clifford Geertz' paper "Religion as a Cultural System," published in M. Barton, ed. *Anthropological Approaches to the Study of Religion,* (New York: F. A. Praeger, 1966), pp. 205-215.

2. Richard E. Palmer, *Hermeneutic*, (Evanston: Northwestern University Press, 1969), p. 193.

3. See Ernest Hocking's "Introduction" to Charles Hartshorne's *Reality as Social Process*, (The Free Press of Glencoe, 1953), p. 14.

4. *Op. cit.*, Hartshorne, p. 29.

5. See Clifford Geertz' paper "The Growth of Culture and the Evolution of the Mind" in Jordan Scher, ed. *Theories of the Mind*, (New York: The Free Press, 1962), p. 713-737.

6. Josiah Royce, *The Problem of Christianity, Vol.II*, (New York: Mac-Millan, 1913), p. 61.

7. *Op. cit.*, Geertz, p. 735.

8. Gibson Winter traces the development of behaviorist models of inter-action between self and society in which a substantive understanding of the "I" structure is supplanted by the socially conformed structure of "me." See his *Elements of A Social Ethic* (New York: The MacMillan Company Paperbacks, 1966) Chap. 1, p. 3-73. This development follows upon a restricted emphasis upon elements in George Herbert Mead's classic explication of the social self in *The Social Psychology of George Herbert Mead*, ed. by Anselem Strauss (Chicago: University of Chicago Press, Phoenix Books, 1956). See also Anselem Strauss *Mirrors and Masks* (New York: The Free Press, 1959).

9. Published as volume I of *The Problem of Christianity*,(New York: The MacMillan Company, 1913).

10. *Op. cit.*, Royce, p. 69.

11. *Ibid.*, p. 214.

12. *Ibid.*

13. See Clifford Geertz' paper "Ideology As A Cultural System," in David Apter, ed. *Ideology and Discontent*,(The Free Press of Glencoe, 1964), p. 62.

14. *Op. cit.*, Hartshorne, p. 70.

15. *Ibid.*, p. 70.

16. *Ibid.*, p. 75.

17. See Charles Hartshorne's *The Divine Reality: A Social Conception of God*, (New Haven: Yale University Press, 1948).

18. From an untitled poem (number 23) by E.E. Cummings, published in *100 Selected Poems*,(New York: Grove Press, Inc.), p. 29.

19. See the article on "The Concept of Culture" by Milton Singer in the *International Encyclopedia of the Social Sciences*,(New York: MacMillan Co. and The Free Press), pp. 527-543. Also see Clifford Geertz, *The Interpretation of Cultures*,(New York: Basic Books, 1973), ch. I, p. 3-32.

20. *Op. cit.*, Royce, p. 216-217.

MONISTIC DIMENSIONS IN HUMANISTIC PSYCHOLOGY: A PROCESS THEOLOGY PERSPECTIVE

by
Don Browning

It has been rumored over the last few years in seminaries and among the learned clergy that there are important affinities between process thought and humanistic psychology. But why would such a suggestion have any importance and what is the supposed gain which follows from it? The answer goes something like this: in recent years,through the leadership of such thinkers as Charles Hartshorne, Schubert Ogden, John Cobb, and Daniel Day Williams, process thought has become an important philosophical ally to Christian theology. Process thought is increasingly popular among scholars and clergy alike as a major resource for the philosophical foundations of constructive Christian thinking. The emerging belief that there are strong similarities between process thought and humanistic psychology holds out a specific kind of promise for the intellectual life and the ministry of the Christian churches. It proffers the hope that a common psycho-philosophical basis might be found for both the intellectual foundations of Christian theology and the practical ministries of the church to individuals and small groups. If something of a synthesis between process thought and humanistic psychology could be established, then the Christian ministry might share a more unified intellectual foundation. This, then, is the gain which might be realized if the alleged affinities between process thought and humanistic psychology can be sustained.

It is my conviction that there are strong affinities between humanistic psychology and process philosophy and theology. But, a closer look will reveal that there are also important differences between these two traditions of thought which must not be overlooked. In this paper, I will clarify one of these differences.

There are connected with some strands of humanistic psychology certain monistic fringes of religious sensibility which are quite antithetical to the major thrust of process theology. Process thought would be critical of these monistic tendencies, and their presence in certain aspects of humanistic psychology seriously strains our first impressions of their spiritual kinship. This note of caution should not be construed as a rejection of the possibilities for creative dialogue between process thought and humanistic psychology. Indeed, in earlier writings, I have helped create the impression of their potential compatability. But I do want to suggest that the fit between these two traditions is by no means perfect and that there are several important "spiritual" differences between them. Furthermore, I will argue that humanistic

155

psychology's contributions will be enhanced if they can be broadened and enriched by the more philosophically adequate psychology
implicit in process thought.

Christian theology has frequently attached itself to
more or less secular psychologies. This was done for a variety of
reasons. Sometimes the motivation was primarily apologetic; it was
thought that expressing Christian truths in the language of a
prestigeous psychology would add to the apparent validity and con-
vincingness of the Christian message. This was certainly in part
the motivation behind Augustine's turn towards Neoplatonic psychology, Aquinas' move towards the philosophical psychology of
Aristotle, Protestant liberalism's use of Kant, and Bultmann's and
Tillich's use of existential phenomenology. Sometimes the motivation was primarily pastoral. This was certainly the case with the
early Christian move toward stoic systems of psychology. Here
there was a search for a practical psychology, more or less system-
atized, which could support the impulse towards the cure of souls
(*cura animarum*).

In the modern period, however, there has been a separation or differentiation of practical psychologies, which aimed at
helping people with problems, from the more philosophical psychologies. The clinical psychologies are concerned with a different
set of problems than those that concern classical modern psychologies, especially those related to the Cartesian or Kantian philosophical psychologies, or the Lockean and Humean tradition of
British empiricism. These latter traditions have been concerned
primarily with the problem of knowledge. The clinical psychologies,
on the other hand, have concerned themselves primarily with generalized personal, emotional, and motivational dysfunctioning.
The clinical psychologies have been concerned with diagnosing and
reorganizing major sections of a troubled person's total personality. The classical modern philosophical psychologies have been
preoccupied on the whole with accounting for how we gain our knowledge or make intellectual and moral judgments.

Since a strong element in the ministry of the church
always has been the guidance of troubled people and the cure of
distraught and spiritually broken souls, it is not surprising that
there has been a significant gravitation towards the secular clinical psychologies. In recent years, the so-called humanistic
clinical psychologies have been of increasing importance for the
ministry of the church, more so than orthodox psychoanalysis and
the behaviorist psychologies. But this has led to the situation
which calls forth the present investigation: is there a significant
relation between the humanistic psychologies which have so influenced the practical ministry of the church and process philosophy
which has influenced the intellectual foundations of Christian
theology?

Humanistic psychology is a movement in the contemporary
behavioral sciences that is complex and difficult to define. And
any remarks about the monism of humanistic psychology do not apply
to the entire range of different psychologies that can lay claim
to a humanistic orientation. Humanistic psychology is generally
defined negatively. The meaning of the phrase as it functions in

contemporary parlance comes from contrasting it with two other
broad schools of psychology, namely psychoanalysis and behaviorism.
These latter schools are thought to be arch typifications of two
kinds of reductionism commonly found in scientific psychology.
Psychoanalysis represents a reductionism in the direction of biological and unconscious determinisms and behaviorisms, and behaviorism represents a reductionism in the direction of environmental
conditioning. On the whole, humanistic psychology refers to any
school of psychology which aspires to study humans without obscuring
their potential freedom, creativity, and individual agency and
initiative. Humanistic psychologies attempt to remain scientific;
they are concerned to chart the regularities of human nature and
the persistent influences which biological constitution and environmental learnings have on human behavior. But they also aspire to
examine such questions as the nature of human freedom, will, creativity, and agency as well as to extend psychology into the study
of such neglected phenomena as artistic, religious, and mystical
activity and states of mind.

There are several strands of humanistic psychology with
varying emphases. Humanistic psychology can include neo-Freudians
such as Adler, Fromm, Horney, and Sullivan, with their heightened
interest in social and cultural factors influencing human behavior.
Although Jung is as biologistic in his own way as Freud, the complexity of his biologism and the seriousness with which he takes
myth and religion often earns him the title of a humanistic psychologist. The existential psychologists such as Sartre,
Binswanger, Boss, May, and many others are often referred to as
humanistic psychologists. They earn this honor because of their
doctrines of human freedom, their theories of human decision and
risk, and their interest in normative visions of authentic human
existence. Psychoanalytic ego psychologists such as Erikson and
Robert White can legitimately be called humanistic psychologists
because of their belief in the initiative and relative autonomy of
the central organizing process known as the ego. Most frequently,
however, humanistic psychology is associated with the psychologists
of self-actualization and human fulfillment such as Maslow, Rogers,
Schutz, and Perls --men also thought to be the grand patriarchs of
the human potential movement.

The remarks in this paper are addressed primarily to
this last group. In the popular mind, psychologists of the ilk of
Maslow, Rogers, Schutz, and Perls are most representative of what
is commonly thought to be humanistic psychology. These are the
names which readily come to mind when it is suggested that humanistic psychology has affinities with process thought. For many
people, these psychologists represent the "heart" of humanistic
psychology. It is not my goal to confirm or deny this judgment.
In fact, there are many reasons to question its legitimacy. But
for the purposes of this paper, I will follow the popular judgment
and aim my remarks at this so-called "heart" of humanistic psychology.

Initial Similarities

In this paper, the term process thought will refer primarily to the philosophical psychologies and philosophies of religion of William James and Alfred North Whitehead. As Eisendrath has pointed out, James and Whitehead have sufficient affinities to justify viewing them as two expressions of a common movement. In addition, James was for a time primarily a psychologist and has recently been rediscovered in studies by Gurwitsch, Wild, Linschoten, Eddie, Wilshire, Reck, and Stevens as one of the greatest philosophical psychologists of all times. In what follows, James will be my primary exemplification of process thought's philosophical psychology and philosophy of religion, although Whitehead will also be cited in order to amplify my remarks. Differences between James and Whitehead will be acknowledged when appropriate.

There is a host of surface similarities between humanistic psychology and process thought. Both are reacting to various forms of philosophical and psychological determinism. Both defend a vision of human freedom and initiative, although humanistic psychology primarily assumes these features of men and makes little effort to ground their possibility conceptually. Both repudiate static, substantial, or essentialistic theories of human identity; they share a view of human existence as primarily a matter of becoming, and both articulate theories of identity that assume the reality of historical and developmental change. There is a tendency in both traditions to use field and gestalt models to articulate aspects of the human self. In this, humanistic psychology has been directly influenced by the gestalt psychologies of Kohler, Wertheimer, Lewin and Goldstein. James and Whitehead independently developed these models out of their respective inquiries into biology and physics. Both traditions tend to ground their theories in phenomenological description. The researches of Wild, Linschoten, Wilshire, Eddie, and Stevens have demonstrated the native phenomenology which runs throughout James' massive two-volume *Principles of Psychology* and his *Essays in Radical Empiricism*. Spiegelberg, Eddie, and Stevens have demonstrated the direct influence that James' chapter on "The Stream of Thought" had on Husserl, specifically James' concept of the "fringe of thought" and his distinction between the topic and the object of thought.[1] It is even better known that Whitehead derived his cosmology in part from a description of the human experience of the transition from inheritance to the integrative moment of decision. There is also a phenomenological aspect in humanistic psychology, especially in the work of Carl Rogers, although it is not rigorous, and there is little awareness of the historical antecedents to his phenomenology.

But these similarities, as profound as they are, should not obscure the fact that the overall vision of man, society, and reality in the two traditions is considerably different. To put it bluntly, the image of the human in the heart of humanistic psychology has much in common with Kierkegaard's aesthetic image of life, whereas the image in James and to some extent Whitehead has more in common with Kierkegaard's ethical and religious stages of life. James often referred to his ideal image of human life as the "strenuous mood" or the "strenuous life."[2]   It was an active, purposeful, and engaged mode of life which emphasized responsibility and care for both the present and the near and distant future. It was the opposite of the "easy-going" and purposeless existence which minimized struggle by minimizing involvement in life and responsible decision.   A similar image of man can be found in Whitehead.   Although the category of the aesthetic is important for both James and Whitehead, they do not promote an "aesthetic" view of life in the Kierkegaardian sense and the dimension of the moral in human life is of crucial importance for them both.

Monistic Fringes

        Although not an explicitly religious movement, humanistic psychology has surrounding it a religious fringe of meaning and sensibility.   On the whole, this fringe of meaning is basically monistic in character.   But what is a monistic religious vision and what difference does it make to suggest humanistic psychology implicitly holds one?   And finally, what is the view of monism held by process thought and what judgments would it make about humanistic psychology if it indeed can be shown to hold such a religious vision?
        Monism is distinguished by two features: 1) the idea that the divinity is a unified, motionless, timeless, unconditioned, and self-caused perfection which is the total and complete cause of all finite realities, and 2) that the human self in its depth is a manifestation of the divine life itself.   Both James and Whitehead vigorously criticized monism, James directly and Whitehead more indirectly.   James' criticism was developed primarily on moral grounds and Whitehead's on cosmological grounds.   James saw monism as depicting an overly secure, inevitably quietistic, and basically indifferent world that extinguishes human freedom, responsibility, and a realistic grasp of the moral evils of this world.   Whitehead shared this moral concern but expressed his criticism more in terms of accounting for both process and unity in a changing world that includes the realms of both history *and* nature.
        But what is the evidence for the belief that there is a monistic fringe of religious sensibility connected with humanistic psychology?   And what are the moral and behavioral consequences of this that would put it in conflict with process thought?
        Two types of evidence can be cited.   First there is a tendency in some expressions of humanistic psychology to equate religious experience with mystical experience and to thereby imply that a monistic view of God and the world is religiously normative. Second, there is a tendency in other expressions of humanistic psychology to collapse the self into a biological actualization tendency and to elevate this actualization tendency to the level of a divine immanence inexorably pushing man towards the good.   This second view borders on monism because there is no authentic self other than this biological actualization tendency, and this tendency, in the writings of some of this school, becomes almost sacralized and easily takes on the aura of an ultimate principle.

Humanistic psychology has affinities with the radical empiricism of James in his desire to be open to all experience and to erect a psychology and philosophy which would exclude no basic fact of experience from consideration. This is why James as a psychologist and philosopher was open to such things as religious experience and even psychic phenomena. Maslow is an example of a humanistic psychologist who has carried the impulse of James' radical empiricism forward and made ground-breaking, albeit impressionistic, studies of such traditionally taboo phenomena as mystical or, as Maslow calls them, "peak experiences." However, Maslow's description of the peak experience has a monistic ring, suggests a monistic view of the world, and even indirectly implies a monistic view of God. According to Maslow, the peak experience is timeless and spaceless just as monistic visions of God depict Him as above the movements and relativities of time and space.[3] Maslow's list of adjectives describing the peak of experience contains such words as "wholeness," "perfection," "completion," and "self-sufficiency," words frequently used to describe the God of monism.[4] Elsewhere he describes the experience as "perfect, complete and needs nothing else. It is sufficient to itself. It is felt as being intrinsically necessary and inevitable. It is just as good as it should be."[5]

In these descriptions, Maslow is primarily trying to distinguish the kind of cognition connected with peak experiences from the cognition of ordinary consciousness. The former he calls Being-cognition and sees it involved with ends and intrinsic values. Ordinary cognition he calls deficiency cognition and sees it as primarily interested in purposes, interests, and means to ends. What is at issue, however, is not Maslow's distinction between levels of consciousness nor his description of the two levels Our concern is his tendency to generalize his description of Being-cognition into a vision of God and the world. One can see this when he writes,

> The philosophical implications here are tremendous. If, for the sake of argument, we accept the thesis that in peak-experience the nature of reality itself *may* be seen more clearly and its essence penetrated more profoundly,

then in the peak experience we may be gaining our most accurate insights into the nature of being.[6] And then he compares the peak experience with the concept of God. "The gods who can contemplate and encompass the whole of Being and who therefore understand it," he tells us, "must see it as good, just, inevitable, and must see 'evil' as a product of limited or selfish vision. . ."[7] In these quotes we see Maslow suggesting that the key to Being or God is the peak experience, that the shape of the world as it stands has about it a certain inevitability, and evil is basically an illusion. These views, as we will see more clearly later, are basic concepts of a monistic religious vision.

James was critical of monism for a variety of reasons. On the whole, however, his criticism was based on moral considerations. A world in which God was the all-enveloping, pervasive,

and solely determinative influence would be so secure, so firmly
in the hands of the divine, that risk, danger, moral responsibility,
and freedom would seem illogical and uncalled for.[8] Quietism,
indifference, and the attitude of "I don't care" can easily become
the fruits of such a vision. In light of these concerns of James,
it is interesting to note that in an article entitled "Some Dangers
of Being-Cognition," Maslow later tries to correct some of the
implications of his early essays on peak experiences. He admits
Being-cognition can sometimes lead to a static and inactive style
of life, that it may make one less responsible in helping other
people, that it can lead to "fatalism" and a "blurring of everyday
values," and to a "loss of taste."[9] In actual practice, Maslow
has found no "peakers" or self-actualizers who are actually like
this. This is because people having peak experiences spend most
of their time in ordinary consciousness, making ordinary decisions,
reacting to the good and the bad, liking some things and disliking
others like most other ordinary people.[10] In fact, according to
Maslow people having peak experiences are only relatively more open,
accepting, tolerant, nonjudgmental and nondeficiency motivated than
other people. Here we find Maslow sensing that his description of
the peak experience, and the monistic world view it implies, logically leads to quietism and indifference, and in a cultural setting
other than the activistic West, might indeed produce such behavior.
He does not understand that the mystical experience is a too narrow
and insufficient ground upon which to build a religious vision of
the world. Both James and Whitehead included the mystical but
constructed a religious vision which made the broadest possible
use of ordinary experience as well.

But there is a second way in which there is a monistic
element at the heart of humanistic psychology. This has to do with
its tendency to equate the self with the actualization tendency of
the organism as a whole and to romanticize and sacralize this tendency. If the actualization tendency becomes elevated to a sacred
ultimate principle, and the self becomes identified with this tendency, then the human self becomes almost absorbed into the divine
immanence implicit in this drive towards actualization.

The writings of Carl Rogers best illustrate my point.
Rogers, as do most of the writers in the heart of humanistic psychology, makes great use of Kurt Goldstein's concept of the actualization tendency.[11] Goldstein devised the concept to explain a
tendency within brain-damaged soldiers to integrate fragments of
impulses and behavior into a functioning whole. Both Rogers and
Maslow have considerably extended the principle. In their hands,
the principle has become the basic biological source for all human
valuations. It has become elevated to the level of becoming the
grounds for value judgments about both the meaning of health and
the meaning of the ethically good.[12] A similar process can be
found in the writings of Fritz Perls and William Schutz.

For Rogers, the major problem with human beings occurs
when the self or self-concept becomes estranged from this actualization tendency. This occurs through the process of socialization
when the infant and child, in an effort to retain the love of
parents and parent surrogates, incorporates within his or her own

self-definition their values or conditions of worth.[13] When this happens, the child gives up his own direct organismic valuations and begins to emulate the values of others. This leads to sickness, conflict, and a final confusion of values. Behind this point of view is the assumption that if the body, its actualization tendency, and its organismic valuations could function unfettered by tradition, culture, and the teachings of parents, there would emerge a free enterprise of harmonious interests which would lead to a healthy society full of healthy individuals. It is further held that in this state of affairs the "self" as a set of differentiated symbols and propositions would gradually become dissolved and finally become identical to the actualization tendency and its organismic valuations. The actualization tendency becomes the normative source for all individual and social values as well as all values related to both health and the morally good. A similar point of view on the relation of the actualization tendency to values is set forth in Maslow's "Psychological Data and Human Values,"[14] and Perl's "Morality, Ego Boundary, and Aggression."[15]
Even if the self becomes identified with the actualization tendency and the actualization tendency becomes the source of all values for the good, one cannot say that these psychologists explicitly deify the actualization tendency. They end in a romantic and idealistic humanism with its vaulted and uncomplicated vision of a pre-existing oneness and harmony in the universe--a humanism with which, as Tillich points out, Protestantism has frequently made alliances.[16] But it is only a small step for the religious imagination to make this humanism of inner harmony a veritable monism of religious sensibility. Maslow's work has doubtless fed various monistic impulses in the more transpersonal mystically-oriented psychologies which he has inspired. One instance of this can be found in the writings of the guru of the encounter culture William Schutz. Schutz in his widely popular book entitled *Here Comes Everybody* admits that he has taken the step from humanistic psychology into spirituality and mysticism. In doing this, he has found God within. Not only has he found God within, but he makes an equation between the self and God.[17]

Process Thought and Monism

Regardless of the many affinities which process thought has with humanistic psychology, the former has taken a variety of steps to guarantee itself against a monistic distortion of its intentions. Throughout James' career, he was concerned to expose the inadequacies of monism. In some of his earliest essays, and especially in his *Will to Believe*, he referred to himself as a pluralist. As early as his "On Some Hegelisms" and as late as his *Pluralistic Universe*, he argued against the tenets of various forms of monistic spirituality.[18] He was critical of both rationalistic monisms associated with the names of Hegel, Bradley, Lotze, Green and McTaggart and a wide range of mystical monisms. The impulse behind both types of monism was the pervasive human need to live in

a secure and harmonious universe. This was finally the motivation
behind the tortuous logic of monistic rationalism as well as the
experiential mystical forms which have more in common with the
incipient monism of our humanistic psychologists. James had sympathy for this need and struggled to accommodate it in his own religious vision. But he did not capitulate to monism in either its
rationalistic or mystical forms. He saw it as spawning an image
of such a static and all-determinative foundation to life that all
individual risk, freedom, decision, and moral responsibility finally
would be rendered meaningless. In his *Pluralistic Universe*, James
developed the outlines of a vision of God's relation to the world
that anticipated the more carefully worked out position of Whitehead
and Hartshorne. He developed an image of a finite God who was related to all creatures, who knew all creatures, who influenced all
things, but who was not the sole determinative influence over all
things.[19] It was a God related to history and time, who was subject to the influence of the world, and who was moved by the passions of finite actualities.[20] In *A Pluralistic Universe*, James
used the writings of Fechner and an analogy from his own psychology
to construct a model of how more inclusive forms of consciousness
organize within themselves simpler forms of consciousness without
completely obliterating them.[21] He applied this analogy to God's
relation to the world in an effort to demonstrate that although God
was related to the world, the world to some extent transcended God
and enjoyed degrees of independence, freedom, and responsibility.[22]
     On the other hand, Whitehead sometimes appears to approach
a monistic religious sensibility. In *Religion in the Making*, he
refers to God as the "nontemporal," suggesting an image of God as
the unmoved mover which is unaffected by time, history or finitude.[23]
But in the last pages of this book[24] and the last chapter of *Process*
and Reality we learn that this is not what Whitehead means.[25] The
primordial nature of God, although the perfect and complete en-
visionment of all abstract possibilities, is itself only an abstraction from the full reality of God. God in his fullness includes a consequent nature as well which brings time, history, and
the actual creativity of finite individuals into the very experience
of God.[26] Hence, the monistic spirituality of certain aspects of
humanistic psychology which sometimes suggests that God or god-
likeness is above time, space, and the polarities of changing experience is shared by neither James nor Whitehead.
     Nor does process thought collapse the self into some near-
divine biological immanence as is widely done in humanistic psychology. James could agree with most of these psychologists that
the interests of the self are deeply motivated by the wide range
of man's biological tendencies and instincts. But James was no
instinctual utopian or romanticizer of man's biological potential.
James was far more situational, ecological, and pluralistic in his
understanding of the biology of humans than are the humanistic psychologists we are reviewing. For James man was the most instinctual
of all creatures, although he, like Freud, believed that man's instincts are highly plastic and easily susceptible to distortion
and disorganization. There were, for James, instincts toward curi-
osity, play, and even toward higher forms of moral and intellectual

judgments.[28] But as Harry Harlowe has recently pointed out, James'
instinct theory was correct in seeing that both the sequence of
their emergence and the pattern of their mutual inhibitions are
crucial in determining which instincts become dominant and habitual
and which languish into confusion or disuse.[29]

James trusted the body but not exclusively. Consciousness
and the self were bodily functions for James but they could be
differentiated from other bodily functions and had a distinct role
to play. Whereas humanistic psychology tries to correct the confusions of consciousness with the intuitions of the body, James
believed it was the role of consciousness to clarify and control
the instinctual confusions of the body.[30]

Nor was there any tendency to identify the self with God.
James did speak in his *Varieties of Religious Experience*[31] and *A
Pluralistic Universe*[32] of our empirical selves as being continuous
with a larger self or "more" which may be a part of the divine life
itself. But continuity was never construed by James to mean identity. In fact, it was precisely this issue of how humans could be
conceived as both related to yet separate from the divine that he
was struggling with so creatively in his Hibbert Lectures. By the
same token, God was never identified with any single biological
impulse or with nature as a whole. God was related to nature as
its ideal tendency, but this never took the form of a single biological tendency which was the source of all values for both health
and the morally good. In the end, James maintained an image of the
"spiritual self" and an "inner principle of personal identity"
which were related to but not identical with either biological tendencies or with God.

Nor is the self in Whitehead identified with any set of
biological tendencies or with God Himself. Biological tendencies
are generally associated by Whitehead with the inheritances of the
past. This would be true even for the more elevated tendencies
such as the tendency towards growth and actualization. The self
is influenced by these inheritances from the past, but is not
completely determined by them. Even though Whitehead believed
that all actual entities contain both mental and physical poles,
he never collapsed the mental completely into the physical or
bodily pole, as some humanistic psychologies are inclined to do.
The self was for Whitehead a particular historical or serial ordering of occasions primarily associated with the mental pole.[33] The
self or soul is dependent on the body for contact with the external
world, and the body is thought to be the soul's immediate environment. But there are various ways in which Whitehead saw the self
as differentiated from all biological inheritances. It was the
seat of the subjective aim of an organism which ordered and selected
from the inheritances of the past. It was in this way that Whitehead tried to account for the possibility of real freedom and real
transcendence of human beings over biological tendencies, even the
most constructive ones. Furthermore, Whitehead made a clear distinction between the subjective aim of an individual and the initial aim that God may have for that individual. The subjective
aim is never completely identified with or determined by God's

initial aim.[34] In this way, Whitehead avoids the mystical and monistic over-identification of the self with the divine.

The weight of these remarks has been primarily historical and comparative. It is my conviction that a longer, more leisurely, and more carefully argued essay could demonstrate the general superiority of the process tradition on the issues discussed. This is not to say that the humanistic tradition of psychology is wrong or not to be trusted. It is, rather, to recognize it for what it is --primarily a clinically based set of psychological concepts which is trying to extend itself into wider areas. Its desire to develop a broadened understanding of psychology is to be commended. But we must be reminded that it aspires to do this without the benefit of careful philosophical criticism and assistance. The affinities between process thought and the "heart" of humanistic psychology are sufficiently apparent to justify a careful dialogue between them. Such a dialogue might be of great benefit to humanistic psychology; it might help to clarify some of its philosophical foundations and some of its implications which, if carried to an extreme, would put humanistic psychology into considerable tension not only with process thought but with the major concerns of Christian theology itself.

If I have demonstrated my case that there is a monistic fringe to certain strands of humanistic psychology, then it is clear that at best it becomes an ambiguous friend to Christian theology. Monism is not only alien to process thought, it is alien to the central impulses of Christian sensibility. The Judeo-Christian tradition in its most authentic moments has consistently emphasized an image of a personal God who is both related to the world and also transcends it. The Old Testament and the New Testament alike portray God as the transcendent creator of the world who also enters into the history of the world--shapes and influences it as well as suffers its pain with it--something like the way one human being enters into the life of another. It has been because process thought has given Christian theology a philosophically powerful way of articulating this image of God that there has grown up this mutual alliance between them. In addition, even though Christianity has at times depicted a most intimate relation between God and the soul of man, it has always resisted stating this relation in terms of an identity. This implication of monistic philosophies is equally at odds with the central witness of the Christian tradition.

All of this suggests that if humanistic psychology is to be used in the context of Christian ministry it should undergo certain philosophical and theological reconstructions. In saying this, I do not mean to suggest that any psychology is wrong simply because it fails to agree with a particular religious tradition, be it Christian or some other. Rather, both Christianity and humanistic psychology must be submitted to a more rigorous philosophical analysis. The process philosophical tradition may be able to provide such an analysis. In the case of humanistic psychology, when this is attempted, certain aspects of its monistic fringe of meaning will come under serious question.

NOTES AND REFERENCES

1. See Aron Gurwitsch, "William James' Theory of the 'Transitive Parts' of the Stream of Consciousness," *Studies in Phenomenology and Psychology* (Evanston: Northwestern University Press, 1966), pp. 301-331; John Wild, *The Radical Empiricism of William James* (New York: Anchor Books, 1970); Hans Linschoten, *On the Way Towards a Phenomenological Psychology* (Pittsburgh: Duquesne University Press, 1968); James Eddie, "Critical Studies: William James and Phenomenology," *The Review of Metaphysics*, Vol. 23 (March, 1970), pp. 481-526; Bruce Wilshire, *William James and Phenomenology* (Bloomington: University of Indiana Press, 1968); Andrew Reck, "The Philosophical Psychology of William James," *Southern Journal of Philosophy*, Vol. 9 (Fall, 1971), pp. 293-312; Richard Stevens, *James and Husserl: The Foundations of Meaning* (Hague: Martinus Nijhoff, 1974).

2. Herbert Spiegelberg, *The Phenomenological Movement* (Hague: Martinus Nijhoff, 1960), pp. 66-69; Eddie, "Critical Studies: William James and Phenomenology," pp. 481-526; Stevens, *James and Husserl*, pp. 24-46.

3. William James, *The Will to Believe* (New York: Dover, 1956), p. 211.

4. Abraham Maslow, *Toward a Psychology of Being* (New York: Van Nostrand, 1962), p. 76.

5. *Ibid.*, p. 78.

6. *Ibid.*, p. 76.

7. *Ibid.*, p. 76-78.

8. *Ibid.*, p. 77.

9. William James, *The Meaning of Truth* (Ann Arbor: University of Michigan Press, 1970), pp. 226-29.

10. Abraham Maslow, *Toward a Psychology of Being*, pp. 110-112.

11. *Ibid.*, pp. 117-18.

12. Carl Rogers, *Client-Centered Therapy* (Boston: Houghton Mifflin, 1951), p. 487.

13. Abraham Maslow, *Toward a Psychology of Being*, pp. 141-156; Carl Rogers, *Person to Person* (New York: Pocket Books, 1971), pp. 4-21.

14. Rogers, *Client-Centered Therapy*, pp. 498-503.

15. Maslow, *Toward a Psychology of Being*, pp. 141-156.

16. Fritz Perls, "Morality, Ego Boundaries, and Aggression," *Complex* (Winter, 1954), p. 145.

17. Paul Tillich, *The Protestant Era* (Chicago: University of Chicago Press, 1948), pp. 115-135.

18. William Schutz, *Here Comes Everybody* (New York: Harper and Row, 1971), pp. 57-63.

19. James, *The Will to Believe*, pp. 263-98; *Essays in Radical Empiricism and A Pluralistic Universe* (New York: E. P. Dutton, 1971), pp. 142-61, 274.

20. James, *A Pluralistic Universe*, pp. 268-69.

21. *Ibid.*, pp. 273-74.

22. *Ibid.*, pp. 185-225.

23. *Ibid.*, p. 269.

24. A.N. Whitehead, *Religion in the Making* (New York: Meridian Books, 1960), p. 88.

25. *Ibid.*, p. 147.

26. A.N. Whitehead, *Process and Reality* (New York: Harper and Row, 1960), pp. 519-33.

27. *Ibid.*, p. 524.

28. William James, *The Principles of Psychology*, Vol. II (New York: Dover Publications, 1950), pp. 383-441; see also Vol. I, pp. 317-25.

29. On the instinctual foundations of intellectual judgments see "Necessary Truths and the Effects of Experience," *The Principles of Psychology*, Vol. II, pp. 625-631.

30. Harry Harlow, "William James and Instinct Theory," in *Willian James: Unfinished Business*, ed. by Robert B. McLeod (Washington, D.C.:   American Psychological Association, 1969), pp. 21-30.

31. James, *The Principles of Psychology*, Vol. I, p. 285.

32. James, *The Varieties of Religious Experience* (New York: Mentor Books, 1958), pp. 385-88.

33. James, *A Pluralistic Universe*, p. 267.

34. Whitehead, *Process and Reality*, pp. 50-52.

35. *Ibid.*, pp. 372-375.

SOCIAL JUSTICE AND THE SERVICED SOCIETY

by
John Fish

In the 1960's the church was involved in struggles for
social justice. My own limited participation in that struggle was
in Woodlawn on the south side of Chicago. Woodlawn was a poor
black community. It was not so much a community as a colony, controlled and exploited by external interests that profited from
neighborhood change and decay. As in similar neighborhoods Woodlawn found itself acted upon by helping agencies that did not help,
representatives who did not represent and service agencies that
were alien and insensitive. A traditional interpretation defined
Woodlawn as a sick community requiring intervention and external
management. Woodlawn's condition, however, was not one of sickness
but of powerlessness. At that time I was doing graduate work at
The University of Chicago where Al Pitcher helped me reappropriate
the wisdom of Reinhold Niebuhr, that the social expression of love
is justice and that justice requires that the powerless be enabled
to check the pretentions and exploitation of the powerful. So,
the First Presbyterian Church along with other churches that shared
this framework entered the struggle for justice and cast their lot
(and resources) with the powerless.

I mention this at the outset because it illustrates an
ethical posture which a segment of the Christian community took on
many fronts, civil rights and war resistance being the most notable
at the time. It was a posture informed, at least for many, by a
Niebuhrian analysis of love, justice, and power in society.

Now is a different social situation. We are closer to
1984 in both ways. The church has retreated from urban struggles
for social justice in the name of "reconciliation." In the place
of justice we have personal solutions for social ills.

In this paper I want to examine our emerging social condition and to suggest that this condition obscures the struggle
for social justice. I will elaborate on what John McKnight of
Northwestern University has called "the serviced society,"[1] and
examine how this serviced society immobilizes us. I will further
suggest that a reappropriation of the insights of Reinhold Niebuhr
might provide us with ways both of recognizing our current dis-ease
and of struggling to deal with it.

It is apparent that we have become a service economy.
In the past two generations we have moved from a society whose
economy was based on the production of goods to a society whose
work force is largely in the provision of services. About 70 per
cent of the civilian job holders in the United States earn a living

serving each other in some way. This trend is expected to continue.
By the year 2000 a small per cent of the labor force in this country
will be able to produce all the goods we use or sell. This trend
is the result of advanced technology in the United States and also
of the relative increase of labor intensive production in countries
where labor is cheaper and less organized. Since fewer people are
needed to grow, assemble and manufacture things, more people will
be helpers, facilitators, communicators, programmers, and planners
in government, finance, education, health care, trade, transporta-
tion, and social services simply to provide means for distributing
income. There are, for example, over 200 careers related to health
care and most of them have been established, with training programs,
professional associations and journals, in the past twenty years.
Each year more emerge. A vivid way of indicating the shift in our
economy is the observation that the cost of each new automobile
includes more health care than steel. That is to say, General
Motors spends more on health insurance for its workers than it does
on steel for its cars. Service has become our major business.
This is clearly where the jobs are.
        The meaning of this emerging service economy is not al-
ways clear. It is generally explained not simply as a necessary
response to avoid high unemployment; it is heralded, rather, as
the pathway to the good society, a society that takes care of its
people, a society where people help each other. To provide services is to do good. To purchase service is to improve your well
being. The social benefits of a service economy are regarded as
the blessing of an advanced culture. We are led to regard the
growth of all the helping professions, a major segment of the service sector, as a good made possible by our affluence and technology and pursued because of our humanistic impulse. This assessment,
I am arguing, needs to be questioned.
        The basic question is not the desirability of or the need
for basic essential services. It is rather the impact of a service-
oriented economy, dominated by over-extended service systems, on
our political, social, and personal lives. It is the contention
of this paper that the benign drift toward a serviced society is
deceptive and ominous. A closer look at some of the major characteristics of a serviced society will reveal the grounds for alarm
and uncover some of the fundamental political, social, and ethical
issues at stake.
        In a serviced society there are people with problems and
needs, there are people who define and answer problems and needs,
and there are institutions or agencies that link service consumers
and service producers. Let us consider these three related parts
of a serviced society - clients, professionals, and service institutions.
        First, consider how a serviced society needs, even
creates, clients. It has been clear how a high production growth-
oriented economy has had to stimulate consumption needs in order
to keep growing. The demand for more and for new products is
based in large part on our ability, through advertising and marketing techniques to create needs for things we produce. As we
have moved into a service economy we have stimulated the consumption of services just as we have stimulated the consumption of goods.

Clients are created because a serviced society needs needs.
         Just as people can be made to feel unfulfilled or un-
successful unless they have certain things, so also they can be
made to feel deficient or deviant and in need of services. Almost
any condition, when defined as a problem, can be a condition in
need of a service. Simply give the condition a name (preferably
in Latin), call it a deficiency (or better yet, a disease), and you
have provided the groundwork for a new service. As traditional
professions expand, new professions emerge, and non-professional
services mushroom, we become in ever-increasing areas of life passive
clients dependent upon experts to execute our foreign policy, fix
our gadgets, or make us feel loved.
         Eric Fromm has often commented upon the effect of a con-
sumption-oriented industrial society on the individual.

> It transforms him into *Homo Consumens*, the total consumer, whose
> only aim is to have more and to use more. This society produces
> many useless things and to the same degree many useless people.
> Man, as a cog in the production machine, becomes a thing, and ceases
> to be human. . . . He is the eternal suckling with the open mouth,
> "taking in," without effort and without inner activeness, whatever
> the boredom-preventing (and boredom-producing) industry forces upon
> him, limited only by what he can afford . . . The passiveness of man
> in industrial society today is one of his most characteristic and
> pathological features.[2]

This pathological passivity, engendered by the consumption of things
in an industrial society, is compounded in a serviced society where
the submissive consumption of services places *Homo Consumens* in a
life-long condition of patienthood taking in not simply the material
goods of the industrial economy but also the therapies and service
goods of a serviced society. One way to characterize the serviced
society, then, is to view it as a client society peopled not so
much by active citizens shaping their destiny as by passive clients
being acted upon.
         Secondly, and implied by the first point, a serviced
society is not only a clientized society but also a professionalized
society. Clients, as McKnight points out are "people who believe
that they will be better because someone else knows better."[3] Professionals are people who "know better." In a serviced society
there is both a proliferation of professions and ever-expanding
systems of professional domination. With the growing complexity
of a technological society more and more segments of life are controlled by experts. The creation of clients and the growing control
of professionals go hand in hand.
         One critic of this move toward professional domination
observed that we have in the past been "inclined to look upon professions as among the wages of original sin," the need for which
was to equip man against "bouts with adversity, with the State and
with his Maker," so that "concessions to exclusive practice were
granted only to medicine, law, and divinity - the 'true' or 'learned'
professions."[4] Now there are not three but hundreds of "professions."
We are no longer suspicious of them. In fact we exalt profession-

alism and use the language of professionalism in almost every field of work. This process of professionalization has several interesting characteristics. One analyst put it this way:

> In the final analysis, professionalization is primarily an achievement of "autonomy" which implies (1) knowing what's best for the client, (2) subjecting one's decisions only to a peer review of colleagues, and (3) establishing all standards of behavior through a professional association.[5]

This sums it up. The professional knows what is best for the client. And the client is allegedly unable to judge the adequacy of professional decisions, behavior, and standards. These are the basic elements of professional control. In a serviced society the role of the citizen is diminished. Not only does the professional know what is best for the client, she/he knows what is wrong with the client.

One of the major tasks of the provider of services is, as I have indicated earlier, to stimulate needs for services. An interesting expression of this task is found in an article in the *Menninger* (Foundation) *Perspective* entitled "Help for the Everyday Problems of Living," where the author makes a case for providing professional help for people's day-to-day "problems." The writer outlines a variety of these problems in everyone's life and argues that:

> Each one of these individuals may at some point devoutly wish that there was a way to get outside guidance and help for his problem. . . People deserve that kind of help. *It is not a luxury but a right. And it is the task of helpers in this day to invent new forms of giving help.*[6]   (Italics added)

This moves us toward the ultimate expression of legitimizing a serviced society, where clienthood becomes a right and professional expansion a virtue. Illich succinctly observed that "in a triumphantly therapeutic society, everybody can make himself into a therapist and someone else into his client."[7] Of course there are incentives for inventing "new forms of giving help." This not only creates clients, it also creates jobs for professionals.

A third characteristic of the serviced society is the concentration of power in centralized service bureaucracies, professional groups, and the corporate interests to which they are often wed. The way services are defined, the manner in which they are provided and the judgments about their effectiveness are increasingly controlled from the top by what might be regarded as service monopolies.

The corporate medical monopoly, once a decentralized "cottage industry," now has major control over (1) the definition of health care and appropriate therapies (primarily "the pill and the knife"), (2) the organization of medical services (primarily in hospitals), and (3) the planning and growth of the system (primarily for the benefit of the providers). Corporate medicine is indeed the result of a complex mix of interests involving insurance,

the medical supply industry, hospitals, research centers, associations of medical professionals, universities, and government. The
result is that Big Medicine is perceived by many as having been
organized primarily around the interests of the providers and sup-
pliers. The interest of system users-- for access, quality and
affordable medical service-- has suffered. Doctors have fled the
inner city and rural areas. Primary care facilities are scarce,
being replaced by the emergency rooms of hospitals. In general,
medical services in urban America are less accessible as they become concentrated in the growing medical empires that are clustered
around our teaching and research centers.

Service institutions and practices in general are shaped
more to meet the needs and interests of the professionals than the
clients. This is especially evident in urban America. The concentration of power in governmental and service bureaucracies--and
the allied commercial interests--is, I believe, directly related
to the destruction of the urban neighborhood. Once the life blood
of the American city, our urban neighborhoods are marked by aban-
doned buildings, high crime, poor schools, faltering services, and
a sense of frustration and powerlessness on the part of the millions who live there. Urban neighborhoods have been cut up by
superhighways, displaced by universities and other institutions,
wiped out by urban renewal, and milked by a variety of real estate
and financial exploiters. But even more devastating is the way
they have been robbed of a capacity to initiate and develop programs and to influence decisions that affect their character and
cohesiveness. Community organizations that have tried to establish
countervailing centers of power and to gain some measure of influence over local affairs have been viewed as a nuisance or threat
by the downtown centers of power and have been undermined, immo-
bilized, bought off or co-opted. As political effectiveness at
the local level is destroyed, our neighborhoods deteriorate. As
communities they are no longer able to enlist the will and energy
or to channel the vitalities and affections of their citizens.

The centralized governing, planning and service agencies,
unchecked by neighborhood interests and values follow their own
institutional, financial and technological imperatives. The result
is the neighborhoods are stripped of communal power, citizens become clients dependent upon centralized institutional services,
and corporate and bureaucratized centers of power gain a monopoly
over our social imagination.

If these three characteristics of a serviced society
appear overstated it has been done both to highlight the dangers
of an apparently benign drift and to isolate specific ominous aspects.

If this gloomy perspective is even partly true why are
we not alarmed at this eclipse of democracy? Why do we not readily
perceive this loss of citizenship? Why do we not resist more vigorously professional and corporate domination? McKnight suggests
that the major reason is that a serviced society wears the mask of
love. Services are a commodity of care and care is the expression
of love. Who can be against love? Services are thus immune from

political debate. They are almost by definition good because they
are seen in terms of caring for and helping people.
        Behind the mask is, for one thing, jobs and control of
jobs. The experience of the Poverty Program in the 60's is a good
example. It was heralded as an expression of care. The nation
was going to help the millions of Americans who were locked in
poverty and had been cut off from access to the American Dream.
To do this the Poverty Program mobilized an army of helpers to
service the poor: teacher aids, case workers, counsellors, mental
health workers, recreation supervisors, therapists, police aids,
land use planners, etc. If the poor were not particularly helped
by this War on Poverty (and they were not) another group of people
was - the helpers. Behind the mask of servicing the poor was a
very real need to provide service jobs.
        Service systems, behind the apolitical mask of caring,
are indeed very political. Politics has to do with who gets what,
how, and when. These systems are clearly ways of allocating power
and resources. Consider again Corporate Medicine. As a system of
caring for health, modern medicine, is questionable. In fact
medicine may have less to do with health and care than most people
imagine.[8] But as a soaring business, approaching 9 per cent of
the GNP and creating an apparently endless array of new jobs,
Corporate Medicine is doing very well indeed. This concentration
of power and resources expands behind the mask of caring which
suggests "the more, the better," and "no cost is too great." The
chairman of Abbott Laboratories, a multinational corporation with
over one billion dollars annual sales of "health care" products
naturally expresses this notion.

> Expanded health care, in the form of sophisticated techological
> advances, will bring benefits in prolonged life and improved health
> which should far outweigh any increased cost.[9] (Italics added)

One can discover many examples of this when-it-comes-to-care-no-
cost-is-too-great ideology. Simply put, in a serviced society,
this apolitical rhetoric of helping-caring-loving-healing-serving
masks a system of allocating money, jobs, and power. McKnight
summarizes the point clearly.

> Behind the mask is simply the servicer, his systems, techniques
> and technologies - a business in need of markets, an economy seek-
> ing new growth potential, professionals in need of an income.[10]

        We should consider more closely how a serviced society
obscures fundamental political and ethical issues. If we look again
at the major characteristics of the serviced society, we can see
that it does so in at least three ways: (1) it becomes a substitute for politics, (2) it can become a denial of authentic caring,
and (3) it obscures issues of social justice.
        1. A serviced society is a substitute for politics.
McKnight points out how a serviced society "translates political
functions into technical and technological problems."[11] Others
also have drawn our attention to what is often referred to as the

"medicalization" of society.12 It is the transformation of people into patients, citizens into clients, social problems into illnesses, problem solving into therapies, and politics into technocratic administration.

In a serviced society, the democratic ideology, which claims for the citizen a measure of power in the body politic, is replaced by a therapeutic ideology. McKnight summarizes the political significance of the therapeutic ideology this way.

> (a) The basic problem is you, (b) the resolution of your problem is my professional control, and (c) my control is your help. The essence of the medical ideology is its capacity to hide control behind the magic cloak of therapeutic help. The power of this mystification is so great that the therapeutic ideology is being adopted and adapted by other interests that recognize that their control mechanisms are dangerously overt. Thus medicine is the paradigm for modernized domination. Indeed, its cultural hegemony is so potent that the very meaning of politics is being underminded.13

In the field of medicine this ideology is most overt (I have illustrated salient features of a serviced society with examples from modern medicine because it is a paradigm for the more general process of medicalization). The use of psychoactive drugs is promoted behind the mask of health care. Valium and Librium are the two most widely prescribed drugs in the United States. These and the other central nervous system agents are used to "treat" problems that by the doctors own admission are essentially social and political rather than physiological. The tensions of modern society, alienation from work, problems at home, anxieties over a variety of social ills are treated as pathological. A study published by a group of medical students issues the warning.

> By redefining social and political problems as medical ones, the doctors who are dispensing these drugs are functioning as agents of social control. . . The drug industry has succeeded in convincing doctors that the symptoms of the ills of our society are actually "personal hangups." The doctors respond by prescribing a medication, implying to the patient that they have defined the problem and can alleviate it. This substituting of a medical problem requiring a drug for a political problem requiring confrontation of oppressive conditions, works as a potent political sedative preventing social change.14

Examples of chemical solutions to social problems are many. The use of "pediatric stimulants" to control children raises obvious questions. Up to one million children receive psychoactive drugs to control their behavior in school. A report alarmed at the use of these drugs observed that:

> The efforts of the educational system to shift attention from its own failure onto its clients, the students, coincided with the drug company's desire to extend the market for Ritalin for children.

Students failed or misbehaved in school, it was claimed because they had a medical disorder, and Ritalin provided the chemical cure.[15]

A good example of a cure in search of a disease, a service in search of a client, a medical solution to a social problem.

This therapeutic ideology, substituting service for politics, although most overt in medicine, is evident in other strategies in a serviced society. A "medical" interpretation of social problems has been applied, for example, to dealing with the poor, especially the black urban poor, whose neighborhoods are defined as sick and for whom service "solutions" are prescribed. The poor are defined as afflicted by a wide range of deficiencies: weak ego strength, pre-conventional morality, limited time horizon, ambivalence toward property, propensity toward crime and more, depending on the particular diagnosis.[16] The essence of this approach is clear. There is nothing wrong with the existing arrangements of power and control in urban America which might require political action. There is something wrong with the poor which requires therapy. Politics is replaced by service.

This substitution obscures the political condition that renders society unhealthy and inhibits action that could address the economic and political causes of our distressing condition.

2. A serviced society is a denial of authentic caring. I have indicated earlier that service is regarded as a commodity of "care." That perception needs to be questioned. Service can be a substitute for care. The caring goals of service become displaced by the institutional needs of the service agencies. We have found out that the health care system cannot provide health. Since it cannot provide health, the medical system, through a displacement of goals, provides something else - access to medical services. The War on Poverty could not provide an avenue out of poverty, but it could provide some access to the poverty services. Access to institutional services becomes a substitute commodity for the rhetorical goals of the service: medicine for health, schooling for education, policing for security, legal services for justice, detention for rehabilitation.

Ivan Illich pushes this argument one step further. Medicine is not only a substitute for health, it is detrimental to health. Illich argues that medical over-expansion is illness-producing. The key to his perspective is the notion of iatrogenic illness, illness induced by the medical system itself. The illness producing aspect of the medical system is not simply the risk of clinical illness related to medical intervention, as great as this is, but also the illness of clienthood when we are stripped of the power to heal ourselves.

Beyond a certain level, the heteronomous management of life will inevitably first restrict, then cripple, and finally paralyze the organism's nontrivial responses, and what was meant to constitute health care will turn into a specific form of health denial.[17]

Authentic help enables and empowers. Service, when mediated through service monopolies, tends to disable and rob of power.

The substitution of service for care tends to become crippling and
render people impotent. The communal resources of mutual help -
in families, churches, neighborhoods, and social groups - are weak-
ened and replaced by institutional services.
        The notion of social iatrogenisis is worth pursuing.
Many of our social problems may be caused, or at least aggravated,
by those institutions that are charged with the task of solving the
problem. We can think of the role of the FHA in urban neighborhood
decay, or how slum clearance in the 1950's led to slum creation, or
how the welfare system serves to sustain the debilitating welfare
cycle. The "solutions" fail but the failure is blamed on the
client. And the client is increasingly powerless to discover or
act upon the real source of the problem. Under the guise of help
and care, services often are help-denying because they expropriate
the power of individuals and groups to help each other. Services
become counterfeit care.
        3. A serviced society obscures issues of social justice.
In a serviced society the love-care-service connection obscures the
fundamental issues of power and justice. When service is regarded
too simply as an expression of love, its demonic aspects are con-
cealed. We need to be reminded of Reinhold Niebuhr's frequent
warning against simple translations of the ideal of love into historical expressions. For Niebuhr, love as the norm of life finds
its historical expression in the principles and structures of justice. As Niebuhr puts it "equal justice is the approximation of
brotherhood under the conditions of sin."[18] Consider the contrast
between a serviced society and what might be called a justice-
seeking society. In a serviced society concentrations of power are
hidden behind the mask of love. In a justice society, power arrangements are exposed because they are regarded as the very instruments and servants of justice. A serviced society has a high regard for the good will of the servicer. A justice society realizes
that "good will" is tainted with self-interest and when unchecked
by alternative interests is justice-denying. A serviced society
often regards inequity as the price of progress. In a justice
society equity is a substantive principle. In a serviced society
ethical inquiry is directed toward issues where the service systems
impinge on the individual. In a justice society ethical inquiry
tends to be directed toward the fundamental and systemic structures
of power which shape the society.
        Consider more fully how a serviced society obscures
issues concerning the power arrangements of society. An increasing
amount of social ethical attention is given to issues at the inter-
face of service systems and clients. In the health care field the
preoccupation with bio-medical ethics is clearly a concomitant
the medicalization process. Certainly genetic engineering, life-
support systems, behavior control technology, organ implants,
chemical foods open up far reaching ethical concerns. They are
issues born out of the extension of technological service systems.
Our ethical attention is directed to questions of how to be a good
professional and how to be a good client and of how to deal with
the intersection of professional control and client rights. The
ethical-legal questions of right to life, right to death, malpractice,

retribution, right to drugs all become centered around the right
to services or the right to protection against services. The triumph of the therapeutic ideology is when ethicists are co-opted into
discussing the refinements of that ideology in terms of the rights
of servicers and the served. Obscured are the systemic issues of
power and justice in the health care system, issues concerning the
concentration of power in a medical monopoly, inequities in the
distribution of resources, and the health-denying aspects of the
medical management of life.

In a serviced society social ethical attention is also
directed toward issues of "reforming" service systems. But these
reform efforts are usually directed at the problems of how to have
better services, more services and less expensive services or with
how to be better users of services, more knowledgeable users of
services, and more frequent users of services. "Each reform,"
McKnight observes in his discussion of medicine, "represents a new
opportunity for the medical system to expand its influence, scale
and control."[19] Here too, the serviced society, with a vested
interest in reform (meaning expansion) obscures the more basic
issues of the arrangements of power and the alignment of special
interests in the service systems themselves.

The critique of a serviced society is based on the contention that such a society subverts democratic politics, is socially
iatrogenic, and obscures issues of social justice.

A reappropriation of the insights of Reinhold Niebuhr can
provide the Christian community with the theological and ethical
grounds for such a critique and also point the way toward a response
to our social condition. Niebuhr's understanding of the relation
of love and justice should help us uncover the mask of love and
direct our attention squarely upon the questions of the concentration, distribution, and use of power. Niebuhr would clearly be
critical of the love-care-service connection as a sentimentalized
mask of power. He was wary of those who made too simple a connection between love and service.

> This positive relation between rules of justice and the law of love
> must be emphasized in opposition to sentimental versions of the love
> commandment, according to which only the most personal individual
> and direct expressions of social obligation are manifestations of
> Christian *agape*.[20]

Love is not a simple possibility. Its historical expression must
be worked out through principles of justice and structures of power
to protect love from becoming exploitation. Niebuhr was always
suspicious of claims of virtue. Ethicist John Bennett wrote of his
colleague,

> Neibuhr rejects the idea that love can take the place of justice, if
> those who love only become more loving. No, there must be structures
> of justice to enable people to defend themselves against the loving
> who are so sure that they know best what is good for others. There
> are none so good that they can be entrusted with unchecked power

over others, for there are too many illusions in any paternalistic love and also too much unacknowledged self-interest.[21]

Niebuhr constantly warns us of the self-serving interests of those who would serve us, interests that become tyrannical when they are based upon inordinant power.

The norm of love is approximated (and also, to be sure, contradicted) in human society through the dynamic tension between the two basic elements of communal life - the organizing principle of power and the equilibrium of power. Socially these are expressed through the organizing centers of power on the one hand and the dispersed "vitalities" of power on the other. These two elements of social life are always in tension and each, when unchecked by the other, is fraught with danger.

> The organizing principle of power may easily degenerate into tyranny.
> It may create coerced unity of society in which the freedom and
> vitality of all individual members are impaired. Such a tyrannical
> unification of life is a travesty on brotherhood. Again, the prin-
> ciple of the balance of power is always pregnant with the possibil-
> ity of anarchy. These twin evils of tyranny and anarchy represent
> the Scylla and Charybdis between which the frail bark of social
> justice must sail.[22]

Unrestrained by communal interests and vitalities, an organizing center of power tends toward tyranny whereby either part of the community dominates the whole or the government itself expands and limits the freedom of all of the parts.

Niebuhr's model provides a framework to perceive the threat of a serviced society where the center dominates the parts. The center is the network of corporate (industrial-governmental-service) systems and the parts are the increasingly homogenized consumers and clients. The center expropriates the power of the parts to define and deal with life issues. This is not so much a "tyrannical unification of life" as it is a benign uniformity. Niebuhr suggests that when unchecked, the center "would be tempted to destroy the vitality and freedom of component elements in the community in the name of 'order'."[23] In a benign serviced society it is not so much in the name of "order" as in the name of "love." But the two may be the same. Those institutions that have been expressions of "communal vitalities," families, neighborhoods, voluntary associations, and smaller interest groups are increasingly robbed of power. As forces in our common life they are subservient to the imperatives of a growth-oriented, technological, and increasingly centralized society. Niebuhr would have liked Illich's use of the notion of *Nemesis*. *Nemesis* was the inevitable response to hubris, to forgetting our limits and presuming to act like God. The good we seek, when we seek it through artifacts of centralized power and professional domination, invites *Nemesis*.

There are resources, both theological and institutional, within the Christian community to respond to the threat of a medi-calized society. A reappropriation of the insights of Reinhold Neibuhr make these evident. I will mention several briefly to urge

more extended charting of the task of the Christian community in
a serviced society.
    1.   One task would be that of unmasking or demythologizing.
Insofar as the therapeutic ideology has become a system of faith in
our society it needs to be probed and exposed.   A Niebuhrian perspective can clarify obscurities, expose false pretentions, and
challenge ideological illusions.
    Howard Moody has challenged us to examine the idolatry
of Scientific Medicine.   He writes:

> The Church - because it suffered some of the same pathologies - can
> be a helpful vehicle in demythologizing Medicine.   Like the medieval
> church, the religion of Scientific Medicine is built on miracles,
> mystery, and authority: the miracle of drugs, organ transplants and
> cure of exotic diseases; the knowledge of mysteries that bring heal-
> ing and cure which cannot be shared with ordinary human beings; the
> authority of unquestioned and unaccountable medical power that mo-
> nopolizes treatment modalities thereby suppressing all "medical
> sects" other than allopathic medicine.[24]

If we see the ideological nature of service systems we will not
confuse Scientific Medicine with health.   We will not confuse
service with care.   Stripped of ideological masks service systems
will be seen as systems of power developed to expand markets,
create clients, stimulate economic growth, and monopolize treatment modalities.   This insight may not change our troubled social
condition but it would allow us to perceive more accurately the
source of our malaise.
    2.   This perspective would lead the Christian community
to direct its critical attention and energies to the systemic
structures of power and control in society.   That is, service would
not be a substitute for strategies of social change.   One clear
example is our response to world hunger.   This is a complicated
issue to be sure and there is no doubt that efforts to feed the
hungry are well intended.   But *Diet for a Small Planet* author
Francis Laape is on target when she observes that:

> More food or even re-distribution programs like food aid and food
> stamps will continue to mean more hunger until we first address the
> question, "who controls and who takes part in the production pro-
> cess?"[25]

    3.   If justice more than service is our goal we will
recognize that justice in an increasingly centralized society requires organizing the interests of those who are stripped of power.
A just society will afford the powerless the means to check the
interests of the powerful.   Niebuhr summarizes this principle well.

> Christianity knows that a healthy society must seek to achieve the
> greatest possible equilibrium of power, the greatest possible number
> of centers of power, the greatest possible social check upon the
> administration of power and the greatest possible inner moral check

on human ambition, as well as the most effective use of forms of power in which consent and coercion are compounded.26

This would direct the Christian community to reclaim the posture of identifying with the powerless and to recover the task of helping to organize the managed, the medicalized, the poor, and the clientized whose voices are muted.

    4.   The Christian community would clarify a social ethic for a society of limits.   It is clear that we live in a society of limits.   We can no longer accept the myth of unlimited growth.   We are facing limits not only of material resources and energy but of services as well.   Particularly in necessary service resources we cannot tolerate unlimited services for some and denial of access for others.   In a society of limits we have to deal with priorities and not seek to solve all problems of inequity by expanding the service systems.   This is what justice is about; addressing squarely the question of equitable distribution of power and resources.

    5.   Finally, the Christian community can direct some of its resources toward a variety of efforts that are seeking to de-velop an alternative understanding and expression of "care" and "help." These alternative expressions or impulses take many forms: self-help, mutual help, alternative life styles, small-is-beautiful, appropriate technology, alternative communities.   And they take shape in collective business enterprises, wholistic health centers, learning exchanges, community radio stations, food co-ops, recycling centers, roof-top gardens, and a growing number of enterprises where people are getting in touch with people.   The one thing these efforts have in common is a rejection of the therapeutic ideology of a serviced society and a determination to break from the domi-nant pattern of consumption and clienthood.   The danger in these efforts - that they become co-opted in a serviced system or that they are regarded as *the* solution of larger problems of social in-justice - needs to be recognized.   But with this awareness, the Christian community can become a center for this kind of subversion of a serviced society.

    Of course there is no assurance that these strategies will reverse our social drift toward a managed and medicalized society.   A Niebuhrian perspective should guard us against the presumption that these efforts would usher in the Kingdom of God.   But the strategies engendered by this perspective do suggest a ministry for the Christian community in our Babylonian Captivity of a serviced society.

NOTES AND REFERENCES

    1. In this analysis of the serviced society I am drawing primarily upon the work of John McKnight: "The Medicalization of Politics," *Christian Century*, September 17, 1975; "Professionalized Service and Disabling Help," (mimeo-graphed, September, 1976); "The Urban Neighborhood 1975," (mimeographed, 1975).
    2. Erich Fromm, *The Revolution of Hope: Toward a Humanized Technology*, (New York: Harper, 1968) p. 39-40.

3. *Op. cit.*, McKnight, "Medicalization of Politics," p. 787.

4. Edward Engberg, "Can the Professions Save Us?" in *The Center Magazine*, November, 1968, p. 13.

5. Carnegie S. Calian, "Ethics and the Professions: Renewal Through Cooperation," in *The American Society of Christian Ethics: 1976 Selected Papers* (University of Montana: Scholars Press, 1976) p. 50.

6. Richard Bollinger, "Help for Everyday Problems," in *Menniger Perspective*, Fall/Winter, 1975, p. 22.

7. Ivan Illich, *Medical Nemesis* (New York: Random House, 1976) p. 121.

8. See selected articles in *Daedalus*, Winter, 1977, *Doing Better and Feeling Worse: Health Care in the United States.*

9. The 1976 Annual Report of Abbott Laboratories, p. 3.

10. *Op. cit.*, McKnight, "Professionalized Service," p. 4.

11. *Ibid.*, p. 15.

12. In addition to McKnight, see Illich, *Medical Nemesis*; Renee Fox, "The Medicalization and Demedicalization of American Society," in *Daedalus, op. cit.*, p. 9-22; Howard Moody, "Demythologizing Medicine: Redefining Health Care," *Christian Century*, September 27, 1975, p. 219-224.

13. *Op. cit.*, McKnight, "Medicalization of Politics," p. 787.

14. "A Hard Look at the Drug Industry," by Concerned Rush Students, Chicago, 1976.

15. Eli Messinger, "Ritalin and MBD," in *Health/PAC Bulletin*, November/December, 1975, p. 3.

16. For example, see Edward Banfield, *The Unheavenly City* (Boston: Little, Brown, and Company, 1970), especially chapter 3.

17. *Op. cit.*, Illich, *Medical Nemesis*, p. 220.

18. Reinhold Niebuhr, *The Nature and Destiny of Man* (New York: Scribners', 1943) Vol. II, p. 254.

19. *Op. cit.*, McKnight, "Medicalization of Politics," p. 787.

20. *Op. cit.*, Niebuhr, p. 251.

21. John Bennett, "Reinhold Niebuhr's Contribution to Christian Social Ethics," in *Reinhold Niebuhr: Prophetic Voice in Our Time*, Harold Landon, ed. (Greenwich: Seabury, 1962) p. 72.

22. *Op. cit.*, Niebuhr, p. 258.

23. *Ibid.*, p. 267.

24. *Op. cit.*, Moody, "Demythologizing Medicine," p. 223.

25. Francis Laape, quoted in *Student Life*, newspaper of Washington University, March 28, 1977, p. 5.

26. Reinhold Niebuhr, "Coercion, Self-interest and Love," in Kenneth Boulding, *The Organizational Revolution*, p. 244.

ECONOMICS AND ETHICS:
THE PROBLEM OF DIALOGUE

by
Paul Heyne

Is economics a science or an ideology? Does it provide trustworthy descriptions and reliable predictions? Or are the descriptions and predictions of economists distorted by ideological presuppositions and commitments?

From Confidence to Confusion

As recently as fifteen years ago it would have been difficult to assemble a session on those questions at a professional economics meeting in this country. There were almost no Marxist economists in academic positions in the United States to press the argument that orthodox economics is bourgeois apologetics.[1] And the "institutionalists," who had vigorously attacked the philosophical and political biases of mainstream American economics a generation earlier,[2] were by 1960 mostly intimidated, converted, compromised, or quarantined.[3] Most economists simply accepted without serious question the position expressed in 1953 by Milton Friedman, that "economics can be, and in part is, a positive science" and that "positive economics is in principle independent of any particular ethical position or normative judgments."[4]

The complacent consensus has been loudly shattered over the last decade. Those economists who remain convinced that economics is a purely positive science have found it increasingly difficult to ignore the charge that the theoretical corpus of their discipline is in large part an elaborate justification of capitalist society.[5] Formation of the Union for Radical Political Economics;[6] the selection by the American Economic Association of a president notorious for maintaining that economics is "a system of belief" and his subsequent presidential address castigating the profession for its blindness, biases, and sterility;[7] the revival of a militant institutionalist movement organized in the Association for Evolutionary Economics;[8] articles and reviews attacking "neoclassical economics" appearing regularly in official publications of the American Economic Association[9]--the evidence is abundant that what was until recently a settled truth within the profession is today a very doubtful dogma indeed. Even the more determined defenders of the positive-normative distinction now admit that the line is extraordinarily difficult to draw.[10]

It would appear that Gunnar Myrdal, after many years of swimming "against the stream" (the title of a recent collection of

183

his essays),11 is now riding triumphantly on the flood. When in the 1920's he was composing his monograph on *The Political\Element in the Development of Economic Theory*, Myrdal believed that it was possible to purge all political, ideological, or other normative elements from economic theory and thereby to construct a purely positive science of economics. But he soon afterward repudiated that position, calling it "naive empiricism." Over the last forty years Myrdal has persistently criticized the implicit and explicit belief of economists "in the existence of a body of scientific knowledge acquired independently of all valuations." He put the criticism succinctly in his Preface to the English edition of *The Political Element*:

> Facts do not organize themselves into concepts and theories just by being looked at; indeed, except within the framework of concepts and theories, there are no scientific facts but only chaos. There is an inescapable *a priori* element in all scientific work. Questions must be asked before answers can be given. The questions are an expression of our interest in the world, they are at bottom valuations. Valuations are thus necessarily involved already at the stage when we observe facts and carry on theoretical analysis, and not only at the stage when we draw political inferences from facts and valuations.12

Myrdal's argument, elaborated subsequent to the 1930's in books, essays, introductions, and appendices, was never seriously challenged. Nonetheless, economists continued to uphold and employ the positive-normative distinction in methodological essays, textbook introductions, and *obiter dicta* until the 1960's, when the tide of opinion underwent a rapid reversal. Thomas Kuhn's *Structure of Scientific Revolutions*,13 assisted by a changing political climate, accomplished quickly what Myrdal's patient arguments had failed to do: convince a substantial number of economists that the science of economics is inescapably grounded upon non-scientific commitments. The new word with which to refute the defenders of a purely positive science became "paradigm." Despite its considerable ambiguity--one careful reader has distinguished at least twenty-one different senses in which Kuhn employed that word14--the concept of a paradigm became for some a philosopher's stone that could transform any and every alleged science into a mere systematic elaboration of particular biases. Whether or not Kuhn intended this interpretation,15 and whether or not those who invoke his authority have actually read him, the entire context within which the positive-normative distinction was used, defended, or criticized by economists did change drastically toward the end of the 1960's.

The resulting situation is unsatisfactory from any responsible point of view. Many economists continue to affirm the possibility of a positive science of economics, continue to assure their students and one another that economists possess or can create a purely scientific, purely descriptive, value-free, logical-empirical system of thought and knowledge, and continue to condemn as unscientific any attempt to derive economic generalizations with

the explicit aid of value judgments.   Such a rigid adherence to
an untenable position severely restricts dialogue and inquiry[16]
and transforms suspicion into conviction for many who are beginning to wonder whether economics is not more ideology than science.[17]

At the same time we find economists and jubilant critics
of economics who, in the words of Robert Solow, "seem to have
rushed from the claim that no social science can be value-free to
the conclusion that therefore anything goes,"[18] or who--the words
are again Solow's--"have corrupted Thomas Kuhn's notion of a
scientific paradigm, which they treat as a mere license for loose
thinking."[19]

The Fatal Distinction

Where can dialogue begin?   Surely it could begin with a
universal agreement to abandon the positive-normative distinction.
It is philosophically untenable, and all attempts to use it lead
to question-begging procedures that stop discussion and impede the
growth of knowledge.   Myrdal's basic argument, that values enter
inevitably into the construction of any scientific generalization,
has never been refuted because it is irrefutable.   The analysis
applies to every science, not just to the social sciences, as has
been amply demonstrated by such distinguished and diverse students
of the history and philosophy of science as E.A. Burtt,[20] R.G.
Collingwood,[21] Alfred North Whitehead,[22] Michael Polanyi,[23] and
now Thomas Kuhn.   The citation of names is hardly an argument; but
the horse is too dead for flogging.   It is *not* possible, not even
"in principle" (that strange phrase economists invoke when they do
not know how to do what they nonetheless believe can somehow be
done) to construct a science of economics that is "independent of
any particular ethical position or normative judgments."[24]

But the next constructive step is not so easy to discern.
Myrdal has maintained that economists have an obligation to reveal
their presuppositions as fully as possible so that readers can more
easily assess the significance and limitations of any piece of analysis or description.   There is an obvious deficiency in this procedure, however, that makes it at least as likely to mislead further
as to reveal more fully.   And Myrdal's own "confessions" demonstrate
the danger.   They tend to tire the reader well before they succeed
in adequately exposing the crucial presuppositions.   Myrdal probably exaggerates the effectiveness of introspection and assigns
insufficient importance to the role of *criticism by others* in de-
tecting the preconceptions that shape our knowledge.   The widespread
neglect for so long of Myrdal's diagnosis may be grounded in large
part in economists' dissatisfaction with his prescription: the constant explication of underlying value judgments.   Lionel Robbins,
for example, has complained of "the minute search for implicit
value judgments, which . . . has even become something of a heresy
hunt--and, like most heresy hunts, something of a bore."[25]   Those
who are in general agreement with Myrdal's analyses may find his
prefaces instructive; but those who consider his analyses inadequate

or misleading will most likely find the same flaws in his presentation of the value framework underlying the analysis.

Robbins' objection suggests another reason why most
economists have not responded to Myrdal's epistemological diagnosis. They believe that the value judgments which enter inevitably into scientific inquiry are trivial or ones which all serious
inquirers hold in common. But if that claim was ever defensible,
it is no longer. The fact is that the guiding preconceptions which
have shaped the development of economic theory *are* being disputed
today, and disputed in quite specific and concrete ways. Economists
are accused of doing economics on the basis of analytical preconceptions that cause them to count as solutions what their critics
perceive as problems and that prevent them from even seeing certain
social relationships as in any sense problematic. If someone were
to suggest, for example, that college professors ought to do their
own typing and a portion of the janitorial work in their own class-
rooms and offices, most economists would invoke the principle of
comparative advantage in defense of present procedures. That is
not an illegitimate response but it is certainly a limited response.
The principle of comparative advantage is at best a clumsy tool for
dealing with the social meaning of work or the alienation that accompanies specialization and the hierarchical organization of labor,
and at worst it is a tool of thought that conceals these problems
altogether.

This is hardly a trivial or peripheral objection. The
principle of comparative advantage is at the very center of price
theory, which is surely the closest thing to a ruling paradigm in
contemporary economic science. It is the pursuit of comparative advantage that makes demand curves slope downward to the right and that
establishes opportunity costs, thereby giving supply curves their
tendency to slope upward to the right. The crucial concept of efficiency is defined in economics in terms of comparative advantage,
and it is the pursuit of comparative advantage that establishes
prices which are indicators of social scarcity, that induces efficient decisions, and that gives meaning to the concept of equilibrium
in price theory. The comparative advantage concept provides a theoretical orientation that is neither trivial in importance nor universally accepted by those who think systematically about social interaction. One may legitimately ask: Can economists defend the significant theoretical decision to view social reality through the prism
of relative price theory and the principle of comparative advantage?

One reply is to say simply that it works; that it yields
good predictions or that it explains what we want to understand.
But that begs important questions. What are we trying to predict
or explain? Which aspects of social reality are brought into prominence by our analytical procedures and which aspects are submerged
or even distorted? Why this and not that?[26]
Economists and other practicing scientists easily become
impatient with questions of this sort and are tempted to reply that
each scientist, including the critic, has the right to study whatever interests him in whatever way he chooses. But such an individualistic, *laissez faire* conception of science is unrealistic.
The separate sciences are not collections of individuals who do as

they please; they are professional communities with definite intellectual standards and substantial power to enforce those standards.
They exercise this power by granting or withholding membership in
the community, the rewards of income and recognition, and opportunities to influence society through the dissemination of research
results. The theoretical decisions of scientists have coercive
power.[27] Moreover, knowledge is always power, and absolute power
corrupts absolutely.

The Criterion of Science

The determination of some economists to find and enforce
unambiguous criteria for genuinely scientific work arises in fact
from their recognition of the social power of science. Genuine
science leads to the progressive accumulation of warranted knowledge
while other modes of inquiry do not--or at least do so less surely
and effectively. And knowledge is useful, not least in the social
sciences, where the inevitable conflicts engendered by opposition
of interests are so often exacerbated by disagreement over matters
of fact. A purely scientific, purely descriptive, value-free,
logical-empirical science of economics could be immensely useful as
an impartial conciliator of social conflict.[28]

The Holy Grail is *objectivity*. The activites, institutions, and achievements of science rest upon the presupposition of
an objective universe, a reality external to each observer that is
what it is irrespective of the opinions people entertain about it;
truth, in other words, is "beyond human authority."[29] This conviction or article of faith has given rise in turn to the concept
of "objective truth." But if by "truth" we mean correct statements
about reality, the phrase "objective truth" is confusing.[30] Statements, propositions, or judgments are made and held by subjects and
are therefore always subjective. It might be argued that they are
"objective" insofar as reality confirms them. But as soon as we
speak less metaphorically we realize that it is always other subjects and never objects that confirm or disconfirm a judgment.
Hypotheses in biology concerning pigeons are confirmed by biologists, not by pigeons; and hypotheses in economics concerning
business cycles are confirmed by economists, not by business cycles.

There is consequently no way to establish the validity of
a proposition in economic science except by persuading other economists. To persuade anyone, it is necessary to begin with what he
is willing to grant and to reply to the objections he raises. *This
is the method of science.* Science is not a purely logical procedure
whereby true judgments are inexorably extracted from objective
reality by automata called scientists. Science is a social activity,
an activity of a community, and the cardinal rule of scientific procedure is: Submit your conclusions without reservation to the
critical examination of others.[31] Scientific knowledge grows by
testing; but it is scientists who do the testing, not "objective
reality."

It is true, of course, that scientists are not at liberty
to accept or reject scientific conjectures on arbitrary or irrelevant

grounds. But it is the scientific community that finally decides
what is arbitrary or irrelevant. Within the confines of what Kuhn
calls "normal science,"[32] such decisions are often made with little
reflection and typically without controversy. But they are relatively simple decisions only because and insofar as members of the
scientific community have no serious doubts about the adequacy of
their ruling paradigm.

The danger lies in the circularity of this system of
community control. One must step outside a paradigm in order to
examine realities that the paradigm overlooks or distorts, but work
done outside the paradigm is not accepted as scientific. *Extra
ecclesiam nulla veritas.* Scientists tend to reject with indignation
the very possibility that someone doing competent scientific work
might be excluded from influential journals or positions because
he adheres to unpopular values. But such a rejection misconceives
the problem. The values at issue are ones that affect the content
and presumptive quality of scientific work. The problem has even
arisen in the natural sciences;[33] it is clearly far more serious
in a discipline like economics where the very perception of problems
to be studied depends so fundamentally upon conceptions of what
human beings and human societies ought to be or can become.

Unfortunately, the view that value judgments cannot be
fruitfully discussed because they are allegedly mere statements of
subjective preference has acquired wide currency within the economics profession. Some economists may be insisting upon the possibility of a purely positive science because they have accepted the
odd notion that "men can ultimately only fight"[34] when their value
judgments conflict, that the issue is then reduced to one of "thy
blood or mine."[35] But it is sheer dogmatism to deny the possibility
that one's choice of a theoretical orientation may have been significantly affected by prior judgments concerning such matters as the
value of freedom versus equality, the relative importance of individual opportunity and social harmony, the merits of democracy
versus some kind of aristocracy, the risks and the possible gains
from conservative and from radical approaches to social reform, or
the nature of man and the meaning of the good life.[36] And obscu-
rantism is added to dogmatism by the strange insistence that such
disagreements can never be resolved through discussion.[37] The soft
side of the positive-normative distinction is the implicit encouragement that it gives to ethical solipsism. Everyone agrees that political or value judgments must be added to positive economics in order
to obtain policy recommendations. The positive-normative distinction
implies that these judgments are essentially arbitrary, mere matters
of personal preference that cannot be tested or revised through
rational discourse.[38]

The preceding argument is a modest one. Economists should
stop talking about positive and normative economics and speak instead simply about the science of economics. Economics is a science
because knowledge about economic phenomena has long been systematically cultivated and continues to be cultivated by a recognized
community of inquirers who read, build upon, and criticize one
another's work. No more is required. Science neither rests upon
nor discovers indubitable truths. The theories and generalizations

of economic science are conjectures; but they are warranted conjectures because and insofar as they have withstood attempts at critical refutation.   Such a conception of science clearly implies that scientists are not entitled to withhold *any* of their conjectures from criticism, and that the disciplinary boundaries within which they will inevitably work must be regarded as potential sources of error as well as guides to the discovery of truth.

Furthermore, economists ought to re-examine their thinking on the whole subject of value judgments. They enter inevitably into scientific work. Their critical examination can sometimes contribute at least as much to the development of warranted knowledge as can the further refinement of data or the logical improvement of formal models. Economists will, of course, shy away from such a challenge if they continue to maintain that value judgments are nothing but statements of subjective preference. But this is itself a dogma that flies in the face of the undeniable fact that people do hold at least some value judgments to be interpersonally valid, that they do offer evidence and reasons to support their value judgments, and that rational discussion often does lead to consensus among people who began by holding (or supposing that they held) conflicting ethical or political positions.

Radicals and Neoclassicals

How does contemporary American economics fare when we apply this criterion, openness to criticism, to determine whether it is scientific or ideological?   Contrary to what most outside observers currently seem to believe, it satisfies the criterion remarkably well.   Despite formal adherence to the positive-normative dichotomy, with all its potential for begging questions and deflecting fundamental criticism, the economics profession over the past decade has encouraged the publication of radical criticism, has paid attention to it, and has publicly responded to it.   This is not enough, of course, for those critics who define as ideological any position incompatible with their own or who distinguish science from ideology by looking at conclusions rather than procedures.   And it will never be admitted by those who, whether from ignorance or malice, persist in caricaturing or flatly misrepresenting what economists are currently doing.[39]

The *Journal of Economic Literature*, an official publication of the American Economic Association, has repeatedly opened its pages in recent years to critics of "establishment" works and ways.   The Association's other journal, the *American Economic Review* has also published, usually in the annual Papers and Proceedings volume, numerous criticisms of orthodox economics.   Other prestigious "establishment" journals, such as the *Quarterly Journal of Economics* and the *Journal of Political Economy*, have offered article reviews, and symposia in which general and specific criticisms were forcefully presented.   The accusation of official indifference or conspiratorial silence in the face of radical criticism simply cannot be sustained by anyone who pays attention to what economists have actually been doing in the last decade.

On the contrary, it is the critics who have tended to substitute dogma for dialogue by failing to modify their criticisms in the light of the responses that have been given to their arguments. Kuhn's concept of scientific paradigms has become in some radical circles a justification for refusing to listen to those who do not begin with the correct presuppositions. The distinguished Marxist economist Paul Sweezy, commenting on Assar Lindbeck's *The Political Economy of the New Left: An Outsider's View*, complained that Lindbeck "has no empathy for the radical position" so that "I, as a radical, find it as irrelevant and boring as most neoclassical economics."[40]   Lindbeck's response was testy:

> If the impossibility of intellectual communication between different groups of social scientists is accepted, these groups belong in (different) divinity schools rather than in social science faculties of universities.[41]

Empathy is essential, of course, to genuine dialogue, but consensus is the goal of dialogue, not its precondition. While passion neither can nor should be excluded from scientific discussion, it does not entail or excuse abusive and *ad hominem* argument. And it surely does not justify a refusal to pay attention to what opponents are actually saying and doing.

Anyone who follows the professional literature and also reads the complaints leveled against it must wonder occasionally about the good faith of the critics. The charge is constantly made, for example, that economists ignore questions of income distribution and that this is an "untouchable" topic. Did the critics perhaps overlook the publication of two comprehensive books on income distribution by two well known economists in 1971?[42]   Or the pair of review articles on these books featured in the *Journal of Economic Literature*?[43]   Or the Richard T. Ely Lecture to the 1974 meeting of the American Economic Association?[44]   Or the research and arguments associated with the names of Lester Thurow,[45] A. Michael Spence,[46] or Doeringer and Piore?[47]   The income distribution studies of Thurow, Spence, and Doeringer-Piore are specifically mentioned here because they have significant non-conservative implications and have attracted considerable attention among economists and others interested in public policy.

The Neoclassical Perspective

Fortunately, an alternative hypothesis to that of bad faith can be constructed. And as we sketch it out we begin to discover the nature of the gulf that currently divides Marxists from so-called neoclassical economists. The radical critics of orthodox economics are reluctant to concede that any research undertaken within the framework of neoclassical theory could constitute genuine investigation of real problems. Not even the radical implications of Thurow's work or of Spence's can redeem research that employs the perspective of marginal productivity theory. Marginal productivity theory is allegedly circular, empty, incoherent, and consequently nothing more than apologetics for capitalism.[48]   But marginal productivity theory is essentially nothing but the neoclassical or orthodox perspective applied to questions of resource pricing and allocation. It is the fundamental perspective of that broader theory to which radical critics are really objecting.

The neoclassical perspective is a way of thinking about social phenomena that conceives society as composed entirely of individuals whose conscious actions aim at maximizing expected utility. People choose continuously among perceived options, weighing the expected benefits and costs of each decision and electing those actions through which they expect to secure for themselves the largest net advantage attainable. Monetary prices are an important set of data for decision makers because they provide a common denominator through which the relative advantage of innumerable options can be precisely compared. The decisions people make entail offers and bids which ultimately establish these prices by moving them toward market clearing values.

Neither selfishness, materialism, nor obsession with money is assumed. The maximization of expected utility can lead to anything from self-sacrifice to self-aggrandizement; the self whose interests are pursued is not prescribed in the neoclassical perspective. Moreover, the notion that economizing is peculiarly directed toward "material" wealth is probably a careless inference from the correct observation that neoclassical economics is centrally concerned with exchange and consequently directs most of its attention to goods that are augmentable and transferable. The substantial role played by monetary costs and monetary transactions in economists' analysis and research is simply a consequence of the fact that the institution of money enormously facilitates exchange.

Why is this perspective so offensive to most radical critics of economics?[49]

To begin with, it assigns fundamental importance to the actual preferences of individuals. Every sensible economist knows that the wants of individuals are the product of socialization and that people's socialization sometimes serves them badly. But neoclassical economists place a heavy burden of proof upon anyone (Galbraith, Nader, Marcuse, or the Federal Communications Commission) who claims to *know* that what individuals want is not in their best interest.[50] Wants expressed in the market are at very least the beginning point for all evaluative judgments.

Secondly, the neoclassical perspective assumes that each party to a voluntary exchange gains from that exchange; otherwise it would not occur. This is not the same as assuming a complete harmony of interests in society, as radical critics repeatedly claim. But voluntary exchange is the focus of attention and voluntary exchange is a method of inducing others to cooperate by *adding to* their range of opportunities rather than subtracting from them. Market interaction secures social cooperation, in short, through persuasion rather than coercion; and orthodox economic theory has developed over the last two centuries largely in an effort to explicate the coordinative potential in voluntary exchange. It must be noted at the same time that this preoccupation of economists with exchange relationships has produced a vast literature on

"market failure" in which the limitations of market arrangements
have been minutely explored. Orthodox economists have paid far
more attention to the deficiencies of market arrangements than
advocates of socialism have paid to the deficiencies of central
planning.
          This is closely related to a third major difference in
approach. The neoclassical perspective views power as an insecure
possession, because the advantages that power confers upon its
possessor will tend to attract additional bids and offers that will
undermine the power base. It is misleading to claim, as radicals
do persistently, that orthodox economists ignore the problem of
power. Ownership of resources is clearly recognized as power, and
resource control coupled with the ability to exclude competitors
is a constant object of study by neoclassical economists. It is
ironic that the critics so rarely see the blindness toward the
problem of power implicit in their own stated preference for a
usually unspecified "social control" of resources. And it is an
empirical question, on which neoclassical theory sheds important
light, whether particular private individuals or organizations in
any society actually possess excessive power through disproportionate resource ownership.
          It is, furthermore, a critical difference between orthodox
and Marxist economics that the former views competition as occurring
between parties *on the same side* of the market. Thus employers
compete against employers, employees against employees. This point
of view is hostile toward notions of "the power of the capitalist
class" or "the solidarity of the working class." But these alternative conceptions so central to Marxist social analysis have not
fared nearly as well as the neoclassical approach in explaining and
predicting observed events. The radical contention that orthodox
economists deliberately conceal the class basis of the distribution
of income ought to be, but largely is not, supported by arguments
and evidence showing that a class-oriented analysis can better explain actual changes over time in patterns of income distribution.[51]
          Finally, neoclassical economics, by focusing on the
efficient allocation of resources, implicitly asserts that the
task of assigning resources to their most advantageous use is a
task of great importance and complexity. This follows from the
almost incalculable variety of presumably legitimate wants that
individuals have and from the infinitely varied ways in which resources can be combined. Marxist economists deny the fundamental
importance or difficulty of the allocative task and assert that
efficient coordination is a relatively simple problem. They do
this by claiming that people's real wants are fairly simple and
uniform and that the appropriate ways of combining resources for
production are largely known data of technology. If the Marxists
are correct, markets are a dispensable social institution and central planning will encounter no major information problems. If the
neoclassical perspective is more nearly correct, the problem of information may not be solvable except through decentralized decision-
making and market coordination.[52]

Conclusion

The thesis of this entire essay has been that the enemy is dogmatism, and the requirements of brevity have at the end led to a manner of statement which is unfortunately dogmatic in tone if not in intent. But perhaps these insufficiently qualified interpretations of the principal radical-orthodox disagreements will serve to focus attention on the depth of the divisions that give rise today to controversies over theory. Debates about marginal productivity theory are symptoms of divergent visions. It could not be wholly a waste of scientific energy for economists to explore, through critical but empathetic dialogue, the conflicting conceptions of human nature and society that the West and, increasingly, the entire world has inherited from the Enlightenment. We might begin, for example, with the French Revolution and ask to what extent liberty presupposes fraternity and the circumstances under which equality is the enemy and the circumstances under which it is the precondition of defensible liberty and genuine fraternity. But that is clearly a task too large to begin here.

NOTES AND REFERENCES

1. See Martin Bronfenbrenner's "Notes on Marxian Economics in the United States," *American Economic Review* (December, 1964), pp. 1019-26, the subsequent exchange with Horace B. Davis, *American Economic Review* (September, 1965), pp. 861-64, and Bronfenbrenner's insightful survey "The Vicissitudes of Marxian Economics," *History of Political Economy* (Fall, 1970), pp. 205-24.

2. Their best known manifesto was *The Trend of Economics*, edited by Rexford Tugwell and published in 1924.

3. A good sense of the situation two decades ago can be obtained from Kenneth Boulding, "A New Look at Institutionalism," with comments by discussants, *American Economic Review* (May, 1957), pp. 1-27; also Fritz Karl Mann, "Institutionalism and American Economic Theory: A Case of Interpenetration," *Kyklos* (July, 1960), pp. 307-23.

4. The quotations are from Friedman's influential essay on "The Methodology of Positive Economics," published in his *Essays in Positive Economics* (Chicago: University of Chicago Press, 1953), pp. 3,4. Friedman's essay triggered an extensive discussion, but the discussion revolved almost exclusively about his claim that the proper test of a theory was the conformity of its predictions to observation rather than the realism of its assumptions. The premise with which he began, that there can be and is a positive science of economics independent of any particular ethical position or normative judgments, went largely unchallenged.

5. The charge that the analytical tools employed by the majority of economists are marred by a fundamental bias in favor of *laissez faire* has been made most often and most vociferously by Joan Robinson, who enjoyed the forum of a Richard T. Ely Lecture for "The Second Crisis of Economic Theory," *American Economics Review* (May, 1972), pp. 1-10.

6. The Minutes of the Annual Business Meeting of the American Economic Association in December, 1970, record one impact of URPE upon the larger profession: *American Economic Review* (May, 1970), pp. 487-89. See also Martin

Bronfenbrenner, "Radical Economics in America: A 1970 Survey," *Journal of Economic Literature* (September, 1970), pp. 747-66.

7. John Kenneth Galbraith, "Economics as a System of Belief," *American Economic Review* (May, 1970), pp. 469-78; "Power and the Useful Economist," *American Economic Review* (March, 1973), pp. 1-11.

8. The Association publishes the *Journal of Economic Issues*. The issues of December, 1975, and March, 1976, will adequately illustrate the militance of the institutionalist renaissance.

9. See the *Journal of Economic Literature* and the annual issue of the *American Economic Review* which publishes the Association's Papers and Proceedings.

10. Friedman's rethinking of his position is discussed in the Introduction, "Why Economists Disagree," to his collection of essays, *Dollars and Deficits* (Englewood Cliffs, New Jersey: Prentice-Hall, Inc., c.1968), pp. 1-16.

11. Gunnar Myrdal, *Against the Stream: Critical Essays on Economics* (New York, New York: Pantheon, 1973).

12. Gunnar Myrdal, *The Political Element in the Development of Economic Theory*, trans. Paul Streeten (London: Routledge & Kegan Paul, 1953), p. vii. Paul Streeten assembled Myrdal's scattered writings between 1933 and 1957 on the role of values in social science and wrote a lengthy introduction for the volume *Values in Social Theory* (London: Routledge & Kegan Paul, c.1958). The most succinct statement of Myrdal's essential position is his note on facts and valuations in Appendix 2 of *An American Dilemma*, reprinted in *Value in Social Theory*, pp. 119-64.

13. Thomas S. Kuhn, *The Structure of Scientific Revolutions*, 2d edition, enlarged (Chicago, Illinois: University of Chicago Press, c.1962, 1970).

14. Margaret Masterman, "The Nature of a Paradigm," in Imre Lakatos and Alan Musgrave (eds.), *Criticism and the Growth of Knowledge* (Cambridge: At the University Press, 1970), pp. 61-65.

15. Kuhn's two contributions to *Criticism and the Growth of Knowledge* pass up numerous opportunities to dissociate himself from this position. See "Logic of Discovery or Psychology of Research," *op. cit.*, pp. 1-23, and "Reflections on My Critics," pp. 231-78.

16. A recent and particularly glaring example of an effort to restrict inquiry with the aid of this distinction may be found in Richard A. Posner, "Economic Justice and the Economist," *The Public Interest* (Fall, 1973), pp. 109-19.

17. In an extended review of Assar Lindbeck's *The Political Economy of the New Left: An Outsider's View* (New York, New York: Harper and Row, 1971), Bruce McFarlane impatiently complains that Lindbeck assumes "objective research" is possible and "ignores what Thomas Kuhn has taught us about the nature of discovery in social sciences, to say nothing of Myrdal who not only maintains that research in the social sciences *is* subjective and based on political values, but especially singles out economics." *The Review of Radical Political Economics* (Summer, 1972), p. 88.

18. Robert M. Solow, "Science and Ideology in Economics," *The Public Interest* (Fall, 1970), p. 101.

19. Robert M. Solow, "Discussion," *American Economic Review* (May, 1971), p. 63.

20. E.A. Burtt, *The Metaphysical Foundations of Modern Science* (rev. ed.; Garden City, New York: Doubleday, c.1932, 1954).

21. R.G. Collingwood, *The Idea of Nature* (New York, New York: Oxford University Press, c.1945, 1960).

22. Alfred North Whitehead, *Science and the Modern World* (New York, New York: The Free Press, c.1925, 1967); *Modes of Thought* (New York, New York: The Free Press, c.1938, 1968).

23. Michael Polanyi, *Personal Knowledge: Towards a Post-Critical Philosophy* (rev. ed.; New York, New York: Harper and Row, c.1958, 1964).

24. Whether or not we choose to designate these preconceptions as value judgments is less important than that we recognize the fact of pre-analytic commitments in scientific inquiry.

25. Lionel Robbins, *Politics and Economics* (New York, New York: St. Martin's Press, 1963), p. 6.

26. The issue is not simply between radical and conservative points of view, of course. The various social sciences employ differing analytical frame-works, with the consequence that one group of scientists may see as a solution what another group takes as its problem. This point is clearly argued and illustrated in Mancur Olson, Jr., "Economics, Sociology, and the Best of All Possible Worlds," *The Public Interest* (Summer, 1968), pp. 96-118. Albert Hirschman has perceptively explored some consequences of the alternative frame-works brought by economists and political scientists to the study of social systems in *Exit, Voice, and Loyalty* (Cambridge: Harvard University Press, 1970).

27. This is one of the themes running through Kuhn's *Structure of Scientific Revolutions*. He has stated that if he were writing the book again he would be-gin by discussing the community structure of science. Kuhn, "Reflections on My Critics," p. 252 and also pp. 237-41. The creative and disciplinary role played by the community in every science has been ably described by John Ziman in *Public Knowledge: An Essay Concerning the Social Dimension of Science* (Cambridge: At the University Press, 1969). Further implications of the fact that most sciences are now integral parts of the industrial and political structure are pointed out in Jerome R. Ravetz, *Scientific Knowledge and Its Social Problems* (New York, New York: Oxford University Press, 1971).

28. This is the argument used by Friedman to support the sharp separation of positive from normative economics in "The Methodology of Positive Economics," *op. cit.*, pp. 3-7.

29. The quotation is from Karl Popper who has consistently criticized both the notion of an authoritative source for knowledge and the absolute relativism which is its polar opposite. See especially Popper, *Conjectures and Refutations: The Growth of Scientific Knowledge* (New York, New York: Harper and Row, 1965), pp. 29-30.

30. The concept of "objective knowledge" is legitimate if it means know-ledge that has been objectified by being expressed in language or some other external form. It is then *public* knowledge. Ziman finds a unifying principle for all of science in the quest for "public and *consensible*" knowledge. *Public Knowledge*, p. 11 and *passim*. If I understand him correctly, this is also what Popper has in mind in *Objective Knowledge: An Evolutionary Approach* (Oxford: At the Clarendon Press, 1972).

31. It is important to guard against the illusion that there can exist in any science methodological rules the mere adoption of which will hasten its progress, although it is true that certain methodolog-ical dogmas . . . may certainly retard the progress of science. All one can do is to argue critically about scientific problems.

K. Klappholz and J. Agassi, "Methodological Prescriptions in Economics," *Economica* (February, 1959), p. 74.

196   BELIEF AND ETHICS

32. "Normal science" means research firmly based upon one or more
past scientific achievements, achievements that some particular
scientific community acknowledges for a time as supplying the
foundation for its further practice.
Kuhn, *The Structure of Scientific Revolutions*, p. 10.
33. Instructive case studies from the natural sciences may be found in
Polanyi's *Personal Knowledge*. The problem is one of implicit beliefs rather
than any kind of bad faith. See also Kuhn, *The Structure of Scientific Revolutions*, especially pp. 77-90, 110-34.
34. Friedman, "The Methodology of Positive Economics," p. 5.
35. Lionel Robbins, *An Essay on the Nature and Significance of Economic
Science* (2d ed.; London: Macmillan, 1935), p. 150.
36. An excellent stimulus for economists willing to reflect on these questions has recently been rescued from the relative obscurity of its initial publication and reprinted as the leading essay in Edmund S. Phelps (ed.), *Economic
Justice* (Baltimore, Maryland: Penguin, 1973): See W.S. Vickrey, "An Exchange
of Questions between Economics and Philosophy," pp. 35-62. This extraordinary
essay was originally published in the first volume of the old Federal Council
of Churches series on Ethics and Economic Life, *Goals of Economic Life*, edited
by A. Dudley Ward (New York, New York: Harper and Brothers, 1953), pp. 148-77.
37. Why do so many social scientists dogmatically assume that criticism
of conflicting judgments (inevitably?) produces consensus in one area but is
altogether useless in another? For philosophically informed discussions of
this issue by economists, see Sidney S. Alexander, "Human Values and Economist's
Values," in Sidney Hook (ed.), *Human Values and Economic Policy* (New York, New
York: New York University Press, 1967), pp. 101-16, and Amartya K. Sen,
Collective Choice and Social Welfare (San Francisco, California: Holden-Day,
1970), pp. 56-64.
38. We must certainly hold fast to the idea of a neutral science of
economics . . . . To have recognized in this connection the distinction between positive and normative judgments is one of the
achievements of thought since Adam Smith and the Physiocrats; and
nothing but confusion could come from any attempt to slur it over.
But the idea that there can be constructed a system of prescriptions
which results more or less inevitably from the results of positive
analysis can involve scarcely less of a confusion: any theory of
economic policy must depend partly on conceptions and valuations
which are imported from outside.
Robbins, *Politics and Economics*, p. 19. But if value judgments are
arbitrary statements of subjective preference and also an inescapable part of
any policy recommendation, then are not all policy recommendations finally
arbitrary? And what then is the value for policy of a positive science?
39. As long as the market for tirades is so much better than the market
for balanced, judicious assessments, the intelligent lay public will continue
to derive most of its notions about economics from books like Robert Lekachman's
Economists at Bay: Why the Experts Will Never Solve Your Problems (New York,
New York: McGraw-Hill, 1975). The reasons for this harsh judgment may be found
in a review of the book in *Worldview* (September, 1976), pp. 53-54.
40. "Symposium: Economics of the New Left," *Quarterly Journal of Economics* (November, 1972), p. 659. Lindbeck's book, first published in 1971, has
been reprinted in an expanded version that contains the contributions to this
symposium plus additional reviews of the book and a further rejoinder by Lindbeck
(New York, New York: Harper and Row, 1977). The book itself, its reception by

economists, and now its republication along with vigorous radical criticism of the book (including a long and hostile review article from *The Review of Radical Political Economics*) are continuing evidence of establishment economists' willingness to confront controversy and honor dissenting views.

41. *Ibid.*, p. 668. The Ethics and Society Department in the University of Chicago Divinity School would surely want to object to Lindbeck's choice of a home for solipsists. If divinity schools are to be sanctuaries for those who wish to work without criticism within closed systems of thought, their faculties are no more entitled to a place in the university than are fundamentalist social scientists. For at least as long as Alvin Pitcher has been quartered in Swift Hall, students in the Divinity School have been urged to criticize fundamentalism of every type, religious or scientific, not to give it a comfortable home. This note offers a good opportunity to thank Al Pitcher for pushing me along the road of dialogue almost twenty years ago and for continuing efforts in the recent past to prevent my straying in the company of economists too far from the straight path.

42. Martin Bronfenbrenner, *Income Distribution Theory* (Chicago, Illinois: Aldine-Atherton, 1971) and Jan Pen, *Income Distribution: Facts, Theories, Policies* (New York, New York: Praeger, 1971).

43. C.E. Ferguson and Edward J. Nell, "Two Books on the Theory of Income Distribution: A Review Article," *Journal of Economic Literature* (June, 1972), pp. 437-53. These are actually two separate review articles. Ferguson was a neoclassical stalwart (he died before his review could be published). Nell writes from a neo-Marxist perspective.

44. Alice M. Rivlin, "Income Distribution--Can Economists Help?" *American Economic Review* (May, 1975), pp. 1-15.

45. Arguments developed by Thurow against the notion of effective wage competition are summarized in his *Generating Inequality: Mechanisms of Distribution in the U.S. Economy* (New York, New York: Basic Books, 1975).

46. Major presuppositions of the "human capital" approach to research on income distribution are sharply questioned in A. Michael Spence, *Market Signaling: Informational Transfer in Hiring and Related Screening Processes* (Cambridge: Harvard University Press, 1974).

47. The authors' theory of dual labor markets is presented in Peter B. Doeringer and Michael J. Piore, *Internal Labor Markets and Manpower Analysis* (Lexington, Mass.: Heath, 1971).

48. A surprising number of Marxists and other radicals who know nothing else about the professional literature of contemporary economics have heard about the Cambridge Capital Controversy and its alleged result: demolition of the marginal productivity theory. But the Cambridge Controversy only showed that marginal productivity theory could not produce a consistent and coherent theory of the aggregative distribution of income between workers and capitalists. The claim that it *could* perform this task was never central to neoclassical theory. No adequate account of the Cambridge Controversy will be easy reading. For good summaries by economists with opposite sympathies, see G.C. Harcourt, "Some Cambridge Controversies in the Theory of Capital," *Journal of Economic Literature* (June, 1969), pp. 369-405, and Mark Blaug, *The Cambridge Revolution: Success or Failure* (London: Institute of Economic Affairs, 1975).

49. But not to all! Some Marxist economists have maintained that neoclassical theory will be an indispensable tool also in a socialist society because it can handle more effectively than Marxist theory problems of efficient planning. See for example the classic statement of Oskar Lange, "Marxian Economics and Modern Economic Theory," reprinted from *The Review of Economic*

Studies (June, 1935) in David Horowitz, ed., *Marx and Modern Economics* (New York, New York: Monthly Review Press, 1968), pp. 68-87.

50. For evidence that neoclassical theory can be used effectively to criticize the outcome of "consumer sovereignty," see Staffan Burenstam Linder, *The Harried Leisure Class* (New York, New York: Columbia University Press, 1970) and Tibor Scitovsky, *The Joyless Economy* (New York, New York: Oxford University Press, 1976).

51. There would seem to be no *a priori* reason to assume that any single theory will best explain both the British and the American economies. The relative preference of British economists for a class-based theory of income distribution may in part reflect the persistence of the class distinctions that were so obvious in David Ricardo's time (the time of Jane Austen).

52. The classic statement of the problem is still the essay of F.A. Hayek, "The Use of Knowledge in Society," *American Economic Review* (September, 1945), pp. 519-30.

MORALITY VERSUS ECONOMIC SCIENCE
IN RELIGIOUS SOCIALISM

by
Clark A. Kucheman

Religious socialism, defined most broadly by Paul Tillich as "the effort to relate the religious principle to social reality and to bring it to form therein,"[1] has been a major concern of mine as a social ethicist and quasi-economist ever since my days as a student under Professor Pitcher's expert guidance. Following Tillich's formula, I have sought to "relate the religious principle" to economic reality and to "bring it to form therein" by showing what kind of economic organization it calls for. Working largely out of Tillich's religious-ethical perspective, but with a different understanding of economic reality's nature and functioning, I have sought to design a new shape for his religious socialism.

To summarize his religious socialism and my proposed revision of it very briefly, the "religious principle" to which Tillich refers in the definition is the "categorical imperative" or "unconditional demand" of morality. Specifically, it is "the unconditional demand addressing itself to every potential personality to become an actual personality."[2] "God is being-itself,"[3] according to him, and the moral imperative to actualize personality is "the ethical expression of the ontological structure of being itself."[4] Moreover, since "all forms of justice are forms that make freedom of personality possible,"[5] the religious principle is also the basic norm by which society should be organized. Since each of us human beings ought "unconditionally" or morally to become, in his words, "a complete self and a rational person,"[6] we each have the corresponding right to conditions of life within which we can do so. Society must therefore be organized and managed in such a way as to secure these conditions; it must provide for "the protection of the individual as a potential personality in a community."[7]

But capitalism does not do this, he argues. Instead, it is a depersonalizing "demonic" power. By using Marxian economic analysis -- "religious socialism stands fundamentally on the ground of Marx's analysis of capitalistic society"[8] -- he finds that "the fundamental 'demonic' phenomenon of the present day is the autonomy of the capitalistic economic system, with all its contradictions, and the mass of disintegration and destruction of meaning in all spheres of historical existence which it produces."[9] Relating the religious principle to economic reality, then, Tillich contends that religious socialism's "most decisive religious task is to participate in exposing and combatting a demonic capitalism"[10] and that "the coming form of society must be a socialist one if it is to be

199

adequate to the actual necessities as well as to the moral demands
of the situation."11
My revised version of religious socialism, to summarize
it even more briefly, incorporates the religious principle, interpreting it as requiring us to become and be -- in a Kantian sense
which deviates somewhat from Tillich, however -- rationally self-
governing agents.12   But I understand economic reality differently
and therefore come to a different practical conclusion.   While I
agree with many of Tillich's specific criticisms of capitalism as
it presently functions, I use neo-classical rather than Marxian economic analysis and consequently "bring [the religious principle] to
form" by advocating a competitive market economy with private ownership of the means of production for the most part, but with certain
socialist aspects,13 rather than, as Tillich does, "a centrally controlled productive process"14 in which "the concentrations of power
now held by privately owned large property . . . are . . . in the
hands of society as a whole."15
This sketchy summary does not convey the substance of either
version of religious socialism, needless to say.   But it does point
to the problem with which I wish to contend.   Both versions, notice,
use and depend upon scientific economic analysis.   Tillich's understanding of economic reality comes from Marxian economics whereas
mine comes from neo-classical, but both of us rely upon economic
science in order to "relate the religious principle" to economic
reality and "bring it to form therein."   In each case, moreover --
and this is the crucial point -- the analysis involved is nomothetic.
That is, both Marxian and neo-classical economic analysis explain
and predict economic events by subsuming them under what are commonly referred to as "covering laws."   And this is where the problem
arises.   By affirming the religious principle -- morality -- religious
socialism in either of its versions presupposes that human beings
have freedom.   For in Tillich's words, "the moral act . . . presupposes the freedom to receive commands, to obey and to disobey them."16
But by using economic science in the process of applying this principle to economic reality, religious socialism also presupposes that
human behavior conforms to economic laws.   For religious socialism
can "relate the religious principle" to the economy and decide how
properly to "bring it to form therein" only if it first understands
the economy's workings and can anticipate the effects of its proposed policies, and it can do these things only if it explains and
predicts economic events on the basis of "covering laws."   Hence
religious socialism presupposes both that human beings act freely
and that they behave in accordance with economic laws, and the problem at issue is whether and how these two apparently conflicting
presuppositions can be justified and reconciled.
This, then, is the problem I shall contend with and try
to solve in this essay.   Since religious socialism depends upon the
truth of both of these presuppositions, I shall first argue in support of the proposition that human beings are free in the needed
sense and then proceed to show how nomothetic explanation in economics must be conceived if it is to be compatible with human freedom.

As I have already suggested, the challenge to religious socialism's presupposition that human beings have freedom comes from nomothetic scientific explanation itself. For as May Brodbeck points out, carried through logically it implies -- or at least seems to -- that "every event occurs in some system of laws such that *if* we knew these laws and the state of the universe at any time, then we could explain the past and predict the future."[17] It implies that "for every event there is a set of laws or regularities connecting it with other events" and, with respect to human beings, that "there are circumstances -- in our constitutions, backgrounds, environment, and character -- that are jointly sufficient conditions for our behavior, including the choices we make."[18] In short, nomothetic explanation seemingly entails determinism.

One obvious but unsatisfactory way to meet this challenge is to evade it. We can argue, with justification, that determinism is not yet itself established scientifically. Indeed we can add that it can never be firmly established, since it is impossible either to know all of the laws of nature -- including human nature -- or to describe in sufficient detail the "state of the universe," both of which would have to be accomplished before determinism's thesis could even be tested. But to take this line is to "cop out." Determinism is "the plainest common sense,"[19] as Brodbeck observes, and we need to meet its challenge directly if we are to support religious socialism's presupposition of freedom in a positive rather than merely negative way.

But perhaps determinism's challenge is not as serious as it seems to be. Perhaps, as "soft" determinism contends, we can hold *both* that "every event occurs in some system of laws such that *if* we knew these laws and the state of the universe at any time, then we could explain the past and predict the future," *and* that we human beings are free.

To put it briefly, soft determinism asserts that human wants, desires, motives, and even choices or volitions can and must be taken into account in nomothetic explanation. Mental states as well as physical states help to determine human behavior. This being so, it appears to follow that freedom and moral responsibility are fully compatible with determinism's claim. For to say that we human beings are free on this understanding is to say -- following Brodbeck again -- that we are not compelled. If we can do as we choose or as we wish, we are free; we act voluntarily. "A man acts," as Brodbeck explains, "when, consciously or unconsciously, his intentions, desires, or reasons are among the causes of his behavior. He has the alternative of doing one thing rather than another; the action he takes depends upon him. He makes a choice. If he had chosen differently, something else would have occurred."[20] Free action is thus to be contrasted not with caused or lawful action but with compelled action. We are compelled -- unfree -- when we are prevented from doing as we wish, for example, by threats, physical constraints, or even psychological compulsions. It follows, then, on this understanding, that we are responsible for what we cause to happen, for what happens in consequence of our choices. "A cause only compels," Brodbeck continues, "if it is of a certain kind in a certain context. If the cause is my own choice, then I am not

compelled. I act freely. By my choice I brought about what happened. If I act freely, then I am responsible for my action."[21]
        This view of freedom and moral responsibility is quite
obviously in harmony with determinism. For it says nothing about
how we happen to have the wants we have or why we make the choices
we do. It admits our wants and choices as determining causes, but
it adds that they may themselves be determined. It is fully consistent with the claim, referred to above, that "there are circumstances -- in our constitutions, backgrounds, environment, and character -- that are jointly sufficient conditions for our behavior,
including the choices we make" (my emphasis). But it is unsatisfactory nevertheless. Properly conceived, the religious principle
--morality -- requires that we have a more radical kind of freedom
than is compatible with determinism.
        Consider moral responsibility. Ordinarily we blame some-
one, including ourselves, for doing something he or she ought not
to have done or for not doing something he or she ought to have done.
We hold the person responsible for the action. When we do so, however, we imply that he or she could have acted otherwise. For example, suppose I have a duty in a given instance to tell the truth.[22]
But suppose also that I tell a lie instead. Upon reflecting about
it afterwards, can I justifiably blame myself for doing what I did?
In the determinist conception of freedom, I am indeed responsible
for what I did. For I chose to do it. I was not compelled; I
could have avoided telling the lie *if* I had so chosen. I was free
in the determinist sense of "free." But am I really responsible?
I could have avoided telling the lie   I could have fulfilled my
moral obligation   according to this view of freedom, *if I had chosen
to*. But I could not have chosen to! According to the understanding
in question the choice was caused by my formed character, my environment, my history, and so on. Anyone who had this information about
me and who was aware of the relevant causal laws could have predicted
that I would do what I did. I could not *not* have done it. Of course,
I could have acted otherwise *if* I had so chosen -- I was not compelled
--but I could not have so chosen. So why should I blame myself or
hold myself responsible for the act? What happened had to happen.
I can justifiably blame myself only for doing what I could *really*
have avoided doing, and not for what I could have avoided doing *if*
I had so chosen.
        Now consider moral obligation itself. So far my discus-
sion has taken it for granted that we do in fact have moral obligations; it has assumed that judgments such as "I ought morally to tell
the truth" can be true. On the determinist view, however, this cannot be so. For as Kant pointed out, ought implies can. If we cannot do something, it cannot be true that we ought morally to do it.
And since determinism holds that our choices -- and therefore our
actions -- are causally determined, it thereby rules out the possibility of our having moral obligations at all, i.e., it makes it impossible for any moral judgment to be true.
        Recall the case of my telling a lie. On the determinist
view I told the lie because I chose to do so, but I chose to do so
because of my formed character, my environment, my history, and so
on. My choice was caused; I could not have chosen to do otherwise.

This being so, however, how could it have been my obligation to tell the truth in the first place? It could not have been. For if I cannot choose to tell the truth -- if I cannot avoid telling a lie -- then, on the "ought implies can" principle, I have no obligation to do so. If I cannot tell the truth, in consequence of the causes determining my choice, then the judgment "I ought morally to tell the truth" cannot conceivably be true. Judgments about moral obligation can be true only if it is possible for us to act on them, and in the case at hand this is precisely what determinism rules out.

Suppose, though, that the factors determining my choice were different. Suppose they caused me to tell the truth rather than a lie. Does this imply that the imperative "I ought morally to tell the truth" could be true after all? For in this case, it seems, I could and did act on it; I told the truth. Remember here, however, that a moral imperative such as this one requires two things. Certainly it requires us to do what it says, in this example, to tell the truth. This requirement was satisfied. But a moral imperative also requires us to act for a certain reason. It requires us to do what ought morally to be done not merely accidentally but *because* it ought morally to be done; we must do our duty for its own sake. In the case at hand, I must tell the truth simply because the truth ought morally to be told. If I tell the truth for any other reason, such as because it is to my interest to do so, or -- what is the relevant consideration here -- if I am caused to do it by my psychological make-up, environment, personal history, and so on, then I have not satisfied this second requirement. I have not done my duty for its own sake; instead, I have acted only accidentally in accordance with the imperative to tell the truth. So in the hypothetical example I have not satisfied this second requirement. Even though I told the truth, I did not do my duty for its own sake. It was impossible for me to act on the imperative, "I ought morally to tell the truth." I did tell the truth, but I did not and could not have done it morally. Hence the problem remains. Moral judgments can be true only if it is possible for us to act on them, and we cannot act on them if our behavior is causally determined.

Religious socialism conceives freedom as "freedom to receive commands, to obey and to disobey them." But freedom in the determinist sense is neither of these. It is not freedom "to obey or to disobey" imperatives of morality, since, according to determinism, "there are circumstances . . . that are jointly sufficient conditions for our behavior, including the choices we make." Nor is it freedom "to receive commands," since there can be "commands" -- moral imperatives -- only if we can act morally, i.e., for the sake of duty, rather than merely as we are caused to act. So what religious socialism presupposes, and what needs yet to be established, is contra-causal freedom. We can be subject to moral imperatives and be responsible for obeying and disobeying them only if we can choose and act independently of causal determination.

So I need to show that human beings have contra-causal freedom if I am to succeed in supporting the religious side of religious socialism.

Tillich rightly points out that human freedom cannot be established by observing human beings as objects in the empirical world. In his words, "If man is considered an object and nothing more than an object, the question of freedom is answered before it is even asked. And the answer is negative. . . . Freedom cannot be explained in concepts taken from a reality that is the opposite of freedom."[23] Invariably we will be able to account for human behavior causally if we begin by looking at human beings as if they were objects like other objects, and this is no doubt the reason why Brodbeck finds determinism to be "the plainest common sense." Instead, Tillich continues, "freedom can be described only in concepts that point to the experience of actual self-determination"; "we can understand [it] only by a sharp awareness of the way in which we act and determine ourselves."[24] In order to support the proposition that human beings are contra-causally free, we must start not by observing external reality but by analyzing our immediate experience of ourselves as thinking and acting subjects.

What we experience immediately are deliberation and decision, and an analysis of these two concepts suggests -- but does not yet prove -- that we are contra-causally free.

> Deliberation points to an act of weighing arguments and motives. The person who does the weighing is above the motives; as long as he weighs them, he is not identical with any of the motives but is free from all of them. . . . The self-centered person does the weighing and reacts as a whole, through his personal center, to the struggle of the motives. This reaction is called "decision." The word "decision," like the word "incision," involves the image of cutting. A decision cuts off possibilities; otherwise no cutting would have been necessary. The person who does the "cutting" or the "excluding" must be beyond what he cuts off or excludes. His personal center has possibilities, but it is not identical with any of them.[25]

Assume, then, following Tillich, that we do in fact deliberate. We deliberate, as he indicates, in order to make a decision. And in making a decision we cut off *real* possibilities; we decide or choose to do one thing rather than another, both of which are possible for us to do. If so, it must be true that we are - or, rather, that we believe ourselves to be -- free.

Suppose, recalling the earlier example, that I am now deliberating about whether to tell the truth or a lie. In deliberating I bring to bear considerations such as, "My duty is to tell the truth," which is a moral reason, or perhaps, "It's to my advantage financially to tell a lie," which is a prudential reason. I weigh these considerations, then, in deciding what actually to do. But if this whole process is to have any meaning for me, what must I believe?[26] First of all, it can make no sense to deliberate about what to do if I already know what I am going to do; if I already know I will tell a lie I cannot deliberate about whether or not to do it. In that case my deliberating would have no point. And it is also clear that I cannot deliberate about what to do unless I believe that what I do is up to me, i.e., that I can either tell the truth or a lie; I must believe, in Tillich's words, that both are "real possibilities" for me. Not only must I be ignorant about what will happen, but I must also believe that what will happen cannot be predicted. I must believe that whether I tell the truth or a lie depends solely upon me. For once again, if this were not so my deliberating would have no point; it would have no meaning for me.

This much is evident. I cannot consistently hold both that I really deliberate and that what I eventually will do is capable -- even in principle -- of being predicted causally. I cannot deliberate and, at the same time, believe that my decisions and actions are causally determined. For I cannot deliberate unless I can also decide, and I cannot decide unless there is something about which to decide, i.e., unless I believe there are "real possibilities." But that there are such "real possibilities" is precisely what determinism denies. Determinism asserts that what I will do can be predicted, at least in principle if not as a matter of practical fact. It holds, instead, that "there are circumstances -- in our constitutions, backgrounds, environment, and character -- that are jointly sufficient conditions for our behavior, including the choices we make" and that "every event [including our decisions and actions] occurs in some system of laws such that if we knew these laws and the state of the universe at any time, then we could explain the past and predict the future." So *if* it is true that I deliberate, determinism has to be false. *If* I do in fact deliberate, I must be contra-causally free.

This analysis does not yet prove that I am contra-causally free, however. To be sure, I feel as though I can and do deliberate; I have the immediate experience of deliberating, i.e., of weighing reasons and motives for the sake of making a decision. But it remains possible for all of this to be illusory. For it could be that my process of deliberating as well as the decision resulting from it is itself determined in accordance with causal laws. Perhaps my deliberating can be explained and predicted on the basis of psychological or even physiological laws. If so, my experience of my self as "above the motive" is an illusion. The fact that I believe myself to be deliberating is not solid proof that I actually am. So a further argument is needed.

Tillich responds to this problem with a dialectical argument. "Both determinism and indeterminism are theoretically impossible," he contends, "because by implication they deny their claim to express truth. Truth presupposes a decision for the true against the false. Both determinism and indeterminism make such a decision unintelligible."[27] If one affirms determinism, he continues, "then his decision for determinism is itself determined, is merely a matter of destiny, has no truth value and should claim none, for he had no alternative."[28] Determinism, Tillich claims, "reduce[s] man to the dimension of the organic-psychological and deprive[s] him of participation in the dimension of spirit, thus making it impossible to explain how he can have a theory which claims to be true -- of which the [determinist] theory itself is an instance."[29] His point, in other words, is that we contradict ourselves if we assert determinism as true. On the contrary, we assert that we are contra-causally free even as we try to deny it by asserting determinism.

To argue in support of determinism is already to prove it false and, at the same time, to prove that we are contra-causally free.

What I am trying to show here, to keep the context clear, is that we do in fact deliberate, i.e., that deliberation is not illusory. For if deliberation is genuine, then our decisions and actions are not -- or at least not always -- causally determined. So how does Tillich's dialectical argument help?

Notice first of all that his argument applies directly not to moral deliberation but to cognitive deliberation. It purports to show not that our conduct is contra-causally free but that our thinking, or knowing, is free. And it might well be objected that cognitive and moral deliberation are so different that to show that we deliberate in the one is not thereby to show that we deliberate in the other as well. But they are not significantly different. We direct our mental activity just as we direct our physical activity. I can decide to think of my cat at this moment, just as I can decide to punch a key on this typewriter, and at least in the long run I can even decide what to believe and what not to believe. Moreover, both cognitive and moral deliberation are done for the sake of making a decision. I deliberate cognitively in order to decide what to believe, what to affirm as true; I deliberate morally in order to decide what to do, what action to perform. And what is crucial here, I can deliberate cognitively, just as I can deliberate morally, only if I cannot predict -- either in fact or in principle -- what I will finally decide to believe. I can deliberate cognitively, just as I can deliberate morally, only if I believe that my deliberating makes a difference. In the one case my conclusions about what is true are at stake; in the other what I will do is at stake. But whether I aim toward a conclusion or an action, the point is that I deliberate in order to attain it.

The issue, then, is deliberation. The question is whether we can and do, at least on occasion, deliberate.

In substance, Tillich's dialectical argument is that all truth assertions imply genuine deliberation. If we cannot deliberate genuinely -- if we cannot "weigh arguments" on their own merits independently of our psychological and environmental conditioning, etc. -- and draw conclusions on the basis of autonomous deliberating, then we can make no truth claims for these conclusions. Since we necessarily make *some* truth claim -- even if it should happen to be in favor of determinism -- it follows, according to Tillich, that we can indeed deliberate genuinely. For to deny that we do is to exclude the possibility that any proposition whatever can be affirmed as true, including this one, which is absurd.

This argument of Tillich's is basically correct, it seems to me, although I prefer to express it somewhat differently. Suppose, for example, that I make a claim to know something. My belief whatever it is, must be not merely true. I may believe my cat to be asleep in his box, and he may well be. But for me to believe this, even if my belief should happen to be true, is not yet to have knowledge of it. My belief is knowledge only if I hold it for the right reasons. If I am to have knowledge that my cat is presently asleep in his box, as contrasted with merely true belief, I must have evidence; I must be able to justify my belief, i.e., to explain why it is true. If I am to judge that my cat is asleep in his box, and if my judgment is to express knowledge rather than accidentally true belief, my deliberation must therefore be free of causal determination; it must be autonomous. For my judgment must be arrived at and supported in a special way; it must be a justified conclusion. It must derive from evidence and the rules of inference, and not from causal determination. A belief that I am merely caused to hold cannot, as such, be knowledge; even if it is true, I do not have knowledge. A hypnotist might cause me to believe that my cat is asleep in his box, for instance, and this belief might easily be true. But the hypnotist cannot give me knowledge of this fact. He can give me true belief, but not knowledge. In order to constitute knowledge a judgment must be a reasoned judgment; I must arrive at it not through a causally determined process but through a process of deliberating in accordance with norms of inductive and deductive logic.

The question involved here is whether the proposition that every event is causally determined can possibly be known. Tillich's answer, and mine as well, is that it cannot. For if the proposition that every event is causally determined is to be justified, i.e., if it is to be known rather than merely believed, then it must be supported by referring not to the causes of our believing it but to the reasons why we *ought* to believe it. But this is just what determinism implicitly rules out. For as Tillich points out, determinism carries the implication that one's "decision for determinism is itself determined"; in supporting the proposition that every event is causally determined, including the event of our asserting this, we can say consistently only that this is what we are caused to believe. If we assert the truth of determinism by citing evidence -- reasons -- in its support, we contradict ourselves, since by citing evidence we acknowledge it to be possible after all to govern our thinking independently of causal determination; we affirm necessarily that our thinking can follow reasons rather than merely conform to causal sequences. Hence to assert determinism is to refute it and, at the same time, to affirm its opposite. By asserting determinism we necessarily affirm nevertheless that we can deliberate rationally and thereby "make a decision for the true against the false."

This raises another question, however. If in deliberating we adhere to logical rules, may it not be possible that this is but another species of causal determination? Brand Blanshard makes this very point as follows:

When a person, starting with the thought of a solid with square faces, deduces that it must have eight vertices, and then asks why he should have thought of that, the natural answer is, Because the first property entails the second. Of course this is not the only condition, but it seems to me contrary to introspectively plain fact to say that it had nothing to do with the movement of thought. . . . I am saying that in thinking at its best thought comes under the constraint of necessities in its object, so that the objective fact that A necessitates B partially determines our passing in thought from A to B.[30]

We are caused to move from one belief to another, Blanshard argues, by the objectively necessary connection between the two. Our deliberation is determined by this connection. Hence in saying that deliberation follows reasons we are making a case not for contra-causal freedom but for a different kind of causation. Our deliberation is determined, although in this case by an ideal standard.

But this objection confuses *objective* and *subjective* necessity. The rules of inductive and deductive inference are of course objectively necessary; there is indeed a necessary connection between a solid's having square faces and its having eight vertices. There is no necessity that our thinking will follow objective necessity, however. For if there were, to borrow words from Carl Hempel, "there would be no logical or mathematical errors" and, in the realm of conduct, "no immoral acts."[31] The fact that we make mistakes in reasoning, and sometimes even deliberately mislead and deceive ourselves, shows that there is a crucial difference between objective and subjective necessity. The rules of logic are objectively necessary -- they are "absolutely and universally valid,"[32] as Tillich says -- but there is no necessity for our subjective thinking to follow them. Deliberately to follow the rules of logic is quite different from being determined by them. Our thinking is not determined by these rules. Rather, we follow them by governing our thinking by them. And this we may or may not do. We may or may not obey the laws of logic. We *ought* to, of course, but whether or not we do is up to us; it is not something that is determined for us causally.

Given that we know anything at all, then, and it is self-contradictory to argue to the contrary, it follows that we can and do deliberate independently of causal determination. We can and do govern our thinking -- and consequently our acting as well, since action is carried out on the basis of thinking -- by reasons, and this implies that we are not merely passive recipients of causes but are contra-causally free agents.[33]

So we do have the "freedom to receive commands, to obey and to disobey them," that religious socialism's religious principle presupposes. But religious socialism is also "the effort to relate the religious principle to social reality and to bring it to form therein," and this aspect of it -- the practical aspect, shall we say -- presupposes that economic reality can be explained and predicted scientifically. Religious socialism presupposes in its practical aspect, that is, that human behavior is lawful after all. Hence we need yet to show how this can be possible in view of the fact of contra-causal freedom. We must reconcile nomothetic explanation and prediction in economic science with the religious principle's affirmation of human freedom.

To begin by looking at Tillich's approach to solving this problem, it is his conviction that human beings have contra-causal freedom that induces him to favor Marxian over what he refers to as "formal" or "liberal," i.e., neo-classical, economic analysis. I shall contend momentarily that he is in error in doing so, but first I wish to show briefly how he reaches this conclusion.

I noted earlier that God, for Tillich, is being-itself and that the moral imperative to become fully personal is "the ethical

expression of the ontological structure of being itself." By becoming fully personal, according to him, we fulfill the "meaning of
being." Being-itself is potentially personal, and "the individual
personality is the place within the whole of being where this becomes
manifest and actual."[34] We are being-itself's agents, so to speak,
and it is our responsibility to fulfill its "meaning" within ourselves. Hence the effort to actualize oneself as "a complete self
and a rational person" is religious. Religion is "directedness toward the Unconditional,"[35] where being-itself is "the Unconditional-
al" -- God -- and morality is "the active realization of the Unconditional"[36] as fully personal being. But morality is religion only
in what Tillich calls *praxis*; it is practical "directedness toward
the Unconditional." We can attend to being-itself theoretically
too, however. We can be religious in *theoria* as well as in *praxis,*
and we are religious theoretically when we attend cognitively to
being-itself. We do this, then, in metaphysics, or ontology. And
just as religion as morality is normative for social organization,
so religion as ontology is normative for knowing in the specialized
sciences -- including economics. Ontology "asks the question of being
as being" and "the answer it provides determines the analysis of all
special forms of being."[37] By describing "the meaning and structure
of being and its manifestation in the different realms of being,"[38]
religion as ontology identifies and characterizes the basic features
of the subject matters of the specialized sciences and thereby governs what methods are "adequate" for knowing them; by describing
being-itself and the grades or dimensions through which it becomes
progressively "manifest and actual," culminating with personal being
-- or "life in the dimension of spirit,"[39] as he also calls it --
religion as ontology is the "vital power, meaning, and blood" of a
normative "system of the sciences according to their objects and
methods."[40]

   We shall not be able to go into the details of his "system
of the sciences" here, of course, but a few quick points should suffice to show why he opts for Marx's conception of economic analysis.
   1. Human beings are potentially and partially actual persons, according to Tillich's ontology, only within a community. "A
person becomes aware of his own character as a person," he explains,
"only when he is confronted by another person. Only in the community
of the I and the thou can personality arise."[41] Hence human life
is necessarily social.
   2. "Community, however," he continues, "transcends personality. Community has a special quality, a power of being of its
own, which is more than the mere aggregate of all the personalities
in the community. It has a life of its own. . . ."[42] A social organism is a "primary gestalt" (ursprüngliche Gestalt)[43] with inner
forms and laws of its own, and "the structural forms and structural
laws of the social organism comprise the subject matter of sociology."[44]
   3. Every social organism performs certain necessary tasks.
For example, it provides for "legal and public administration" by
means of a political system, and it "preserves and develops itself"
by means of an economic system.[45] These "social functions" (Sozial-
funktionen),[46] as Tillich calls them, are the subject matters of

political science and the science of economics respectively. Unlike the social organism itself, however, its "social functions"
are derivative rather than "primary" gestalts. They are gestalts,
i.e., they behave as structural wholes, but they are created by
rather than merely given to human beings; they are products of
contra-causally free human activity rather than naturally given entities.
        4. Hence whereas there are "sociological laws which hold
for every social community,"[47] there are no general laws regulating
the behavior of the political and economic "social functions." Political and economic systems behave in accordance with laws, but
political and economic laws are relative to the specific kinds of
political and economic gestalts in which they operate. Specifically,
Tillich argues,

> Economic laws come about only when partly conscious and partly uncon-
> scious technological will has created economic institutions within
> which these laws are effective. Economic laws are laws of the tech-
> nologically formed economic function of society, and they change when
> purposes and programs change. . . . The idea of a "pure" economic
> science is an impossible abstraction.[48]

Human freedom creates society's economic system. Once created, an
economic system has its own inner behavioral laws, but there are no
"economic laws in the sense of [universal] laws of being."[49]
        It is this notion that economic systems are human creations,
then, that induces Tillich to favor Marxian over neo-classical economic analysis. Both Marxian and neo-classical economic analysis
are nomothetic; both explain and predict economic events in terms of
economic laws. But whereas Marxian analysis is aware, as Engels
says, that it "deals with material which is historical, that is,
constantly changing,"[50] neo-classical analysis approaches every possible economic system as if it behaved in accordance with the same
laws. "Merchant adventurers, companies, and trusts; Guilds, Governments and Soviets may come and go. But under them all, and, if need
be in spite of them all," as Hubert Henderson puts it, "the profound
adjustments of supply and demand will work themselves out and work
themselves out again for so long as the lot of man is darkened by
the curse of Adam."[51] So the Marxian, and not the neo-classical,
conception is in line with Tillich's notion of economic systems as
human creations with changing laws of behavior. "Marx's method of
analyzing economic phenomena," he explains, "is a sociological method:
it takes into consideration, in every moment, the human and social
factors and denies the escapist attitude of formal [neo-classical]
economics which hides the fact that economic action is human action."[52]

> [Marx] puts the so-called economic laws into the context of man's
> total behavior as it develops under special sociological conditions.
> He does not believe in the abstract functioning of these laws, but
> shows that their validity depends on the structure of the society
> in which they operate. Thus his method is concrete, dynamic and
> critical, in contrast to the attempts . . . of theoretical economists

to formulate [universal] economic laws according to the pattern of mathematical physics."53

So this is how Tillich reconciles contra-causal human freedom and nomothetic explanation and prediction in economic science. Human freedom creates economic systems; a society's economic order comes into being by virtue of collective human activity. Consequently, economic systems are historical. Not only do they come and go over time,but their structures and behavior vary with human purposes and programs. Nevertheless, economic systems are gestalts. That is, once instituted by human action,they are structural wholes which behave in accordance with inner laws of their own. Human freedom and nomothetic economic analysis are therefore compatible, Tillich maintains. For while human beings are free to create various kinds of economic systems, the science of economics can discover and formulate the special laws regulating the behavior of whatever economic system is thereby created.

We do not have to go into the details of Tillich's Marxian analysis of economic reality to see that this is not a satisfactory solution to the problem at hand, however. It does not reconcile contra-causal freedom with economic law. For while Tillich's understanding acknowledges a freedom on the part of human beings collectively to set up different kinds of economic systems, it still views human behavior *within* a given system as determined by the structural laws of that system. It thinks of an economic system as a kind of organism within which individual human beings function as constituent parts or members. The system behaves as a whole -- as a gestalt -- and its parts, namely, individual human beings, conform to the inner laws of the whole. Hence, on this understanding, there is no place -- or at least not a significant one -- for contra-causally free activity by individual human beings. But it is precisely the contra-causal freedom of individuals that we need to reconcile with nomothetic economic explanation. And this reconciliation cannot be achieved by showing,as Tillich tries to do, economic laws to be "laws of the technologically formed economic function of society."

Where Tillich goes wrong, I suggest, is in conceiving of economic analysis as an analysis primarily of the behavior of economic systems as wholes or gestalts and only secondarily -- if at all -- as an analysis of the economic activity of individual human beings. For to do this is already to think of individuals not as freely acting persons but as largely passive functionaries of the whole. When economic laws are thought of as the whole's inner structural laws, then the activity of individuals must be thought of as determined by these laws. So if this is his error, the solution to the problem of reconciling human contra-causal freedom with nomothetic economic explanation must be found by starting from the other direction. We should start not by analyzing the behavior of the whole, i.e., a given "economic function" of a society, but by analyzing human activity itself and then building up from this analysis a theory of how economic systems behave as wholes. We should conceive of economics as a science primarily of human action and only secondarily or derivatively as a science of a society's "economic function."

So how can this be possible? If human beings have contra-causal freedom, as I have agreed with Tillich's ontology in assert-ing, how can there be laws of human action from which laws of eco-nomic systems as wholes can be derived? The answer is that the activity of contra-causally free human beings is not random. Free-dom and randomness are not the same at all! On the contrary, as I argued earlier, to be free is to govern one's activity rationally, at least in some degree, and rational activity is -- in a sense -- lawful. "There are no laws regarding the content of economic be-haviour," as economist Frank H. Knight points out, "but there are laws universally valid as to its form. There is an abstract ratio-nale of all conduct which is rational at all, and a rationale of all social relations arising through the organization of rational activity."[54] This "abstract rationale" is the law of the economic activity of individual persons, and the laws of society's "economic function" derive from it. And it is a law *of* human action, not a law *over* human action; it is a "rationale," not a causal determinant.

To illustrate this notion very roughly, suppose I perform a free action. My action, as free, is goal-oriented. Unlike plants and lower animals, I choose an end -- a state of affairs I aim to bring about -- and in acting I then use means in order to achieve this end. And in doing this I am acting rationally insofar as my means are appropriate for reaching the end.

But I have more than one end I wish to attain; I have many goals in mind. And the means to my ends are scarce; that is, I can-not attain all of my ends. So I "economize." I allocate the means at my disposal in such a way as to maximize my total goal-attainment. I arrange my various goals in their order of importance to me and allocate my means so as to attain the most important goals first. Economizing is thus an aspect of my free activity. I allocate scarce means (which have alternative uses) among my several ends for the sake of maximizing my total goal-attainment.

Here, then, is the "rationale" or "form" of my activity. First I decide the value to me of each means -- each consumer good, to use the language of neo-classical economics. I decide the value of each book, each gallon of gasoline, each hamburger, and so on. I do this by determining each unit's "utility" to me for achieving my goals, for maximizing my total "satisfaction." And the utility or value to me of each succeeding unit of the same good necessarily declines. For since I have my goals arranged in the order of their importance to me, the first unit of the good satisfies the most im-portant goal; the second unit satisfies a goal of less importance, and so on down the ranking of my goals.

Although I have expressed it crudely here, this is what neo-classical economics refers to as the law of diminishing marginal utility. But it is not a law by which I am causally determined. On the contrary, it is a part of the "rationale" of my contra-causally free activity. It is a principle I follow in order to achieve my chosen ends.

The means to my ends are not simply there in the world for me to take and use, however. For the most part I have to produce them, and on the (unrealistic, to be sure) assumption that I am the sole producer and consumer of means, I must determine the cost to me

of producing them. I must estimate as best I can the cost to me of
producing each unit of books, gasoline, hamburger, and so on. And
my productive resources -- time, energy, and materials -- are limited.
I therefore have to allocate them; I cannot produce all I need of
every means to my goals. To the extent that I produce books I must
forego producing gasoline and hamburgers, for example. Hence the
cost to me of producing another book is the satisfaction I would
have gotten if I had produced other means instead. Cost of production is foregone satisfaction. I gain satisfaction by consuming
the book, but I lose the satisfaction I would have obtained from
extra units of gasoline and hamburger. This loss of satisfaction,
then, is the marginal cost of producing the extra book. So just as
marginal utility -- value -- declines with the consumption of each
successive unit of a means, the marginal cost of producing a means
to my ends rises. Rising marginal cost is the other side of diminishing marginal utility.

Taking diminishing marginal utility and increasing marginal cost into account I then determine what means and in what
amounts actually to produce and consume. I produce and consume the
means to my goals in amounts such that the value to me -- the utility,
that is -- of each unit of a means is just equal to the marginal cost
of producing it. I will produce and consume means in quantities
such that the contribution to my goal-satisfaction of the last unit
of each means is just equal to the satisfaction I forego by virtue
of producing this means rather than another. For if I produce and
consume a means in a quantity less than this, I can increase my
total goal-satisfaction by producing and consuming more, because
the satisfaction gained would then be greater than the satisfaction
given up by changing my resource allocation. Conversely, if I produce and consume more than this quantity I can gain in total satisfaction by cutting back, since by shifting my production and consumption to something else I gain more value than I lose. I maximize my total goal-satisfaction -- I am in equilibrium, as economists
say -- when I equate the marginal utility of a means with its marginal cost.

Putting all of this into the language of neo-classical
economic analysis, I have a "demand" and a "supply" of each means
I produce and consume. Expressed geometrically, my demand for a
means is a schedule sloping downward to the right from a vertical
axis representing value toward a horizontal axis representing quantity, and my supply of a means is a schedule sloping upward to the
right from the horizontal axis along the vertical. The downward
sloping demand schedule reflects diminishing marginal utility; the
upward sloping supply schedule reflects increasing marginal cost.
And the point where these two schedules intersect expresses my equilibrium position. This point shows both the value to me of each
means and the quantity of it that I produce and consume. I determine the value to me of each good as well as the quantities to produce and consume by my demand for and supply of each.

It should be clear from what I have said here that my activity, even as contra-causally free, is not random but lawful. Indeed it is lawful precisely because it is free. Free activity is
rational activity, and rational activity has a "form" or "rationale,"

as Knight rightly points out. And "there are laws universally valid
as to [this] form," for example, the laws of diminishing marginal
utility and increasing marginal cost. They are laws *of* but not *over*
my activity. They do not determine my activity; rather, my activity
determines the laws.

Of course an "economic function" of a society, to use
Tillich's term, is vastly more complex than my individual economy.
But its "rationale" remains the same. Production and consumption in
a social economy are separated. Producers produce for others' consumption, and consumers consume goods and services -- means -- produced
by others. Production is specialized. People specialize in the production of some particular good or service which they then exchange
through the market for goods and services produced by others. Even
so, demand and supply regulate output and price (value). Borrowing
Henderson's words again, "the profound adjustments of supply and demand will work themselves out and work themselves out again for so
long as the lot of man is darkened by the curse of Adam." Just as
in my individual economy, the equilibrium prices and quantities of
goods and services in a social economy will be the prices and quantities at which the quantities demanded by everyone are equal to the
quantities supplied by everyone. For no matter how much more complex a social economy may be it is comprised of individual human
beings acting in the way described above, and consequently its behavior can be explained and predicted by the same laws of diminishing marginal utility and increasing marginal cost.

What I have been doing here of course has been to describe roughly the approach to economic reality which, as Tillich
rightly points out, "attempts . . . to formulate [universal] economic
laws according to the pattern of mathematic physics." The laws by
which neo-classical economic analysis explains and predicts economic events are indeed universal. To be sure, they "work themselves
out" in a variety of different ways, depending in part on how a particular society's "economic function" is organized. For example,
the manager of a publicly owned monopolistic industry will no doubt
make different price and output decisions than will the manager of a
privately owned one. But the underlying "rationale" remains the
same. "Merchant adventurers, companies, and trusts; Guilds, Governments and Soviets may come and go" -- but they all behave in accordance with the laws of diminishing marginal utility and increasing
marginal cost. Nevertheless, these laws are fully compatible with,
and in fact come from, contra-causally free human activity. For
"there is an abstract rationale of all conduct which is rational at
all, and a rationale of all social relations arising through the organization of rational activity." The laws are universal because
the "rationale" of human action is universal, but they are laws *of* --
and not *over* -- human action.

So religious socialism's religious principle can be reconciled with nomothetic economic explanation and prediction. It can
be, that is, if the laws by which economic analysis explains and
predicts economic events are conceived as laws of human action itself. For in that case, the religious principle's presupposition of
contra-causal freedom is compatible with economic science's presupposition that human behavior is lawful.

NOTES AND REFERENCES

1. Paul Tillich, *Gesammelte Werke*, Vol. II: *Christentum und Soziale Gestaltung* (Stuttgart: Evangelisches Verlagswerk, 1962), p. 175. Hereafter this work will be referred to as *XSG*.

2. Paul Tillich, *The Protestant Era*, James Luther Adams, ed. and trs. (Chicago: The University of Chicago Press, 1948), p. 118. Hereafter this work will be referred to as *PE*.

3. Paul Tillich, *Systematic Theology*, 3 Vols.(Chicago: The University of Chicago Press, 1951-1963), I: 237. Hereafter this work will be referred to as *ST* I, II, and III respectively.

4. *PE*, p. 118.

5. Paul Tillich, *Gesammelte Werke*, Vol. I: *Fruhe Hauptwerke* (Stuttgart: Evangelisches Verlagswerk, 1959), p. 325. Hereafter this work will be referred to as *FH*.

6. *ST*, I, p. 183.

7. *ST*, III, p. 386.

8. Paul Tillich, *Political Expectation,* James Luther Adams, ed. (New York: Harper and Row, 1971), p. 48.

9. Paul Tillich, "The Kingdom of God and History," *The Kingdom of God and History*, The Official Oxford Conference Books, Vol. III (Chicago, New York: Willet, Clark and Co., 1938), p. 132.

10. *Political Expectation*, p. 50.

11. "The Kingdom of God and History," p. 107.

12. My argument on this is expressed in an essay entitled "Rationality and Moral Obligation," to be published soon in a collection of essays tentatively titled *Religious Liberal Perspectives on Morality*.

13. See my essay "Toward a Theory of Normative Economics" in *Social Ethics: Issues in Ethics and Society*, Gibson Winter,ed. (New York: Harper and Row, 1968), pp. 83-103.

14. *XSG*, p. 361.

15. *Ibid.*, p. 363.

16. *ST*, III, p. 40.

17. May Brodbeck, "Freedom, Determinism, and Morality," *Readings in the Philosophy of the Social Sciences*, May Brodbeck, ed. (New York: The Macmillan Co., 1968), p. 669.

18. *Ibid.*, p. 671.

19. *Ibid.*, p. 670.

20. *Ibid.*, pp. 672-673.

21. *Ibid.*

22. Concrete duties such as the duty to tell the truth derive, for Tillich, from the reverse side of the imperative to actualize personality, i.e., from the right of persons not to be treated as mere things, and, for me, from a duty to act only on maxims which can be willed as universal law (Kant's "categorical imperative").

23. *PE*, p. 116.

24. *Ibid.*

25. *ST*, I, p. 184.

26. My argument here is guided by Richard Taylor's. See his *Action and Purpose* (Englewood Cliffs: Prentice Hall, Inc., 1966), pp. 167-184.

27. *ST*, I, p. 183. Indeterminism, i.e., the view that some events are completely random, is of course equally incompatible with freedom conceived as self-determination.

28. Paul Tillich, *My Search for Absolutes* (New York: Simon and Schuster, 1969), p. 79-80.

29. *ST*, III, p. 38.

30. Paul Blanshard, "The Case for Determinism," *Determinism and Freedom in the Age of Modern Science*, Sidney Hook, ed. (New York: Collier Books, 1961), pp. 27-28.

31. Carl Hempel, "Some Reflections on 'The Case for Determinism'," *Determinism and Freedom in the Age of Modern Science*, p. 174.

32. *FH*, p. 128.

33. I am not suggesting here of course that we have unlimited freedom. Our contra-causal freedom is limited, as Tillich points out, by our destiny.

34. *PE*, p. 118.

35. Paul Tillich, *What is Religion?*, James Luther Adams, ed. (New York: Harper and Row, 1969), p. 162.

36. *FH*, pp. 269-270.

37. *ST*, I, p. 163.

38. *PE*, p. 88.

39. *ST*, III, p. 38.

40. *FH*, p. 117.

41. *PE*, p. 125.

42. *Ibid*.

43. *FH*, p. 171.

44. *Ibid.*, p. 172.

45. *Ibid.*, p. 174.

46. *Ibid*.

47. *Ibid.*, p. 173.

48. *Ibid.*, p. 190.

49. *Ibid*.

50. Frederick Engels, *Anti-Duhring* (Moscow: Foreign Languages Publishing House, 1959), p. 203.

51. Hubert Henderson, *Supply and Demand* (Chicago: The University of Chicago Press, 1958), p. 14.

52. *PE*, p. 259.

53. Paul Tillich, "How Much Truth is in Karl Marx?", *The Christian Century*, LXV (September, 1948), p. 906.

54. Frank H. Knight, *The Ethics of Competition and Other Essays* (London: George Allen and Unwin, Ltd., 1951), p. 135.

THE TASK OF SOCIAL ETHICS

by
George W. Pickering

According to my reckoning, social ethics made its appearance on the American scene in the late nineteenth century in the work of Francis Greenwood Peabody, William Jewett Tucker, Graham Taylor, and Charles Richmond Henderson. These men all set out to provide intellectual discipline to the confrontation which was taking place in their time between the various claims of the Christian faith and the sundry issues of the industrial corporate order. They were exceedingly confident that the Christian faith had the resources not only to provide imperatives for social action but also -- and this is what was new about them -- to provide descriptive and interpretive insight into the dynamics and issues of the emerging social order. They were unwilling to grant any radical distinction between normative and descriptive concerns. At least in the cases of Peabody and Tucker, social ethics had emerged from homiletics. By the 1890's these men had carried the problems of speaking into the problems of acting and had there encountered the problems of the emerging and not well understood social structure. Tucker developed a theory of 'social economics'; Peabody a theology of social order; Taylor a theory of religion and democratic social action; Henderson seems to have cast his mind on the problems of social planning although he does not seem to have settled on a theory.[1]

None of these men succeeded in leaving behind him a durable discipline or intellectual enterprise. In a sense, their work was swallowed up in what is conventionally called either "the social gospel" or the "progressive era." Walter Rauschenbusch, generally taken to be the epitome of the marriage of the social gospel and progressivism, actually reversed the inner movement of these men's work and decisively carried social ethics back to homiletics. Both the churches and the rest of the culture, it seems, were more comfortable with that arrangement.

Consequently, while there have been persons working on problems in social ethics, Christian ethics, and theological ethics --in various mixtures of each-- we do not find today that we stand in any line of development toward a focussed discipline of social ethics. There have been changes, to be sure, as the styles of theology, social science, and social action have changed; but disciplined developments are hard to find.

It is to be hoped that scholars will not have to look back, yet another hundred years hence, and give the same report. Perhaps it is to be feared that they may. The task of social ethics, after all, did not pass away with the progressive era. Indeed, in the meantime it would seem that its possibilities have enlarged, even though its practice has been largely episodic.

As I see it, the task of social ethics is to discipline the concern for moral standards as they appear in the culture at large, to identify the sources and structures of moral problems encountered in the life of the society as well as in the course of an individual life, to describe the normative conflicts as well as the normative structures which are embodied in our common life as a people, and·to reason normatively about the practical alternatives available within the culture; in short, to view the social order as morally and intellectually serious but unfinished business.

There is time enough for the methodological complications of this task; but I doubt very much that we will get around to them in the next hundred years any more than we have in the last century unless we gain some vision any or grasp of the cultural and religious significance of the project.

This past century in America has been a period of sustained cultural and religious transformation. Americans have seen the world of the corporation emerge as a powerful but not always identified competitor to the worlds of the republic and the covenant. The liasons between these latter two had always been somewhat uncertain and uneasy anyway. In the competition with the world of the corporation, they have been elevated to the status of "ideals" which need to be compromised from time to time, i.e., daily, in the name of "realism," i.e., the imperatives of the corporate world. Descriptively, the world of the republic has been reduced to a question of who gets -- what, where, and how. Similarly, the world of the covenant has been empirically relegated to a "private sphere" where ultimate meanings can be entertained on a personal or confessional basis without any serious confrontation with the obvious meanings structured in the social order. Such is the fate of ideals which end up in a world where competitive values have the advantage of presenting themselves as facts.

One of the lessons of cultural relativity is that in every age and climate "realism" wins. It is the fantastic array of realisms which needs to be explained. There never was a "realism" that did not have a moral universe of some sort embedded within it and consequently, enacted through it. It is not, however, always easy to get at that moral universe, disguised as it is as nothing but matter-of-fact common sense, and protected as it is by socially embodied, culturally articulated structures of faith and reason.

Uncovering those socially embodied and culturally articulated structures of faith and reason is, therefore, the first task of social ethics. Raising them up to a level of awareness through disciplined discourse is an important prerequisite to the clarification of the moral problematic. While it is true that the religious and the moral are not the same thing, it seems also to be true that each requires the other to be understood and, what is more, to be enacted.

Our forebears in the late nineteenth century were on the right track when they thought that there was something religiously problematic about the oncoming industrial corporate order; but it was more than a question of the adequacy of the Christian faith to relate normatively and descriptively to the emerging society. Nor was it, as their latter-day protagonists supposed, a question of the viability of religious commitments in a secular society. It was a question of the religious meaning of the new world which was then appearing. That question was, and is, important, not because it offers a wedge for re-establishing the relevance of traditional religious language, but because it offers the possibility of understanding the transformations which have been experienced in the actual forms of our common humanity.

By the late nineteenth century, Americans were accustomed -- even if they were not intellectually accommodated -- to a religiously pluralistic culture. This radical relativity of religious structures, which was not only implied but enforced by the situation, had not yet, however, become an object of religious thought. William James' *Varieties of Religious Experience* is exceptional in this respect. For the most part, evangelical Protestants responded with a drive to leave their distinctive mark on social institutions, while American Catholics responded with an equally strong drive to preserve their own distinctive religious traits. While these groups have paid some attention to each other -- sometimes antipathetically, sometimes ecumenically -- neither has paid much attention to the religious character of the basic situation to which they were responding. On the whole, they have accommodated themselves to the apparently secular aspects of it. They have preferred strategies of liberalizing or theologically representing their doctrines in the attempt to maintain their own claims to universality. Meanwhile, the irreversible relativity of the situation has continued to take its toll on their credibility either as moral guides or as articulators of the human spirit.

That, however, is not the most serious aspect of the situation. Caught between their own claims to distinctiveness *and* universality, these religions have tended to make themselves the objects of religious attention while the other -- and in many ways spiritually more formative -- religious dimensions of the culture have gone unattended, not only by the representatives and critics of these religions, but by other scholars of our common life as well. Consequently, we are left with a void in the understanding and interpretation of our culture, our social order, and even our personal lives.

Whether the traditional religions are, or can be made, relevant to modern social conditions is not the primary religious question for persons in our time. If that were the question, it could be answered rather easily. The answer is: yes, they can be and there is a wide variety of ways in which this can be accomplished. There is only one pre-requisite which all these ways share and that is this: treat these religious realities as dependent variables and any number of life-styles and continuing identities can be worked out for them. In this pluralistic culture's house, there are many mansions. If it were not so, it would have been obvious long before now.

The primary religious question is much more unsettling and possibly more enlightening than that. It has to do with the presence and elaboration of structures of faith which do effectively give form and substance to the human spirit, but which are not recognized as religious and are not, therefore, subject to the disciplined attention which is accorded to recognized religious meanings.

This culture is shot through with principles, values, beliefs, symbols, rituals and associations by which the preferred and pre-eminent modes of being are defined among us. The problem for religious thought is to bring the forms of thought into focus on the actual forms of being that have arisen among us, that is, on the actual forms of our common humanity. It is silly nonsense to continue the fiction that somehow faith and reason got a divorce when they encountered the world of the corporation. There never was a structure of faith which did not have as an essential dimension of it a corresponding doctrine and exercise of reason. The reverse is also true. There never was a structure of reason -- even in the purest Kantian world -- which did not entail a world of faith. We know this in the abstract. The problem in the modern world is to trace its meaning into the concreteness of those relations in which we live and move and have our actual being.

Structures of Faith and Reason as an Empirical Problem

Strange to say, but in the analysis of our time and the interpretation of our culture and the assessment of our prospects, questions of faith are rarely taken to be serious factors, elements, or dimensions in the structure of our predicaments. This is strange because we are really quite sophisticated at perceiving the mixtures of faith and reason in other ages and in other cultures and at interpreting the world-creating and world-limiting functions of this mixture for other peoples. When it comes to our own situation, however, we seem to have lost track of the forms which faith has taken in our own midst. By contrast with other periods in our history, we seem to be much more aware of the forms of faith which we have lost and which these other periods presumably had than of the forms which we have produced. When, in the struggle of "cosmos and history" or "sacred and profane," history and the profane seem to dominate -- as they do among us -- we seem not to notice the continuing functions of faith and religious meaning, except insofar as they are seen to take refuge in some "private sphere" or other. This is unfortunate because, far from yielding a clear view of our "objective situation," the result is an almost total mystification of the actual content of our common humanity, to a point where we even doubt its existence, which is to say, our own being. Strange to say, stranger yet to live with; but apparently true.

It is amazing how many of our recent religious histories are stories of loss. Sidney Mead, Cushing Strout, Sidney Ahlstrom, Robert Handy -- each is viewing our religious history with an eye to lost opportunities, lost syntheses, lost coherences, and lost hopes. It is equally amazing how many of our projections of the

future have turned bleak in their assessment of the prospects for
advancing humane values. Futurologists, like historians, seem to
be dividing between those who see the need, but not the resources,
for some new beginning and those who deny the need and therefore
do not miss the prospects. Robert Heilbroner could stand as a
representative of the first type and the president of almost any
multi-national corporation as a representative of the latter. The
division of the world into optimists and pessimists is an almost
certain sign that some fatal blow has been struck to our powers of
empirical inquiry.

It may be that concepts of faith and reason are ultimately
normative concepts. I am prepared to agree with that. It is no
corollary, however, that concepts of faith and reason -- including
structures of faith and reason -- are therefore intrinsically subjective, arbitrarily variable, socially unstructured and empirically
unspecifiable. Neither does it follow that no such normative concepts either apply or operate just because it can be seen that some
previously normative configurations of faith and reason have been
driven from the center to the margin of the structure of culturally
formative action and, even in their attenuated presence, have been
so radically transformed in the transition to specifically modern
conditions as to have lost their historic significance. Something
of the same functional order has taken their place; and it is an
empirical question what that is. We need, however, some descriptive concepts of faith and reason to guide the inquiry.

It will not suffice, empirically, to translate the notion
of a structure of faith and reason into a mere configuration of beliefs or other subjectively held "values." That may suffice to
account for the fate of traditional faiths under modern social
conditions; but it will not shed light on the profoundly human
dimensions which are embodied, endangered, and hidden under the
notions of "common sense" which attend modern social conditions.
The exclusion of the forms of faith and the structures of faith
and reason from the world of disciplined inquiry into our empirical
situation only succeeds in concealing critical dimensions of our
common humanity while rendering the other dimensions less than intelligible.

The argument here presented is not an apologia for any
particular, and most assuredly not for any universal, structure of
faith, although it will become advocative before all is said and
done. It is an argument that any society will exhibit socially
structured and empirically specifiable forms of faith and reason
and that understanding these structures is as much a descriptive
task as understanding the patterns of kinship or the distributions
of political power or even such abstract functions as pattern
maintenance, role performance, class conflict or the maximization
of self interest.

Such structures will be found wherever there are real
social relations which embody, imply and evoke principles, values,
beliefs, symbols, rituals, and associations which represent a claim
as to the preferred and pre-eminent modes of being by which a community either is or should be characterized. These are the forms
which faith and reason take in our common life.

There is no need to suppose that there is only one such
structure in any given society, certainly not in ours. There may
be many. It is an open question whether some kind of unity threads
itself throughout the apparent multiplicity. That is an empirical
question, not surely an analytical one as Durkheim supposed. Indeed, divergent structures of faith and reason may account for
some of the conflict experienced by individuals, groups and societies in the modern age -- not just the conflict between these,
but the conflict within them as well.

One more *caveat*. There is no necessary connection between structures of faith and reason and any explicit or even implicit reference to or articulation of the Sacred, the Holy, the
Ultimate Height or Depth. These symbolisms may or may not be
present and it is important to know if they are and how they are;
but even when they are present, they are not necessarily definitive,
either historically or generically, even of the religious realm.
If the past century of studies in the histories of religions has
yielded anything besides voluminous details of diverse orientations,
it would seem to be this: that the humanistic import far outweighs
the transcendental mysteries in sacred orientations; and, indeed,
that it is the humanistic import which shines through and is enacted
through the sacred orientations; in short, that the varieties of
religious experience, encounter, and expression which prevail among
a people are best understood as defining for that people the nature,
the limits, the importance and the content of their common humanity.
It is the actual forms of common humanity which have become the
basis for understanding the diverse orientations which we have
discovered in the history of religions. It is the constitution of
the everyday world in terms of its preferred and pre-eminent modes
of being which lies at the final outcome of orientations to the
sacred. The constitution of the everyday world in terms of its
preferred and pre-eminent modes of being is a structure of faith(s)
and reason(s). It is a realm of religious meaning with or without
the benefit of a transcendent referent or supervening unity.

What, then, are we to look for in cultures like ours
which, it is commonly agreed, are de-sacralized? It seems that we
may have lost any over-arching or supervening orientation toward a
commonly perceived or articulated sacred point of reference. According to our historians, we have certainly lost our historic
configurations of sacred belief and meaning. Bits and pieces may
survive, but the configurations which held them together have dissipated. According to Luckmann we stand as consumers before a vast
array of historically developed "ultimate meanings," filling our
lives, like shoppers with market baskets, with prepackaged religious meanings from the shelves of our super-market culture. If we
follow his line of thought, we are led to the conclusion that the
de-sacralization of the society and the culture is a correlate of
the sacralization of the individual, articulated as autonomous,
mysteriously atomized in a "private sphere," sustained by the
structured promise of a personal but private identity. The preferred and pre-eminent modes of being are the private ones; and the
nature, limits, importance, and content of common humanity are seen
in terms of their availability for private uses, in this world and

any others. This, surely, is a structure of faith and reason and
the various schools of economics and existentialisms provide some
of the theologies for it. It is not at all clear that a sacred
orientation toward the autonomous individual is necessary either
as an affirmation or even as an implication for the continuity or
the religious meaning of this situation.

    This preoccupation with the private as the pre-eminent
may be partially descriptive but it is also problematic. The
public remains intrusive even at the normative level as the bearer
of competitive religious meanings. In the brief compass of this
essay, we can only suggest a couple of examples of the intrusive
public. Both are religious, that is, structures of faith and
reason. Both are in some conflict with each other and with any
primary definition of the individual as his/her private identity.
The two which we shall discuss are (1) the color line and (2) the
democratic prospect. In examining these, we shall see that even
at the descriptive level the private sphere is a good deal less
private than might be supposed or, for that matter, desired. In
the process perhaps a point or two can be made, simply on the scale
of empirical adequacy, for the value of viewing such things as
structures of religious meaning.

The Color Line as a Structure of Faith and Reason

    The color line creates a world that makes sense. That
is its most important characteristic which needs to be explained
or understood. It is a normative function. It will help to explain this otherwise elusive and apparently seductive characteristic if we approach the color line not only as a social structure
-- which it undoubtedly is -- but also as a structure of religious meaning, a structure of faith and reason, a structure of
principles, values, beliefs, symbols, rituals and associations by
which color is defined as a preferred and pre-eminent mode of being
around which it seems acceptable to organize significant aspects
of our common humanity.

    Faith and reason, like facts and values, may be logically
distinct but they are everywhere found mixed in activities, events,
and structured contexts. Indeed, they are found so mixed that
there is always an empirical as well as a theoretical question,
which is which? This is not an easy question to settle. It is
some advantage just to know that it is a question.

    What, for instance, are the "facts" of the color line?
Well, one of the irreducible facts is that in every epoch of
American history, we have embodied, however reluctantly or en-
thusiastically, some major institutionalization of the color line
to the point where that institution made sense and opposing it
seemed unreasonable. Today we look back on slavery as an obvious
miscarriage of human relations; but in its own time, that was far
from obvious. As late as 1863 it was not clear that the Union was
prepared to abolish slavery. Nor was there any clear idea as to
what form a future without slavery could take. Today we look back
on Jim Crow as an obvious miscarriage of the legal and social

system. As late as 1963, however, scholars and newspapers were
still arguing over whether American institutions were in fact
segregated,and they were still having more doubts about the propriety of civil rights tactics attacking segregation than about
the continuing resistence to integrated alternatives by what were
still called "responsible" public officials. Today we look out
upon the metropolitan areas and take it for granted that the color
line is an essential ingredient in their institutional arrangements. It is just part of the matter of fact situation which
supports a whole world of common sense activities. In fact, the
"metropolitan area" is the latest institutionalization of the color
line. Three quarters of the American people live in those metropolitan areas and, while they are aware of many problems in their
social and institutional life, abolishing the color line does not
appear to most of them to be much of a solution to the many problems they experience. Quite the reverse.

If we can abstract ourselves from it for a moment, we
shall see that this color line is no mere figure of speech. It
is an elaborate arrangement of socially structured reasons for its
own continuance. These reasons appear to be nothing but configurations of facts, highly valorized facts to be sure; but it is in
the guise of facts -- social facts and experiential facts -- that
the color line provides one of the "realisms" by which we arrange
ourselves as a people. It is a self-fulfilling prophecy of antag-
onism and inequality which binds us together as a people while
seeming to keep us apart as "races." The dimensions of this color
line are as follows:
(1) Continued or increasing *separation* of the "races"
geographically, socially, and institutionally;
(2) Continued or increasing *subordination* of black
people, Native Americans, Puerto Ricans, Chicanos and others in
terms of their access (a) to basic life needs, (b) to high quality
public institutions, and (c) to structures for political freedom
and power;
(3) Continued or increasing *denial of ordinary status*
to these groups within the social order and within the culture;
(4) Continued or increasing *abasement* and *fear* of non-
white life by the dominant white society;
(5) Continued or increasing legitimacy for and recourse
to *violence* in the making, the keeping and the consequences of the
color line;
(6) Continued or increasing *capacity to rationalize*
these dimensions, their consequences and their claims to a future.

Such homely stuff as this may seem an unlikely candidate
for so noble a position as a structure of faith and reason; but that
is the role in which it is here being presented. Each of these
dimensions interacts with the others with cumulative force to define color as a preferred and pre-eminent mode of being, to associate
all sorts of other characteristics with color, and to organize the
life of the community as an expression of that principle. It is
the color line itself which produces the experiences which validate
its beliefs, which creates a world which supports its meanings, and
which structures the activities which fulfill its vision of common
sense.

The *separation* is a fact, an obvious social fact of every metropolitan area. It is also a principle, a value, a belief, a symbol, and a ritual of association. Whether in slavery, Jim Crow, or the metropolitan areas, the principle of separation has been symbolized, and ritualized, and rationalized in a wide variety of ways by the other dimensions of the color line. For reasons having largely to do with the other dimensions, this separation has been a value to almost everyone; but the separation itself is not without value. It provides one of the necessary conditions for the availability of color as a principle of personal identity. We see this in phrases like "free, white and twenty-one," "black is beautiful/dutiful," "honkey white boy," "all a nigger wants..." Plus or minus, a matter of pride or derrogation, separation, whether geographical, social, or institutional, assures a differential distribution of experience and association; and experience and association are the stuff of personal identities. In the metropolitan areas, the heavy emphasis on domestic separation has created one of the most solid social facts in an otherwise incredibly dynamic and changing situation. In many of these areas, even the commercial experts are uncertain about where the ultimate "downtown" will be or if there will even be only one; but anyone can tell you where the color line is and is going.

The separation sets the stage for "us" and "them" competitive relations in which *subordination* is the rule for nonwhites. The results are documented quarterly by the government printing office in terms of everything from infant mortality to longevity, from unemployment to types of employment and salary scales, from value of housing to commercial ownership and so forth. This subordination in terms of access to basic life needs is so regular that banks, insurance companies and realtors at all levels of the industry have converted statistical generalizations of it into principles to guide and justify their own operations. To them it seems like realism to which they are only responding; and they are aghast that there are people who call this "red-lining" and see it as an active cause of neighborhood disruption. But this subordination in access to basic life needs carries with it a subordination in access to high quality public institutions. The schools, crucial as they are to the children's future possibilities, are but a case in point. For more than twenty years now, plaintiffs have been proving in court that their children are caught in segregated and inferior schools. The condition which affects these children is systemic to the metropolitan area as a set of interacting institutions; but attempts to remedy the situation on the scale that it exists, appear to be "forced" and artificial resolutions. They will continue to be perceived that way as long as the color line itself, of which this subordination is such an important dimension, does not appear to be the problem. This subordination in access to high quality institutions results both from and in subordination in access to political power as well. Within the world of the color line, all this seems natural, merely a matter of fact. In the metropolitan areas, the Supreme Court has trouble finding discriminatory intentions at work. It's just the way things are.

The highly visible separation and subordination, then, appear to provide a factual and reasonable basis for the *denial of ordinary status*. It seems to be confirmed by experience that "these people are different." Symbols and rituals, commemorating, marking, and deepening these differences, abound to the point where they enter prominently into the definition of the individual's location in the social order. Those who can take their ordinary status for granted are free to focus on the problems of individual achievement and personal mobility, while those who find ordinary status withheld can never be quite sure that even their positive achievements will count on their behalf. Enlightened self-interest seems to lie in making the most of this status which is ascribed on the basis of color.

Given the separation, the subordination, and the denial of ordinary status, we seem to have a situation in which it makes sense to ask questions of better and worse. Because of the subordination, there is a situation of practical superiority for whites, and this affects the social psychology of "race relations" and the perceptual structure of the interactions. Whites get better jobs, housing, schools, public services, and the like, not *apparently* through any special treatment, but -- at least as they see it -- through working hard as individuals within the system. Their inclination, therefore, is to look for -- and to find -- special deficiencies in those groups who do not better themselves through working hard as individuals within the system. They focus, not on their good fortune, but on the practical inferiority of others. This practical inferiority -- the statistically demonstrated higher frequency of poverty, family and community disorganization, lower scholastic achievement scores, higher crime rates, and the like -- represents everything that Americans want to avoid. Whenever these symptoms appear, they spread an atmosphere of *fear*, a social psychology of avoidance and threat, and a social dynamic of mutual *abasement* in which each party, in peering across the color line, sees and provokes and responds to what is worst in the other. Avoidance becomes the most sensible policy.

But *violence* becomes the most likely outcome. Violence has been endemic to the color line in all its forms -- slavery, Jim Crow, and now the metropolitan areas. Nobody wants to live under the daily threat of great bodily harm. Common sense, therefore, dictates that families and businesses have a propelling interest in putting as much distance as possible between themselves and the violence of this color line. Translated into practical alternatives this means that blacks, for instance, will try to move, if they can, beyond the violence of the ghetto while whites, if they can, will want to get away from non-white areas or, failing that option, will try to prevent the movement of blacks into "their" areas. Either way, the violence goes on; and for the people caught up in it, far from having any interest in opposing the color line, they seem to have an urgent interest in extending it.

By such reasoning as this does the *rationalization* of the color line proceed. It does not require bizarre claims on nature, history, or the divine to rationalize the color line although these

may be invoked and called upon to buttress its defense and provide
yet another layer of justification for the color line's claim to
a future. Even in the absence of such claims, nonetheless, the
socially structured and produced facts become reasons for their
own existence, values calling for their continued existence,
symbols interpretive of our common humanity, rituals of degradation
and justification, and principles governing the forms of association
which prevail -- from the most intimate to the most corporate, from
the utterly private to the most fully public. These all add up to
an apparently rational "realism" whose moral universe is disguised
as nothing but a matter-of-fact common sense which obscures its
character as a culturally articulated structure of faith and reason.

The Democratic Prospect as a Structure of Faith and Reason

There is, running alongside and sometimes co-mingled with
this color line, yet another structure of faith and reason, institutionalized in the Republic and generally called the Democratic
Faith, the Religion of the Republic, the American Creed, or something of that sort. Like the color line, this is not just a bundle
of ideas which some persons happen to hold. It too is an amalgam
of institutionalized principles, values, beliefs, symbols, rituals,
and associations; but it points to alternative claims as to the
preferred and pre-eminent modes of being by which the community both
is and might be characterized. Although we all participate in both
of these structures every day, they are not "in principle" compatible. One of them has to be compromised for the other to be
advanced. Their conflict is a daily enacted crisis in the constitution of our common humanity. What is more, the democratic
prospect, less amenable to single-mindedness than the color line,
is more inherently problematic. In the first place, its concerns
are more catholic. In the second place, it may not be as completely
assimilated to the world of the corporation as is the current structure of the color line. Its great strength lies in its highly
visible embodiment in the institutions of the Republic. This is
also its potential weakness. Woven as it is into the status quo
in institutions which represent a vision of order, there is a
question whether it can also provide a structured vision of change.
In spite of its impressive embodiment and achievements in American
history, this structure of faith and reason seems empirically much
more questionable, ambiguous, and compromised than does the color
line. This is a rather new development.
During the late 1940's, UNESCO undertook a serious examination of the ambiguities and ideological cross-currents involved
in the concept of "democracy." Through the analysis of differences
arising from divergent cultural histories and political practices,
a world-renowned group of philosophers and social scientists surveyed the diversity of meanings ascribed to democracy. One of
their conclusions was surprising then and it is worth recalling now:

> In spite of the violence of conflict concerning basic social and
> political ideas and concerning means of international cooperation,

there are abundant indications of fundamental agreements....The
agreements are themselves involved in the ideological conflict.
Yet the unanimity which appears in the statement of aims is an
impressive fact. For the first time in the history of the world,
no doctrines are advanced as anti-democratic....This acceptance
of democracy as the highest form of political and social organization is a sign of a basic agreement in the ultimate aims of
modern social and political institutions....[2]

A generation later, in spite of a dramatic lessening in
"cold war" tensions, it is doubtful that a similarly distinguished
group could come to the same conclusion. The democratic prospect
has come under question at home, as it were, by persons and parties
within the Western democracies who actively doubt that the democratic commitment can deal with the issues that lie before us.
In his *Inquiry Into the Human Prospect* (1974), Professor
Robert Heilbroner raises the possibility that we may have to sacrifice the democratic prospect in order to secure even a minimal
"human prospect." It seems to him that the changes required for
human societies even to survive the combined impact of resource
scarcities, on the one hand, and rising demands for the redistribution of resources, on the other hand, may require authoritarian
regimes.
"Candor," he says, compels him "to suggest that the
passage through the gantlet ahead may be possible only under governments capable of rallying obedience far more effectively than
would be possible in a democratic setting." In support of this
idea, which is much more than a mere suggestion in the context of
Heilbroner's perspective, he continues:

If the issue for mankind is survival, such governments may be unavoidable, even necessary. What our speculative analysis provides
is not an apologia for those governments, but a basis for understanding the critical support that they may be able to provide for
a people who will need, over and above a solution to their difficulties, a mitigation of their existential anxieties.[3]

If that is not an "apologia" then I am at a loss as to
the meaning of the word. In what seems to be a hazard of his profession, Heilbroner, the economist, systematically reduces values
to mere preferences while elevating probabilities to the status of
principles. Thus are the values of democracy brushed aside as
pious wishes in the name of a corporate realism of efficiency and
obedience, the "hard facts" of our "human nature" according to
Heilbroner. The result is a cogently argued up-dating of the case
for the Leviathan and against the Republic. Madame Gandhi could
not have stated it more reluctantly nor more gently.
While there is more to be said about the interplay between the human prospect and the possibilities of democratic order
and change, Professor Heilbroner does seem to have a preponderance
of social theory and political practice on his side, even though
he is more candid than most about the implications of his position.

It is as if, over these past thirty years, -- assuming that McKeon
and his associates were right in their conclusions for UNESCO --
anti-democratic "realisms" of various sorts have eroded any effective distinction between what is likely and what is even possible,
let alone desirable.

Letting "The Future" (as if it already existed) substitute for moral and political thinking is an old American habit
with an undistinguished history. It functions to avoid the difficult issues of the present moment. The Future was supposed to
take care of slavery. In fact, it took a dreadful war. That progressive optimism has now given way to eschatalogical pessimism
as regards the future, does not alter the moral and political
function of such futurism.

No doubt the human prospect will vary with the degree to
which groups and societies are able to intervene in events and leave
the stamp of human purpose on them; but I see no point whatsoever --
indeed, I see grave moral and political problems -- in doubting a
priori, as Heilbroner and so many other contemporaries do, "whether
any society can bring about alterations of this magnitude through
the conscious intervention of men, rather than by convulsive changes
forced upon men."[4] It remains very much to be seen not only the
degrees but the kinds of purposes to which the issues of our time
may yet be susceptible. With so much hanging in the balance, it
would seem the wiser course to assess the alternatives than to
assume the outcome.

But how shall we assess the alternatives? It is not only
conceptually but empirically, as well, that the democratic prospect
has been eroded as a structure of faith and reason. At least since
the mid-nineteenth century, the principal forces for social and
political change have seemed to emanate from the structure of advancing industrial and technological economies -- and they are
anything but democratically organized, consumer sovereignty to the
contrary notwithstanding.

Even in the United States where democratic values have
at least some institutionalization and popular support, the rise
of an urban *cum* metropolitan, industrial *cum* technological social
order has made the notion of democratic social change difficult
even to understand, let alone to pursue and perchance achieve.
The social order is dynamic and full of changing forms, but only
some of that change has been deliberately pursued and even most of
that could hardly be called "democratic social change."

If the democratic prospect is still a socially embodied
structure of faith and reason it certainly seems to lack the matter-
of-fact common sense realism that so greatly enhances the effectiveness of the color line. Or does it? Part of the strength of the
color line lies in the fact that its cumulative and interacting
dimensions are not perceived with the full force of their inner
unity and coherence. It benefits from a certain amount of uncon-
sciousness. I shall try to suggest, very briefly, that there are
cumulative and interacting dimensions to the democratic prospect
too; but that it redounds to the weakness of the democratic prospect that these dimensions are not perceived as parts of the same

thing. Unlike the color line, the democratic prospect has something to gain from critical attention.

The preferred and pre-eminent modes of being toward which
the democratic structure of faith and reason is oriented are empirically complex and apparently internally ambiguous. The expectation of self-respecting citizens in a self-governing community is
perhaps the most general statement of the orientation; but the
vision of citizens is rooted in a perception of individuals as
possessive but perfectible and probably ultimately private while
the vision of community is rooted in a reliance on majorities to
check the power of the few and on rights-based procedures to check
the power of the majorities. Embedded within these expectations
is a transcendent vision of a public which is ambiguously and
ambivalently articulated, in some respects as the sum or balance
of the many private interests, in other respects as a body -- the
people - with a life and interests and dignity of its own.

This structure of faith and reason is embodied in certain
matter-of-fact common sense activities which are not always consciously associated with each other nor with the overall orientation
which they articulate. There is, for instance, the much remarked
but little studied penchant of Americans to articulate their purposes, public as well as private, through the formation of voluntary
associations. Through these associations, Americans create various
forums in which to exercise their rights of free speech and assembly
in relation to all manner of issues in order to persuade friends
and enemies alike of the rightness of their concerns and to test
as well as to display the strength of their purpose and resolve.
There is hardly an issue in American life which has not gained
access to public attention through the formation of associations
determined to be the voice of the people. This is one of the most
competitive aspects of American life. Even large corporations,
in other ways so unquestioned in their exercise of power, find it
necessary to defend and advance some of their most important interests in this arena.

For all the individualism, real and alleged, there is a
built-in behavioral connection between the perception of issues and
the formation of associations. In the everyday world, this is what
Americans mean by their "natural rights." Freedom of speech,
action, and even religion translate as a matter of common sense into
the opportunity to pursue issues as one sees them in the company of
others who more or less agree.

It is taken for granted that all this should be within
the law, in some sense, even when changing the law is part of the
purpose. Since the laws are considered amenable to orderly, democratic change by means of pressures generated within this voluntary
sector, it is also taken for granted that activities are to be
limited by respect for the rule of law. This is a kind of matter-
of-fact consent, not to the status quo necessarily, but to the
capacity of the people as a whole to deal fairly, albeit forcefully sometimes, with the issues arising in their midst, the rule
of law being both the source and the symbol of that consent.

At the same time, both the law and the people in general
relate to persons as individuals. At least for moral purposes,

each person is considered -- and on the whole, considers him/herself -- as a morally responsible agent of his/her own life. This is taken for granted in everyday activities and it has to be proven in some way or other if there are circumstances which might mitigate this forcefully structured assumption. That each person is the bearer of his/her own conscience tends to be the center of explicit moral concern.

It is taken for granted that the individual is committed to "bettering" him/herself. This emphasis on improvement (or its opposite) is expressed in mobility -- personal mobility through the life cycle and social statuses, social mobility expressed in highly visible but private, domestic arrangements which are publicly symbolized geographically.

That any person can make a new beginning is a counterpoint to the structural pressure that each individual is the responsible agent of his/her life. An emphasis on natality accompanied by all sorts of ways of staying young and a fascination with changing fashions in all spheres of life, produces an interest in children, not in themselves but as the Future, an ambiguous role for already existing beings. It is also an ambiguous role for the future. Since so much is expected of it, the "future" becomes a present reason for dealing with people who seem to be in the way of it. American violence is typically the strongest when the drive for a new beginning, personal or political, seems threatened or thwarted. This gives us a history of violence that seems to be justified because it is believed to have been a "last resort" to preserve or prevent some new beginning.

In the democratic structure, not only violence, but reason, too, has been defined by its function in relation to new beginnings. Much of the so-called anti-intellectualism in American life is really an impatience with theoretical speculations abstracted from life's events and problems. The orientation is toward practical reason, toward reason in its capacity to inform and guide decisions and actions, toward reason as an instrument of governance, management, and control. Within this structure of faith and reason, violence begins where reason cannot secure the new beginning, where conscience feels encroached by hostile forces, where consent appears to be withdrawn or undermined, where persuasion is at an impasse, where associations still feel strongly about their purposes but futile about their powers. Perhaps this is the deepest ambiguity: that this vision of self-respecting citizens in a self-governing community generates some of the very forces which most threaten its fulfillment.

Structures of Faith and Reason as a Normative Problem

We began with some remarks on the failure of social ethics to develop as a discipline in spite of a century of continuing attempts and in spite, I should add, of some really brilliant intellectual but finally individual enterprises aimed in that direction. In the main I believe that this situation has resulted from a preoccupation with the search for definitive normative principles without a corresponding concern for the empirical subject matter on which such a discipline could appropriately focus. Normative problems, however, do not arise in the abstract. They arise in particular, though generally structured, situations; and the first problem in the clarification of norms and of normative conflicts is an empirical one.

I have proposed that there are such things as empirically specifiable, social structures of faith and reason; and I have submitted, however briefly, two examples of the kind of thing I have in mind. I hope that no one will suppose that I think these are the only two structures of faith and reason at work in American society. I submit them because they are two of the more prominent ones. At the very least, there are also the denominational structures of faith and reason which do seem to gravitate toward the private as the pre-eminent even though they are capable, even on that basis, of generating concerns for political justice and the general welfare of the community. There is also the sexist structure of faith and reason which has only begun to be analyzed for what it is. And towering above all these in terms of its global dynamic and institutional consolidation, there is the massive world of the corporation with its managerial faith and its work ethic. It remains to be seen what others there may be; but it seems to me that this subject matter invites inquiry on a broad scale.

It seems to me that our most serious normative problems arise in the form of issues generated by the conflicting claims of these structures of faith and reason and that our task is to build up a realm of moral discourse around those issues. This brings us, however, face to face with the problem of historicism which, for the past century, has seemed to present us with an impasse when it comes to alternative or conflicting normative claims that are also "faith claims." Whether it is put in Weber's terms of an ultimately irrational value orientation or in Troeltsch's terms of a concrete absolute, it has seemed in sociological and theological circles that there comes a point beyond which inquiry cannot advance, a point where the origins of ultimate orientations are rationally unaccountable and, as a corollary, where these orientations can only be either observed by "outsiders" or confessed by "insiders." At this point, if we follow the historicist logic, we are at the end of effective or meaningful normative discourse except for the apologetic purposes either of making oneself understood to others or possibly of converting the others to one's own viewpoint. This is the historicist impasse: history seems to present us with divergent claims to ultimacy and importance which "history" cannot resolve and which do not allow of neutral ground from which to evaluate these claims.

The dominant schools of social science have welcomed this impasse as legitimating the restriction of their purview to the description of normative matters while excusing their avoidance of the normative problematic. Unfortunately, in spite of this heroic attempt at asceticism, there is no more reason to suppose that there is descriptively neutral ground than there is to suppose that there is normatively neutral ground. As a result there is a problem with the descriptive adequacy of a social science that attempts to exclude normative concerns per se.

On the other hand, the dominant schools of theology and religious thought have responded to the historicist impasse by restricting their attention to the problem of clarifying the nature and sources of their norms and working out various applications which those norms might have or should have in the empirical world. Having avoided the empirical problematic, however, their imperatives seem singularly uninteresting to those who do not share their stance, except insofar as they manage to become associated with one of the "realisms" which is recognized in the culture at large.

In both cases, the empirical structure of the moral problematic in the culture goes largely unattended, with the result that moral questions seem singularly marginal to the life of the culture. Everything gets accounted for in other terms -- social, political, economic, and sometimes religious. This is truly amazing and ironic given our well-known and well-deserved reputation as a people for moralism.

What we have here, in both popular and academic culture, is a problem of misplaced absoluteness. It is not the principles or their sources or the fact that they are believed that is absolute. Neither is it the personal or social attachment to them that is absolute. It is the fact that they have consequences, that in becoming principles of action, they take on lives of their own and become structural factors in the lives of the rest of us, imposing themselves beyond those who hold them. Their origins may or may not be unaccountable; but their consequences are certainly accountable. Even the most unreconstructed idealist, recalcitrant positivist or intense existentialist will agree that it is not sufficient that principles either be or be thought to be good in the abstract. Some argument needs to be advanced about what would be better in the concrete. The value of utilitarianism, in spite of its rather low repute of late, was that at least it was a position that included within moral discourse the question about the actual empirical meaning of moral principles. To be sure, the slogan about "the greatest good for the greatest number" seemed to open more grounds for moral evasion than seriousness; but at least it held open a tension between the abstract and the concrete meaning of moral principles and did not absolutize the abstract. If anything is absolute, it is not the abstract and universal. A more likely case can be made for the concrete. At least there we are dealing with the stubbornness of actuality, the irreversibility of action and the irretrievability of the spoken word. In that sense, absolute means something definite.

I believe, with the historicists, that we are presented by history with divergent claims to ultimacy and importance. I think that within and between cultures these claims can be empirically investigated both in their integrity -- if they have any -- and in their intermingling. I also believe, with the historicists, that there is no neutral ground from which to evaluate these divergent and frequently conflicting claims. However, it is my view that this is the starting point for truly serious and finally interesting normative discourse, not the end of it.

        It is doubtful -- it may not even be desirable -- that
we could ever arrive at a common set of principles even within our
own culture, let alone in our relations with the rest of mankind;
but we can develop a critical awareness of the principles that are
enacted and embodied in the structures of faith and reason which
have so much to do with the shape and substance of our common
humanity whether we "believe" in them or not. The substance of
our common humanity is an empirical as well as a normative question.
We are having great difficulty getting at the normative question
because we have neglected the empirical one.
        There is, of course, a sense in which we do have a common
set of principles, that is to say, principles to which we are
commonly subject in a problematic way. At the very least we can
argue about these, about the value of the actual forms of common
humanity in which they are embodied and in which we find ourselves.
We can trace their persistence to the structures of faith and
reason which sustain them. In some respects, for instance, we are
a democratic public. In other respects, we are a people of the
color line. It is a normative question whether we want to be either
of these, just as it is an empirical question what else we are and
what options we really have. Our task is to bring our forms of
thought into focus on the actual forms of being that have emerged
among us. To do this, I believe that we can develop our moral
discourse around the forms of common humanity which given principles, given actions, given structures of faith and reason produce, not only for those who "accept" these givens, but for the
rest of us as well, the community at large, the people, the public.
        Developing the normative function critically requires
seeing it in the context of competing structures of faith and reason.
The plurality of moral standards imbedded within the matrix of the
culture, its institutions, and our personal lives is the first object of attention if there is to be much clarification of the moral
problematic.
        The critical normative function is impeded to the degree
that there are moral principles operating under the guise of facts.
They need to be seen for what they are if we hope to improve our
capacity to deal with them. As things now stand, we are suffering
from a mystification of the everyday world, a strange mixture of
the bizarre and the decent, the demonic and the humane -- structures of faith disguised as "realisms." I do not say that such
clarification would solve any of the normative problems that plague
us; but I do believe that it would be a worthwhile advance in establishing the focus and, perhaps, the standards for discourse about
the problems of social ethics.

NOTES AND REFERENCES

1. See, for example: Francis Greenwood Peabody, *Jesus Christ and the Social Question* (New York, New York: Macmillan, 1900); William Jewett Tucker, "Social Economics: The Outline of an Elective Course of Study," *Andover Review*, Vols. XI (1889) - XVI (1891); Graham Taylor, *Religion in Social Action* (New York, New York: Dodd, Mead, 1913); Charles Richmond Henderson, *The Social Spirit in America* (Meadville, Pennsylvania: Chataqua-Century Press, 1897).

2. Richard McKeon, ed., with the assistance of Stein Rokkan, *Democracy in a World of Tensions*, A Symposium Prepared by UNESCO (Chicago, Illinois: University of Chicago Press, 1951), pp. 522-23.

3. Robert L. Heilbroner, *An Inquiry Into the Human Prospect* (New York, New York: W.W. Norton, 1974), p. 110.

4. *Ibid.*, p. 95.

TOWARD BELIEF: A PROCESS PERSPECTIVE ON THE SOCIAL SCIENCES AND ON SOCIAL ETHICS

by

W. Widick Schroeder

Introduction

Process thought, involving a transposition of the Platonic tradition, has had slight impact on the social sciences to date. The theoretic foundations of the modern social sciences emerged primarily in Europe in the nineteenth and early twentieth centuries. Karl Marx, John Stuart Mill, Herbert Spencer, August Comte, Emile Durkheim, Sigmund Freud, and Max Weber are among the seminal thinkers contributing to their emergence in that epoch. In spite of the internal diversity between these cited figures, they shared one characteristic; none of them thought it was necessary to appeal to a God who was in some sense *sui generis* to interpret human life. All were interested in religion and sought to interpret it, but their approaches to the study of religious phenomena were phenomenological, residualistic, or reductionistic.

These early emphases continue, for today only a few social scientists are informed by the Platonic, Aristotelian, or Christian traditions. Broadly viewed, contemporary social scientists have more intellectual kinship with Democritus or the Sophists than with Plato, Aristotle or classical Christian thinkers.[1]

The voluntaristic facet of contemporary social science, rooted in the tradition of Max Weber primarily, and John Stuart Mill and other nineteenth-century English liberals and some evolutionists secondarily, has more in common with a process view of the social sciences than the more causally oriented views rooted in the traditions of Karl Marx, Sigmund Freud, and Emile Durkheim. At the same time, the staunch phenomenological and interactionist views of contemporary voluntarists differentiate them from process perspectives; for process thinkers have to appeal to a Divine Reality to discern a locus for potentiality, to explain the human experiences of the lure for harmony and intensity of feeling, to interpret the mediation of data from one creature to another, and to delineate the ultimate receptor of all that has become.

This essay explores some of the implications of process thought for the social sciences and social ethics. It deals primarily with the ordering of the social sciences in the mode of process thought, the understanding of human nature and human experience from this perspective, and the bases for a process social ethic. This focus on generic notions will permit readers to contrast this

237

perspective with their own understandings and with the views of the social theorists whom they happen to know.

Although the reader not possessing a knowledge of the basic categories of process thought can follow the overall sequence of the discussion in this essay, he may encounter some difficulty in certain passages; for space limitations have precluded a full elaboration of every notion employed.[2]

A Resume of the Ordering of the Sciences in the Perspective of Process Thought

The complexity of actual entities and groupings of actual entities in societies has given rise to the hierarchical ordering of nature discernible in this cosmic epoch. It is the basis for the ordering of the sciences.

Metaphysical propositions apply to all creatures. They constitute the matrix in which more specialized propositions applying to particular entities and societies are set. Theological proposi- tions apply to the Supreme Subject-Object, for from the perspective of process thought God exemplifies the metaphysical propositions supremely. Thus, a reciprocal relation exists between theology and metaphysics -- a fully adequate theology awaits a fully adequate metaphysics. Since limitations of insight and language preclude the full realization of the latter, the former is likewise precluded.

Mathematics deals with geometric relations and derivative notions. Insofar as mathematics is exploring potentiality, it is "pure." In its "applied" form, mathematics seeks to discern the forms of definiteness associated with particular creatures in this cosmic epoch.

The physical sciences are saliently concerned with geo- metric forms and with measurements involving intervals and ratios. The biological sciences retain these interests, but organismic pur- pose becomes increasingly important. In the human sciences, such interest becomes central.

This pattern of increasing complexification is grounded in the natures of the creatures and societies of creatures constituting the subject matters of the several sciences. All creatures are dipolar. Excepting God, they begin their experience with their ap- propriation of data from the world. This physical phase is sup- plemented by a mental phase in which creatures appropriate forms of definiteness embodied in God's primordial nature. Guided by its subjective aim, the emerging creature synthesizes these two phases into an integrated unity.

The hierarchy of nature is twofold. First, there are substantial differences in the importance of the supplemental phase in the lives of various creatures. Some creatures and some soci- eties of creatures merely reproduce their pasts in their presents with a modicum of novelty. They convey the impression of stability, endurance, and relative changelessness. So-called "inorganic" societies are composed of such creatures. Other creatures respond with greater novelty to the context in which they find themselves. Some creatures in so-called "organic" societies are illustrative.

They are "alive." As the presence of viruses and other transitional
societies indicates, the dividing line between organic and inorganic
societies is not clear cut.

Second, there are substantial differences in the complexity
and structuring of groups of creatures. Some entities, such as gases,
are less structured than others, such as solids. Living organisms
involve the integration of groups of societies and sub-societies
and are sometimes co-ordinated to support an entirely living nexus.

Human beings are the most complex creatures of which we
have any direct knowledge at present. The human is comprised of a
large number of living and nonliving sub-societies, co-ordinated in
such a way that there are reciprocal relations between the regnant
center and the rest of the organism. This regnant center, a "form-
less form" so protean that it can "contain" the sequence of ultimate
percipient occasions constituting it, is of very high grade. The
supplemental phase is greatly enhanced in the creatures constituting
it, so humans are able to respond to and to shape their initial
data with a very substantial measure of novelty. Subjective species
of eternal objects and a welter of subjective forms are enhanced in
high grade organisms, so feelings and meanings loom large in human
life. Purposiveness and intentionality are also salient in human
experience. Any rendering of the human sciences that loses sight
of these foundational experiences is suspect, for their recognition
is too widespread in the life of civilized humankind to be put aside
as mere error.[3]

The Relation Between Internal and External Factors
in Human Experience

When social scientists consider emotions, meanings, and
actions, they are considering other people's emotions, meanings,
and actions. Their *own* emotions, meanings, and actions are provisionally excluded from consideration. Such exclusion is fitting
and proper, for it is possible to analyze values and social structures, discern the intensity of other people's feelings, and examine
other people's actions provisionally without evaluating them.

This provisional distinction, however, is ultimately only
heuristic, for the internal and external dimensions of experience
are inextricably intertwined. According to the principle of relativity, fundamental to process modes of thought, every being is a
potential for every becoming. Consequently, what a creature *is*
cannot be separated from *how* a creature functions. Creatures begin
their process of becoming with the *valuation* of the data they appropriate.

It is arbitrary to distinguish absolutely between the
analytical and descriptive and the synthetic and evaluative sides
of social scientific theory, for the social scientist also participates in the pervasive attraction towards beauty, truth, and goodness which is at the base of things. If he ignores or denies these
experiences in his study of human life, he is going to distort his
interpretation of the human situation. Social scientists confront
the question of the adequacy of their foundational perspective more

forcefully than natural scientists (though natural scientists also
confront the issue), for in a more direct way than is the case for
studies of sub-human subject-objects, both the findings of specific
social scientific studies and also the general conceptual schemata
employed by social scientists affect their subject-objects.[4]

Human cultural phenomena have both objective and subjective dimensions. As objects for study, they are part of the subject matter of the social sciences. As sources and expressions of
meaning, cultural objects -- artistic products, musical compositions,
and thought forms -- are necessarily related to human internal experiences. Both dimensions need to be explored in the elaboration
of a more adequate human science.

In the context of the social sciences, the inner side of
experience gives rise to morality and the science of morals -- for
human behavior is concerned with the good.

Since the good (action pertaining to the seasonally relevant future) is intimately related to the beautiful (the actualization of harmony and intensity of feeling) and to the true (the
elaboration of propositions fitting to various subject-objects),
experiences in one dimension may elicit or reinforce experiences in
the other dimensions. Religious experience involves the sensitive
response to and/or awareness of these dimensions of experience. It
both surpasses and also shades off into experiences heightening
human awareness of the beautiful, the true, and the good.

This paper does not consider the ordering of the aesthetic
disciplines or the ordering of the natural sciences; it is focused
on the implications of process modes of thought for the social
sciences. For the reasons noted in the preceding paragraph, these
omissions are somewhat arbitrary. They have been dictated by the
author's specialized interest in the implications of process thought
for the social sciences and by space limitations.

The Spheres of the Social Order:
The Subject Matter of the Social Sciences

INTRODUCTION

As noted previously, the external and internal factors of
experience are interrelated. The drop of experience constituting
our conscious self begins to become by appropriating facets of other
creatures in its causal past. In the supplemental phase of its becoming it appropriates forms of definiteness embodied in God's primordial nature and not necessarily actualized in other creatures.
The emerging creature is aiming at satisfaction, a focus lured forth
by God's subjective aim.

The organizing regnant center of an individual human being
constitutes the subject matter of psychology. Social institutions,
meanings, values, and norms in the several spheres of the social
order abstracted from the individuals comprising them constitute the
subject matter of the other human sciences.

The meanings, values, and norms giving shape to social
institutions in the several spheres of the social order cannot be
definitively separated from the humans shaping them and participating

in them, for function and meaning are interrelated; both are rooted
in human decisions. As noted earlier, this interrelation makes an
evaluative consideration of societal norms, art objects, and scientific and philosophic thought forms -- the fruits of inner human
experiences of the good, the beautiful, and the true -- integral to
an adequate social science.

The good is especially related to norms and institutions
in the familial sphere, primary and quasi-primary group spheres,
the economic sphere, and the political sphere. In the cultural
sphere, the beautiful is related especially to art objects; and the
true is related especially to scientific and philosophic thought
forms.

In the religious sphere, the beautiful is especially related to constitutive acts of worship giving rise to religious
institutions. The reality of God needs to be considered in an
adequate interpretation of religious institutions, for they are
grounded in human experiences of a Divine Reality who is, in some
senses, *sui generis*.

The intrinsic interrelatedness of the beautiful, the true,
and the good means these distinctions are equivocal, but the priority
of factors in the various spheres of the social order legitimates
the distinctions and sustains the differentiations of the spheres.

The interdependency and interrelation of the spheres are
reflected in the evolution of various "hybrid" disciplines such as
demography, geography, social psychology, and urban and regional
studies. They are also reflected in the tendency for each of the
social sciences to incorporate facets of other disciplines in their
own work.

The remainder of this section sketches the bases for the
ordering of the "major" social scientific disciplines. They are
grounded in the biological, social, intellectual, aesthetic, and
religious characteristics of humankind. These characteristics give
rise to the several spheres of the social order and provide the subject matters for the various social sciences.

THE ORGANIZING CENTER OF HUMAN BEINGS: THE SUBJECT MATTER OF PSYCHOLOGY

The subject matter of psychology is the regnant center of
the human being. Psychology is the most concrete social science,
for feelings, attitudes, values, beliefs, norms, and decisions are
ultimately referable to the human beings in which they are rooted.
The hierarchy of nature noted earlier gives some guidance about the
degree of precision to be anticipated in various sub-disciplines of
psychology. Sub-disciplines dealing with the impact of the body on
the regnant center are apt to develop more precise "laws" than sub-
disciplines focusing primarily on the regnant center itself. The
latter sub-disciplines deal with attitudes, values, beliefs, and
actions involving intentionality, purpose, and decision.

Consequently, physiological psychologists may expect to
develop theories possessing more predictive power than social psychologists. Theories predicting the impact of certain drugs on
sense perception, for example, are more precise and less culture-
bound than theories predicting the impact of social attitudes on
electoral behavior.

THE ABSTRACTIVE NET OF HUMAN RELATIONS: THE SUBJECT MATTER OF THE OTHER SOCIAL SCIENCES

The subject matter of other social sciences is the entire net of human relations in the social order abstracted from the concrete relations of human beings comprising the net. Individuals are inextricably interrelated with social institutions in the several spheres of the social order, for the defining characteristics of social institutions are immanent in the human beings comprising them. As individuals surpass the structures reflected in the several spheres of the social order, studies of social institutions in one sphere cannot be isolated from studies of social institutions in all the spheres or from the actions of individual humans. The social sciences must deal with human meaning, intentionality, and social structures in their interrelatedness.

Sociology is an inclusive abstractive social science, for it is concerned with forms of social organization in all the spheres of the social order. Various other social scientific disciplines may be distinguished by the special attention they give to one or more spheres of the social order. Economics, political science, and anthropology are often related to the economic, the political, and the cultural spheres, respectively.

THE FAMILIAL SPHERE, THE QUASI-PRIMARY SPHERE, THE ETHNIC SPHERE, AND THE SOCIAL SPHERE: A SPECIAL DOMAIN OF SOCIOLOGY

It is arbitrary to limit the actual interests of sociologists to groups in the spheres of the social order composed of familial and of the quasi-primary groups, ethnic groups, and status groups, for in fact sociologists study forms of social organization in all the spheres. This sequence of discussion is shaped by the desire for systematic clarity and is not intended to be an accurate empirical description of the subject matters sociologists actually study.

The *family* is rooted in biological necessity and in human trans-rational social needs for intimate, diffuse, primary relations. Human sexual and social needs account for the multiplicity of forms of family organization, shaped by values, beliefs, and norms. Other small primary groups, grounded in human trans-rational social needs for intimacy, emerge in all societies.

Biological and socio-historical factors working in concert with human capacity for feeling and thinking contribute to the development of persons who feel they belong to particular *ethnic* or *racial* groups. Racial groups are defined by real or imagined common biological characteristics, and ethnic groups are defined by commonly shared historical experiences.

Human beings have the capacity to shape sentiments and values in relation to particular socio-historical groupings. As a result, people develop varied and distinctive life styles to which honor or prestige is differentially accorded. Persons in the same *status* group manifest comparable styles of life. Though status groups are frequently reinforced by values associated more directly with one of the other spheres of the social order, members of the same status groups may be drawn from different groups in the other spheres of the social order.

Sociologists have made innumerable studies of familial and other primary groups, ethnic and racial groups, and status groupings. As noted earlier, they also study economic, political, and religious groups as well. Two of these spheres -- the economic and the political -- have been the special subject matter of other social scientists.

THE ECONOMIC SPHERE: THE SUBJECT MATTER OF ECONOMICS

Human creativity, reason, capacity for novelty of response, and biological necessity combine to create and to sustain institutions in the economic sphere of the social order. Human economic behavior and institutions in this sphere constitute the subject matter of the·science of economics.

Rational calculation in a means-ends pattern is salient in this sphere. "Technical" reason is predominant in the economic sphere.[5]

The data on which economics is based ultimately refer back to the human beings from which they have been abstracted. For this reason, the predictive capacity of economic science -- even in those societies in which calculating reason is forcefully accentuated -- is less than in the sub-human sciences.

Humans, embodying both technical and ontic reason, reproduce some values for extended periods, so economic analysis is possible and often useful. Nonetheless, humans surpass technical rationalism, and contemporary human decisions surpass the past, so the tales told by laws in economics and the other human sciences are less certain than the tales told by laws in the sub-human sciences.

THE POLITICAL SPHERE: THE SUBJECT MATTER OF POLITICAL SCIENCE

Human creativity, human reason, human capacity for novelty of response, and social necessity combine to create and to sustain institutions in the political sphere, the subject matter of political science.

The rational side of the political sphere includes the objectification of the values sustaining particular forms of political organization, the principles of justice, and the rules and regulations of justice. Groups rooted in any of the other spheres of the social order may and do become political groups, for they may seek to attain group objectives through political processes. In these processes, they both compete with and also cooperate with other groups.[6]

The subject matter of political science differs in specificity from the subject matter of economics. Economics, especially in industrial societies, focuses on highly rationalized relations, so its subject matter is relatively specific. This specificity, coupled with the widespread tendency of most people in some societies to follow reasonably well the rules of a rational economic game, enhances the predictive power of economics in such societies.

Political science studies trans-rational decisions and "power" relations directly, so its subject matter is more diffuse. The unique character of crucial decisions and actions of political leaders more sharply limits the predictive capacity of political science than is the case for some of the other social sciences.

THE CULTURAL SPHERE: THE SUBJECT MATTER OF THE "SCIENCE OF CULTURE"

The cultural creations of human beings constitute the subject matter of the "science of culture." Human reason and the human

capacities for novelty of response interplay with inner experiences
and the conditions of human existence to produce human culture, for
fundamental beliefs, values, and norms give shape to the forms of
social organization in every sphere of the social order.

Disembodied cultural objects, which some define as the subject matter of anthropology, are human products. Social scientists
reifying these concepts or dealing with the objects independent of
the creatures in whom they are embodied deal inadequately with the
science of culture. From the perspective of process thought social
scientists separating the *function* of moral, aesthetic, and intellectual objects from their *meaning* to the creatures embodying and
creating them are acting arbitrarily. The especially human character
of culture accentuates the need for a broader conceptual scheme with
which to interpret intellectual, aesthetic, and moral objects than
is currently fashionable in the social sciences.[7]

The disciplines are embryonic or non-existent within the
social sciences, but a "science of belief," a "science of aesthetics,"
and a "science of morals" to study the cognitive and ideational side
of the science of culture can be envisaged. Each of these disciplines
would have an external side, analyzing the extant objects, and an
internal side, considering the inner grounds for human creation of
objects, norms, and principles. Thus, these sciences ought to have
both analytic and descriptive dimensions and also normative and evaluative dimensions.

Because of its pertinence here, the evaluative and normative dimensions of a "science of morals" are elaborated briefly in
the following section of this essay. This "science" is related to
all of the social sciences, for it would seek to evolve normative
forms of social organization in all the spheres of the social order
to permit an evaluation of existing forms of social organization
and to lure forth more adequate forms.

THE RELIGIOUS SPHERE: THE SUBJECT MATTER OF THE "SCIENCE OF RELIGION"

Religious rituals, symbols, beliefs, and institutions constitute the subject matter of the "science of religion." These subject matters are often studied in the sociology of religion.

As noted earlier, religious experience arises as a human
fuses its physical and conceptual experiences into an emerging unit.
This foundational experience constitutes the basic subject matter
of the psychology of religion. Rituals, emotions, symbols, beliefs,
and institutions emerge out of and contribute to human religious experience. Because of these reciprocal relations it is arbitrary to
separate sharply the sociology of religion from the psychology of
religion.

The science of religion should study both the conceptual,
moral, and aesthetic objects arising from religious experience and
also the forms of religious organization evolved in relation to human
religious experience.

If function and meaning are intertwined, as has been
affirmed frequently here, social scientists ought to study the inner
meaning of and grounds for religious experience. These analyses
will lead ultimately to analyses of the nature of religious experience and its relation to human experiences of the beautiful, the

true, and the good and to a consideration of the relation of these
experiences to the Divine Life. Facets of this exploration are
developed in the final portion of this essay.

THE INTEGRATED WHOLE: THE SUBJECT MATTER OF HISTORICAL STUDIES

Conceived in its broadest sense, history is the discipline
studying the factors giving rise to the cosmos at a given state of
its becoming. Insofar as the factors giving rise to the present
state of the cosmos can be rationalized by explaining how successors
are determined by causal antecedents, historians may attain some
success in their efforts. Since there is no reason intrinsic to
the historical process for the necessary actualization of a given
flux of forms, historians cannot fully and adequately rationalize
history; they simply must accept it as "given."

Human history may be conceived more narrowly as the discipline tracing the interplay between human decisions and social-
institutional configurations. Causal analysis in human history incorporates human decisions as part of the causal factors. For this
reason historical study is necessarily *post facto*, integrative, and
wholistic.

Historians should seek to interpret the values, decisions,
and actions of particular people in their relation to particular
social institutions in particular societies in particular historical
epochs. In this disciplined artistic synthesis, the historian draws
on data provided by the other social sciences. Since a whole is
more than the sum of its parts, history is the social science most
able to delineate the character of the various epochs constituting
the history of civilized humankind. The historian performs both a
most difficult and also an indispensable role in the interpretation
of human life.[8]

This *resume* of the status of history concludes this outline of the ordering of the subject matters of the social sciences
dealing with the external side of human community-in-individuality.
As previously noted, the question of *how* an entity functions cannot
be divorced from the question of *why* an entity becomes. Efficient
cause and final cause are inter-related; an analysis of function
cannot be separated from an analysis of meaning.

Morality is intimately related with the internal side of
human meanings. These meanings shape forms of social organization
and norms of human conduct. The concluding section of this essay
elaborates the shape of a process social ethic.

Morality in a Process Perspective: The Bases for a Social Ethic

INTRODUCTION

The lure to accentuate harmony and intensity of feeling
in the future is at the base of morality. Although one may be a
bit oblivious to morals at certain times and in certain places, the
lure for aesthetic satisfaction, truthful formulations, and good
actions constitutes a basic trinity inherent in the nature of things.
Prescription and interpretation are as intrinsic to an adequate
social science as are description and analysis.

Morality incorporates both formal and volitional dimensions. The delineation of principles of justice, the elaboration of the relations between form (justice), dynamics (power), and unification (love) in various interpersonal and intergroup relations, and the description of the forms of familial, social, economic, political, cultural, and religious organizations normatively desirable for human beings constitute the formal dimension. The social sciences provide empirical data to help humans discern the probability of actualizing the normative forms in a particular context and the probable consequences of alternative actions and policy.

Human moral decisions, guided by but surpassing factors included in the formal dimension, constitute the volitional dimension. This contrast between volitional and formal dimensions is one facet of an "isness-oughtness" contrast, a part of the experience of all humans.

The more fundamental contrast is rooted in human intuition of the primordial nature of God, one facet of human experience of the lure for the beautiful, the true, and the good. Humans are persuaded by the lure for harmony embedded in this dimension of experience and in some facets of their causal pasts to enhance the beautiful, to seek the true, and to try to do the good. They are also coerced by finitude and ignorance, i.e., the limitations of existence, so harmonious and disharmonious experiences are both part of human experience. Persuasion is a more desirable kind of power than coercion, but the two kinds are intermingled in human experience. Insofar as is possible in a given context, persuasion rather than coercion should be exercised.

Finitude, ignorance, sloth, and lethargy combine with inordinate self-interest to preclude the possibility of a perfect harmony of life with life under the conditions of existence. The only "perfect" harmony is the ordering of the forms of definiteness by God's subjective aim, and this harmony is deficient in actuality.

Evil involves experiences of disharmony and of loss. Loss is the more fundamental evil, for discord may signal the dawn of an emerging order that is richer and more complex than its predecessors. As the ultimate receptor and synthesizer of all that has become, God retains everlastingly and without loss all the creatures of the world. In this fashion, that which appears to be lost or evil from the human perspective is transformed and retained in Divine Life.

THE FORMAL SIDE OF MORALITY

Forms are an integral part of every experience. Humans may surpass particular forms as they become, but they must appropriate some forms in their becoming. The primacy of the category of creativity in process thought gives it a dynamic bias, but this primacy is balanced by the necessity of the presence of some forms of definiteness in all creatures.[9]

In the introduction of this section the three dimensions of the formal side of morality were cited: the principles of justice, the relations between form (justice), dynamics (power), and unification (love) in various interpersonal and intergroup relations, and the normative forms of social organization. These dimensions are considered in this sub-section.

The Principles of Justice[10] -- There are three formal
principles of justice. These principles are based on the universality of the experience of the unification of a formal dimension
in the dynamic process of the becoming of creatures. These principles are: *self-determination* informed by excellence, *equality*
appropriate to form, and the *order, love and peace* harmonizing the
other two principles.

At the metaphysical level, the dynamic process is rooted
in the creativity which is at the base of things; the formal dimension is grounded in the forms of definiteness envisaged by God and
embodied in creatures; and the unification dimension is grounded in
God's subjective aim and is manifest in the emerging creatures' aims
for harmony and intensity of feeling.

These general principles are embodied in the rules and
regulations of justice of a living community through its decision-
making processes. Humans then have to apply these rules and regulations of justice to particular contexts.

Because of this movement from the more general to the more
specific, the general principles of justice are less ambiguous than
the rules and regulations of justice. For the same reason, the rules
and regulations of justice are less ambiguous than the application
of the rules and regulations in a given context. The "power" component of the form-dynamic couplet is salient in the actualization
of the principles of justice in concrete situations.

*Relative Priority of Form (Justice), Dynamics (Power),
and Unification (Love) in the Spheres of Human Life* -- Form, dynamics,
and unification are three-in-relation, so these factors are each
present in every sphere of human life. Even so, the saliency of the
factors differs, permitting an assessment of the potential contribution of social institutions in the several spheres to interpersonal
and intergroup life. There are six possible priorities of relations
between these factors: dynamics, unification, and form; form, unification, and dynamics; form, dynamics, and unification; dynamics,
form, and unification; unification, dynamics, and form; and unification, form, and dynamics.

In human life, dynamics refers to power or self-determination informed by excellence; form refers to defining characteristics
and principles of justice; and unification refers to the harmony or
love uniting dynamic and form.

The sequence of priority "dynamics, unification, and form"
points to the emergence of the novel creature *per se*. Any emergent
creature (dynamics) with its subjective aim fostered by God (unification) seeks to actualize itself by harmonizing the universality
of this sequence; a sequence of priority may be made in human life
and in human social relationships.

The sequence of priority "form, unification, and dynamics"
points to the priority of factors in interpersonal relations. The
priority of the principle of equality appropriate to form is dominant,
so a person can be treated more fully as a person in small primary
and quasi-primary groups than in any other contexts. Among these
groups, the family is paramount. Love, involving sensitive and
empathetic response to the needs of the other, is second in emphasis.
Self-determination, involving the actualization of one's own aims,

is third in emphasis; for one's own aims are intimately related to
the aims of the other members of the primary group.

The sequences of priorities "form, dynamics, and unification" and "dynamics, form, and unification" relate to social institutions and groups abstracted from the concrete network of relations in which human beings are enmeshed. This abstraction precludes fuller human relations in the racial, ethnic, status, economic,
political, and cultural spheres. Groups in these spheres may become
vehicles for more inclusive interpersonal relations, but in themselves they do not permit the fuller and richer human interplay
characterizing interpersonal relations in small groups.

In every sphere except the political sphere, the sequence
of priority is "form, dynamics, and unification," for groups in the
other spheres are dominantly shaped by defining characteristics
(form). These defining characteristics are sometimes enhanced by
actions rooted in the political sphere. People will to belong to
these groups (dynamic), and they have a sense of shared values and/or
common participation (unification).

In the political sphere, the sequence of priority of
factors is "dynamics, form, and unification." Power considerations
(dynamics) are leading; but the state, which is the organizing
center of a society, gives shape to the structures (form) defining
relations between groups in a given geographical territory. To
facilitate this effort, the state develops rules and regulations of
justice (form). Citizens of a state participate (unification) in
common values and at least tacitly approve of political leadership.
Leaders trying to impose their wills (power) without regard to justice
(form) or to the expectations of the citizens (unification) may
succeed for a while, but eventually such leadership will be deposed.

The state seeks both domestic and international order and
harmony. Harmony in the international sphere is especially difficult,
for there is little consensus about justice (form) and minimal sense
of the common destiny of humankind (unification).

The sequences of priorities "unification, dynamics, and
form" and "unification, form, and dynamics" refer to God-world relations. From the Divine point of view, the former sequence applies;
from the human point of view, the latter sequence applies. Love,
power, and form delineate the sequence of sensitivity of response,
lure for feeling, provision of seasonally relevant forms, and objectification of the world characterizing the Divine functioning in the
world. Love, form, and power delineate the sequence of sensitivity
of response, development of subjective aim, appropriation of forms,
and self-actualization characterizing the realization of creatures
in the world.

Institutions in the religious sphere are grounded in human
religious experience and in interpretations of that experience. The
priority of the sequence "unification, form, and dynamics" from the
human perspective on God-world relations provides criteria to guide
the relation of religious institutions to other social institutions
and groups. The Divine Reality functions by suasion, and institutions lured forth by that reality should do likewise. Religious institutions should not use force or violence, and they should become
involved directly in the political sphere most infrequently. The

priority of form over dynamics implies that reason contributes
positively to human experience of the Divine Presence, but the
salience of unification or love implies that religious experience
is more fundamental and elemental than any analysis of it or of the
Supreme Subject-Object of religious devotion. Consequently, faith
precedes reason in human religious experience, but reason may help
elicit or may reinforce faith.

Due to the relative priority of factors in the spheres of
the social order and in the networks of human relations, the fulfillment of human life is most realizable in interpersonal relations
and in the everlasting objectification of creatures in the Divine
Life. Desirable forms of familial, social, economic, political,
cultural, and religious organizations may foster richer human life,
but social institutions and groups cannot be the end or fulfillment
of human life.

In some ways, the more the spheres are differentiated,
the more intense the sense of disharmony becomes between interpersonal and intergroup relations. In most modern societies in
which high technology is predominant, the differentiations are very
substantial. A qualified critique of inordinate social differentiation may be appropriate, but it is a mistake to criticize inordi-
nately forms of familial, social, economic, political, cultural, or
religious life on the grounds they prevent full humanness. Some
forms of social organization are more adequate than others and should
be fostered, but the most any form of social organization can ever
do is to provide a more congenial environment for the development of
richer, fuller, and more harmonious human life. Temporal fulfillment
of human life surpasses institutional forms and historical groups
and is embodied in individual human beings through concrete relations
with other human and non-human beings; eternal fulfillment of human
life surpasses the perishing of the temporal and is manifest in the
everlasting objectification of creatures in the Divine Life.

Normative Forms of Social Organization -- Even though
human life surpasses social institutions, desirable forms of social
organization may contribute positively to human life. The delineation of normative forms of familial, social, economic, political,
cultural, and religious organizations developed in this sub-section
is based on a consideration conjointly of the principles of justice,
the relative priority of form, dynamics, and unification in the
spheres of the social order, and the conditions of human existence.

The dominantly bi-sexual character of human beings and
the necessity for sociability among them give rise to the family,
the fundamental and elemental unit in the social structure. The
biological basis of the family is the diadic character of human
sexual relations. The social basis is the necessity for continuity
and intensity of social interaction to elicit intensity and contrast of feeling among people and to provide a stable sustaining
environment for the development of children. Monogamy is the form
of family organization best able to harmonize biological and social
necessity.

Diverse racial, ethnic, and status groups are a part of
the life of any complex society. Racial, ethnic, and status pluralism is desirable, for it provides a context for a more diverse and

potentially richer societal unity. The diversity is limited by the self-understanding of the diverse groups and by the possibilities for integration into a reasonably harmonious whole.

It is not possible to state the limits of diversity formally, for the limits depend on the nature of the society. Some societies are able to sustain greater complexity harmoniously than others. Too much complexity fosters disintegration of a given society; too little diversity results in a dull and monotonous whole. Racial, ethnic, and status groups rejecting a pluralistic harmony are least desirable and cause the most difficulty for a society.

No normative form of economic organization can be delineated, but some guidelines can be indicated. Greater direction can be provided negatively than positively. The decisions of the persons in the system should provide some direction for the allocation of resources, so any non-primitive economic system should contain supply-demand pricing mechanisms insuring a relatively efficient allocation of resources. The system should also permit some measure of individual and group self-initiation in the production of economic goods and services. Finally, the system should not abuse unduly the nature of the human beings who participate in it.

Representative democracy is the form of political organization best able to harmonize self-determination informed by excellence and equality appropriate to form. Because these principles of justice are partially contradictory, neither an egalitarian society nor a rigidly stratified one is desirable. Some social differentiation is essential, but it must be balanced by a measure of equality. As the state integrates and harmonizes community-individuality, it necessarily develops rules and regulations pertinent to institutions in the other spheres. The state must retain a monopoly on the legitimate use of force in a society, but its use of force must be subject to careful review by a multiplicity of agencies.

As there is no single mode of perfection in the cosmos, a qualified cultural pluralism is desirable in a society. The "best" society is the one which can harmonize the greatest cultural diversity, but there are limits to the degree of diversity sustainable in a society without personal and corporate disintegration. No narrowly conceived notions of artistic, educational, or literary uniformity can be supported, but no sharp judgment about the desirable diversity of creations can be made independent of a context.

In a good society, most of its citizens will share some common unifying beliefs and values transcending the diverse ones of sub-groups. A relatively "better" society is one in which the large majority of its participants share the normative forms of social organization outlined here.

This necessity for unifying integrative values limits the range of social and cultural pluralism a society can tolerate. No society can escape some limitations on pluralism without anarchical disintegration into conflicting groups. In efforts to impose order, governments may become tyrannical. Humans should try to chart a course of unity and diversity in values, avoiding the polar opposites of tyranny and anarchy.

Because the Subject-Object to which religious institutions
bear witness is supreme, the religious sphere should be separated
from the other spheres. Worship, education, and the fostering of
close interpersonal relations are direct responsibilities of religious institutions. The religious institution should uphold principles of justice and cultivate an *ethos* which fosters rich human
life, but it should not impinge directly in particular issues in
the political sphere except in the most extraordinary circumstances.
Religious institutions should seek to give direction to a society,
but they should refrain from giving directives to a society.

The religious professional possesses no unique sacerdotal
role, but through his training and special skills he may contribute
positively to the life of a worshipping community. Voluntarism is
especially prized in the religious sphere, for people cannot be
coerced to worship. Some structures beyond local religious institutions are necessary to provide them with a broader breadth of
vision and a higher level of excellence. As in the political sphere,
some type of representative democratic structure is desirable.

No human society reflecting perfectly those normative
forms of familial, social, economic, political, cultural, and religious organization has existed or will exist. Clearly delineated
normative forms are not even possible in the social, economic, and
cultural spheres.

The normative forms of social organization developed here
presuppose creatures possessing human characteristics. Some of
these defining characteristics will shift in due course, and new
normative forms of social organization will then emerge. If sexual
relations were triadic or quadratic, for example, new normative forms
of family organization would evolve.

Some of these normative forms have been more adequately
institutionalized in Western democracies than in any other part of
the world. Persons in those societies in which monogamy, social
pluralism, a modified enterprise economic system, representative
democracy, cultural pluralism, and religious pluralism and voluntarism are institutionalized tolerably well should seek to preserve
and to improve such patterns.

Some of these normative forms are obviously not seasonally
relevant in many countries at the present time. Persons who live
in such countries must balance the vision of normative forms with
their social context as they decide what forms of social organization are most appropriate in their situation. In every instance
they may be guided by a concern for the proper balance between self-
interest and the common good.

People have to make judgments about the forms of social
organization they seek or support in a given society; they also have
to make innumerable moral decisions about interpersonal and intergroup relations in their existing social order. This reality leads
to a consideration of the volitional side of morality.

THE VOLITIONAL SIDE OF MORALITY

As people seek to decide what to do to enhance harmony
and intensity of life with life in a given context, they cannot
attain unqualified guidance by intellectual analysis and interpretation. Contexts change, and there is no single mode of perfection

in the universe. Informed by their understanding of the principles
of justice, the relative priority of form, dynamics, and unification
in various spheres of the social order, and their view on seasonally
relevant forms of social organization, they must make judgments
about the most appropriate mode of action in their situation.
        Progress is possible in morality, for forms are a neces-
sary part of moral decisions. Perfection is impossible in morality;
for no form fits a context perfectly, and finitude, ignorance,
sloth, lethargy, and inordinate self-interest preclude the possibility of the perfect harmony of life with life.
        Human moral experience -- the sense of a "rightness" of
fit between form and context elicited by God's evocation of harmony
-- shades off into religious and aesthetic experiences. People are
sustained in their awareness of the impossibility of an unqualifiedly
proper moral decision by their awareness of the presence of the One
Who is able to make the best of whatever is offered to Him and Who
is able to retain everlastingly all the world offers Him. In this
fashion, one may interpret disharmonious elements in human experience as contrasts in a broader, richer, and more complex unity.
At the same time, since each person contributes his bit to the Divine
Life, he is sustained in his quest for love and justice in the life
of civilized humankind.
        Without such a Supreme Referee, all is ultimately sound
and fury, signifying nothing.

NOTES AND REFERENCES

        1. For extended discussions of these issues see, for example, Gregory Baum,
Religion and Alienation (New York: Paulist Press, 1975), Robert W. Friedrichs,
A Sociology of Sociology (New York: The Free Press, 1970), W. Widick Schroeder,
Cognitive Structures and Religious Research (East Lansing: Michigan State
University Press, 1970),and Gibson Winter, *Elements for a Social Ethic* (New York:
Macmillan, 1966).
        2. As this essay is primarily a constructive one, no references are made
to other theorists in the body of the text, and space limitations prevent discussion in the "Notes and References" section. The following texts have been
most suggestive in raising and/or illumining the problems addressed here:
        Ernest Barker, *Reflections on Government* (New York: Oxford University
Press, 1958).
        Emil Brunner, *The Divine Imperative* (Philadelphia: The Westminster Press,
1947).
        Emile Durkheim, *Sociology and Philosophy* (Glencoe, Ill.: The Free Press,
1953).
        T.S. Eliot, *The Idea of a Christian Society* (New York: Harcourt, Brace
and Company, 1940).
        The Federalist Papers
        Milton Friedman, *Capitalism and Freedom* (Chicago: University of Chicago
Press, 1962).
        Hans Morgenthau, *Politics Among Nations* (New York: A. Knopf, 1948).
        Reinhold Niebuhr, *The Children of Light and the Children of Darkness*
(New York: Charles Scribner's Sons, 1944).

Reinhold Niebuhr, *The Nature and Destiny of Man* (New York: Charles Scribner's Sons, 1949).

Reinhold Niebuhr, *The Structure of Nations and Empires* (New York: Charles Scribner's Sons, 1960).

Talcott Parsons, *The Social System* (Glencoe: The Free Press, 1951).

Plato, *The Republic*.

Paul Tillich, *Love, Power and Justice* (New York: Oxford University Press, 1954).

Paul Tillich, *Systematic Theology* (Chicago: University of Chicago Press, 1951, 1955, 1963).

Max Weber, "Politics as a Vocation" and "Science as a Vocation" in C. Wright Mills and Hans Geuth, editors, *From Max Weber: Essays in Sociology* (New York: Oxford University Press, 1946).

Max Weber, *Theory of Social and Economic Organization*, translated by A.R. Henderson and Talcott Parsons (New York: Oxford University Press, 1947).

Alfred North Whitehead, *Adventures of Ideas* (New York: Macmillan, 1933).

Alfred North Whitehead, *Process and Reality* (New York: Macmillan, 1929).

Alfred North Whitehead, *Science and the Modern World* (New York: Macmillan, 1925).

Other writings by the author of this essay which compliment and supplement the present discussion include:

Cognitive Structures and Religious Research (East Lansing: Michigan State University Press, 1970).

"A Constructive Interpretation: Authentic Religion, America's Public Faith and the Religions of American Suburbia" in W. Widick Schroeder, Victor Obenhaus, Larry A. Jones, and Thomas Sweetser, S.J., *Suburban Religion* (Chicago: Center for the Scientific Study of Religion, 1974).

"The Development of Religious Research: Retrospect and Prospect," *Review of Religious Research*, Vol. 13, No. 1 (Fall, 1971) pp. 2-12.

"Measuring the Muse: Reflections on the Use of Survey Research Methods in the Study of Religious Phenomena," *Review of Religious Research*, Vol. 18, No. 2 (Winter, 1977) pp. 148-162.

"Religious Institutions and Human Society: A Normative Inquiry into the Appropriate Contribution of Religious Institutions to Human Life and to the Divine Life" in Philip Hefner and W. Widick Schroeder, editors, *Belonging and Alienation* (Chicago: Center for the Scientific Study of Religion, 1976).

Where Do I Stand? (co-authored with Keith A. Davis) (Chicago: Exploration Press, 1975).

Whitehead's *Process and Reality* is the primary text for an appropriation of the basic categories of process thought.   Valuable interpretations of White-head's thought include William Christian, *An Interpretation of Whitehead's Meta-physics* (New Haven: Yale University Press, 1959); John Cobb, Jr. and David Ray Griffin, *Process Theology: An Introductory Exposition* (Philadelphia: West-minster, 1976); and Donald W. Sherburne, *A Key to Whitehead's Process and Reality* (New York: Macmillan, 1966).

3. For this reason the voluntaristic facet of social science theory rooted in the tradition of Max Weber and manifest in various phenomenologies has more in common with process views than the causal facet rooted in the traditions of Durkheim, Pareto, Freud, Marx, and other strongly causally oriented theorists.

4. The fact-value disjunction, manifest in the neo-Kantian understanding of social scientific theory associated with Max Weber and his followers, is spurious.   The inner and exterior factors in human experience are necessarily related.

5. In its broader meaning, "reason" refers to human participation in forms of definiteness embodied in God's primordial nature. This "ontic" reason, coupled with human capacity to think by a method of difference and by the exercise of negative judgments, enables humans to analyze and to interpret human experience.

Technical reason is grounded in ontic reason, and in appropriate contexts the two meanings of reason should be explored. Such explorations are currently not fashionable among economists or, for that matter, among social scientists generally.

6. In a society in which technical reason is highly valued, the legal order may be richly elaborated. Lawyers and the "law" become very important in such societies.

7. This interdependence is the basis of a process critique of structural-functional analysis.

8. Needless to say, his formulations also must be set in the context of a more inclusive interpretative scheme. The notion of the historian writing history as it really was is a figment of the imagination.

9. The relatively "conserving" nature of the version of a process social ethic elaborated here is grounded on a relatively greater emphasis on the formal side of experience than is the case for most process thinkers addressing this problem.

10. Space limitations dictate the propositional character of the delineations advanced here and preclude an extended elaboration and clarification of these propositions in this essay.

THE MEANING OF CITIZENSHIP: AN EXERCISE IN CONSTRUCTIVE POLITICAL THEORY

by
Douglas Sturm

The social and political sciences in the West are gradually and haltingly undergoing a process of reconstruction. Richard J. Bernstein has documented this process in a rich and creative way in two recent studies in which he notes a convergence of direction among a number of seemingly distinct intellectual movements. In the first study, Bernstein demonstrates how Marxism, existentialism, pragmatism and analytic philosophy all tend toward a theory of person as agent.[1] In the second study, he shows how movements in the social sciences, linguistic analysis, phenomenology, and the critical school all press toward a new understanding of the status of theory and the problematic of the theorist.[2] Among other things, these movements tend toward a reconsideration of the relation between theory and practice. They raise serious questions about the possibility of a pure science of society. While there are significant differences among these movements, they force us to see that there are various forms of interpenetration between how we think and what we do.

Interpenetration means influence running both ways. On the one side, one's life-situation is an inescapable place from which thought begins. This is not to say that all thought is in all respects determined necessarily by historical or socioeconomic location. But it is to admit that there is a perspectival character to what one perceives and how one conceives. On the other side, what and how one thinks has an impact on one's activity. Words, images, symbols are of practical import. As the author of a recent study of political linguistics noted

> While language is the medium of politics, it is far from a neutral
> instrument. Our own words and vocabulary affect us politically.
> Language is more than a tool for manipulating others. In ways
> often undetected, it structures our ideas about those with whom we
> interact. The medium of politics is itself political.[3]

The naming of an event, a person, a group, a movement is often an act of practical significance, for it indicates whether the referent is to be honored or damned, exalted or degraded, encouraged or ignored. The practical significance of naming is evident in many areas of social discourse. In legal processes, criminal and civil, for instance, once a mode of identification has been affixed by judge or jury, there are consequences that flow

255

directly therefrom. As an example of the acknowledgement of this
process from ancient times, Confucius' doctrine of the rectification
of names was an effort at far-reaching social reform.

One conclusion to draw from this understanding of the
practical significance of names is that the social and political
analyst has a moral responsibility to consider the consequences and
implications of the theoretical constructs and categories of interpretation that are employed for research. While this proposition
seems fairly tame, persons in Third World countries would point to
the wide divergence in understanding and action that results from
the decision to use categories of either developmental theory or
dependency theory to interpret their political and economic situation.

Against this background, I shall explore the meaning of
citizenship in an effort to formulate an understanding of the political agent that has been neglected. Other recent studies of the
"terms of political discourse" have probed the meanings of power,
interest, influence, and authority,[4] but these are qualities of
relationship among political agents. It would seem wise to have
some sense of what it means to speak of political agents as citizens
and what the implications of citizenship are. Indeed, this would
seem to be particularly important because of what Robert J. Pranger
has called the "eclipse of citizenship" in the Western world.[5]

Pranger distinguishes two types of political culture--a
politics of power and a politics of participation. A citizen's
main task, he asserts, is "to be himself and to participate directly
and spontaneously in creating public business."[6] This task, however,
cannot be performed in a political culture characterized as a politics of power. But that is the form of politics that currently
prevails, at least in the West. The democratic myth notwithstanding,
the actual role of the citizen has been sharply curtailed. The presumed citizen is propagandized and socialized rather than provided
with effective opportunity to engage in the affairs of the public
realm. The bureaucratization of organizational life in political
and economic spheres sharply delimits the possibility of participation. The concentration of power within all major areas of social
organization leaves the citizen in the passive role of subject.
These processes are at the root of the widespread sense, and in
some cases the actual condition, of political alienation and political oppression.

There is another side to the eclipse of citizenship. As
noted in a study of political analysis and its normative implications:

> For whatever reason, recent and contemporary political science has
> adopted an essentially unidimensional conception of politics.
> Specifically, politics is viewed as oriented toward the maximiz-
> ation of personal interests within the constraints imposed by
> organized society. Accordingly, the political process, at any
> level, becomes a matter of bargaining for policies designed to
> achieve this end.[7]

Interest theory in effect factors out the role of citizen. The
political agent is viewed as a representative of a demographic
sector or socioeconomic class or pressure group. One is black or
white, male or female, labor or management, wealthy or poor, con-
servationist or industrialist. The political process is viewed as
a means of mitigating conflict, effecting compromise, maintaining
a *modus vivendi* among contending groups, but all within a framework in which the distribution of political power remains relatively
constant. This view of politics is deemed realistic, that is, as
portraying the process as it actually operates at least in Western
democratic societies. The political agent is thus defined in terms
of interest and power. There is no definitive role of the citizen
as such.

     Hence by dint of both the force of modern political cul-
ture and the trend of modern political analysis, each reinforcing
the other, the meaning of citizenship has been eclipsed. In light
of the political situation as portrayed, it would appear to be
naive and unrealistic to talk about citizenship as such. But to
talk about citizenship would be naive and unrealistic only if one
accepts the presuppositions about the character of the political
world that underlie current practice and theory. It would not be
naive and unrealistic if in exploring the meaning of citizenship
one uncovers dimensions of reality that continue to have valence
even if largely ignored or even suppressed. The counter-thesis to
the charge of naivete is that the restoration of the meaning of
citizenship is related to the restoration of humanity, that citizenship is the political face of personal existence, and that to the
degree to which citizenship is twisted and perverted, the question
of whether it is realistic to engage in an exploration of the sense
of citizenship is thus the question of whether it is meaningful to
reflect about the political character of personal existence and
whether such reflection is of practical import in shaping perceptions and in reinforcing movements within the historical process
that run counter to a politics of power and interest.

     The predominant part of the procedure I have undertaken
in this exploration is historical in the sense that I intend to
appropriate meanings of citizenship that are present in past American experience. As a prior exercise, however, I shall characterize the "way of appropriation" as a means of using the historical
past for ethical reflection. In the concluding portion of the
essay, I shall indicate very briefly how the meanings of citizenship appropriated from the American past might be construed as
grounded in a theory of human action. Thus in the sections that
follow, I shall characterize the way of appropriation; describe
three principles that constitute the form of citizenship, a liberal
principle, a communal principle and a principle of transcendence;
and, finally, relate these three principles to an understanding of
human action construed as communication.

I. The Way of Appropriation

Karl Mannheim has observed that there are two ways of writing the history of thought. The first is the narrative. It tells the story of the passage of ideas from one thinker to another in chronological fashion. The second is the depiction of styles of thought. It characterizes clusters of ideas that cohere under the direction of a dominant intention and that recur with some continuity at various times and places.[8] Without denying the usefulness of either of these ways, I would suggest a third that is relevant to political and ethical thought. It is a method actually employed in legal processes and religious communities. According to the way of appropriation, past historical movements of thought are not simply dead hands of the past. Rather, they persist as possibilities that can be taken up afresh. Appropriation is not the same as repetition. Repetition means to reiterate the same pattern of thought or action without alteration. Repetition is habitual reenactment. Appropriation, on the other hand, is a creative act. It involves reflection. It entails discerning possibilities out of past times and past writings for present consideration and action.

The same historical data may be handled in all three ways. Thus one may examine writings of Aristotle as part of the development of classical Greek thought, as initiating a style of thought that has recurred at various times and places in the West, and as presenting a method and doctrine for creative thought and action in the present. The third is the way of appropriation.

Anglo-American common law is a classic instance of the way of appropriation. While the principle of *stare decisis* can be invoked to support an uncritical traditionalism, a precedent normally has authority within the common law not merely because it is a precedent, but because it is discerned as a relevant and compelling possibility for the case before the courts. If it is so appropriated, it is not simply repeated, but is given a fresh formulation for the case at hand. The precedent so employed is both a continuation and a reconstruction. It is taken up from the past, but it assumes new form in the present. If a precedent is rejected, the case before the court is distinguished or the precedent is overruled and a new beginning is initiated. But if accepted, it constitutes an instance of the way of appropriation.[9]

Religious ritual is another instance of the way of appropriation, an instance that is particularly pertinent to politics for there is an analogue, and perhaps more than an analogue, between political ritual and religious ritual.

Religious ritual, as Mircea Eliade has indicated, is related to religious myth and religious tradition. At the root of religious tradition is a determinative moment--a theophany, an event of the appearance of the sacred. To the religious person, the presence of the sacred is central. It establishes a point of orientation. It creates a world. It institutes a structure of meaning. It marks a passage from chaos to cosmos. It constitutes a base from which to perceive and to evaluate other realities. Indeed it determines what reality is.

The religious myth is the story of that time and that place in which the sacred has appeared. It is a statement of what occurred during that special, creative moment. But myth is not only descriptive; it is not merely an answer to a theoretical question. In Eliade's terms, "the supreme function of the myth is to 'fix' the paradigmatic models for all rites and all significant human activities--eating, sexuality, work, education, and so on."[10] The religious myth, while re-presenting the theophanous moment, is directive. It commands the religious person to act in conformity with the dictates of that moment. It induces the religious person to imitate the divine.

The point of central religious rituals is to re-enact what is told in the myths. The religious ceremony is an imitation of the mighty acts of the gods. It revivifies the story. It commemorates the time when the world began. It is therefore a remembering that is more than a remembering, for it has a transformative effect on the participant. By reminding the participant of the foundation of his existence in the world, it restores his being. It is at once a return and renovation. To use the language of a linear conception of time, the ritual brings the past into the present for the sake of the future. The one who participates is born again and is oriented toward the regeneration of reality.

By way of example, the Eucharistic celebration is a participation in the Last Supper and in the crucifixion and resurrection of Jesus Christ. Through this means, the Atonement becomes efficacious and reconciliation is accomplished. Further, the Jew who participates in the Seder at Passover relives the event of Israel's liberation from enslavement in Egypt and becomes committed afresh to the continuing tasks of liberation. Hence "this night" becomes "different from all other nights."

In celebration, therefore, the religious past becomes a creative possibility in the present for a new future, a possibility for overcoming the effects of sin, perversion, forgetfulness, a loss of the sense of the sacred, and for beginning anew. That, at least, is the serious intent of religious ritual.

There are illuminating parallels between religious rituals and political rituals. Political holidays are intended to fulfill the same function. This is particularly true of political holidays that represent and signify new beginnings--Bastille Day in France, Independence Day in the United States. Compared with religious holidays, they may more easily become trivialized and their intended ground forgotten. But they nonetheless possess, in principle, the character of recapturing the past as possibility and inducing the participants to think and to act in accordance with the celebrated qualities of that past.

There is another feature of the way of appropriation that should be mentioned, the feature of critical reflexivity. That is, it is in conformity with the way of appropriation to turn a normative symbol derived from a past event back upon the event itself. This is one way of construing Lord Mansfield's maxim that the common law purifies itself, or Lon Fuller's notion that the judicial process over the centuries may be characterized as the collaborative articulation of shared purposes. There are, for instance, two ways

to react to those founders of the United States who proclaimed the
equality of all persons yet continued to hold slaves and failed to
enfranchise women. One way is to charge them with hypocrisy and
to reject the principle they proclaimed. The other way, an exercise in critical reflexivity, is to appropriate their proclamation
as a possibility still worthy of respect, but be honest and critical
about the inconsistency between their proclamation and their practice.

The bicentennial year in the United States was an instructive case of the way of appropriation even though the year's celebration was gravely distorted through commercialization and huck-
sterism which is, perhaps, to be expected in a dominantly business-
oriented culture and consumer society. Still, the bicentennial
year was meant to be a time of remembering and restoration. I
mention the bicentennial year because its focus was on the American
Revolution, a key event in the origins of this nation, and I intend
to appropriate certain sentiments and meanings from that event in
this exploration of the meaning of citizenship. Those who were
principals in the Revolution insisted it was not primarily a
military event; it was a cultural movement that would not be complete unless and until it permeated the institutions of the society
and the morals and manners of the people.

Thus John Adams wrote in a letter to Hezekiah Niles,

> What do we mean by the American Revolution? Do we mean the American
> war? The Revolution was effected before the war commenced. The
> Revolution was in the minds and hearts of the people; a change in
> their religious sentiments, of their duties and obligations. . . .
> *This radical change in the principles, opinions, sentiments, and*
> *affections of the people was the real American Revolution.*[11]

Benjamin Rush, signer of the Declaration of Independence and founder
of the first American antislavery society, was not so sure the
radical change had taken full effect. He wrote in 1787,

> The American war is over: but this is far from being the case with
> the American revolution. On the contrary, nothing but the first
> act of the great drama is closed. It remains to establish and per-
> fect our new forms of government and to prepare the principles,
> morals, and manners of our citizens for these forms of government
> after they are established and brought to perfection.[12]

Both Adams and Rush agree, however, that the American Revolution
was a matter of principle and that the concern of the Revolution
was to have a transformative impact upon the citizenry. Indeed it
was to create a citizenry.

In the sections that follow I shall assert that there are
three principles discoverable within the sentiments and meanings
expressed at the time of the American Revolution that constitute
the meaning of citizenship--the principles of liberty, community,
and transcendence. The principles derive from three traditions of
political belief: liberalism, conservatism, and constitutionalism.

II. Liberalism and the Principle of Liberty

Throughout its variations from country to country and from time to time, liberalism has been controlled by a single, dominant, defining aim: the freedom of the individual. During some periods, liberalism assumed a more negative form, opposing forces of arbitrary authority. During other periods, liberalism presented a more positive front, encouraging free self-expression. But throughout all its variations, liberalism's primary concern has been liberty, a concern clearly present in the minds of the American Revolutionaries. Bernard Bailyn, in his masterful interpretation of the ideological origins of the American Revolution, demonstrates that liberty was a vital, perhaps the most vital, category in the political literature of the pre-revolutionary years:

> The primary goal of the American Revolution. . .was not the overthrow or even the alteration of the existing social order but the preservation of political liberty threatened by the apparent corruption of the constitution, and the establishment in principle of the existing conditions of liberty.[13]

In the context of the pre-revolutionary years, liberty is understood as the antithesis of power, but power is conceived not merely as the capacity to be and to act. Power is dominion, "the dominion of some men over others, the human control of human life: ultimately force, compulsion."[14] As such, power tends to become malignant because of the propensity of persons in positions of dominion to exploit their office for the aggrandizement of themselves at the expense of others. Power tends to enslave, that is, to create a condition by which one is obliged to act in accordance with the arbitrary desire or will of another. To the revolutionaries, the prevailing political powers in England had explicit designs to control and ultimately to enslave the American colonies and all the inhabitants of the colonies. Whether or not there were such designs, that was the belief of the revolutionaries. Thus the cause of the revolutionaries was the cause of liberty, political liberty, the capacity of individuals to act freely within the framework of the natural rights of humankind and those social laws, but only those social laws, duly established by the people or their representatives.

The language of liberty and power was synonymous with the language of individual and government. The citizen is an individual, at liberty to act as she or he pleases, subject to some restraints, but only those restraints needed to prevent the obstruction of the liberty of other citizens. According to the liberal tradition, government may be useful for some purposes, but for the preservation of genuine citizenship, those purposes should be limited and the reach of governmental power carefully circumscribed. Government should be viewed always as a potential enemy of individual liberty, for often it becomes an actual enemy, enslaving individuals, denying or depriving them of the rights and privileges of citizenship.

Thoreau's essay on "Civil Disobedience," originally delivered as a lecture entitled "On the Relation of the Individual to the State," presents this position with the force of personal profession.

> I heartily accept the motto--"That government is best which governs least"; and I should like to see it acted up to more rapidly and systematically. Carried out, it finally amounts to this, which also I believe--"That government is best which governs not at all"; and when men are prepared for it, that will be the kind of government which they will have.[15]

Political progress is "progress toward a true respect for the individual," "toward recognizing and organizing the rights of man." Thus, to Thoreau,

> There will never be a really true and enlightened State, until the State comes to recognize the individual as a higher and independent power, from which all its own power and authority are derived, and treats him accordingly.[16]

The state rests on the consent of the individual. When it fails to acknowledge this fact in its institutional operation, then the citizen as citizen may determine "to refuse allegiance to the State, to withdraw and stand aloof from it effectively." That is what Thoreau himself did, announcing, "I quietly declare war with the State, after my fashion."[17]

Thoreau's essay-lecture was presented as a justification for his refusal to pay the head tax in Massachusetts for which he spent one night in the Concord prison. His description of this experience manifests something of the character of the liberal spirit.

> I saw that, if there was a wall of stone between me and my townsmen, there was still a more difficult one to climb or break through, before they could get to be as free as I was. . . .I could not but smile to see how industriously they locked the door on my meditations, which followed them out again without let or hindrance, and *they* were really all that was dangerous. . . .I saw that the State was half-witted. . . .that it did not know its friends from its foes, and I lost all remaining respect for it, and pitied it.[18]

Upon his release from jail, Thoreau joined others to pick huckleberries; in a short time they were "in the midst of a huckleberry field, on one of our highest hills, two miles off, and there the State was nowhere to be seen."[19] Thoreau's prison meditations and the huckleberry field are symbols for one side of the liberal understanding of citizenship. To be a citizen is to be at liberty, to be autonomous, to have private space in which to pursue one's own thoughts and activities in one's own way without "let or hindrance" by governmental power. This is the logic that connects liberalism with both civil liberties and property rights.

But there is another side to Thoreau's understanding of citizenship which would also seem to be part of the creed of liberalism. Thoreau was not content with the right to be left alone. Through vigorous opposition to slavery and the Mexican wars, he manifested a felt duty to extend the quality of liberty to others as well.

> I cannot for an instant recognize the political organization as *my* government which is the *slave's* government also. . . .When a sixth of the population of a nation which has undertaken to be the refuge of liberty are slaves, and a whole country is unjustly overrun and conquered by a foreign army, and subjected to military law, I think that it is not too soon for honest men to rebel and to revolutionize.[20]

Subsequent to Thoreau, these two sides of the meaning of citizenship, the right to private space and freedom of thought and the duty to liberate the oppressed, so intimately related in Thoreau's mind and joined in the American Revolution, became disjoined. Thus, in our time, many who oppose big government are at the same time indifferent if not antagonistic to drives for liberation by ethnic groups, Native Americans, women, blacks, and colonized peoples throughout the world. The individualistic base of liberalism proved inadequate to integrate rights for self with duty to others. Furthermore there has been a failure to extend the principle of liberty and rights to forms of dominion that are non-governmental but no less enslaving.[21]

However inconsistent contemporary liberals may be and however limited their vision, there is nonetheless an important insight in the liberal spirit that should be preserved as a principle of citizenship. There are, in Hocking's phrase, "lasting elements of individualism."[22] In an age that is so dominantly nationalistic, corporativistic, and militaristic, in an age in which the bureaucratic form has permeated our common life, there is persuasiveness to Mark Roelofs' plea for renewed attention to the individualistic dimension of citizenship, albeit on a new religious and metaphysical grounding more appropriate to modern times.[23] In this connection, Harold Laski was led several years ago to suggest in an essay on "The Recovery of Citizenship":

> If democratic government is to survive, it must discover means of restoring to the individual citizen his personal initiative and responsibility. For it is difficult not to feel that the scale of modern civilization has of itself done much to deprive him of his freedom. He cannot hope, in populations of modern size, that his own voice will be clearly heard. To want effectively, he must be part of an organization wide enough, and significant enough, to be able to make its impress upon political authority. The citizen who stands alone today is lost. It is as part of a group that he secures the power to fulfill himself.[24]

To have space for individual creativity, to have civil
liberties for protection against arbitrariness, and to have opportunity for political expression and participation--these are among
the constitutive elements of citizenship derived from the tradition
of liberalism.

III. Conservatism and the Principle of Community

The principle of community is a second dimension of the
meaning of citizenship. What liberty is to liberalism, community
is to conservatism. Conservatism is a deep-seated tradition in the
United States alongside liberalism, although it is not always acknowledged as such, and when it is acknowledged, by supporters or
detractors, its basic insights are often misunderstood.
The American Revolution was a conservative event. Recall
the statement by Bernard Bailyn already quoted: "the primary goal of
the American Revolution. . .was not the overthrow or even the alteration of the existing social order but the preservation of political
liberty threatened by the apparent corruption of the constitution."[25]
The American colonists cherished the rights of Englishmen. Their
primary grievance in the years preceding the outbreak of the revolution was that they were being deprived of those traditional rights.
They did not want to change constitutional expectations. They wanted
to correct perversions of those expectations. In political pamphlets
during the years of crisis (1763-1776), they invoked seventeenth-
and early eighteenth-century English writings by opposition thinkers
who were expressing grave concern over the erosion of "England's
ancient heritage."[26] The colonists, this is to say, were grounding
their argument on tradition. Their claim was not to break with
political tradition, but to bring the principles of that tradition
to life in judging the perversity of prevailing political powers.
It must be remembered that the classic English conservative, Edmund
Burke, himself vigorously opposed England's colonial policy and
thought the American Revolution was, while unfortunate, justified
on conservative grounds.
Conservatism is traditionalism. But tradition is honored
by conservatives not for its own sake. It is honored as essential
to the substance of human existence. It is honored as necessary
for the continuation of community, and human existence is impossible apart from community. The fracturing of long-standing relations and expectations is destructive of humanity. It entails
alienation and separation from the community of one's identity and
one's belonging. Rootlessness is fatal to the development of personality.
Conservatism thus gives voice to a dimension of human
existence neglected by liberalism. William Ernest Hocking has
argued that, with all its virtues, liberalism suffers from several
glaring defects. It is lacking in a keen sense of the ambiguities
and fragilities of human association. It tends to stress individual rights to the neglect of duties and responsibilities. And it
fails to provide a basis for social unity.[27] To the liberal, relations between individuals are artificial and external. They may

be created and broken upon demand. Associations are all voluntary and contractual. One makes contracts to associate at will. But that understanding of the character and texture of human relations and human existence is naive and unreal, however much one might wish it were true. Human beings are instead very much a part of one another. An individual's perceptions and thoughts, feelings and sensibilities, hunches and ideas, joys and sorrows, values and actions are all profoundly shaped by prior generations, present companions, and anticipated associations. The community--past, present, and future--is a presence even in one's solitariness, even in Thoreau's huckleberry field.

As an aside, it might be noted that Karl Marx, whose *Communist Manifesto* was first published the same year Thoreau delivered his lecture on "Civil Disobedience" (1848), understood the interdependency of persons in the economic and political order and the interrelatedness of past, present, and future in a way that Thoreau did not. Marx's depictions of the conditions of mankind in modern capitalistic society show him as more of an historical and social realist than Thoreau. Marx understood the solidarity of human life. He knew that we are members one of another, that our destinies are intertwined, and that what we are and what we shall become are not matters subject simply to our individual determination.

From the standpoint of classical conservative political thought, the communal spirit consists of several features.[28] A society is understood as a complex and concrete organism with its own life, its own history, its own laws of development. A society is not dependent on the particular individuals who are members of it, for the social organism goes on as individuals are born, die, or emigrate. On the other hand, individuals depend on society not only for sheer existence, but for nurture, education, identity, fulfillment. There is no isolated individual. What we call abstractly the "individual" is in concrete reality parent or child, teacher or student, poet or worker, outlaw or undertaker. One is always a member of society. Indeed the various dimensions of a society are related as parts of a whole. A change in one belief, institution, or norm has some impact on all others.

Political policies should be oriented toward the fulfillment of the needs of the social organism and its members, not toward the protection of individual rights. The appropriate method for interpreting and evaluating persons and institutions is therefore functional: they are of value to the degree to which they contribute to the needs of the society and they are discounted to the extent to which they are not.

Within the same framework, small social groups, families, and neighborhood communities are important in developing loyalties and providing support for persons. Without such groups, persons are faceless and the people becomes a mass. Any large scale effort to reorganize or to rationalize the social order will lead to anomie and finally to social disorganization, for persons do not live by reason alone. If a society is to survive, a people's traditions and loyalties, rituals and symbols, motivational commitments and religious sensibilities must be cherished and respected.

Finally, from the classical conservative perspective, a healthy society will be hierarchical in form. Each person has his or her own status and function within the social order. There is a natural inequality among persons, and not all can or should occupy positions of authority, but authority is necessary for social survival and is legitimate when it originates in and serves to reinforce the customs of a people.

Thus to the conservative the citizen is one who knows and accepts his or her place within the social organism. The citizen is the loyal and devoted member of the body politic standing in opposition to those forces that would, by intention or effect, destroy it. Citizenship consists not in the protection and enjoyment of individual rights, freedoms and liberties, but in the duty to contribute one's energies, mind, and whole being toward the fulfillment of one's social function. As citizen one is responsible to and, within the scope of one's status, responsible for, the social whole. Not liberty, but responsibility is the key characteristic of the citizen. As John F. Kennedy cast it in a felicitous but controversial phrase, ask not what your country can do for you, ask what you can do for your country. This is the meaning of citizenship from the viewpoint of classical conservatism.

Among the principals in the revolutionary period in the United States, there were devotees of both liberalism and conservatism. Thomas Jefferson and Thomas Paine were more of the former persuasion; Alexander Hamilton, John Adams, even James Madison were more of the latter. Revisionist historians properly remind us that all these persons, with the possible exception of Paine, were illiberal in actual political plans and policies. But the difference in stated intention was present, and both movements· of thought constitute data for an exploration of the meaning of citizenship.

I would claim it is possible to distinguish in the conservative movement what is primary from what is secondary. What is primary is the central and governing concern of conservatism, the concern for *communitas* as essential to the development, maintenance, and fulfillment of human existence. What is secondary is everything else--features of custom, tradition, status, authority, inequality. These features of social life are required by conservatism, or what I shall call critical conservatism, only so far as they are needed for and contribute to the development and enrichment of communal existence. If one intends to form "a more perfect Union," one may invoke the ancient heritage of rights and expectations--those rights and expectations that constitute the community, that hold it together, that compose its identity--but raise to a point of critical reflexivity those principles of that heritage that are of a genuinely liberal and communal character. It may be noted that paramount among the principles invoked in the American Revolution was that ultimate political authority (sovereignty) rested with the people.[29] The people as a people is the basic political association. Government is meant to be an agent of the people, grounded in its consent, created to protect its rights and to serve its welfare, subjected to its criticism and alteration in light of its judgment. It is the traditions, experiences, aspirations of the community, understood as embracing all conditions, kinds, and groups, that should rule.

What I am suggesting is that liberalism and conservatism might be conjoined and that the meaning of citizenship might be understood as including both the principle of liberty and the principle of community. The principle of liberty is the basis for civil liberties and private space. The principle of community is the foundation for the citizen's loyalty to the people, for as the community past has informed one's mind, so the condition of the community present and the community future depend on what one is and what one does, what one thinks and what one values.

IV. Degenerate Forms of Liberalism and Conservatism

There is an all too obvious tendency for both the liberal and the conservative principles of citizenship to degenerate into delimited and perverse forms. On the one hand, liberalism's fundamental commitment is to the liberty of the individual. It is often transformed into sheer individualism and is understood as implying that everyone has a right to her or his own opinion, that judgments and choices are grounded in subjective feelings, and that all opinions, judgments, and choices are equivalent. Liberalism in this form is subjectivism. It is grounded in what R. M. Unger has called the "principle of arbitrary desire"[30] and the "principle of subjective value."[31] Thus liberalism results in a politics of interest and power which assumes particularly virulent form when large groups and corporations are legitimated as *persona ficta* and invested with the privileges and respect of individual persons. Each individual and group, it is urged, has its own interests which it rightfully promulgates, presses, pushes, and promotes within the political arena employing whatever means it can to fulfill those interests. Liberty becomes license. Rights become a warrant to pursue one's own purposes or the purposes of one's corporate group with studied indifference to the impact of that pursuit on the rest of the world. Liberalism in this form, especially when joined with a maldistribution of social power, has lost the nobility one finds in classical declarations of human rights and has become a self-serving, narrow-minded, destructive political philosophy.

On the other hand, conservatism's fundamental commitment is to the community of belonging. With that basic commitment, conservatism is usually identified with historicism. As Joseph de Maistre quipped, he has seen Persians, Russians, Germans, Poles, but never a human being. Individuals are discerned as belonging to concrete historical communities from which they derive their identity and in the absence of which they suffer from separation anxiety and meaninglessness. Individuals are unable to cope with life satisfactorily apart from their historical communities which is what makes the case of refugees and displaced persons so poignant   Hence the preservation and survival of the community become the dominant, overriding political task. Nation, race, religion, ethnic origin are the keys of political identity and political responsibility. The community of one's origin or

orientation with its given historical symbols and institutions defines one's political role. Conservatism in this form results in
a politics of nationalism, racism, ethnicity, or religious orthodoxy. As such it is a politics of the *status quo* unless seriously
threatened, when it is easily transformed into a radicalized,
frenetic politics of violence. Conservatism in these forms is
without the qualities of mutuality and compassion. It has become
the philosophy of a tribalistic, closed society.

V. Constitutionalism and the Principle of Transcendence

Over against the degenerate forms of liberalism and conservatism stands a third principle of the meaning of citizenship,
the principle of transcendence. This is a principle I would
attribute to constitutionalism, another of the strains of thought
one can discover in the American Revolution.

By claim the American Revolution was neither self-serving
nor nationalistic. It was intended as a revolution of principles,
principles characterized by objectivity and universality. While
the principles articulated deeply felt desires of the colonists,
and while they were transmitted through "England's ancient heritage,"
they were presented as objective in ground and universal in application. That is, at least, the appearance of the beginning passages of the Declaration of Independence.

> We hold these truths to be self-evident, that all men are created
> equal; that they are endowed by their Creator with certain unalien-
> able rights; that among these are life, liberty, and the pursuit of
> happiness. That to secure these rights, governments are instituted
> among men, deriving their just powers from the consent of the gov-
> erned; that, whenever any form of government becomes destructive
> of these ends, it is the right of the people to alter or to abolish
> it, and to institute a new government, laying its foundation on
> such principles, and organizing its powers in such form, as to them
> shall seem most likely to effect their safety and happiness.

We have learned, of course, to be both suspicious and
critical of these statements declaring independence. They derive
from an outmoded style of thought--the Enlightenment. They were
a cover for bourgeois interest. It is uncertain what it means for
truths to be self-evident. Granting valiant efforts by John Rawls
and others, the principle of equality has fallen on hard times.
In most policy decisions, there is an open balancing and qualification of rights, making them somewhat less than unalienable. It
is debatable what justice is and whether there is any meaningful
and effective way whereby the governed ever did or ever can give
consent to the government.

Yet there is a dimension of thought captured in these
statements that deserves attention in exploring the meaning of
citizenship, the dimension of transcendence. At first blush, the
notion of transcendence has the connotation of that which is beyond, which excels, which is independent of one's ken or control.

The transcendent is the "above." It is what one cannot attain or reach. However, as Roger Hazelton has observed, the nouns "transcendence" and "transcendent" are derived from a verb which means to climb over or to cross over. To transcend an obstacle is to overcome it. To transcend a difficulty is to rise above it. In a curious etymological twist, the noun "transcendence" has come to mean an obstacle that cannot be overcome. Here, however, the word shall be used in its more active, verbal sense.

Transcendence is a beyondness, but a beyondness that lures one out of oneself, that moves one to reach across boundaries, that lifts the horizons of one's mind and opens new possibilities for thought, feeling, and action. The experience of transcendence is that of moving onto a new plane of existing.[32] The experience of transcendence is not, however, necessarily rare or extraordinary. It is involved in all creative action and genuine understanding. To understand another person, culture, mode of thought, or form of life, for instance, one must cross over from one's self to another with the result that the self is not and cannot remain the same. Education, at its best, entails transcendence, for education informs and transforms the mind through discovery.

The phrases of the Declaration of Independence, if taken seriously, are meant to provoke an act of transcendence. They provoke a moving beyond immediate political interests to a consideration of truths about the condition of mankind in the world. They provoke a moving beyond one's immediate community of belonging to a consideration of the universal human community. By inference, the principles of the Declaration announce the insufficiency of citizenship governed by personal opinion and group politics, national security and power considerations. This is not to say that matters of opinion, group interest, security and power are unimportant or inappropriate to political reflection and action. It is only to affirm that they are finally inadequate as political norms.

The phrases of the Declaration shift the level of political discourse from considerations of desire, expediency, ethnic pride, and *raison d'Etat* to considerations of the principle of humanity. They require the mind to consider political questions within a universal human context, and thus they require of citizenship a spirit of transcendence, a going beyond previously defined interests and given communities of belonging.

I have attributed this spirit of transcendence to constitutionalism. Traditionally, constitutionalism has been understood as meaning a form of political procedure in which the sphere of governmental action is deliberately limited through institutional arrangement and legal definition. Over the course of its development, constitutionalism has included the principles of rule of law, mixed government, separation of powers, an independent judiciary, the primacy of Parliament, and the legalization of human rights. Constitutionalism thus has the reputation of a negative political form because it creates limits and specifies exact procedures for governmental action. But at its best the historic impact of constitutionalism and its basic reason have been not the delimitation but the opening up of the political process, not the constriction but the extension of political participation. The principles of constitutionalism have been invoked in reaction against closed government, rigidity in government, oppressive government. The import of constitutionalism is to overcome elitist politics for the sake of humanist politics. Indeed, Scott Buchanan argues that the ultimate import of constitutionalism goes even beyond the limitations of humanist politics to a form of cosmic politics, a "constitutional kingdom of nature."[33] Constitutionalism on its negative side involves the establishment of prohibitions and restraints in government but for the sake of the positive side of constitutionalism--the creation of channels of communication. We shall attend to this motif of communication again in the final section of this essay.

In general I am suggesting that in the intentionality of the constitutionalist tradition,[34] the liberty of liberalism becomes a process of constant liberation and the community of conservatism becomes the open society. A passage from Henri Bergson captures this point about the principle of transcendence in constitutionalism:

> The open society is the society which is deemed in principle to embrace all humanity. A dream dreamt, now and again, by chosen souls, it embodies on every occasion something of itself in creations, each of which, through a more or less far-reaching transformation of man, conquers difficulties hitherto unconquerable. But after each occasion the circle that has momentarily opened closes again. . . .(Each new stage in that process aims) at opening what was closed; and the group, which after the last opening had closed on itself, was brought back every time to humanity.[35]

The meaning of citizenship includes the principle of transcendence. It contains the dream of an open society.[36] It embraces the drive for liberation, for a crossing beyond the boundaries, for the correction and critical transformation of political consciousness.

A challenge by Vernon Bettecourt, leader of the American Indian Movement, may be interpreted as illustrative of the drive for transcendence within the context of current American politics.

> To put this event (the bicentennial) in its proper perspective we must ask that it be looked at as not 200 years of celebration, but 200 years of deceit and shame because the nation massacred America's original people, the Indians, and built a nation on lands taken from the Indians. . . .You must remember as you celebrate your revolution of 1776 that you only took off the yoke of colonial rule, and placed it squarely around the neck of our Indian nations. . . .Only when America is willing to accept these truths, will America be able to enter a period of reconciliation with Indian people. . . .If America is willing to end its longest undeclared war against the original people, our lands, resources and way of life, then we must enter into this era of reconciliation.[37]

Vernon Bettecourt was voicing the need for a transformation of political consciousness, the need for an appreciable alteration and extension of the political system to acknowledge the human rights and the human presence of groups that had long been excluded and held down. He was asking for an extraordinarily difficult exercise of the mind, but an exercise that is part of the meaning of citizenship. He was asking that his hearers change their perceptions, transform their expectations, and reevaluate their political visions in light of realities previously ignored. He was asking for a kind of political conversion.

The principle of transcendence is vital to the meaning of citizenship because the final arena of politics is the ever-changing cosmopolis. The final loyalty of the citizen is not to one's own individual liberties alone nor the national community alone. It is to the community of mankind and beyond, even to the entire community of nature. This is why Edmond Cahn has avowed that sometimes political and legal loyalty properly takes the form of "principled recalcitrance."[38]

The principle of transcendence does not contradict the principles of liberty and community. Rather it corrects, expands, stretches them. It drives the mind to attend to realities outside the immediate purview of one's concern and it instructs the mind to acknowledge that "New occasions teach new duties/Time makes ancient good uncouth" (James Russell Lowell). Past requirements of liberty and community may lose their force in new circumstances. It is even conceivable that the implications of the principles of liberty and community become clear only over the course of time, which is a possible explanation of the incongruities between the rhetoric and the realities of American politics during the long, violent, still unfinished process of minority groups in this country struggling for emancipation and acceptance. The principle of transcendence produces a sense of humility, restlessness, searching, openness. The point of constitutionalism is to create institutional structures amenable to the probing character of the principle of transcendence, even though we must admit that constitutionalism, like liberalism and conservatism, is often known in perverse form.

In summary to this point, I have declared that out of the traditions of liberalism, conservatism, and constitutionalism present in the American past, one may appropriate three principles of the meaning of citizenship--a liberal principle, a communal principle, and a principle of transcendence. To be clear, I have not declared that the political institutions and policies of American history, in the revolutionary period or in the present, conform to these principles. Nothing could be further from the truth. The perversions of these principles in the American political experience are too evident to rehearse. The tragedy of America is that what it has been and what it has done contravene the promise with which it began. Yet there is point to the analogue drawn earlier in this essay between the way of appropriation and religious ritual, for a vital part of the ritual of remembrance and renovation is confession of sin. While the principles of the meaning of citizenship may not have been and are not now embodied in

the institutions and agents of the political process, they nonetheless possess the reality of possibility and judgment. Through
a procedure of critical reflexivity, they enable one to discern
past conditions as denials of liberty, corruptions of community,
and rejections of transcendence. And they stand before one with
the challenge to engage in the never-ending task of forming and
transforming the conditions of common life including both institutional structures and the structures of our own thought and conduct as political agents.

VI. Citizenship and Personal Existence

        In this final section, I return very briefly to the thesis
stated at the beginning that the eclipse of citizenship is the perversion of the principle of humanity and, conversely, that the
restoration of the meaning of citizenship is related to the restoration of a humane, personal existence.
        In the preceding sections of the essay, the American
tradition was explored through the way of appropriation to construct three principles of the meaning of citizenship. One may
properly raise a question about the status of the result. Is it
merely a subjective or historical reconstruction of meaning? This
question is related to one of the primary concerns of the work of
Jürgen Habermas.[39] He has asked whether and how there is any basis
for moving beyond historicism; whether and how there is any ground
for a critique of ideology; whether and how there is a foundation
for political criticism and reconstruction. He claims there is
such a basis in what he calls the ideal speech situation. His
argument is that all forms of communicative interaction, however
deceptive and systematically distorted they might be, presuppose
and anticipate an ideal speech situation, that is, a situation in
which persons are enabled by their own competence and by supportive
institutional settings to engage in free, open, sincere, serious
argumentation, seeking a resolution of whatever question is at hand.
The ideal speech situation, the possibility of communicative competence, is therefore a norm derived directly from social intercourse, a norm rooted in the emancipatory interest that motivates
persons to speak inquiringly with one another. In the ideal speech
situation, I would suggest, the principle of liberty undergirds the
rights of each speaker, the communal principle pertains to the
maintenance of the community of discourse, and the principle of
transcendence underlies the aspiration to attain new levels of
understanding and new possibilities for political action. Thus
the meaning of citizenship is implicit in the ideal speech situation
which, in turn, is implied wherever there is political communication.
        David Bell urges that politics generally should be under-
stood as forms of communication, in which context he asserts:

> In an ideal political community. . .people listen to each other's
> talk, especially their urgent words, rendering violence unnecessary
> as a form of political communication. The humanization of society
> consists of our learning to talk and to listen together. Thus a

prime educational task for political linguistics concerns the
necessity of understanding how political communication can make
political community, both within the nation states and among them,
possible.[40]

David Bell does not carry through with this broad hint. But, were
it carried through, it might be possible to argue that communication is not only an essential component of politics, it is, in a
special form, the fundamental pattern of human existence; that the
more fully political relations assume that pattern, the more humane
they become; and perhaps even that this understanding of the character of human existence has a theistic implication.
    According to Henry Nelson Wieman, for instance, creative
intercommunication is the process by which all that is distinc-
tively human comes into being and is sustained in being.[41] To be
sure, as he notes, there are many obstacles, social and psychological, that obstruct the communicative process--social and political
oppression, resistance to change, deep-seated feelings of guilt,
futility, and meaninglessness. Yet there can be no human existence
at all without some degree of creative interchange. The question
is how to remove the obstacles, overcome the obstructions, and
thereby release the workings of this process toward the increased
realization of human good. To Wieman one of the ways of release
is faith, that is, commitment to the process itself which, as a
result, enhances one's freedom (liberty), engages one more fully
in communal interchange (community), and moves one to new levels
of appreciative consciousness (transcendence). In this sense, the
meaning of citizenship derived from the traditions of liberalism,
conservatism, and constitutionalism is directly related to the
realization of human good. To be citizen is an expression of one's
humanity.
    As a final note, I shall take an argument from John
MacMurray's theory of the form of the personal.[42] In MacMurray's
radical reversal of the philosophical task which bears directly on
the reconstruction currently underway in the social and political
sciences,[43] to be a person is not primarily to be thinker but to
be agent. Reflection is a function of action. Theory is a function
of practice. One's thinking about the world is a function of one's
presence in the world. But action in the world has reference always to an Other. To be an agent is to be in relation to and in
touch with an Other which is what MacMurray means when he writes
that "communication is fundamental in all personal experience and
determines its form."[44] To act as a citizen means normally to act
in concert with and in relation to others in a variety of associations and relations ranging from local voluntary groups to nation
states, from parties to international organizations. Yet, in the
final analysis, the total field of action is the universe in the
sense that one's action is part of the whole complex of actions
that determine the immediate future. While various planes and
levels of action may be distinguished, and while some may appear
more immediately and obviously relevant than others, each act is
a contribution of a present moment to the future of the entire
world. But, asks MacMurray, how is one to characterize that

dimension of action, how is one to represent the Other in relation to which one acts as participant in the universe? His answer is, God, the One who calls the universe into being and in relation to Whom the world can be thought of as one action, as a total dynamic community united by God's intention.[45]   So far as one can take this step, then the ultimate responsibility of citizen is to God. The rights of citizen are the rights necessary for human agency; the community of belonging is the universe; and the transcendent aspiration is the intention of God.

NOTES AND REFERENCES

1. Richard J. Bernstein, *Praxis and Action: Contemporary Philosophies of Human Activity* (Philadelphia: University of Pennsylvania Press, 1971).
2. Richard J. Bernstein, *The Restructuring of Social and Political Theory* (New York & London: Harcourt Brace Jovanovich, 1976).
3. David V.J. Bell, *Power, Influence, and Authority: An Essay in Political Linguistics* (New York: Oxford University Press, 1975), p. x.
4. Besides David V.J. Bell's book cited in footnote 3, see William F. Connolly, *Terms of Political Discourse* (Lexington, Mass.: D.C. Heath and Co., 1974).
5. Robert J. Pranger, *The Eclipse of Citizenship: Power and Participation in Contemporary Politics* (New York: Holt, Rinehart and Winston, 1968).
6. *Ibid.*, p. 17.
7. Arthur L. Kalleberg and Larry M. Preston, "Normative Political Analysis and the Problem of Justification," *Journal of Politics* 37, 3 (August, 1975), p. 652.
8. Kurt J. Wolff, ed., *From Karl Mannheim* (New York: Oxford University Press, 1971), pp. 132ff.
9. See Edward H. Levi, *An Introduction to Legal Reasoning* (Chicago: The University of Chicago Press, 1949). For a more recent and provocative grappling with the intellectual and practical issues involved in legal reasoning, see John T. Noonan, *Persons and Masks of the Law* (New York: Farrer, Straus, and Giroux, 1976), especially chapter 5, "The Alliance of Law and History."
10. Mircea Eliade, *The Sacred and the Profane: The Nature of Religion* (New York: Harper and Row, 1961), p. 98.
11. Bernard Bailyn, *The Ideological Origins of the American Revolution* (Cambridge: Belknap Press, 1967), p. 160.
12. *Ibid.*, p. 230.
13. *Ibid.*, p. 19.
14. *Ibid.*, p. 56.
15. As published in Hugo Bedau, ed., *Civil Disobedience: Theory and Practice* (New York: Pegasus, 1969), p. 27.
16. *Ibid.*, p. 47.
17. *Ibid.*, p. 43.
18. *Ibid.*, p. 40.
19. *Ibid.*, p. 43.
20. *Ibid.*, p. 30.
21. See, for example, Arthur Selwyn Miller, *The Supreme Court and American Capitalism* (New York: Free Press, 1967) which is concerned with the application of constitutional principles to the modern corporation.

22. William Ernest Hocking, *The Lasting Elements of Individualism* (New Haven: Yale University Press, 1937).

23. H. Mark Roelofs, *The Tension of Citizenship: Private Man and Public Duty* (New York: Rinehart & Co., 1957).

24. Harold Laski, *The Dangers of Obedience and Other Essays* (New York: Harper and Brothers, 1930), p. 59.

25. *Op. cit.*, p. 19.

26. *Ibid.*, p. 46.

27. *Op. cit.*, chapter II.

28. For characterizations of conservatism, see Karl Mannheim's essay, "Conservative Thought," in Kurt Wolff, ed., *op. cit.*; Robert Nisbet, *Tradition and Revolt* (New York: Random House, 1968), chapter 4, "Conservatism and Sociology"; and Clinton Rossiter's essay, "Conservatism" in the *International Encyclopedia for the Social Sciences*.

29. See Bailyn, *op. cit.*, p. 228.

30. Roberto Mangabeira Unger, *Knowledge and Politics* (New York: The Free Press, 1975), p. 42.

31. *Ibid.*, p. 76. See also p. 119.

32. Roger Hazelton, "Relocating Transcendence," *Union Seminary Quarterly Review* 30, 2-4 (Winter-Summer, 1975), pp. 103, 105.

33. Scott Buchanan, "Natural Law and Teleology," *Natural Law and Modern Society* (Cleveland: World Publishing Co., 1963), p. 150.

34. On stages in the development of the constitutionalist tradition, see Douglas Sturm, "Constitutionalism: A Critical Appreciation and An Extension of the Political Theory of C.H. McIlwain," *Minnesota Law Review* 54, 2 (December, 1969), pp. 215-244.

35. Henri Bergson, *The Two Sources of Morality and Religion* (New York: Henry Holt and Co., 1935), p. 256.

36. See Dante Germino and Klaus von Beyme, eds., *The Open Society in Theory and Practice* (The Hague: Martinus Nijhoff, 1974), especially the opening paper by Germino, "Preliminary Reflections on the Open Society: Bergson, Popper, Voegelin."

37. Quoted in the *National Catholic Reporter*, November 21, 1975, pp. 1, 5.

38. Edmond Cahn, *The Moral Decision: Right and Wrong in American Law* (Bloomington, Indiana: Indiana University Press, 1955), p. 178.

39. See Jürgen Habermas, *Knowledge and Human Interests* (Boston: Beacon Press, 1971) and "Towards a Theory of Communicative Competence," *Inquiry* 13 (1970), pp. 360-375.

40. David V.J. Bell, *op. cit.*, pp. xi, xii.

41. Henry Nelson Wieman, *Man's Ultimate Commitment* (Carbondale, Illinois: Southern Illinois University Press, 1958).

42. John MacMurray delivered the Gifford Lectures in 1953-54 under the general title, "The Form of the Personal." They were published in two volumes: *The Self as Agent* (London: Faber and Faber, 1957) and *Persons in Relation* (London: Faber and Faber, 1961).

43. See the initial paragraph of this essay. See also Stuart Hampshire, *Thought and Action* (London: Chatto & Windus, 1970) for a similar turn toward understanding person as agent.

44. John MacMurray, *Persons in Relation, op. cit.*, p. 66.

45. See *ibid.*, chapter 10.

A THEOLOGY OF CREATIVE PARTICIPATION

by
Gibson Winter

A controversy has been developing in the Americas over the proper locus of theological work. It surfaced dramatically in Detroit during August of 1975 when the conference, Theology in the Americas, drew together theologians, practitioners, and social scientists concerned with liberation in the Americas. Theologians, ethicists, and social scientists working in the South American struggle for liberation confronted those working for black liberation, women's liberation, Puerto Rican liberation, Chicano liberation, radical movements in labor, and many concerned with the lethargy of the Christian churches before the growing economic and social oppressions within the United States. In these confrontations, which spread all through the Conference in different forms, there was tacit agreement that theological work should be related to the "struggle for liberation." The first question to be asked of a theologian or social scientist was where and how he or she was located in "historical praxis."

Three Styles of Theological Work

Gustavo Gutiérrez identified three major styles of theological work in his book, *A Theology of Liberation*.[1] He spoke of theology as "wisdom," theology as "rational knowledge," and "liberation" theology or theology as "critical reflection on praxis." He interpreted these styles historically, each with a permanent contribution to make to the *ecclesia* in the struggle for liberation. He located theology as wisdom in the early centuries, as above all monastic, characterized by concern for the life of spiritual perfection. In his interpretation he is thinking of this style as dominant until the later medieval period, yet certainly much of Augustine's work was founding a style of theology as rational knowledge. However, Gutiérrez identifies theology as rational knowledge with the emerging concern for theology as science in the twelfth and thirteenth centuries. The balance which Thomas Aquinas struck between theology as wisdom and theology as rational knowledge soon dissipated, and scholastic theology became concerned with systematization and the use of reason in achieving clarity of exposition. Gutiérrez notes the permanent aspects of these styles of theological work by stressing the continuing importance of spirituality, which is now strengthened by Biblical renewal and stress on lay spirituality. He sees the importance of theology as science in the

disinterested use of reason in theological understanding of faith
as well as in the work of the biological and human sciences. In
the conclusion of this discussion Gutiérrez states what he takes to
be the permanent aspects of theology as wisdom and rational knowledge in the new epoch of theology of liberation:

> Theology as a critical reflection on Christian praxis in the light
> of the Word does not replace the other functions of theology, such
> as wisdom and rational knowledge; rather it presupposes and needs
> them. But this is not all. We are not concerned here with a mere
> juxtaposition. The critical function of theology necessarily leads
> to redefinition of these other two tasks. Henceforth, wisdom and
> rational knowledge will more explicitly have ecclesial praxis as
> their point of departure and their context. It is in reference to
> this praxis that an understanding of spiritual growth based on
> Scripture should be developed, and it is through this same praxis
> that faith encounters the problems posed by human reason.[2]

       This final statement indicates the ancillary role in which
theology of liberation places the other styles of theological work.
It accounts for the polarization that is being experienced between
academic theology and theology of liberation.
       Gustavo Gutiérrez summarizes this whole position on the
new way of doing theology as follows:

> ...Theology as critical reflection on historical praxis is a liber-
> ating theology, a theology of the liberating transformation of the
> history of mankind and also therefore that part of mankind--
> gathered into *ecclesia*--which openly confesses Christ. This is a
> theology which does not stop with reflecting on the world, but
> rather tries to be part of a process through which the world is
> transformed. It is a theology which is open--in the protest against
> trampled human dignity, in the struggle against the plunder of the
> vast majority of people, in liberating love and in the building of
> a new, just and fraternal society--to the gift of the Kingdom of
> God.[3]

       Theology thus understood sets a radically transformative
context for theology as wisdom and as rational knowledge. In fact,
it can only lead to increasing polarization of these theological
styles unless some broader context is perceived for the total theological task. I propose here, as an hypothesis, a context for re-
interpreting our theological task.

A Post-Religious or New Religious Age

       The hypothesis on which I shall proceed is that our
modern age, at least in the West, has erased the experiential base
of religious faith, including Christian faith, which is to say that
our everyday mode of thinking is such that any sense of the religious has fallen into the collective unconscious. Further, the

modern West has been experiencing for over a century a new, conscious mode of religious experience which has yet to make an impact
on everyday thinking. In brief, we live in a post-religious age
in process of becoming a new religious age. In this interim period
we are experiencing a crisis of religious faith and religious
thought, a crisis at the very moment in history when humankind is
teetering precariously on the brink of environmental and political
disaster. In some ways these are familiar hypotheses. I shall
try to explicate them under several broad themes which have been
dealt with in great depth by others in recent generations.
     The erosion of the experiential base of religious faith
has been discussed for several centuries. This insight was dominant for many generations among philosophers and humanists. In
our own time this erosion has penetrated the everyday world and
created a strange ambivalence in our common life. "Experience" is
taken here to signify possibility of meaning. Thus I treat "experiential base" as involving symbols, language and communicability.
To experience something is to be able to name it, to give it expression in one or another mode of speech and action. The human
species is understood here as a symbolic species, experiencing and
sharing a world of meanings in language. Elemental, synthesizing
symbols and linguistic discourse constitute a shared and interpreted
world. In saying the "experiential base" of religious faith has
been eroded, one is not arguing then that deep feelings of the
divine life have been erased from human species life but only that
this sensibility is blocked from communicable experience and thus
ensconced in a collective unconscious. Put somewhat differently,
religious sense including sense of Christian salvation becomes a
private, highly individualized matter of subjective feeling. Thinking about such deep sensibilities or acting upon them is viewed as
inappropriate or pointless; indeed the "religious" becomes the
non-rational and incommunicable realm of the lonely soul.
     What then was the experiential base of religious faith
that was eroded? It was the sense of participating* an unseen
world of powers in and behind all appearances. Owen Barfield has
called this mode of being-in-the-world "original participation," by
which he means an unconscious sense of the immediacy of presence of
unseen powers in and through all of life and nature.[4] In its purest
form this is the religious sense of archaic peoples that has been
so brilliantly explicated by Mircea Eliade. The world of the
sacred hierophanies that Eliade unfolds is a world of original
participation, a world of the being of peoples to which they belong
rather than a world of self-consciousness.[5] The spiritual reality
of this world, the ancestral spirits that participate this world
with the people, are far more real than the things and tools with
which the people work, though even such a distinction would probably
distort the sense of interpenetration in one world of human, natural,
and sacred realities. This is not to fall back into the evolutionary notion that dominated earlier anthropological thinking about
the emergence of human species life from proto-scientist to scientist
*"Participate" is used in a transitive sense following earlier usage
and the interpretation developed by Owen Barfield.

in the gradual ascent of humankind from ignorance to science. It is rather to say that archaic, primordial humankind felt and imagined, thought and acted in a world in which the divine powers ever struggled against profane darkness and chaos, a world in which the people had the burden and joy of repeating the cosmogonic process in myth and ritual, thus participating the re-creation of things, participating the restoring of primordial powers that brought all things into being. The human person, or self-consciousness as we would say now, was at most a stopping-place of this unseen power, not a center or perspective or project in the world over against such reality. In this sense Eliade can speak of the archaic hungering for being, by which I take him to mean gravitating to power and reality, to the sacred center, to true being.[6]

In its debased form, as Mircea Eliade has observed, this participation could degenerate into mechanical repetition, in loss of sense of the sacred power and in mechanical attempts to calculate and control the powers. This is the emergence of what with Barfield we might call alpha-thinking, which is to say thought about things as independent of participation.[7] This rudimentary alpha-thinking in early civilization, borne by priestly and elite groups, was still ensconced within original participation, and indeed drew such powers as it possessed from such participation. For example, the remarkable astronomical and calendric achievements of the Maya can be understood as the development of alpha-thinking within the sacred cosmos of original participation. Reading the heavens was an extension of that participation. To what extent the collapse of the Maya civilization can be attributed to the loss of this original participation will probably never be known, but it certainly ranks as an important hypothesis in the interpretation of that sudden collapse.[8]

Alpha-thinking about things, about nature and technique, is undoubtedly very ancient in human species life, but in earlier civilizations it served original participation rather than contradicting it. In discussing these matters in his insightful monograph, *Poetic Diction*, Owen Barfield has proposed that the high point of great cultural productivity occurs historically where alpha-thinking has developed to a significant stage, and original participation still informs the ethos of the people.[9] This intersection of two modes of encountering one world releases creative imagination, sustained by original participation in spiritual life. Be that as it may, the Western world moved into a period of alpha-thinking in recent centuries which gradually eroded original participation from symbols, language, and everyday experience. This scientific thought which began gradually in late medieval times, depending upon how one traces such an evolution of the modern consciousness, achieved unchallenged prominence in the Enlightenment and is without rival in our own time. Science and technology have now joined forces. They constitute the ideology or *mythos* of modernity.[10]

There is something special about this development of alpha-thinking in the Western world, at least so far as we know, though similar developments may have occurred in civilizations long

perished. The evidences for this special character of the phenomenon can be adduced from the remarkable scientific and technical
achievements of this period. The peculiar character of this alpha-
thinking is the notion that reality is external to the human subject and accessible only to objectifying thought. This is to say
that things in themselves are reality. They are independent of
consciousness. They can only be truly known by scientific method
which discerns the laws that govern them. Further, the advancement
of science will vest in humankind the rule of the cosmos through
science-based technology. Many modern scientists would of course
reject such notions, since many of them in the wisdom of their
labors have concluded that all we can know of nature is the theory
which we project upon the universe; thus, in searching the universe we discover ourselves as in a mirror. Further, many would
forego notions of truth and causality, settling for the workability
of our formulae, acknowledging that many of their notional models
may never (if that is not too strong a word) be subjected to tests
of workability. However, here I exceed my own grasp of the
puzzling realm in which they are plunged.

Our everyday experience has been radically reshaped by
the sense that reality is *in* things external to, independent of,
us. Yet we are living with a cosmos of energies which underlies
all of these things, eluding any meaningful integration in our
common-sense world. Thus, the peculiar character of the alpha-
thinking of modernity is that it has granted ultimate reality to
things, assuming that its concepts give it access to these things,
while the science that generated this consciousness deals only with
energies and even then only with its notional models of this infra-
structure. Our common-sense world conceals any sense that language
and symbolization bring a world to presence through our participation, through our figuration and imagination. In actuality, we
participate things and one another. We are internally related with
all things in the cosmos. Yet we live with a language and everyday
consciousness that suppresses that participation, isolating consciousness in autonomous entities externally related to a meaningless cosmos.

Two aspects of modern everyday life need to be accented.
We have already noted one aspect: our sense of participating the
coming to be of the world, and particularly any sense of original
participation or participating the unseen spiritual realm of which
things are mere manifestations, has eroded. We have fallen into a
kind of idolatry, since the only reality is in things. The other
side of this process is the emergence of an independent human consciousness, a self-consciousness over against the world of nature
and society. This independence of consciousness led to historical
consciousness, for a people looking out upon a world other than
itself is also a people living self-consciously with images of that
world. This emerging historical consciousness generated a sense
that nature and consequently history were not merely given by an
ineluctable fate but arose in the struggle of human species life.

As self-consciousness emerged with the triumph of alpha-
thinking and erosion of original participation, the mind turned

critically to the relation of the human consciousness to things, moral values, and ultimate realities, leading to a Copernican revolution in thought. This critical reflection is designated beta-thinking by Owen Barfield.[11] The human subject was recognized as a constitutive element in the coming to be of the world. Here the stage was set for social and political revolutions, for historical praxis. The stage was also set for a new kind of participation, a creative participation which could replace the original participation that had been eroded from language and everyday experience. However, this new participation has yet to penetrate our everyday world. If I understand the inaugural lecture by my colleague Diogenes Allen, Leibniz grasped both the power of alpha-thinking at which he was so adept and also the higher, encompassing ranges of human imagination which that very alpha-thinking was silencing and extruding from intellectual respectability.[12] And if I understand him further it is no wonder that Leibniz' contributions to science and mathematics were circulated and appreciated while these deeper probings of his creative imagination were ignored for centuries.

One further observation may enable us to perceive the strange predicament and unique religious possibilities of our modern era. Our hypothesis stated that original participation fell into the collective unconscious in our modern period. Mircea Eliade has spoken of this phenomenon in one of his rare and insightful reflections on our modern era.[13] Freud and Jung in different ways identified the powers of the unconscious, still within the framework of alpha-thinking. They opened to modern thinking the unconscious powers in which our lives are embedded. We are far from ready to say much yet about the character of these powers, but it can be hypothesized, and I take it to be Owen Barfield's major hypothesis, that the collective unconscious embraces that cosmos underlying and pervading all of reality, a "sea of cosmic wisdom" as he puts it, in which we participate one another and the divine life.[14] This is to say that the unconscious in which our lives are embedded is the mode of our participating one another, nature and the divine life. This collective unconscious is then pregnant with meaning, ready to light up through the powers of creative imagination. Following Jung, we could say that our sense of this collective unconscious is mediated and filtered through symbolization and language, making it accessible to experience on the conscious level, at the same time obscuring and even distorting its potentialities. This is to say, symbols and language are ambiguous mediations of the cosmos, bringing to light and darkening, revealing and concealing, ever in need of reflection and critical reinterpretation, "giving rise to thought" as Paul Ricoeur has said so well.[15]

Following this hypothesis, we could say that the magnetic energies of the natural world and the instincts of human species life, this unconscious realm that seems to recede ever more and more under the most powerful scrutiny of alpha-thinking, is not alien to consciousness but potentiality for consciousness, for creative imagination and illumination. The divine life urging and luring us to creativity is *logos* of this collective unconscious.

Creative imagination, the creative participation of consciousness, which has made science possible and empowered the brilliant achievements of our technology, not to speak of our artistic, poetic and imaginative accomplishments, this power need no longer be consigned to merely human will to power nor left adrift in a meaningless and boundaryless cosmos. Creative participation is a liberating moment in the evolution of consciousness.

This raises two questions for us before we return to a consideration of the theological task within this religious horizon of creative participation. First, the release of creative imagination under the conditions of modernity is an ambiguous historical phenomenon and, indeed, may endanger species life as we know it on this earth. Secondly, the roots of modern self-consciousness in the Biblical heritage, and thus the anchorage of the creative imagination in the divine purposefulness, the notion thus that the collective unconscious can be thought of as the utterance of the divine *logos*, this is anything but obvious. This second question relates directly to the first issue, for it pertains to the humanizing and normative direction that might guide our creative imagination in modernity.

The first issue needs almost no comment. We can take almost as fact that human species life today is vested with enormous powers to control and manipulate, and indeed is reshaping nature according to its own desires. Experiments with recombinant DNA, which only follow on similar work in less advanced stages, pose the possibility of creating new species, not to say the dire possibility of releasing forms of life that could overrun and destroy life as we know it on earth. We only have to think of the Nazi era and the holocaust, the pattern bombing of Viet Nam and the destruction of so many millions by our forces in Southeast Asia, to realize that creative imagination can be destructive as well as humanizing, demonic as well as divine. Hence, each step along the way in this new era poses the question of guidelines in the cultivation of human powers.

Does creative participation, conscious bringing to expression of the possibilities of cosmos which we participate through the collective unconscious, centering participation in the inwardness of human species life, have its roots in our Biblical heritage? This constitutes a somewhat different interpretation of some of our Scriptural materials, but one that is consonant with certain strands of the Biblical heritage. The prophetic strand of the Hebrew Scriptures and its roots in the Covenant of Sinai are a direct challenge to the original participation of the peoples of that settled land as well as the Israelite bonds to Near Eastern life. This struggle against original participation persists through most of Israelite history, it is a challenge to idols, not in the way of alpha-thinking in the modern world, but in the sense of acknowledging an Otherness of the mystery while recognizing the gift of crops, law, and common life in divine grace. Although we comprehend the world of original participation only dimly through imaginative reconstruction, we share in many ways a common world with Israel, however much their imagination was filtered through an original participation.[16]

The same holds for the figure of Jesus Christ in the New Testament. Although the world in which He came was, so far as we can tell, a world of original participation and apocalyptic expectations shaped in part by a primitive mode of alpha-thinking; nevertheless, the proclamation and the life we encounter there is one of an inward sense of the Father's presence, of the Kingdom, conjoined with a profound sense of the Otherness of the Father. We are here at what could be called a turning point, fully in accord with Israel's struggle against idolatry, in which the divine Word became flesh and opened the way toward a slowly deepening sense of the divine presence and human share in the divine work of love.[17] I make no case here that this begins to take up the many problems that face a critical hermeneutics if this hypothesis of modernity is taken seriously, but I do urge that modernity as creative participation is not alien to the Word of God in Scripture and further that only as that symbolization can guide and direct, criticize and shape, the creative imagination of modernity will we be able to anticipate a historical praxis that is liberating rather than destructive.

Within this broad hypothesis on the character of modernity as a new religious age, I believe we can grasp somewhat more adequately the difficulties facing theology as wisdom and as rational knowledge, to use the categories employed by Gutiérrez, and the possibilities of synthesis among these styles of theology.

The Transformation of Theology

Theology as wisdom or cultivation of the spiritual life has undergone radical transformation in the modern world. On the surface, this transformation would seem to be a consequence of the developments in psychotherapy and the appropriation of a dynamic understanding of personality in the field of pastoral theology. In terms of our hypothesis, the emergence of dynamic psychology itself is an aspect of the developing self-consciousness of modernity, a dawning awareness of the collective unconscious in which consciousness is embedded. This has been a slow process and much distorted by the idolatry of things that informed so much alpha-thinking, yet it has been an inexorable and creative process in the modern imagination. Two characteristics mark this development: the sense that the images and representations in which our everyday world finds expression may conceal and often distort the deeper levels of our experience; and, further, the sense that human nature or personality is historical, not a once for all given but rather a dynamic given, open to reshaping and liberation through reflection and re-experiencing in its symbolic depths. These two characteristics are closely correlated, since it is precisely the concealments on the level of consciousness which have to be penetrated in the re-experiencing of potentialities for healthy development.

Speaking as an appreciative but non-specialized student of this region of modern theology, I would argue that this form of pastoral theology cultivates creative participation in which symbolic repressions are decoded and resymbolized in healthful directions through collaboration between counselors and clients, through release of creative potentialities of the collective unconscious. This decoding of distortions and resymbolization in ways which bring to expression the creative potentialities of the unconscious furnish a paradigm for the integration of thought and action in the world of creative participation.

Theology as rational knowledge is in a somewhat less propitious condition in our time. If ours is an era of creative participation, so far as it is opening on a new religious horizon, then the problem of any theology will be the matter of experience, of praxis, of participating divine creativity in life and work. We have already noted that psychotherapy opened the door on this experiential level of creative transformation of personal life for pastoral theology, exploring the conscious and unconscious meanings in existential struggles. The same cannot be said for theology as rational knowledge, although its attention has turned more and more to the hermeneutic of religious symbols, thus attending to the modern mode of religious experience. The Biblical symbols arose in the struggles between original participation and a counterpart to our modern creative participation, but the language and theological tradition presupposed original participation. Despite the intention of hermeneutic theology to recover the heritage in modern context, it comes out too often looking like theological reflection on revealed truths and doctrines, since the experiential base has eroded and no experiential mode of creative participation has replaced it.

This critical situation in systematic theology or theology as rational knowledge can be illumined by considering the theological models that are proposed by David Tracy in his book, *Blessed Rage for Order*.[18] We can recast the five models that he proposes in the context of our hypothesis: the erosion of original participation, the emergence of the idolatry of modernity and its technical rationality, and the opening of a horizon of creative participation. Then we find an interesting pairing of the models. The *orthodox* and *neo-orthodox* models have a center of gravity in the Biblical symbols and tradition. This is to say that the traditional symbols are held to be valid in their own terms. The changed consciousness of modernity creates difficulties, but it is not allowed to enter as an equal partner in the dialogue with the tradition. These two models implicitly deny the erosion of the experiential base in original participation; that is, no radical historical change in human consciousness is acknowledged. To be sure, the stress on hermeneutics would seem to point to serious dialogue, but neither of these models moves toward a radical hermeneutic, at least as Tracy delineates them.

Another pairing of models yields *liberalism* and *radical, secular theology*. Liberalism in the tradition of Harnack, Ritschl and Troeltsch attempted to live with the rationality of the modern world. It sought to sustain a religious consciousness as at least a moral dimension of human life. The erosion of original participation and the destructiveness unleashed in the twentieth century by the creative powers of an uprooted human imagination gradually discredited this liberal approach. Its partner under these

conditions of despair has been the secular, "god-is-dead" style of
theology which emerged with the failure of neo-orthodoxy. Here
again the idolatry of modernity is taken for granted as the only
world we have and the only rationality with which we can work.
Religion is relegated to a "Blik" or subjective feeling.[19] Neither
liberalism nor secular theology offers a serious critique of modernity. Both try to salvage a trace of religious life, however reduced or irrational, while leaving the idolatry of modern rationality untouched. So far as they perceive the horizon of creative
participation into which our world is being lured by the divine
life, it is reduced to creative technology.

David Tracy offers a "Revisionist" model as "philosophical
reflection upon the meanings present in common human experience and
the meanings present in the Christian tradition."[20] This sounds
like an attempt to reach the experiential base of modernity in
creative participation, but the model is a blend of liberalism and
orthodoxy. It locates the religious dimension in "limit questions,"
i.e., grounding of thought, founding of morality, and everyday
"rumors of angels." God is located on the outer edges of reality.
Thus, we are not yet in discourse with the "mature" consciousness
of modernity but dwelling in the negativities and irrationalities,
the residual world left to us when original participation collapsed.
Further, this revisionist model which promises to take praxis
seriously, ends in the usual position of Western metaphysics,
resting praxis on *theoria*; "so the practical theologian's task becomes the rigorous investigation of the possibilities of praxis
which a reconstructed *historia* and a newly constructed *theoria* may
allow."[21]

We are, in other words, still under the domination of
alpha-thinking in its metaphysical form, revising orthodoxy with
the tools of hermeneutics, depending upon existential interpretations
of the human dilemma arising in modern idolatry, but not dealing with
either the erosion of original participation which undergirded such
a metaphysics nor the emergence of creative participation which is
the stuff of modernity. Revisionism thus becomes a half-way house
toward creative participation, its significant point being the
awareness that there are modes of discourse other than scientific
rationality which have validity as well as human meaning. This is
an important step, since it is the other side of the critique of
modern idolatry. Nevertheless, creative imagination in poetic and
praxis, the experiential base of the religious life of modernity,
remains an appendage of an updated metaphysics.

It would be a happy situation if we could turn to the
various theologies of liberation and find there the resolution of
the difficulties besetting systematic theology. Unfortunately, theology of historical action or critical reflection on historical
praxis is just beginning to emerge and is caught in many of the
difficulties confronting theology as rational knowledge. Nevertheless, theology of historical praxis joins pastoral theology, extending it to the common life of the human community, our participating one another. Moreover, this social view of the human
transforms its notion of sin and grace. The understanding of sin

now encompasses the structural oppressions of systematically distorted communication and access to life chances. Grace is taken
to mean the divine power to overcome these distortions through
revolutionary actions and institutional innovations. Institutions,
including the free market, are now envisioned as being made for
and by humanity rather than humanity being made for institutions.
Thus, the understanding of sin and grace begins to open out upon
the world of historical action and creative participation.

This opening on the new religious horizon does not solve
the problem of dialogue with the religious symbols which are
bearers as well as concealers of the creative and redemptive power
of the divine life. Liberation theologies with rare exceptions
have been rather traditional in their appropriation of these
symbols, thus creating a strange dissonance between their involvements in historical praxis and their interpretation of the heritage.
The important contribution of liberation theology to our theological task is the opening of the realm of historical action, the
realm of creative participation, to theological reflection. Where
theology found itself adrift after the erosion of original participation, theology of liberation undertook the work of love and social
transformation, servanthood of the *ecclesia* and creative political
action, unveiling the experiential base of the new religious age.
This radical opening on a new religious horizon has profound implications for the appropriation of the heritage, but the implications
are only dimly perceived at this point. Dialogue with the symbolic
heritage in liberation theology is difficult, since the Western
theological tradition is couched in a language much more appropriate
to the salvation of individual souls than to the transformation of
the public world through creative and religiously responsible action.

The common ground for the dialogue of creative participation and the originary giving of the symbols could be found in
the return to the origins of our own religious life today, to the
depths of the collective unconscious in its archetypal structures,
to the life of Spirit in which that potentiality awaits expression,
to the very beginnings in which the grace of creative love is experienced, furnishing ground in our meditations for appreciating
the intentionality of the original symbols of the Hebrew and
Christian Scriptures. This inwardness of the divine life has its
counterpart in the rituals and institutions of the common life,
and only as those public expressions conform to the creative love
and openness of that inward life can they become vehicles of the
new creation.

This return to the origins, to the beginnings, is the
work of poetic creativity, for poetry, as Gaston Bachelard observes,
places us at the origin of language, at the original naming in
which a world comes to be. The counterpart to poetry and symbolic
discourse in historical praxis is action which begins anew, which
arises out of the freedom of the origin. This is the action of
which Hannah Arendt spoke so eloquently in her monograph, *The Human
Condition*.[22] It is the action that Adolphe de Waehlens speaks of
as one's being the origin of transforming self and world, inner and
outer worlds.[23] It is precisely what one would mean by creative

participation as sharing in the divine creative word, bringing to
expression the potentiality of the collective unconscious as itself
the utterance of the divine word through the historical action of
humankind. If history is the realm of freedom, the realm of action
in this fundamental sense, then historical action is the unfolding
of cosmos through creative participation. To return to Hannah
Arendt's indictment of the modern world as given over to production,
to labor as a realm of necessity and bondage, we could say that
modernity lacks both historical and political life, for its activity
is the technical manipulation of means in a ceaseless round of production and consumption, amassing and distribution of energy, mechanical repetition of technical processes in the name of progress.
The liberation of our globe from this self-destructive, mechanical
repetition can come only with the grace of creative participation,
with the release of the power of the revelatory symbols, release
to the promise and hope of the divine Word become flesh and dwelling
among us. This means going to the origins of our own experience,
to the source of our creativity and hope in the utterance of the
divine life, in the transforming power of love that engenders
servanthood and opens communication in place of greed and oppression. It means theologically founded, historical praxis.
     The return to origins, the work of creative partici-
pation, poses the radical question of *source* for the creative
imagination of modernity. We can participate our origin, but we
cannot get behind it, we cannot subsume it under a concept and
master it, for our origin like our birth ever lies behind us. The
origin like the end involves the totality of a life or a history,
a totality we can participate but not transcend. In this sense,
the creative imagination of modernity is torn between striving to
be its own origin, the will to power and mastery, or participating
the divine source as creative participation which is guided and
informed by a critical appropriation of the symbolic heritage. The
will to power is manifest today as the relentless extension of technological mastery. The path of creative participation is an unfolding of meditative thinking, poetic speech and deed, institutional transformation, and celebration of life.
     How then do things stand with theology as rational know-
ledge? So far as this theological style has operated as "systematic
theology," there are obvious difficulties in a transitional period
toward a new religious horizon. Systematic theology can easily become an academic substitute for serious theological work when the
experiential base of the life of faith has eroded. Then theological work comes to look like a play with abstractions, like a "game
of glass beads." Nevertheless, the inner drive to system in understanding is rooted in the phenomenon of symbol itself. It is not
simply an aberration of alpha-thinking.
     Mircea Eliade's hermeneutic of archaic religious symbolism
explores the structural coherence of symbols on the premise that
symbols arise in system.[24] There are two temporal-spatial aspects
or horizons to symbolization that constitute the possibility of
system in understanding. These horizons can perhaps be exemplified
in an example drawn from the educational work of Paulo Freire. He

found that he could teach literacy to peasants in Brazil by taking
words that expressed basic interests of a local group, working
with the parts of those words and gradually composing new words.[25]
The key to the method was the involvement of people in terms or
symbols that played a crucial role in their common life and even
survival. Take for example a "bridge" as one practical need felt
by villagers! Around this symbol and several others, the education
in literacy could proceed, building into the linguistic work the
sense that the world itself could be shaped and reshaped through
local action even as words could be broken up and composed. The
symbolism of the "bridge" creates two major horizons of experi-
encing--the inner horizon of its constitution and the outer horizon of its interrelatedness with the whole of a people's life. The
constitution of terms out of parts in particular relations reveals
a verbal mode of the inner horizon of sequence and relationship.
The correlation of the term "bridge" with other terms such as exchange, sharing labor, access to certain needed resources, possibilities of wider communication, etc. reveal an outer horizon of
coherence or what goes with what. Literacy for the villager,
political cooperation toward common goals and understanding as
entering into the inner and outer horizons of meaning, all point to
system in the rich sense of consistent and coherent acting and
thinking. The center of this systematic gathering is symbol.
        Mircea Eliade refers this system to the inherent poten-
tiality of symbol, in our own terms to the potentiality of the
collective unconscious as utterance of the divine *logos*. This
suggests that when Paul Ricoeur proposes that the "symbol invites
(or evokes) thought" he is pointing to the lure to understanding
constituted by the inner and outer horizons of symbol. A debase-
ment of alpha-thinking arises, then, from substituting its own logic
of system for participating the symbol. Then system becomes abstract logic. This problem can be further specified in terms of
correspondence between thought and reality.
        The inner and outer horizons of thought presuppose par-
ticipation of thought in symbol, otherwise alpha-thinking becomes
a play of fantasies. Robert Lindner, the psychiatrist, told a
dramatic story in his book, *The Fifty-Minute Hour*, about a physicist
who had become so engrossed in an interstellar world of his imagination that he lost contact with his everyday tasks in high security defense work.[26] He pursued the battles and political progress
of that interstellar world logically with all the powers of his
mathematical mind. The only thing missing was any referent outside
his imagination. When the experiential base of religious faith
erodes, theological work can become just such a play of illusions,
out of touch with realities. But what is the basis of correspondence of thought and its objects? Whence the contact between theological discourse and participating the divine reality? Truth as
correspondence presupposes disclosure, the coming to presence of
that presence which alpha-thinking examines. This coming to presence
is truth as disclosure or unveiling, the revelatory origination of
things and persons and meanings. At this origin is language and
symbol, the poetic naming that lets come forth and be gathered into

presence. We participate the coming to presence in the gift of
naming. Poetic, praxis and originary thinking are primordial
modes of participating world and the divine *logos*. This originary
coming to presence is an ecstatic spatial-temporal horizon, the
being at the source of giving of world. This ecstatic horizon
founds a world, constituting the inner and outer horizons of
discourse and understanding.

There is a tendency today to abandon understanding in
religious life. This reaction stems partly from the erosion of
original participation. The turn to experience, to religious
imagination as well as historical praxis, reflects the new religious horizon of creative participation which we have tried to
identify. Yet, theology as rational knowledge has important
functions in this era of creative participation, despite the
tendency to repudiate understanding. For one thing, alpha-thinking
has no exclusive claim to the psychotic world of fantasy. Creative
participation can move easily into realms of illusion, especially
when it becomes oriented to the spiritual world at the cost of
concrete historical struggles for a more human world. This is the
gnostic strand in Christian history, an ever-present danger. It
attracts many privileged, alienated classes today. Creative participation easily becomes "spiritual" escape from the social and
political realities of oppression and exploitation. Alpha-thinking
turned toward the *relation* of the experiencing human community to
its foundations in symbol and revelatory history, what we have
called beta-thinking, provides an indispensable critique of such
mystification.

Beta-thinking applies as well to historical praxis.
History has a way of testing out and crushing flights of fancy,
yet historical projects can delude and destroy before such tests
are effective as we saw vividly in the Nazi movement and the invasion of Viet Nam by United States' forces. The symbol is embedded in culture and history; to this extent, it is subject to
critique both as mystification and as ideology. But the symbol
also transcends history and culture. This is its historically constitutive and transformative power. In an age of creative participation, new symbolization and enriched symbols--for example, "democratic socialism"--open new historical horizons. Although no critique can obviate the commitment and risk in which such symbolism
is participated, coherence with other elements in the religious
heritage is a crucial testing of the spirits. This is an indispensable work of a hermeneutic theology, a work that presupposes involvement in praxis *and* anchorage in the heritage. We are familiar
with such work in participant observation within the human sciences.
In theology it means breaking with the specializations that have
divorced theology and ethics, thought and practice, for these
dichotomies have been imposed by alpha-thinking.

Beta-thinking, taking its departure from the experience
of humankind, theologically from the experiences of the paradigmatic
Biblical history and the life of faith in the churches, is indispensable in testing creative participation as historical praxis.
We are on the threshold of a release of human powers beyond any-

thing previous generations might have imagined. Now more than at any time in the past, we need dialogue between systematic inter- pretation of the Biblical symbols in the history of the church and our historical praxis. *Ad hoc* appropriation of the heritage can radically distort praxis as well as *logos*. In this sense a polar- ization of theology as rational knowledge and theology as critical reflection on historical praxis would constitute a grave peril for the churches and the world. Critical reflection on historical praxis could be taken to include this role of systematic theology, but it is precisely the selective appropriation of symbol in liber- ation theology which distorts life in and through the ideological manipulation of symbol. Mutuality and equality are necessary in authentic dialogue. Praxis cannot be supplementary to *theoria* and *historia* as David Tracy argues. In an era of creative participation, hermeneutic theology of Biblical symbols and history cannot be prior to nor ancillary to historical praxis. Once we say "mutuality," however, we indicate that both historical praxis and symbolic heritage will undergo transformation in the creative work of the divine *logos*. Here we part company with orthodoxy and neo-orthodoxy, even as we left liberalism and secular theology as uncritical col- laborators in modern idolatry. Creative participation takes history as unfinished, thus participating the divine creating in symbol and praxis.

In his concluding remarks at Detroit, Gustavo Gutiérrez drew attention to the central task of the churches today, the re- discovery of God as love. In many contexts this might seem Chris- tian sentimentality. In the struggle against oppression in South America it is a call to the nth degree of heroism in the churches, a call to participate the creative power of the divine life in liberating humankind. Such a work can only be accomplished in con- flict and struggle. This is the style of historical praxis as creative participation. This is the verification that gives evidence of the creative work of God in our new religious age. It is the verification of disclosure, of the coming to presence of the Word of life and truth in historical praxis.

NOTES AND REFERENCES

1. Gustavo Gutiérrez, *A Theology of Liberation: History, Politics and Salvation* (Maryknoll, New York: Orbis Books, 1973).

2. *Ibid.*, pp. 13f.

3. *Ibid.*, p. 15.

4. Owen Barfield, *Saving the Appearances: A Study in Idolatry* (New York, New York: Harcourt, Brace & World, Inc., 1965) esp. Ch. VI.

5. Mircea Eliade, *The Sacred and the Profane: The Nature of Religion* (New York, New York: Harcourt, Brace & World, Inc., 1959), pp. 11ff.

6. *Ibid.*, pp. 64f, 80, 92, 106.

7. Owen Barfield, *op. cit.*,

...The second thing, therefore, that we can do with the represen- tations is to think about them. Here, as before, we remain unconscious

of the intimate relation which they in fact have, as representations, with our own organisms and minds. Or rather, more unconscious than before. For now our very attitude is, to treat them
as independent of ourselves; to accept their "outness" as self-
evidently given; and to speculate about or to investigate their
relations *with each other*. One could perhaps name this process
"theorizing" or "theoretical thinking," since it is exactly what
is done in most places where science is pursued, whether it be
botany, medicine, metallurgy, zoology or any other. But I do not
think the term is wide enough. The kind of thing I mean covers
other studies as well--a good deal of history, for instance. Nor
need it be systematic...Therefore, at the like hazard as before, I
propose to call this particular kind of thinking alpha-thinking.
pp. 24f.

8. See *The Classic Maya Collapse*, edited by T. Patrick Culbert,
(Albuquerque, New Mexico: University of New Mexico Press, 1973), esp. pp. 474ff.
9. Owen Barfield, *Poetic Diction: A Study in Meaning* (New York, New York:
McGraw-Hill Book Co., 1964). This theme is more fully explicated in *Saving the
Appearances*.
10. Jürgen Habermas, *Toward a Rational Society* (Boston, Massachusetts:
Beacon Press, 1970) Ch. 6 "Technology and Science as Ideology"; William Leiss,
The Domination of Nature (Boston, Massachusetts: Beacon Press, 1974).
11. Owen Barfield, *Saving the Appearances, op. cit.,*

Thirdly, we can think about the *nature* of collective representations
as such, and therefore about their relation to our own minds. We
can think about perceiving and we can think about thinking...it is
also part of the province of philosophy. It has been called reflection or reflective thinking. But for the same reasons as before, I shall reject the simpler and more elegant term and call it
beta-thinking. p. 25.

12. Diogenes Allen, "Leibniz' Relevance for Today's Christianity," Inaugural Lecture, Princeton Theological Seminary, October 6, 1976 and remarks in
conversation with the faculty.
13. Mircea Eliade, *op. cit.*, pp. 209ff.
14. Owen Barfield, *Saving the Appearances, op. cit.*, Ch. XX and pp. 154ff.
15. Paul Ricoeur, *The Symbolism of Evil* (New York, New York: Harper & Row,
Publishers, 1967) "Conclusion: The Symbol Gives Rise to Thought."
16. Owen Barfield, *Saving the Appearances, op. cit.*, Ch. XVI. Israel.
17. *Ibid.*, pp. 125-127.
18. David Tracy, *Blessed Rage for Order: The New Pluralism in Theology*
(New York, New York: The Seabury Press, 1975) Ch. 2 "Five Basic Models in Contemporary Theology."
19. See Paul Van Buren, *The Secular Meaning of the Gospel* (New York, New
York: Macmillan & Co., 1963).
20. David Tracy, *op. cit.*, p. 34.
21. *Ibid.*, p. 240.
22. Hannah Arendt, *The Human Condition* (Chicago, Illinois: The University
of Chicago Press, 1958).

23. Alphonse de Waelhens, "Vie Interieure et Vie Active," in "Les Droits de l'Esprit et Les Exigences Sociales," *Rencontres Internationales de Geneve*, 1950 (Neuchatel: Editions de la Baconniere).

24. See the discussion of this aspect of Mircea Eliade's work in David M. Rasmussen, *Symbol and Interpretation* (The Hague, Netherlands: Martinus Nijhoff, 1974), pp. 32f.

25. Paulo Freire, *Pedagogy of the Oppressed* (New York, New York: Herder and Herder, 1970).

26. Robert Lindner, *The Fifty Minute Hour* (New York, New York: Rinehart, 1955).

Part Three
Ministry in the Public Sphere

POLITICAL COMMUNITY:
AN ALTERNATIVE TO WAR

by
Lowell Livezey

It is relatively easy to specify conditions which, if achieved, would fulfill the goal of the United Nations Charter, "to save succeeding generations from the scourge of war." But it is quite another thing, and much more important, to determine what has to change to bring those conditions into reality. Indeed, in the absence of serious, practical reasoning about how to achieve a world without war, the goal itself appears hopelessly utopian, and the energies required for its achievement are lost. Therefore, I wish to argue for a program of action by United States citizens and their organizations in the last quarter of the twentieth century to establish this goal and contribute to its achievement.

Action for a peace requires difficult choices at a number of levels. Because a world without war could, in principle, be achieved in a variety of ways, we must determine which concrete global conditions are both desirable and attainable. Moreover, change as fundamental and pervasive as abolishing the institution of war will require the involvement of a wide variety of actors, and it will be a major task to sort out their various roles and devise a coherent and effective strategy of change. Cutting across both sets of choices is the problem of United States foreign policy -- that is, what means should the United States employ to promote conditions for a world without war, and how can citizens and their organizations most effectively advocate such means?

The assertion that there are many ways of achieving a world without war will be questioned by many, in view of the widespread doubt that the goal can be achieved at all. But there are many visions of a peaceful world that are credible in principle. The pacifist dictum that "wars will cease when men refuse to fight" is incontrovertible, though one must ask how in fact to get the "men" to refuse. The Biblical vision of Shalom, of whole community, is plausible as a world without war because in whole community, by definition, conditions are sufficiently satisfactory, and the sense of justice so thoroughly shared, that war is superfluous. But one must ask how such ideal conditions can be achieved. Similarly, the so-called political realists' conception of a stable world in which war is prevented by the threat of war has a certain undeniable logic. If military power is kept perfectly in balance, each unit effectively checked by another, then that military power will not be used. But the question must be asked, how can the balance be maintained, and why, in view of past failures, might we think it likely?

297

It is my central thesis that the institution of war can be abolished through the creation of a world political community. In such a community, political institutions and processes would replace the global military system. They would serve as alternatives to violence in the resolution of international conflict and the struggle for justice, and would prevent resort to war. The logic, again, is flawless. If such a political system can be created, war can be ended. But as with pacifism, Shalom, and the balance of power, the important questions are not questions of logic but of practice. Can it be done? How? And by whom? It is to these questions that the rest of this essay is addressed.

The idea that political institutions can provide an alternative to war is an old one. It has been modified and developed considerably during the course of its adventure through modern history, and it has won considerable support. In his late eighteenth century essay "On Perpetual Peace," Immanuel Kant argued for a supranational government that would prevent war among nation states.[1] A century later, as Charles Chatfield has shown, work for peace became a "respectable avocation" among influential Americans who promoted international arbitration and international law as means of dealing with international conflict.[2] About the same time, members of the United States Congress were joining the Interparliamentary Union and by the early twentieth century, State Department officials were advocating development of a world court and other international organizations. The creation of the League of Nations and the United Nations represented imperfect attempts to embody the idea of a world political community.

Now in the late 1970's significant constituencies and a wide range of organizations are still committed in principle to the idea of a world political community. Organizations specifically constituted on this basis -- the World Federalists, the Members of Congress for Peace Through Law, the United Nations Association and the World Without War Council -- are not the only ones for which this is true. For example, the Roman Catholic Church and many of the largest Protestant and Jewish organizations are formally committed to promoting peace through some form of global politics. It is also true of business organizations, such as U.N. We Believe, and many national labor unions and professional associations.

Nevertheless, despite its impressive history and its numerous exponents past and present, the idea of a world political community as an alternative to war has been realized only in fragments. Its most powerful exponents use their influence primarily for other purposes, and its most ardent supporters are politically marginal, poorly organized, and even more poorly funded. The idea itself is mutilated and confused, inadequate in its present form for providing either the substantive basis of policy or the inspiration for effective political action.

The confusion of the idea is indeed one of the main reasons that commitment in principle so often fails to generate political influence or public policy. The problem is in part a lack of conceptual development. Insufficient thought has been given to the concrete institutions, structures, and processes needed to replace the world military system. This is a practical problem which provides part of the agenda of action itself. It will be discussed later in this essay as a responsibility of colleges and universities. But the prospect for effective action depends fundamentally upon clarity about the ideas of politics and of political power which shall be offered as alternatives to war and military power.

The idea of politics as an alternative to war rests upon two interrelated distinctions: the distinction between violence and political power, and the distinction between violence and conflict. The distinction between violence and political power is obviously necessary because it would be self-contradictory to replace a system of global violence with a new system that incorporates the violence it sought to replace. Yet if we are to avoid the contradiction, we must reject the common notion of politics as the struggle for power, the power which "grows out of the barrel of a gun."

Fortunately there is another time-honored political tradition upon which the idea of a world political community can be built without contradiction. It was embodied, however imperfectly, in the Athenian city-state and the United States Constitution. In this tradition political power rests on public consent which is achieved by persuasion, compromise, and a search for the common good. Hannah Arendt succinctly summarizes the relationship between political power and violence in this political tradition near the end of her brilliant study, *On Violence*:

> ....Politically speaking, it is insufficient to say that power and violence are not the same. Power and violence are opposites; where the one rules absolutely, the other is absent....it is not correct to think of the opposite of violence as nonviolence: to speak of nonviolent power is actually redundant. Violence can destroy power; it is utterly incapable of creating it.[3]

Thus the sources of political power, whether in a city, a nation, or the world community, are destroyed by violence, not created or acquired by it; and political power is an alternative to military power, never its extension or consequence.

The development of politics as an alternative to war also rests on a distinction between violence and conflict. This distinction is possible because of the nature of conflict; it is necessary because of the nature of politics.

Conflict is simply a situation in which two or more parties have purposes that are, or appear to be, incompatible. But the parties have a variety of options. They can fight, to be sure, and if they are nations they can go to war. One of the parties can yield to the other. But they can also negotiate, compromise, reason with each other, seek to persuade one another, or search for a new, mutually compatible solution. The point is that the use of violence to resolve conflict is a matter of choice, and not inherent in the nature of conflict.

Politics is born of conflict, it is a means by which a number of parties, beginning with different and incompatible purposes, arrive at common terms for living together. It is a particular means of dealing with conflict. So if there is to be politics

without violence, it follows that violence and conflict must be distinguished.

In sum, world political community as a means to a world
without war, will seek to eliminate only war, not the conflict from
which it springs; and it will be based on public consent, not on
domination through violence.

The tangible elements of a world political community have
to be determined by the people and political units that constitute
it, so it is impossible to say in advance precisely and finally
what these elements will be. Yet it is possible and necessary to
posit goals for action that can be modified in the process of their
achievement. Drawing on both the history and the idea of world
political community and the experience of political community at
the local and national levels, it is clear that the institution of
law will be central. In any political community, law is the formal
expression of the terms of life together, the terms established
through the non-violent resolution of conflict. And law implies
procedures for application and enforcement, and for determining
what the law shall be.

The question arises as to whether world political community is really just another name for world government, for it obviously will involve governmental institutions at the global level.
Some form of limited world government is necessary for the elimination of war through politics. Yet government is insufficient,
for not all conflicts can be resolved and not all common terms
established at the global level or within a single institution.
Therefore, a world political community will involve a network of
political and legal institutions at various levels and will evoke
the participation of various sectors of the world population. The
heart of the matter is not world government as such, but political
authority legally instituted with sufficient scope and variety to
provide an effective alternative to war.

Political and legal institutions, however, do not exist
in a vacuum, and their capacity to attain the consent of their constituents and to resolve conflict depends substantially upon the
conditions in which they exist. I believe the three conditions
most determinative of the possibilities for world political community are the economic conditions of the poor, the status of human
rights, and the level, character and control of armaments. Each of
these must be changed in the process of achieving a world political
community.

It has been said that the propensity for violence is
directly proportional to the gap between rich and poor and to the
degree of awareness of this gap. Although this equation is over-
drawn, there is no doubt that the conflicts arising from the sense
of economic injustice entail such a strong propensity for violence
that, as a practical matter, no strictly political process could
contain it. Quite apart from humanitarian motivations, the creation
of world political community requires economic progress for the poor,
and grounds for their hope that political processes will enable them
to work effectively for justice. Nothing will be gained, however,
if the economic progress is promoted by means which destroy the
emergent political community.

The human rights issue is more complex. First, the denial of human rights is a source of severe conflict which may lead to violence. Second, the exercise of human rights is necessary for the expression of public consent upon which the world political community must be based. Finally, because in the world today there is so little agreement about the substance of human rights, a global political process is needed in order to establish generally satisfactory definitions and means of enforcement. In the meantime progress toward world political community requires increased affirmation of human rights by means which build the legal institutions ultimately needed.

Finally, the sheer existence of massive armaments erodes the function of politics based on consent. The existence of armaments cannot be separated from their potential use, so those who have armaments have a tremendous capacity either to dominate or to prevent domination by others. They do not have political power by virtue of their arms, but they cannot help but prevent the emergence of political power. Thus, as the world's capacity for military destruction increases, its capacity for the political determination of its future is eroded. So while disarmament can be completed only when political alternatives to war are established, the converse is also true. Disarmament, then, must be considered a practical task in building a world political community.

In sum, a world political community is in essence a global fabric of legal and political institutions which will provide alternatives to war in the resolution of international conflict, ameliorate the conditions that engender resort to violence, and eliminate not only the use but the means of violence on a massive scale. And since each of these elements of a world political community depends upon the others, progress on them must be made simultaneously, and it must begin at once.

Now if an idea has been publicly discussed for at least two centuries and its advocates are still politically marginal, why would one propose it as a practical route to a world without war? In part, the answer lies in the fact that more of the requisites of political community have been realized at the global level than ever before. The code word for the new situation is interdependence. In short, the development of systems of interaction through communications, travel, and trade provide a dramatic increase in the common experience and mutual understanding that help make politics possible. At the same time, the emergence of common problems and problems that require global solutions, coupled with the accelerated dangers of international violence, have made global politics necessary. So the fact that there have been wars and rumors of war from the beginning of time, and that the idea of politics, at least in rudimentary form, has long been available as an alternative, need not discourage us. New conditions have emerged, and with them, new possibilities.

Interdependence requires new modes of being together on the planet. That is unavoidable. Among the various possibilities, political community should be attractive to most of the world's people. It affirms the diversity of people and respects cultural and religious differences and national idiosyncrasies. It does not

require, nor does it promote, a common ideology. It is sufficiently
similar to political community at the local and national level that
most of the world's people have either experienced it or learned
about it through the experience of others, so it will not come as
a totally new idea. Finally, political community is self-limiting
and self-correcting since it requires a high degree of public consent in order to proceed. Therefore, in the inevitably difficult
progress toward its realization, there will be opportunities to re-
vise and reconstruct, and the world will be protected against the
imposition of new structures by any single nation or bloc.

There are also a number of reasons why American citizens
in particular should readily support, and work for, creation of
political community at the global level. It is congruent with the
most fundamental values upon which this nation was founded. The
Constitution itself represented the creation of a political community out of previously autonomous political entities, and the
terms of the community it created included the rule of law, equality
under the law, and the protection of human rights. Moreover, world
political community gives the best practical expression to an ideal
shared by many of us, that the unity of the world is more fundamental than its divisions, and that this unity is compatible with
its diversity. Whether we are religious people affirming the "brotherhood of man," socialists affirming the worldwide unity of the
working class, entrepreneurs viewing the globe as a single market
place, or environmentalists educating their fellow citizens to the
idea of the world as a closed system, we generally affirm forms of
unity that transcend our divisions. Political community gives expression to that affirmation without denying our diversity or under-
estimating our conflicts.

Finally, and perhaps most important, political community
fulfills American moral ambitions. We aspire to be a "light to the
nations," a positive example to the rest of the world. Our experiment with political community in North America provides a plausible
analogy to what political community might be at the global level.
To help design and create a world political community would be
deeply satisfying to the American people, and this fact adds to the
potential for the development of a supportive public constituency.

In practice, world political community can be created
only as widespread public support for it is expressed, and as consent to the world military system is withdrawn. In short, a political constituency must be created. Indeed, the most important
reason to be hopeful of a world political community may be negative:
of all the work needed to create a constituency, so little has been
done that no one can really tell how great is its potential. Let
us therefore consider specifically what kinds of change are needed,
and who can make the change occur. Our analysis is necessarily incomplete, for it is concerned with the action only of United States
citizens and their organizations. But United States citizens and
organizations have as much capacity as any -- and more than many --
to create a dynamic in the international system that will evoke
reciprocation from other countries and the growing consent of the
world's people.

Action for a World Political Community

Responsible participation in a world political community
would require momentous change for the United States -- as it would
for any country. Participation in the *creation* of a world political community is even more difficult, requiring change predicated
partly on hopes and ideals and imposing transitional costs and dis-
ruptions. Adventure into the unknown is difficult even for an
adventurous people.

The needed change must pervade the society, so the agents
of change will inevitably be diverse and their actions will affect
each other. The focus of change is, of course, United States foreign
policy, and the immediate agent of change is the United States government. But "foreign policy" is really a collection of policies
affecting the international and transnational activities of the
United States and its citizens, organizations, and institutions.
It is natural, therefore, that the making of foreign policy -- or
foreign policies -- is substantially decentralized.

Second, United States foreign policy is in an important,
though imprecise, way related to public opinion, and shapers of
public opinion are therefore potential change agents for -- or
against -- a world political community. The most important of these
agents are probably the media, educational institutions, voluntary
associations, and the government itself. The fact that the government simultaneously reflects, is constrained by, and shapes public
opinion is but one of the complexities of the relationship between
public opinion and public policy.

A more fundamental problem lies in the relationship between public opinion and public consent. Public policy, even in a
legitimate democracy, depends on opinion only to the extent that
opinion affects consent. Traditionally, the pervasive view that
"politics stops at the water's edge" has led most citizens to consent to foreign policy regardless of their judgment. Thus most
politicians were responsive to opinion on domestic issues because
they knew that on these issues consent could be readily withdrawn.

An escalating and costly arms race, the Vietnam War, the
events loosely called "Watergate," and the increasing interaction
between foreign and domestic policy have done a great deal to make
consent more dependent upon favorable public opinion. In building
public consent for a world political community, it will be critical
not to be satisfied with a positive but passive public attitude toward it. Citizens will also need confidence in their ability to
judge foreign policy issues and in their capacity for effective
action on those issues. Therefore, the task of opinion-making
agents is not simply to project a positive image of a world political community, but to engender a sense of responsibility and public efficacy on the part of the citizens who become committed to
it.

Finally, the character of the public discussion needs to
change, and for this, both government and opinion-shaping institutions bear responsibility. The "character" of the discussion is a
matter of what is at issue and what is assumed, of how clearly the

assumptions are articulated, and of how imaginatively alternatives and new possibilities are set forth.

Most of the public discussion of foreign policy in the 1960's and 1970's has focused on relatively specific, short-term issues and has assumed more or less uncritically the broad goals of policy. We as a nation have debated Strontium-90, troop strength in Europe, the defense budget, the B-1 bomber, and the control of the CIA, for example, but we have not debated seriously and publicly the goals and assumptions of our policy. We have not publicly examined our operative assumption that security can best be achieved through a combination of nuclear deterrence and geopolitical power balances. Yet it is precisely at this level that the public debate on a world political community must take place.

Whether to build a new fleet of bombers is an issue -- that is, it is a genuine question for which and against which reasons can be given -- regardless of whether the nation's overall goal is a balance of power or a world political community. But the reasons will be different and the priorities will be different according to which goals are affirmed. (Given other goals, such as isolationism or passive non-resistance, the B-1 would not even be an issue, but in the progress toward a world political community the military function would decline gradually and systematically, not abruptly.) And because world political community requires such pervasive change, the most important factor is what goals provide the reasons and criteria for determining specific issues. A decision not to build a new fleet of bombers on the grounds that it is too expensive, or not cost-effective, or unreliable, or not needed for deterrence does nothing to advance a world political community, because a less expensive weapon which is more efficient, reliable, and capable will be proposed in its stead. But a debate on a fleet of bombers in which the goal of world political community is articulated and affirmed by a significant and growing public -- such a debate will aid our cause, because it will demonstrate that a growing part of public consent in America will be reserved for those policies which mark progress toward the creation of a world political community.

The public discussion of foreign policy needed in the future differs from the current discussion not in the issues addressed, but in the way they are defined. Specifically, the choice of general goals must become a public matter, and this will require significant change on the part of public officials, the media and the various advocates of alternative policies -- including proponents of a world political community.

It should be evident by now that movement toward a world political community requires change in a great variety of organizations and institutions, from a local church social concerns committee to the United States government. We are about to identify some of the changes that are most critically needed. But it should be clear at the outset that neither the capacity for initiating these changes nor the responsibility for building the needed public constituency is evenly or equally shared.

Although the government obviously has the authority to make and change policy within the limits of public consent, we are talking here about a fundamental change in policy for which public

consent has not even been seriously tested, much less expressed.
It is as if we were advocating the abolition of slavery in 1820:
We simply cannot say, "Let the government do it," for the government does not have the public mandate to enact the policy we propose.   Rather, we can call upon the government to provide leadership in the exploration of alternatives, to test the public's
willingness to support innovative policies.

        In American society it has traditionally fallen to the
voluntary associations to put new possibilities and purposes on the
public agenda, to nurture novel ideas and preserve them for the
more receptive publics of the future, and, at the right time, to
initiate public discussion and activities which evoke the consent
required for a purpose to become a policy.[4]   The abolitionists, the
suffragettes, the opponents of child labor, the early trade union-
ists -- all these and many more were gathered in associations, and
the fact that their goals are now largely embodied in public policy
is a tribute not only to the effectiveness of their associations but
also to the function and stature of associations in American political life.

        The prospects for the goal of world political community
becoming embodied in public policy depend heavily upon the readiness
and ability of a few voluntary associations to assume the leadership
that proponents of great purposes have assumed in the past.   Nothing
is more important than to strengthen the organizations whose central
purpose is advancement of this goal.   These organizations need
friends who will provide funds, who will serve as their advocates
in other parts of the society, and who will help develop and test
the ideas that chart the course between the current situation and
the goal.   And they need sustained, high quality leadership, so that
through good times and bad, and however confusing the political
climate and however inhospitable the cultural conditions, they will
continue steadfastly in their task.

        It is not that voluntary associations can do the job alone,
for there is little hope that those devoted to world political community will have sufficient strength for that.   Rather, these associations are the principal agents of change in the whole range of institutions that reflect and shape the society at large.

        Effective action for world political community requires
an analysis of what changes are both needed and possible in a wide
variety of institutions -- in government, the media, schools and
universities, and citizen organizations.   In what follows we shall
outline a minimal set of action objectives for citizens and their
associations that are devoted to promoting a world political community.   There is little point in seeking change that is either
greater or more fundamental than necessary, and there is a great
danger in setting impossible goals.   The necessary and possible are
quite enough for the remaining years of this century!

        GOVERNMENT.   In the last quarter of the twentieth century,
the United States government has the opportunity to enact policies
that will help create some of the elements of a world political
community and that will invite the participation of other countries
and political units in the same process.   It can do so in ways that
encourage a public examination of the goals of our policy and test

the readiness of the American people to support a policy whose central goal is the creation of political community at the global level.
Citizens and associations now committed to this goal must call upon
the government to seize this opportunity.

The elements of a world political community are already
at issue in international relations; the opportunity lies in the
capacity to act in a new way. The strength and character of the
United Nations system, the structure of the world economy, the status
of human rights, and the extent and limits of world armaments are
all changing rapidly, for better or worse. The question is, can
this country influence the change in ways that will eventually eliminate war and develop political alternatives?

The United Nations system embodies enough of the formal
political institutions needed for world political community that
it may serve as a stepping stone. But it can only do so if some
of its major participants, such as the United States, provide a
strange combination of firm support, severe criticism, and creative
leadership. In light of the United Nations' central purpose, "to
save succeeding generations from the scourge of war," its record
has been an obvious disappointment. And, as if to compound passive
failures, the organization has in recent years explicitly and will-
fully violated its own purposes by endorsing war (in Namibia) and
by distorting principles of human rights. Support for the United
Nations as a potential element in a world political community, therefore, requires severe criticism, but not criticism in the absence of
constructive alternative proposals. With respect to Namibia, for
example, a host of non-violent, political initiatives might have
been employed, but none were even seriously advocated. Self-
government might well have been advanced by an economic boycott,
or a world citizens' tribunal, or an international team observing
military movements across Namibia's borders, or a suit in the International Court of Justice. Initiatives such as these, which could
be advanced by the United States, might help the United Nations find
a way between acquiescence in racist repression, on the one hand,
and support of a war, on the other. In the process the United
Nations would increase in prestige and authority and develop its
political procedures. In general, the United States should engage
vigorously in the politics of the United Nations system, consistently advocating and supporting measures that will enhance that
system's capacity for non-violent resolution of conflict.

Structural issues of the international economy are unavoidable. This is true partly because of the pressure for a "New
International Economic Order." It also results from the fact that
so many corporations have outgrown the political contexts within
which they previously functioned. Finally, there is the increased
realization of the need to harmonize the development, allocation,
and consumption of resources with the limits on their availability.
As the United States responds to the realities and to the fact of
one-half billion people suffering acute malnutrition, it must do so
not only with financial resources but with a view toward establishing
more adequate international economic processes. Whatever the merits
of the market system, it is a blunt instrument for allocating available resources to meet the basic needs of people who lack money,

and it is incapable of adequate long-term conservation and allocation in a situation of scarcity. Therefore, during the coming
decades, the United States should support an international process
of economic planning, not as an alternative to the market, but as
a means of requiring that economic choices serve politically established social goals -- including abolition of hunger and conservation of non-renewable resources -- as well as profit.

There is no simple way to establish such a process, but
several measures would point in the right direction. The United
States should help establish a world food reserve system under international control. It should significantly increase economic aid,
and use this support to strengthen the United Nations Development
Programme as an institution engaged in planning as well as in action
to prevent poverty. It should increase support for the International
Development Association, the major development section of the World
Bank, and support the Bank's efforts to improve development strategies in impoverished regions. The specific opportunities are many
and diverse, but in general, advocates of a world political community
should be working for the United States policies that will promote
world economic development by means that increase the role and influence of international political institutions in reshaping the
world economy to serve commonly established social goals.

To promote human rights in a way that builds world political community, the United States must not allow its commitment to
human rights to be distorted by ideological and geopolitical considerations, and it must support not only the substance of human
rights but also better and stronger international institutions to
enforce them.

Because geopolitical and ideological factors cannot be
avoided, citizens and associations seeking direct United States
support for human rights in a given area must accept responsibility
for interpretation. For example, action for religious freedom and
political dissent in South Korea that ignores North Korea's denial
of the same rights often serves the geopolitical and ideological
needs of the Soviet bloc. An organization supporting Soviet dissidents without criticizing political repression by rightist dic-
tatorships tends to strengthen anti-communist attitudes. Opponents
of the Vietnam War who refuse to inquire into alleged human rights
violations by the Hanoi government undermine their professed commitment to human rights. As a practical matter we often need to
focus on particular violations in particular countries, but it is
essential to do so without obscuring our commitment to general human
rights principles. United States policy must be tenaciously even-
handed, lest its commitment to human rights as such be -- or appear
to be -- compromised.

If we had better international human rights institutions,
distortion for ideological and geopolitical purposes would be more
difficult. The United States can help develop these institutions
by ratifying many of the human rights conventions and treaties already adopted by the United Nations, and by supporting creation of
the office of a United Nations High Commissioner for Human Rights.
It can bring human rights violations before the International Court
of Justice or the United Nations Commission on Human Rights.

The international human rights machinery is so ineffectual at present that United States action for human rights should also use bilateral channels. But even bilateral action ought to be coupled with action through available international institutions. If we withhold economic aid because of human rights violations, why not simultaneously bring charges before the United Nations Commission on Human Rights? Citizen advocates of human rights should foster a policy with both bilateral and multilateral channels of action on most human rights issues.

A United States policy aimed at world political community must reestablish the goal of general and complete disarmament as the central criterion by which to evaluate the success of arms control negotiations and the adequacy of arms control agreements. Citizen action for such a policy must therefore support successive reductions in the quantity and destructive capability of armaments, not just a more precise or more stable balance in the military capacities of nations. At the same time, it must support comprehensive and effective international agreements, ensuring that reductions are in fact multilateral and do not give any nation or bloc substantial military advantage. In general, action for military reductions by the United States which are not a part of a strategy toward internationally agreed disarmament are either irrelevent or detrimental to the prospects of disarmament and world political community.

The problem of citizen action for disarmament is therefore complex -- as is the policy it seeks to affect. But it is possible to effect military reductions in ways that encourage reciprocation and eventual agreement. In 1963, President Kennedy announced a moratorium on nuclear testing in the atmosphere that would remain in effect as long as no similar Soviet test was detected. This unilateral, non-military initiative helped create a new context for negotiation in which the Partial Test Ban Treaty was signed a few months later. Such initiatives do not, of course, always produce the desired result. But there are numerous opportunities which could be tried with limited risk in the next few years. For example, how might the level of forces in Europe be reduced? A major unilateral reduction by the United States could be highly destabilizing, increasing anxieties in Western Europe, encouraging Soviet pressures on the West and repression of dissidents in satellite countries, and increasing NATO's reliance on the nuclear threat. But a marginal reduction of NATO forces, coupled with a public pledge to repeat the reduction if the Warsaw Pact reciprocated in kind, might start a process of deescalation which could later be formalized in an arms control agreement. Similarly, major unilateral reductions in the United States defense budget could indicate a failure of American nerve, creating undue hopes in the Soviet Union and unnecessary anxiety among our allies, and increasing our reliance on the nuclear shield. But a modest transfer of two or three billion dollars from the military budget to an international economic assistance agency, announced as an initiative that would be repeated if reciprocated by the Soviet Union, could set in motion a process leading to mutual reductions, cooperative economic development efforts, and eventual agreement.

Since the mid-1960's, citizen action has been largely divided between advocates of a stronger military establishment and advocates of unilateral reduction of military spending. The cause of disarmament, however, requires support for unilateral measures aimed at multilateral reduction and agreements leading to disarmament.

The United States government's role in creating a world political community must be designed to affect not only international relationships but also domestic politics. It is not yet clear whether or not, to what extent, or under what conditions, public consent to the goal of world political community will be forthcoming. And this is to be expected, for much more is at stake than a set of options on specific issues. It is the goal itself -- a world political community, not a balance of power or Shalom or the elimination of all violence -- that is crucial. Every policy that seeks to further that goal, therefore, is necessarily partly a test of public readiness to support it and a demonstration to the public of how steps might now be taken to achieve it.

Responsibility for public discourse about the goals, as well as the immediate details of policy, fall to both the government and to the public. It is essential that enough information be available that the public will have a basis for intelligently assessing those explanations. But perhaps most important, the government must provide occasions for general examination and reexamination of the broad goals of the policy. Moreover, the public must be included in the process, for it is at this level that public consent is most needed -- and most obviously lacking.

Citizens and associations working for a world political community must do their utmost to get this goal under public discussion and to permit it to be weighed and tested by comparison with other goals of foreign policy. They should call upon the government to engage in public dialogue about the goals of policy, to examine optional goals, to explain specific actions in terms of the goals they are intended to advance, and to provide access to information sufficient for critical examination.

In addition, citizen actions on specific issues should be designed to illustrate the goal of world political community. They should provide occasions for the evaluation of this goal in comparison with its alternatives. This will sometimes require painful decisions to eschew coalitions which, though devoted to a sound policy, would obscure or undermine the general goal of world political community. And it will require extremely judicious selection of issues -- issues that not only advance the goal of world political community but can be readily seen by the public to contribute toward it.

In short, citizen action for a world political community must recognize that evoking public consent and building a reliable, broad based constituency are much more important than achieving victory in immediate issues. The critical role of constituencybuilding not only affects the kind of action needed to influence government policy. It also means that advocates of world political community need to influence the whole range of shapers of public opinion.

MEDIA. The process of public consent for policy oriented
toward world political community faces two major problems which are
partly caused by the media but which the media could help solve.
One is the problem of thinking about policy in terms of fundamental,
long-term goals, and not simply in terms of immediate choices. The
second is the problem of initiating discussion of what is, from the
perspective of the general public, a novel idea. Both of these
problems are general problems, faced by advocates of fundamental
change on a wide variety of social issues, so collaboration with
associations in other fields may be possible. The agenda of action
for a world political community, however, is the criterion for collaboration, and it includes the following.

First, advocates of a world political community must be
concerned about the dominant images of the world which the public
receives. Does war appear to be a fact of life or a matter of
choice? Whose choice? Is it in any way amenable to action by citizens? What appears to determine the course of human events? Force,
violence and war, or more civilized means of effecting change? These
general images, repeated and reinforced daily, probably have a much
greater influence on political attitudes than would occur if world
political community advocates could get every news story they thought
important on network news. Yet we are without systematic analysis
of the way the overall content of news and comment relate to the
policies, issues, and goals of a world political community. This
analysis, coupled with an appropriate critique and alternative proposals, is a major and urgent requirement for action.

Second, we must persuade and help editors, producers, and
writers to articulate issues in terms of their long-term effects
and of the general goals they imply. This will be much easier when
and if official justifications of policy are provided in those terms,
but thoughtful journalists could be doing much more to show what is
"really" at stake, what are the issues behind the issues. In this
context, we can press for news coverage and comment on action for
policies aimed at world political community even if immediate public
involvement is modest.

Finally, we must point out that action that deserves attention is extremely diverse and is of importance to diverse audiences.
For example, education for a world political community in schools,
churches, and synagogues should be reported in the religion and
education sections and in professional journals. And it is extremely
important to help the media present to the public an image of their
country in which action for world political community is not relegated to peace organizations and policy makers alone, but is taking
place -- or could take place -- throughout the fabric of the society.

UNIVERSITIES, COLLEGES, AND SCHOOLS. The prospects of
public support for world political community depend upon educational
institutions that treat war as a problem to be solved rather than
as a fact to be accepted. Within this context it is essential that
world political community be interpreted as one possible means, not
the only means, and not a means which is sure of success. A world
political community, and a United States capable of being a constructive participant in a world political community, both need,

above all, citizens who can think creatively about the problems they face in common and critically about the options that seem to be available.

Educational institutions not only provide information and skills needed for citizenship, but influence fundamental attitudes and values. If schools are to help students appreciate war as a problem -- that is, as a reality they can do something about -- all aspects of the educational experience must be engaged. By means of in-service training of teachers, development and dissemination of new instructional materials, and creation of new contexts for learning, advocates of world political community can contribute to constructive innovation in teaching.

Briefly stated, we should encourage teaching about past wars in ways that show the elements of choice involved, and we should encourage teaching about "wars which didn't occur" -- about severe conflicts that were resolved by other means. We should work for more attention to the problems, prospects and techniques of non-violent conflict resolution and to specific occasions in which the United States could contribute to those possibilities. Images of the world that exphasize the interdependence of its peoples and the interrelationships among its problems support a more accurate understanding of war and alternatives to it than a fragmented and nationalistic approach.

Students should be helped to clarify and think critically about their own fundamental values and to explore the implications of those values for choices they may face as a result of the problem of war. The heritage of values from the world's political, cultural, and religious traditions should be examined critically.

Finally, students need to relate their own capacities for action to the problem of war. Whether they become involved in the American Legion or the local peace council is less important than their need to do so thoughtfully and critically and in a way which gives them a sense of their own efficacy.

Colleges and universities represent a great deal of this country's resources for basic and problem-solving research. In view of the need for further clarification and development of the idea of a world political community, its advocates should call upon colleges and universities for help. Research on disarmament must begin to compete more favorably with research on military strategy, weapons development, and even arms control. Research on international law related to human rights and conflict resolution should be increased in comparison both to domestic law and to international law serving commercial and national interests. Economic research should place greater emphasis on the changes needed to feed and clothe the world's population and to develop global institutions adequate to a more just and viable economic order. To propose this agenda is not to belittle or contradict current critiques of the "military-academic complex," but to suggest a positive agenda as a needed corollary to an essentially negative one.

VOLUNTARY ASSOCIATIONS. Only a few American voluntary associations are working for a world political community. Most are organized for different purposes: for study, worship, the advancement of a profession or a trade, the preservation of ethnic or racial

identity, sport, advancement of an ideology, and companionship.
Yet most of them influence the political thinking and enhance the
political influence of their members. Therefore, many and diverse
associations have capacities which could be engaged in the cause
of world political community. Citizens and associations devoted to
this purpose would do well to seek their collaboration and support.
        It is important to recognize that voluntary associations
are strongest and most effective when they are consistent with their
essential purposes, when they fulfill the objectives for which their
members belong. Their only real power is their people. Thus, voluntary associations can only be seriously engaged in the task of
building world political community on a voluntary basis. The key
to this is a sensitive identification of activities that are consistent with the associations' purposes, that will tend to increase
and use the strengths of the organization and that will help people
think constructively about, and act effectively for, a world political community.
        Associations are so diverse that a more specific formula
for their engagement can be provided only on a case by case basis.
Churches and synagogues, for example, will contribute most to a
world political community if their religious purpose is at the core
of their activity. They should be called upon to proclaim and interpret their faith explicitly as a resource for thinking and acting
in response to the problem of war. And if this essentially religious
core is maintained, it should be possible to place the problem of
war on the education and worship agenda, and not relegate it to the
usually marginal social action group. Since people, however religious, must address the problem of war in their capacity as citizens,
churches and synagogues must take responsibility for the political
consequences of their programs. Political and religious education
must go hand in hand, for each is important in its own right, and
each needs the other. Advocates of a world political community will
be most effective if they not only make a political analysis, but
also respect the fundamental religious premises of the organization
they seek to engage and have the skills to help develop programs
that strengthen educational and worship experiences.
        Similar analyses are needed for any organization that
could help the cause of world community,but for the sake of brevity I
will limit the rest of this discussion to those associations loosely
called "the peace movement." The relationships among peace organizations have been problematic throughout the history of the movement,
so it should come as no surprise that the potential relationship of
most peace groups to the cause of a world political community is a
sensitive practical problem and a complex substantive issue. It is
indeed so sensitive and practical that terms of worthwhile relations
cannot be set forth in general, or in advance of concrete discussions
of action, and they are so complex that only the broad outlines of
the problem can be suggested here.
        Broadly speaking, the three rules that apply to associa-
tions in general -- consistency with purpose, engagement of institutional strength, and fidelity to the idea of world political community -- all apply to engagement of peace organizations. Because
of this, the division and fragmentation within the peace movement is

the natural result of the diversity of purposes and strategies of
the organizations that make it up. And it remains to be seen which
of these organizations can work productively together on the task
of building support of a world political community.

Can pacifists and pacifist organizations be part of a
broad movement for a world political community? Possibly, for although a world political community incorporates limited violence
(national and international police forces) it would drastically reduce the levels of violence. Would religious people energized by
the vision of Shalom be drawn to the task of building a world political community? Possibly, for it might well be seen as the best
approximation of the Shalom ideal that could actually be achieved
in the next generation. In both cases, the necessary compromises
might be made in order to translate a utopian ideal into an achiev-
able goal, and advocates of a world political community should enter
into a searching dialogue with their more idealistic counterparts.

A different kind of question is posed by those within the
peace movement who seek change in United States policy but not in
the policies of other countries or in the structures and processes
of international relations. To them advocacy of a world political
community may seem either presumptuous (America has no right to try
to shape the world) or naively idealistic (it's hard enough to
change America, so why take on the world?). Others limit their
critique to American militarism because they are really partisans
of America's adversaries or because they oppose corporate capitalism
which, they believe, benefits from military spending. But many may
agree that the United States military establishment is, as a practical matter, unlikely to be reduced as long as most nations are
heavily armed and while most international relationships are determined by predominantly military factors. Therefore, advocates of
a world political community should seek actively to cooperate with
those who now focus exclusively on diminishing the strength of the
Pentagon. And we should seek to cooperate in activities in which
the aim of mutual disarmament in the context of adequate world political processes is both clear and credible.

The organizations and institutions identified here are
of course not the only actors whose political influence must change
if world political community is to become a reality. We have focused
on those that are generally recognized to have responsibility for
educating the public or shaping public opinion or public policy in
ways that promote the common good. In the end many others -- notably
business and organized labor -- will have to exercise their political influence differently in order to build toward world political
community. And as the list of needed actors grows, it may become
more evident why a politically effective movement for world political community has never been created. Perhaps the task is just too
difficult.

On the other hand, since an adequate course of action has
never been attempted, it should come as no surprise that a world
political community has not been achieved. Ideas, however great,
do not become reality by thought alone. The challenge facing advocates of a world political community is enormous. But it is the
challenge to undertake a constellation of very practical tasks --

tasks which can in fact be accomplished if sufficient energies can
be mobilized and sustained, and if the guiding vision is kept clear.
And in meeting these conditions -- energy and vision -- the role of
voluntary associations committed to world political community is
crucial.   Individuals acting alone usually cannot achieve the impact
or keep a sufficiently clear sense of direction to create the needed
momentum.   On the other hand, the major mainstream institutions are
absorbed in other purposes and are not potential sources of initiative for world political community.   The major initiative will come,
if it comes at all, from a small group of associations, whose purpose and potential impact are infinitely greater than their numbers
and their wealth.   That initiative will be possible if there is a
constituency of supporters who sustain the associations.   And it
will be effective if there are receptive individuals, not only in
government but in schools, colleges and universities, in the media,
in churches and synagogues, and in a host of non-governmental organizations -- individual citizens who will see both the importance
and the possibility of a world political community, and will help
engage their institutions in realizing that possibility.

NOTES AND REFERENCES

1. Immanuel Kant, *Perpetual Peace*, ed. Lewis White Beck (Indianapolis:
The Bobbs-Merrill Company, Inc., 1957).

2. Charles Chatfield, "More than Dovish: Movements and Ideals for Peace
in the United States," paper delivered at the Conference on 200 Years of American Thinking on War and Peace, sponsored by the Department of International
Politics, the University of Wales, at Gregynog, Wales, 5-8 July 1976.

3. Hannah Arendt, *On Violence* (New York: Harcourt, Brace and World, Inc.,
1969), p. 56.

4. In my interpretation of the role of voluntary associations in American
political life, I am particularly dependent upon the work of James Luther Adams.
See, for example, Professor Adams' essay, "The Political Responsibility of the
Man of Culture," *Comprendre*, No. 16, (1956), and also *On Being Human Religiously*
(Boston: Beacon Press, 1976). A summary of much of Adams' interpretation of
voluntary associations is provided by James D. Hunt in "Voluntary Associations
as a Key to History," *Voluntary Associations*, ed. D. B. Robertson (Richmond,
Virginia: John Knox Press, 1966).

THE MORAL AND POLITICAL SIGNIFICANCE OF THE BLACK CHURCHES IN AMERICA

by
Peter J. Paris

Social scientists have long acknowledged the importance of the black churches as social institutions. W.E.B. DuBois was the first to attribute to them a place of primacy in the black community. He said that "as a social group the Negro Church may be said to have antedated the Negro family on American soil."[1] E. Franklin Frazier concluded that "it is difficult to imagine organized social life among Negroes without the important role of the religion and the Negro Church."[2] Mays and Nicholson described the black churches, past and present, as institutional loci where blacks could be relatively free from white domination.

> The church was the first community or public organization that the Negro actually owned and completely controlled. And it is possibly true to this day that the Negro Church is the most thoroughly owned and controlled public institution of the race.[3]

And in his comprehensive study of race relations in America, the Swedish sociologist Gunnar Myrdal described the widespread respect with which the black community regards its churches in the following way:

> The solidarity behind the abstract church institution in the Negro community is simply amazing....Few question the church as such, its benevolent influence and its great potentialities.[4]

Clearly, there is an impressive body of scholarship concerning the functions of the black churches in the development and maintenance of a structured social life among black Americans.[5] But, unfortunately, very little is known (though much is assumed) about their ethical significance.[6] Now, the cause of this lack must not be attributed to the social sciences (the sources of much of our empirical knowledge about the black churches) since they claim no methodological skills for studying the qualitative dimensions of social reality. Rather, those spheres of inquiry are the rightful subject matter of social ethics. Such a distinction, however, need not imply any rigorous cleavage and/or contradiction between the methodologies of the social sciences and of social ethics. In fact, the latter is often dependent in important ways on the findings of the former. That is to say, the subject matter of social ethics, i.e., morality and politics, is always located ir

315

some societal situation and, hence, subject to those unchanging and controlling social regularities that the social sciences seek to clarify. Thus, social ethics must be allied with social science since it cannot illumine the quality of human action and its possible enhancement in isolation from an accurate knowledge of societal conditions.[7]

This inquiry into the moral and political significance of the black churches will proceed in the following way: (a) a brief statement will describe prominent sociological perspectives on the functions of the black churches; (b) "authority" in the black churches will be analyzed as a key for understanding their moral and political significance and hence, the ground for their sociological functions; (c) the implications of our findings for morality, religion and politics in the black experience will be explored.

Major Sociological Interpretations of the Black Churches

It is a well-known fact that black Americans have had a long history of involuntary racial isolation from white Americans. Following three hundred years of slavery, the practices of racial discrimination and segregation determined the relations between the races for nearly a century. The result has been the gradual solidification of two parallel cultures characterized by race: the one white and the other black.[8] This fact was clearly identifiable at the turn of the century when DuBois described the black community in Philadelphia as a "city within a city."[9] Further, one-half century later, St. Clair Drake and Horace Cayton manifested their indebtedness to the same concept when they entitled their comprehensive study of the black community in Chicago, "Black Metropolis" in order to symbolize its relationship to "Midwest Metropolis." "On eight square miles of land a Black Metropolis was growing in the womb of the white...Negroes were building an attractive home-life and society of their own."[10] But, more importantly, they did not consider that situation peculiar to Chicago alone. Rather, they concluded what has been taken for granted by all other subsequent scholars:

> The Negro community in Chicago began as a haven of refuge for the escaped slaves. It emerged a century later as Black Metropolis inhabited by the grandchildren and great-grandchildren of slaves. In the years between, it had become a citadel of economic and political power in the midst of Midwest Metropolis - an integral part of the city political machine and a reservoir for industrial labor and personal domestic servants. The story of the growth of Black Metropolis between the Civil War and the Depression is, with minor variations, the story of the Negro in New York, Detroit, Philadelphia, Pittsburg, and a number of other cities in America's northeastern and east-central industrial areas. During the Second World War it became the story, too, of San Francisco and Los Angeles as Negroes streamed to the West Coast to help man the arsenal of democracy.[11]

Hence, in our day, terms such as "black community," "ghetto," "inner city," (to mention only a few) are contemporary synonyms for the separate black culture that has emerged within the American society. In many respects, black America is a phenomenon created and maintained by the practices of white racism. More specifically, its physical boundaries and many of its pathological conditions are direct results of deliberate racist policies. But the community itself displays an amazing resiliency evidenced in its self-understanding, the nature of which reveals an astounding transcendence over the impact of racism. And the black churches have played no small role in shaping and nurturing that under-standing.

Historically, the churches have performed the many and varied functions of governance within the black community. The importance of those functions cannot be overemphasized. Constrained in every dimension of their common life by the dehumanizing con-ditions of white racism, blacks made their churches agencies for teaching them how to respond in creative and constructive ways. E. Franklin Frazier has described the internal activities of the black churches as forms of compensation for the denial of freedom experienced by blacks in the larger society. He viewed the churches as crucial social institutions for the maintenance of civility, self-respect and communal belonging, i.e., identity.

> The Negro Church was not only an arena of political life for the leaders of Negroes, it had a political meaning for the masses. Al-though they were denied the right to vote in the American community, within their churches, especially the Methodist Churches, they could vote and engage in electing their officers. The election of bishops and other officers and representatives to conventions has been a serious activity for the masses of Negroes. But, in addition, the Church had a political significance for the Negroes in a broader meaning of the term. The development of the Negro Church after Emancipation was tied up, as we have seen, largely with the Negro family. A study of Negro churches in a Black Belt county in Georgia in 1903 revealed, for example, that a large proportion of the churches were "family churches." Outside of the family, the church represented the only other organized social existence. The rural Negro communities in the South were named after their churches. In fact, the Negro population in the rural South has been organized in "church communities" which represented their widest social orientation and the largest social groups in which they found an identification. Moreover, since the Negro was an outsider in the American community it was the church that enlisted his deepest loyalties. Therefore, it was more than an amusing incident to note some years ago in a rural community in Alabama, that a Negro when asked to identify the people in the adjoining community replied, "The nationality in there is Methodist." We must remember that these people have no historic traditions and language and sentiments to identify them as the var-ious nationalities of Europe. For the Negro masses, in their social and moral isolation in American society, the Negro church community has been a nation within a nation.[12]

The above passage has been quoted at length because it aptly describes many of the governance functions of the black churches. Further, it reveals one of Frazier's most important and perceptive arguments, viz. that the identity which black communities have gained from their churches is comparable to that which European immigrants have inherited from their respective nationalities. In other words, he likened the functions of the black churches to those of nations.[13]

Now, C. Eric Lincoln has described another dimension of the black churches, the implications of which have immense political significance. In a recent monograph he argues that there has always been an integral relationship between the churches and the community at large. In fact, he claims that among black Americans there is no radical dichotomy between the sacred and the secular spheres of life. Rather, the cleavage that has characterized so much of Protestantism simply does not apply.

> To understand the power of the Black Church it must first be understood that there is no disjunction between the Black Church and the Black community, whether one is a "church member" or not is beside the point in any assessment of the importance and meaning of the Black Church....The Black Church then, is in some sense a "universal Church," claiming and representing all Blacks out of a long tradition that looks back to the time when there was only the Black Church to bear witness to "who" or "what" a man was as he stood at the bar of his community. The church still accepts a broad-guage responsibility for the Black community inside and outside its formal communion. No one can die "outside the Black Church" if he is Black. No matter how notorious one's life on earth, the Church claims its own at death - and with appropriate ceremony.[14]

Further, Lincoln argues a point that has been reiterated by several others[15] and which has important implications for ethics and politics. He concludes, "the Church is still in an important sense the people, and...the Church leaders are still the people's representatives..."[16]

Thus, the diverse governance functions of the black churches justify the claim that the latter have been, in many respects, virtually governments within the black community. They have been the basic source of identity for many of their constituents. They have attempted to minister to all the needs of their people - social, economic, political, religious.[17] They have been diligent in protecting their community from the multifarious abuses of racism by comforting the wounded, by restoring hope to the despairing, by redirecting those bent on inculcating attitudes of bitterness and hatred or contemplating actions of violence, and by devising and implementing forms of protest against the inhumanity of white racism. They have advocated the support of black businesses, established and maintained educational institutions, strengthened family life, and have been closely allied with the many civil rights organizations. In short, they have a long and impressive history of institutional primacy in a racially segregated situation.

But, more importantly, we contend that the black churches
have a unique history in being the single most important institutions embodying goals and purposes that pertain primarily to the
welfare of black people. That uniqueness is significant because
in America there have been no other enduring institutions with such
purposes. Rather, white institutions have always aimed at the welfare of whites even when they espoused causes that were seemingly
focussed on the welfare of blacks. Alexis de Tocqueville perceived
that fact nearly one hundred and fifty years ago in his startling
conclusion regarding the crucial question of abolitionism: "It is
not for the good of the Negroes, but for that of the whites, that
measures are taken to abolish slavery in the United States."[18]
Clearly, Tocqueville's position implied that the welfare of whites
is not the same as that of blacks, though the latter may receive
some indirect benefits as a result of increased gains on the part
of the former. Tocqueville may have thought similarly when he
argued that white America would never grant blacks equality and
that their eventual emancipation from slavery would initiate the
beginning of an alternative form of subjugation already firmly
evidenced (in his day) among the "free persons of color."[19]

The Nature of Authority in the Black Churches

Clearly, any effective exercise of the many and varied
governance functions of the black churches must imply the consent
of the black community at large. Otherwise, the churches would be
experienced as tyrannical forces bent on self-gratification, exploitation, and domination. But, on the contrary, the community
at large views its churches as "race institutions," i.e., being "for"
the race and not against it. Thus, the community not only legitimates their actual functions but it expects them. The obvious circularity in this argument illustrates the harmonious relationship
between the social functions of the churches and the community's
expectations. Now, we do not wish to imply, however, that the community always agrees with the substance of those functions. Rather,
it is our claim that the churches are formally legitimated in the
performance of their governance functions. Though there are probably many reasons for that legitimation, one is definitely primary,
viz. a tradition that has always been normative for the black
churches and the black community. It is not the so-called "Western
Christian Tradition" as such, though that is one important source
of it. But, more accurately, it is the "Black Christian Tradition."
Now the terms "Western" and "Black" designate two different but very significant modifications of Christianity. Each
signifies a particular socio-political context in which the Christian religion has been appropriated and shaped. Since religious
experience is always conditioned (in important ways) by its socio-
political context, it follows that significant differences in the
latter imply significant differences in the former. Consequently,
since the black churches were racially segregated from their white
counterparts, it should not be surprising to discover the reflection
of that reality in black religion; similarly, with the religion of

whites. But, one should not assume (as many have done)[20] that the
pathological conditions of the black community are the only forces
shaping social reality. Rather, the Black Christian Tradition
evidences the lie of that assumption. It represents the empirical
transcendence of the human spirit over the dehumanizing power of
white racism.

Now, there should be no equivocation concerning the black
churches and the Black Christian Tradition. The two are closely
related though not synonymous. The Black Christian Tradition became institutionalized in the Black Churches during the period following the American Revolutionary War.[21] Prior to that event, the
desire and quest for freedom and equality (together with their concomitant resistance to slavery and racism) had no enduring public
form. Formally accepted by the churches as standard and norm,[22]
the substance of the Black Christian Tradition (freedom and equality
of all persons under God) has been experienced by blacks only within
the black churches.

Out of the crucible of racial segregationalism the Black
Christian Tradition emerged as a non-racist appropriation of the
Christian faith. As such it represents the astounding transcendence
of the human spirit over the impact of the multifarious conditions
of racial oppression. But it also represents a principle of opposition to racism which radically challenges the latter in all
spheres of its influence: social, religious, moral. Thus, the
Black Christian Tradition is essentially prophetic, utilizing prophetic powers to effect religious and moral reform in a specific
societal context.

The Black Christian Tradition stands in opposition to the
Western Christian Tradition as represented in white American
churches. It has always been the source of inspiration for black
churches in their persistent attempts to reveal the fundamental
depths of racism, i.e., that racial segregation and discrimination
(not to mention slavery) are not merely a social issue, but, rather,
are rooted in values that are morally and religiously false. Hence
the black churches have pointed to the self-contradictory nature of
the problem. Ironically, their basic source of authority has been
the Biblical Scriptures which they inherited from their slave
masters. But, more specifically, the basis of that authority has
been that to which blacks have been unreservedly committed, viz.
their understanding of a Biblical anthropology that strongly affirms
the equality of all persons under God regardless of race or any
other natural quality.[23] This doctrine is the essence of the Black
Christian Tradition and the most fundamental requirement of its
churches. The discovery of this doctrine soon revealed to blacks
the basic contradiction implicit in the religion of white Americans.
The internal conflict between the Biblical Scriptures and the
practices of the white churches has always been the strongest
weapon of the black churches against the racism of their white
counterparts. In short, the Black Christian Tradition posits a
fundamental moral and religious dilemma at the heart of white Christianity. It (the Black Christian Tradition) was born in opposition
to that dilemma.

The moral and political significance of the black churches is derived from their common source of authority, i.e., the Black Christian Tradition. In the latter, the thought and practice of religion, politics and morality are integrally related.[24] That is to say, the one always implies the other. Whenever they are isolated from one another the tradition itself is severely threatened.[25] But, further, whenever individuals and/or groups betray the basic principles of that tradition, whether by direct assault or by some insidious compromise, the self-integrity and group meaning of the black community per se are undermined. Such a threat is due to the fact that the community's self-understanding is intrinsically tied up with the moral and political dimensions of the Black Christian Tradition. In other words, the latter is not only normative for the black churches but is the basic principle of meaning for the community at large.[26]

Now, regardless of the measure of success betrayers of the Black Christian Tradition may achieve, they never gain full legitimacy within the black community. At best they are received ambivalently. At worst, they become liable to the community's most opprobrious epithet, "Uncle Tom." Such persons and/or groups gain no permanent honor, but, rather, have the destiny of becoming insignificant enclaves in the black community.

Thus, the moral and political character of the black churches is based on an authority that is not the controlled possession of the churches themselves. Rather, it transcends them as both lure and judge. In fact, the churches are either praised or blamed by the community-at-large in accordance with their faithfulness to that tradition. As we have seen (above) those that betray the tradition not only violate their own religious principle of authority but they become vulnerable to the charge of forsaking the community's trust and choosing not to be its true representatives. Faithfulness to the principle of human equality under God and its implied opposition to racism determines the integrity of the churches and their relationship to the black community. Now, let us look more closely at the concept of "authority" implied by the Black Christian Tradition.

Many contemporary political scientists describe authority as the essence of government. Consequently, they view it as synonymous with their understanding of power and define both in terms of coercion, force and violence. In fact, it is commonplace today for such scholars to view government as necessarily based on the capacity to apply physical force and/or to command its use as a threat.[27] Hence, those who equate authority with physical compulsion understand government to be the legitimate exercise of control over others. Similarly, many others understand the authority of the family, professional associations, churches, etc. in terms of their various capacities for applying coercion or its threat in order to secure obedience.

As we have seen (above) it is generally agreed that the black churches exercise authority[28] in the black community. But, unlike nations, they command no militia. Rather, the authority of the black churches is not in any way based on coercion or force. Consequently, it must have a different meaning.

Contrary to the scholarly opinions of many, Hanna Arendt defines authority in terms other than those denoting physical force and coercion. She is fully aware that her understanding has reference to a phenomenon that has almost vanished from the Western world. She writes that "authority precludes the use of external means of coercion; where force is used, authority itself has failed.[24] Further, she defines authority as a relation between the one who commands and the one who obeys: a relation based on a common experience which transcends both and which is respected by both. Thus, she writes:

> The authoritarian relation between the one who commands and the one who obeys rests neither on common reason nor on the power of the one who commands; what they have in common is the hierarchy itself, whose rightness and legitimacy both recognize and where both have their predetermined stable place.[30]

Thus, Arendt argues that the acknowledgment of authority not only precludes the use of coercion and force, but it also excludes the use of persuasion. Those who do not acknowledge authority can neither be forced nor persuaded to do so. But, further still, Arendt rightly contrasts the appearance of authority with that of tyranny by arguing that the tyrant always rules in accordance with his/her own interest and will, while authority is always bound by principles and/or laws that set the legitimate terms of governance.

> The source of authority in authoritarian government is always a force external and superior to its own power; it is always this source, this external force which transcends the political realm, from which the authorities derive their "authority," that is, their legitimacy, and against which their power can be checked.[31]

The distinction Arendt makes between power and authority is significant. Surprisingly, she states that "the most conspicuous characteristic of those in authority is that they do not have power."[32] All legitimate power is grounded in authority. But those who are in authority always *represent* it. They do not establish it, nor do they possess it. The President of the United States represents the authority of the nation, i.e., the constitution. His oath of office is a vow of obedience to that source. His signing of bills authorizes their enforcement. The authority he represents is external to both him and the people he rules. Hence, we are able to distinguish between the "President" and the "Presidency." The former changes regularly while the latter endures. Similarly, a separation of power and authority is vividly seen in the polity of congregational churches. The assembled church is the autonomous source of power for all official decisions including the hiring and dismissal of ministers. But the office of the latter represents the church's authority. While power resides in the congregation, authority transcends both minister and congregation. Hence, we distinguish between the "minister" and the "ministry."

As we have seen (above) all authority implies some form of hierarchy and that of the black churches is no exception. In

fact, the pyramid image is an appropriate one for describing not
only their internal activities but also their external functions
in the black community. Egalitarianism is not a prominent feature
of the black churches in spite of certain formal structures implying
the contrary. Actually, inequality permeates the many and varied
relations within the churches from the minister to the newest member.
But, the inequality pertains to function alone and not to persons
qua persons. Within the arena of the Black Christian Tradition
inequalities of function never imply inequalities of persons because the Tradition is grounded uncompromisingly in the belief that
all persons are equal under God. Further, the Tradition demands
expression in all human relations.

Thus, the inequalities implied by authoritarian relations
are morally preferable to those implied by totalitarian relations.
In the former case freedom is no threat but, rather, is preserved
and promoted in accordance with rules and principles that transcend
those who are in authority. But, in the latter, freedom is a fundamental threat and must be forcibly hindered and actually destroyed
in order to secure the ruler's arbitrary control. Further, the inequality of function implicit in authoritarian relations contrasts
vividly with the permanent state of inequality (i.e., subordination)
to which all are necessarily reduced in totalitarian situations.

Clearly, the Black Christian Tradition has been the life-
line of the black community. Apart from it blacks would not have
been able to survive the dehumanizing force of chattel slavery and
its legacy of race oppression. It has stimulated the interests and
shaped the pursuits of countless artists, scholars, religionists,
reformers, etc. Embodied in the community's primary institutions,
i.e., the churches, it has been the source of ultimate meaning for
their many and varied social functions. Surely the end of racism
would imply the beginning of a new era for the Tradition -- an era
in which the Biblical understanding of humanity would continue to
be proclaimed by the black churches as normative for all people,
but the proclamation would issue from a different vantage point.
That is to say, the validity of the basic principle of the Black
Christian Tradition would not be altered by the removal of the experiential condition of racism because the tradition itself is
grounded in the truth of God which is eternal. Therefore, as a
formal principle it is applicable for all time. But, as a living
principle it requires institutional embodiment. Historically, in
this land, the black churches have served that function, i.e., those
that have been faithful to the Black Christian Tradition.

Implications for Morality, Religion and Politics
in the Black Experience

First, let us consider the implications of the above
analysis for morality. Clearly, those black churches that have
been faithful to the Black Christian Tradition are moral institutions. Their raison d'etre is inextricably tied to the function of
opposing the beliefs and practices of racism by proclaiming the
Biblical view of humanity as they have appropriated it, i.e., the

equality of all persons under God. Thus, their moral aim is theologically grounded. In other words, the doctrine of human equality
under God is, for them, the final authority for all matters pertaining to faith, thought, and practice. In short, its function in
the black experience is categorical, i.e., unconditional, absolute,
and universally applicable. Consequently, all action (religious
or political) that is aimed at correcting the social injustice of
racism is viewed as moral action. But, there is an important modi-
fication. The Black Christian Tradition justifies no acts of
violence against other humans. To do so would be self-contradictory
since the Tradition itself is rooted in the understanding that all
persons are equal under God. Such a high estimation of human nature
is always contradicted whenever humans destroy one another, however
righteous the cause might be. Further, that which is gained by
violence and the threat of violence must be maintained similarly.
That is the way of nations in both their conquests and defenses.
But, though the black churches have always known that the black community has been formed and controlled in all dimensions of its life
by the application of violence and its threat, they have chosen to
oppose those forces by alternative methods, i.e., non-violent methods.[33] Under the norm of the Black Christian Tradition they have
fostered opposition to racism that has been both vigorous and creative. Their forms of action have tended always to be life-protecting,
life-enabling, life-respecting. In short, their opposition to racism
has contributed to the creation and preservation of community not
only among blacks but between blacks and whites.
   The ubiquity of racism has had a prominent influence on
the way in which the black churches have defined themselves. As
we have seen, they came into being to embody and express the Biblical
understanding that all humans are equal under God. Throughout their
institutional life that ideal has functioned as a norm in their experience, inspiring their imaginations and governing their thought
and action. Further, the norm has been their greatest potential
source of unity since all have long agreed that racism is a profound
evil that must be resisted (in some form) by every self-respecting
human being.
   Though there are many theological implications of these
facts, two are of the greatest importance. First, the black churches,
under the norm of the Black Christian Tradition, are characterized
by their common quest for human justice, i.e., the equality of all
persons under God. But, second, that aim implies a strong doctrine
of sin in relation to the problem of racism. But, it also implies
a strong doctrine of virtue in relation to those who oppose racism.
This dialectic becomes more graphic when one views its respective
empirical poles. In other words, the empirical referent for the
doctrine of sin is white racism (i.e., as practiced by white people
and their institutions in the main) while black resistance (i.e.,
as practiced by black people and their institutions in the main) is
on the side of human virtue.[34] Thus, those black churches under
the norm of the Black Christian Tradition have no radical doctrine
of sin[35] that readily implicates all people (white and black) in
the same way. Rather, the thought of the black churches distinguishes the sins of black people from that of white racism. Though

the doctrine of human equality under God implies that none (including blacks) are justified in their attempts to subordinate the humanity of others, its application to blacks is often obscured because the experience of white racism is so prevalent. Thus, though blacks are guilty of oppressing other blacks (rarely are they in positions of power over whites), the churches give their attention to the fact that all blacks are oppressed by the greater force of white racism which is considered the greater evil and possibly the source of all sin.

Finally, it is politically significant that the Black Christian Tradition justifies all action that is in opposition to racism in so far as its quality is commensurate with its goal, i.e., affirming and establishing the equality of all persons under God. In other words, means and ends must be integrally related. Clearly, the Black Christian Tradition puts forward a formal principle of opposition to racism that is lacking in content. The nature of that content must be decided in every context and hence, must vary - not in its moral quality but in its practical relevance. That is to say, while certain forms of protest may have been appropriate in one period, they may not be appropriate in another. The demands of justice and the substance which it seeks to embody must vary according to the possibilities afforded by specific situations. Clearly, the task of striving to effect legal guarantees for the civil rights of blacks was the rightful preoccupation of the churches and others in earlier decades. But, the facts of social change may render those former goals and methods inappropriate for our present time. Rather, the contemporary situation may demand the development, preservation and enhancement of power (social, economic, political) in all dimensions of our common life. Like every situation the present is characterized by its possibilities which necessitate clarification, specification, and the utilization of many and varied skills for effective decision and action. Churches faithful to the Black Christian Tradition will waste no time in questioning the moral and religious value of political engagement, i.e., running for elective office, campaigning, active party membership, lobbying, etc. Rather, they will measure the validity of such activities only in terms of practical wisdom as guided by their norm. Those who do otherwise reveal their alienation from the Black Christian Tradition.

NOTES AND REFERENCES

1. W.E.B. DuBois, *The Philadelphia Negro: A Social Study*, (New York: Schocken Books, 1967), p. 201.

2. E. Franklin Frazier, *The Negro Church in America*, (New York: Schocken Books, 1966), p. 82.

3. Benjamin Mays and Joseph Nicholson, *The Negro's Church*, (New York: Institute of Social and Religious Research, 1933), pp. 278-279. This point has been argued by many other scholars not least of whom is John Hope Franklin. See his monumental treatise, *From Slavery to Freedom: A History of Negro Americans*, (New York: Alfred Knopf, 1967), p. 561.

4. Gunnar Myrdal, *An American Dilemma, The Negro Problem and Modern Democracy*, vol. 11, (New York: Harper and Row, 1962), p. 877.

5. *Op. cit.*, See John Hope Franklin, pp. 404ff; 560ff.

6. Gayraud Wilmore's recent book, *Black Religion and Black Radicalism: An Examination of the Black Experience in Religion*, (New York: Doubleday and Co., 1972) is an important contribution to this area of study and it deserves a much more serious review than it has hitherto received.

7. Any complete demonstration of this argument would reveal my indebtedness to Gibson Winter's constructive work, *Elements for a Social Ethic: The Role of Social Science in Public Policy*, (New York: MacMillan Co., 1968).

8. This fact was graphically revealed as one of the conclusions of the *Report of the National Advisory Commission on Civil Disorders*, (New York: Bantam Books, 1968), p. 407. See also *op. cit.*, John Hope Franklin, pp. 559ff.

9. W.E.B. DuBois, *The Philadelphia Negro: A Social Study*, p. 5.

10. St. Clair Drake and Horace R. Cayton, *Black Metropolis: A Study of Negro Life in a Northern City*, vol. 1, (New York: Harper, 1962), pp. 80-81.

11. *Ibid.*, vol. 11, p. 655.

12. E. Franklin Frazier, *The Negro Church in America*, p. 44.

13. It is important to note that this notion is not peculiar to the black churches alone. Rather, the sociologist Will Herberg has aptly described the way in which the churches became the "primary context of self-identification and social location for the third generation, as well as for the bulk of the second generation of America's immigrants, and that meant, by and large, for the American people." See his *Protestant, Catholic and Jew*, (New York: Doubleday & Co., 1960), p. 31.

14. C. Eric Lincoln, *The Black Church Since Frazier*, (New York: Schocken Books, 1974), pp. 115-116.

15. In a mimeographed paper entitled, "Our Heritage and Our Hope" delivered and circulated among the members of the Society for the Study of Black Religion at its annual meeting held in Jamaica, W.I., November 1976, Gayraud Wilmore has written,

> ...there is no essential discontinuity between Africa and Afro-America, between black culture and black religion, between the Black Church and the Black Community.

Similarly, in a special feature article K.M. Smith was quoted as having said, "All members of the black community do not belong to the church, but the church belongs to all the community. And everybody knows it." See *Time* magazine, September 27, 1976, p. 87. It appears to this writer that the thought of both Wilmore and Smith (as well as that of Lincoln) is strikingly similar to Myrdal's conclusion several decades ago when he wrote, "...it must never be forgotten that the Negro Church *fundamentally is an expression of the Negro community itself*." (See his *American Dilemma*, vol. 11, p. 875.

16. *Op. cit.*, C. Eric Lincoln, p. 116.

17. It is important to emphasize again the fact that we do not wish to imply in this inquiry that the black churches are unique with respect to their social functions or their integral relationship with the total life of their community. Rather, we concur with Will Herberg who claimed that such characteristics were dominant in the American ethos:

American religion and American society would seem to be so closely inter-related as to make it virtually impossible to understand either without reference to the other.

(See his *Protestant, Catholic and Jew*, p. 3).   Further, we are sympathetic to his claim that the religious communities of the ethnic groups in America tend to revolve round sociological rather than theological issues and concerns. (*Ibid.*, p. 36ff.)

18. Alexis de Tocqueville, *Democracy in America*, vol. 1, (New York: Alfred A. Knopf, Vintage Books, 1945), p. 375.

19. *Ibid.*, pp. 394ff.

20. Many behaviourists have attended only to those pathological forces in their descriptive analyses of the black community and have made them, alone, determinative of social reality.   Consequently, they have often viewed the churches as products of those pathological forces, i.e., evidences of social pathology.

21. It is important to note that this thought is not novel.   Rather, it has been put forth by such scholars as (a) Gayraud Wilmore who writes:

All of this is to say that the independent Church movement among Blacks, during and immediately following the period of the Revolutionary War, must be considered, *ipso facto*, an expression of Black resistance to white oppression - *the first Black freedom movement.*

(See his *Black Churches and Black Radicalism,* p. 108); (b) John Hope Franklin who writes:

Although Negroes took the initiative in bringing about separation, it appears that such steps were not taken until it was obvious that they were not welcome in the white churches.   This keen sensitivity to mis-treatment and the consequent organization of separate and independent religious organizations of their own were to be the cause for the church occupying such an important place in Negro life in the nineteenth and twentieth centuries.

(See his *From Slavery to Freedom,* p. 164); (c) Eugene D. Genovese writes:

When the black slaves of the New World made it their own, they transformed it into a religion of resistance - not often of revolutionary defiance, but of a spiritual resistance that accepted the limits of the politically possible....whereas the whites asked Jesus for forgiveness, the blacks primarily asked for recognition.

(See his *Roll, Jordan, Roll: The World the Slaves Made*, (New York: Pantheon Books, 1974, p. 254); (d) Harry V. Richardson who writes:

Yet from the beginning the church served as the main outlet through which the slaves could express their sufferings and dissatisfaction. Although it was done covertly, the church rendered two great needed services to the slaves: first, it kept alive the consciousness that the slave system was wicked; and second, it kept alive the hope that in the plan of a good, just God, the wicked, brutal system under which they lived would have to pass away.

(See his essay "The Negro in American Religious Life," in *The American Negro Reference Book*, edited by John P. Davis, (New Jersey: Prentice-Hall, 1966), p. 401.

22. It is important to note that the black churches may contradict (as many have done) that norm and thus manifest their own victimization rather than transcendence over the destructive force of racism. But, that fact must be demonstrated elsewhere.

23. Lawrence Jones argues similarly when he writes the following:

> Black churches are also the product of the positive, self-affirming
> attitudes of Blacks toward themselves. They testify to the fact that
> Blacks had heard and believed the Gospel teaching that God is *no respecter
> of persons*. They were early aware of the distinction that had to be drawn
> between Christianity as practiced and preached by some whites and Chris-
> tianity as proclaimed by its Founder.

(See his article, "Black Churches in Historical Perspective," in *Christianity and Crisis: A Christian Journal of Opinion*, vol. XXX, No. 18, November 12 and 16, 1970, p. 228.)

24. For reasons different from our own, Kenneth B. Clark has described the relationship between religion and politics in the black community as not only a historical fact but as unavoidable. See his *Dark Ghetto: Dilemmas of Social Power*, (New York: Harper and Row, 1965), pp. 175ff.

25. Such threats are always present in the face of political movements, organizations, etc. that devalue the importance of religion or reject moral concerns while deliberating about methods for attaining desired goals. Similar threats attend those religious groups that devalue political involvements, i.e., those whose aims are primarily "other-worldly." Both are alien to the Black Christian Tradition and fail to receive the legitimation of the community at large.

26. It is important to note that the Nation of Islam has characteristically explained itself to Black Americans in terms of the Black Christian Tradition, explicating its symbols and sources while condemning the churches for their presumed apostasy.

27. See Marian D. Irish and James W. Prothro, *The Politics of American Democracy*, (New Jersey: Prentice-Hall, 1968), p. 6 whose definition of authority is representative of large segments of the discipline:

> Government consists of the structures and processes through which rules
> or policies are authoritatively determined for society as a whole. These
> rules may be directed toward realizing such contradictory goals as con-
> tinuing peace or military victory...But whatever its substantive goals,
> public government differs from private governing agencies in that it can
> legitimately rely on physical compulsion, which means that its rules are
> *authoritatively* prescribed.

28. This fact is disputed by all those who would understand authority simply as physical coercion. They view the black churches as void of any actual authority, though some are willing to attribute potential power to them by virtue of their capacity to assemble large numbers of blacks on a regular basis; see Kenneth Clark, *Dark Ghetto, Dilemmas of Social Power*, pp. 174ff. But, many others conclude that the immense growth of organizations among blacks in the twentieth century have forced the churches into a less prominent position than

that which they formerly enjoyed.   Thus, they argue that their authority has been reduced considerably.

29. Hanna Arendt, *Between Past and Future: Six Exercises in Political Thought,* (New World: World Publishing Co., 1963), p. 9.

30. *Ibid.*, p. 93.

31. *Ibid.*, p. 97.

32. *Ibid.*, p. 122.

33. Thus, the concept of non-violence as promulgated by Martin Luther King, Jr. was not alien to the black churches.   None resisted it.   In fact, King was merely explicating and implementing the traditional means of protest long practiced by the black churches under the Black Christian Tradition. King's novelty was his attempt to relate the concept of non-violence to the thought of Gandhi and his method of mass demonstrations.

34. This has been one of the most disputed aspects of *Black Theology* which has been accused of bestowing ontological and ultimate significance on the concept "blackness" in contradistinction to that of "whiteness."

35. The Black Christian Tradition represents an alternative position to that of many neo-orthodox Protestant thinkers who draw radical distinctions between Divine and human virtue.

THE PERSONAL AND SOCIAL DIMENSIONS OF ABORTION

by

E. Spencer Parsons

The relationships that exist between the exercise of personal freedom and the stability of the social order have long attracted the attention of theologians, ethicists, and political theorists. In the seventies the abortion issue has forced to the surface of public debate a number of implicit assumptions which have previously been obscured by the rhetoric of self-justification between the pro-abortionists and the anti-abortionists, or, as they prefer to identify themselves, the pro-choice and pro-life advocates.

Parties to the dispute have enlisted professional ethicists and theologians in their ideological warfare. On the practical side clergymen, social workers, and physicians have been increasingly involved in helping women think through the implications of their pregnancies and assisted them frequently in implementing their decisions. The existential circumstances of these women along with the medical, moral, judicial, and legislative implications of their decisions, however, have not always been appreciated in the formulation of just and viable public policies.

In this essay, I have chosen to examine the personal moral choices women make as these relate to the legitimate, though limited, interest of the society to guarantee its continuity as a humane commonwealth.

That each side of the controversy tends to ignore the legitimate claims of the opposition may be natural, but it is not necessary. Those who are concerned for the quality and cogency of our ethical decisions during the remainder of the twentieth century would do well to give serious consideration to the problem of abortion in its personal and social dimensions.

The issue is of substantial importance to those who are engaged in the quest for truth and justice. For those who are academically concerned with the development of a process of decision-making which involves personal, professional, and public values, the abortion issue provides an almost ideal model of interconnections

The issue is important for religious communities because if they cannot provide moral norms for their constituencies on this question, then they will have relegated the area of human sexuality and reproduction to the peculiarities of individual preferences or consigned them to the bondage of public laws which may or may not take into account those values and principles that need to be weighed if freedom, justice, and order are to prevail in our society.

331

The early debates in the 1950's tried to maintain that the abortion question was simply a personal, medical matter. Whenever someone claims anything to be *simply* this or that, our critical faculties should be alerted. The issue is now recognized as being more complex than was initially perceived. The category of the personal soon came to include the dimension of the religious, and the religious was finally understood to include, at least for Christians and Jews, the institutional expressions of churches, synagogues, and national church bodies.

To pretend that the issue is not a judicial, legislative, and political concern is absurd, since in the first instance the abortion law reformers and those seeking repeal of all such laws used the instruments of representative government and the courts to overturn the pre-1973 statutes of the states in the hope of establishing the constitutionality of the right to abort.

United States Supreme Court Decision, 1973

It was in January of 1973 that the Supreme Court of the United States rendered its historic decisions regarding abortions.[1] It declared that during the first trimester of pregnancy (about twelve weeks) the abortion decision was one which properly belonged only to the pregnant woman and her physician. While recognizing that there were other interested parties, such as husband and family, the Court declared that the final choice should be made by the woman and that the state had no compelling reason to intervene between her and her physician. During the second trimester (approximately between the twelfth and twenty-fourth week of gestation) the states could regulate the conditions under which abortions were to be performed, but only to the extent necessary to protect the health of the pregnant woman. Finally, in the third trimester (from approximately the twenty-fifth week to full term) the Court granted the states the right to prohibit abortions except in those instances where the life and health of the pregnant woman were at stake.

The legal consequences of those decisions were to strike down in whole, or in part, almost all the existing anti-abortion statutes, except those in New York which already had the most liberal abortion laws in the country.[2] The medical consequences were that despite the unfettered right physicians now had to perform abortions during the first trimester most of them recognized that the procedure required particular skills and that the unexpected complications could best be handled in well-equipped clinics or the outpatient departments of general hospitals. In the large metropolitan areas clinics were rapidly established; some public hospitals, and a lesser number of private hospitals began doing abortions. Of course, Catholic hospitals refused to do abortions, and many community hospitals yielded to the religious pressures of their staff, trustees, or community groups and refused to permit abortions in their operating rooms. Physicians were even threatened with the loss of their affiliations with these hospitals if they performed abortions in other hospitals or clinics.

Religiously the results of the Court's decisions were instantaneous. The Roman Catholic Church through its hierarchy and its "Right to Life" organizations took the public lead and denounced the Court and vowed to seek a Constitutional Amendment to reverse the decision.[3] The ground of their opposition was theological for they believed that once a new life entity had been generated in the human species such a life was already a human being. Recent Roman Catholic pronouncements have presumed that the humanity of the embryo is not problematic and that its personal rights to life are derived from its potential citizenship in society and its incorporation into the life of the church as a child of God at the moment of its conception. Believing this, it is understandable why the leaders of the Roman Catholic Church could not give consent by remaining silent to a judicial decision which allowed what they believed to be acts of human genocide against the unborn children of the society of which they were an important and substantial part. While initially seeking to base their objections on civil and human rights issues, it soon became evident that their objections were basically religious.[4]

The reluctance of the Roman Catholic Church to acknowledge the theological grounds of their objections is of course due to the widely held assumption in the United States that public law is not to be based upon the theological peculiarities of any religious sect. This widely held feeling finds its expression in the much publicized doctrine of the "separation of church and state." This doctrine is based on the First Amendment to the Constitution which declares that "Congress shall make no law respecting an establishment of religion, or prohibiting the free exercise thereof."[5]

However much the Church was criticized for violating the spirit of the First Amendment in seeking to overturn the Supreme Court's rulings on abortion, it is interesting to note that their opponents always found it to their advantage to forget the guarantee that there were to be no prohibitions against the "free exercise thereof." Certainly the right to practice one's religion presumably includes the right to seek the enactment of laws which religious groups deem necessary to preserve the civilized character of society. There is ample precedent for such political and legislative activity on the part of all the major denominations in America since the early days of the colonists.[6]

The months following the Court's decisions were tumultuous. Penultimate, if not ultimate, issues were at stake for both sides, and the emergence of the "abortion issue" in the national elections of 1976, catapulted there by the efforts of the National Conference of Catholic Bishops, is the public evidence that religion and politics, and not simply private conscience and medical technology are involved in this issue.[7]

At the present level of commitment by all parties to this struggle, there is no expectation that a once-and-for-all solution will soon be reached. The leadership in the struggle is young enough and sufficiently resourceful to keep the matter in the courts for many years to come. It is the nature of important questions that they are not as easily resolved as the partisans to the debate are tempted to believe. Yet this essay would contend that there are legal compromises which could be reached that would respect the deepest, if not all, the moral sensibilities of both the pro-choice and the pro-life advocates.

The Pregnant Woman and Her Inalienable Rights

George Anastaplo of The University of Chicago and Rosary College whose interests in law, morality, liberty, and the rights of conscience are exhaustive was once asked to "consider what ought to be done with our knowledge of human behavior and with our ability to modify it." He replied, "There is a short and simple prescription of what we ought to do about that. . .we ought to think about it. That is, we ought to try and understand what it all means..."[8]
Perhaps no better preface to a discussion of the abortion issue could be written. Too often we seek political change based on parochial considerations or laws designed to serve only the narrowest self-interests. To think about this issue is to seek for personal and social norms for the sake of personal integrity and social justice.
Preceding any analysis of the abortion dilemma by churchmen, lawyers, politicians, and physicians, it should be acknowledged that the problem is existentially and initially one which involves a living woman whose humanity is not problematic. Her physical, psychological, and spiritual condition constitutes the primary data with which she and the community must deal. Her inquiries, her concerns, her fears, her anxieties, and her self-disclosures provide the point of entry into any discussion or analysis of the abortion issue. This is so because only as a woman testifies in confidence or in public as to whether she believes herself to be, or is in fact, pregnant are any second parties, such as husband, family, church, or community involved. All discussions about the "right" or "good" are critically dependent upon her revealing that she is pregnant.
This point of beginning does not presume to suggest that the woman became pregnant by herself. She is obviously pregnant because of a relationship with another human being and both of them are members of a larger community of persons who ultimately belong through the mystery of creation to the power "by which all things are" to recall a phrase from Richard Niebuhr.[9]
Yet, whatever may be the social character of all individual life, there is, at least in the abortion controversy a persistent tendency to ignore the primary subject, the pregnant woman. She is the person whose interests are theologically and sociologically pre-eminent,at least during the early days and weeks of her pregnancy, despite every effort to reduce her to an abstraction.
The pregnant woman and her situation then become the primary data for theological reflection because she is the one who first wrestles with the meaning of her awareness of her possible pregnancy. She and no one else responds initially to the mystery and miracle of new life; and it is she who first experiences a deep sense of joy or fear in the face of the possibility that she may be pregnant. Her cries, her prayers, whether silent or spoken, raise

the ultimate questions about her own identity and destiny. Whenever questions of such magnitude are dealt with seriously they are
inevitably theological in character. While the reflection may
eventually involve others, nevertheless she is the first theologian
in the debate.
        The miracle and mystery by which new lives are brought
into the world are awesome to ponder. Counselors are aware that
the pregnant woman turns the fact of her pregnancy and its possibilities over and over in her mind in the early dawn, in the full
light of day, and in the darkness and loneliness of the night -
sometimes alone, though often with others whom she loves and trusts.
        Whatever personal choices may have been involved in the
initial sexual activity by which she became pregnant, now in the
moment of realization that she is pregnant, there is the overwhelming awareness that something is happening to her over which she has
only limited control. She is changing, her mensus has ceased, her
breasts are tender and enlarged, and she may experience nausea.
She is now bound into a process the consequences of which affect
her in ways even she can only partially comprehend. Her inner
fears, hopes, and joys, as well as her employment, her education,
her relationships with her partner, her family, and her colleagues
may all be involved in this thing which is now happening to her.
        Under these circumstances the critical questions are
asked. *Now*, what is the meaning of human freedom and the right to
direct one's own life? *Now*, what does it mean to make moral decisions? *Now*, what does it mean to find oneself a willing or an
unwilling partner in a biological process one may not have intended
to initiate?
        If she is a married woman certainly she has a right to
presume that the sexual intimacy in which she engaged was justified
for purposes other than procreation. The celebration of life together in love and trust has been affirmed by most Protestant
Christians and Jews for centuries and finally by the Roman Catholic
hierarchy itself.[10] That human sexuality is a more inclusive category of human experience than human reproduction is the basis upon
which non-Catholic couples have practiced responsible birth control
for decades. Indeed for most Protestant Christians, Jews, and
sensitive humanists birth control has been understood to be more
than morally permissible; it is a moral necessity for the sake of
personal, family, and indeed, society's welfare.

Inviolable Rights

        In the United States, at least, the state feels bound to
respect the choice of a woman to continue her pregnancy on the
grounds that such a choice is protected by the fourth amendment to
the U.S. Constitution in granting "The right of people to be secure
in their persons..."[11] Such a provision has long been interpreted
to mean that no medical medication or surgery can be undertaken
without the patient's "informed consent." If then nothing can be
done to her body without her consent, can it not be assumed that
she has the right to determine whether she will permit her body to

be used as a means of sustenance for any other life?[12]   The terms
of the debate frequently turn on whether the embryonic or fetal life
within her also has inviolable rights to life.   It may be argued
that the life within, for all practical purposes during the early
weeks of pregnancy, is to be recognized in a special way as being
a part of her own body or such a primitive form of life as to be
without the values we ascribe to born persons and the rights our
society has conferred upon its citizens.

Since the pregnant woman's full humanity and personhood
are not in question, her inalienable right to "life, liberty, and
the pursuit of happiness" could only be denied by people who could
establish that their rights as persons were being violated by her
decision to abort.[13]   The undisputed recognition of her humanity
contrasts sharply with the widely admitted problematic nature of
the personhood of the embryo or fetus.   This difference requires
that the political debate always be pursued in relation to her
"nearly absolute value" as a person who enjoys inalienable rights
under the United States Constitution.   Therefore any maneuver which
would remove her from the central position in the debate over abortion would seem to be a denial of her previously acknowledged primacy - biologically, psychically, and now legally.

In terms of the Christian tradition her responsibility to
make moral choices must be viewed as the proper exercise of her
freedom within the community of faith.   While her conscience does
not function in a moral vacuum, her choices in matters of such personal intimacy as her own sexual and reproductive life once again
require that she remain central in the decision-making process.
Such a recognition does not imply that she enjoys absolute and final
authority over all decisions relative to her life as a person, or,
in this instance, as a pregnant person.   Such a presumption would
deny the social nature of our life as human beings before God and
each other.   What this essay hopes to show is that, despite this
qualification, there are times when persons do have a nearly absolute and final right to determine what shall happen to them.   This
apparent ambiguity hopefully can be resolved as we move into an
examination of the developmental nature of human life.

Defining Abortion

Abortion is not as unambiguous as many assume.   The classic
definition of abortion is that it is the spontaneous or intentional
emptying of the female uterus of embryonic or fetal life sometime
after fertilization and usually before the beginning of the third
trimester of pregnancy.

The United States Supreme Court used the word "abortion"
to describe the termination of any pregnancy between fertilization
and normal full-term delivery.   Regretfully the Court based its
definition on a relatively narrow medical tradition since most
medical opinion would use the word "abortion" to designate a procedure, either spontaneous or induced, only between fertilization
and the beginning of the third trimester.   After the fetus has
reached a weight of approximately 900 grams, or arrived at the stage

of human viability, any action to separate fetal life from maternal
life has normally been undertaken with the intent of sustaining the
life of both the woman and the newly delivered child.[14] Such procedures have been classified as "intentional induction" or an "induced delivery" of a premature or immature child or as a Cesarean
section. Responsible physicians and hospitals have presumed that
such procedures would be undertaken only under the most extraordinary circumstances for what were judged to be medically compelling
reasons.[15]
     Again, no person's rights are absolute under all circum-
stances. By virtue of the developing pregnancy a woman's rights
are increasingly circumscribed both morally and legally, and in each
case the degree of limitation is directly related to the time frame
of the pregnancy. While the Supreme Court noted the distinction
between the beginning and the end of pregnancy, most partisans to
the controversy have never taken the developmental character of
pregnancy with sufficient seriousness to clarify the problem.

Birth Control - Contraception and Abortion

     Let us now turn to the time period just prior to preg-
nancy and carry our inquiry through the first few weeks, totally
within the first trimester. Within the Protestant Christian and
Jewish communities there are only a very few people who would deny
a woman the right to use birth control methods of her choice to
order the biological processes within her own body. Few would argue
that it is not morally and medically acceptable to use an IUD to
prevent the implantation of an already fertilized egg in the wall
of the uterus, though it must be admitted that many people "don't
want to know how an IUD works" lest they find themselves practicing
a birth control method which is inconsistent with their anti-
abortion stand! Few would object either morally or legally to a
woman taking provera or stilbestrol following a rape in order to
prevent having an unwanted child. Since there would be no way of
knowing whether fertilization had actually taken place, many would
rationalize the use of these drugs as permissible, "because there
is no way of knowing." These people apparently presume that there
is moral virtue in not knowing, which would be removed if the action
were based upon knowing that fertilization had indeed taken place.
     The Pill, as it is commonly called, is another pharmaceu-
tical medication which prevents child-birth. Its three modes of
operation are, first, it controls the female reproductive cycle in
such a way as to prevent an ovum from being released into the fal-
lopian tubes where fertilization might take place during coitus.
Secondly, it thickens the cervical mucus so as to impede the passage of the male sperm through the cervix into the uterus. Thirdly,
it alters the lining of the uterus so as to make implantation of
any egg that *might* have become fertilized impossible.[16] It is the
third function of the Pill which makes its birth control properties
somewhat ambiguous. Strict adherents to only pure contraceptives
would rather not know that the Pill acts, in part, as an abortifa-
cient along with the IUD, provera, and stilbestrol. Calculated

ignorance, it may be noted, is often used as a licence for many
actions in areas far removed from the problems of sexual and reproductive health.

In any case few Protestant Christians and Jews would prohibit on legal grounds or be critical on moral principle of women
who choose to control their reproductive life with any of these
mechanical or pharmaceutical birth control measures. More importantly, most Protestant Christians and Jews would regard any interference by the state or condemnation by the community of their
choice of controls as an unwarranted intrusion into their private
lives. However, though the courts have declared these choices to
be outside of the interests of the state, some people would insist
that there is a significant moral distinction between those birth
control measures that are pre-conceptive and those that are post-
conceptive.17

Yet despite the availability of most of these methods,
failures do occur and women become pregnant either because of a
technical failure in the device or medication,or a human failure in
the proper use of a method. If pregnancy does occur under these
circumstances, what now are the options?

While the pregnant woman has only two options at this
point, either to continue the pregnancy or to terminate it, the process by which she arrives at either of these decisions has both
moral and legal implications. Morally she cannot pretend that it
is only *her* concern. It must be remembered that she became pregnant
as a consequence of a relationship with another human being, therefore as she decides what to do, she must weigh the interests and,
hopefully, the loving concern of her partner. If she is a person
who has other children, their interests must be weighed. To argue
that there are other interests beyond her own, however, does not
imply that any of the others are overriding, but only that her life
and her perception of her welfare, though primary at this early
stage of pregnancy, are not absolute in the sense of being uncon-
ditioned by any of these or conceivably other considerations.

What frequently happens is that in acknowledging the social
nature of pregnancy people ascribe rights to secondary and tertiary
parties that have the effect of abrogating the pregnant woman's primary rights. The male partner cannot be said to have no rights, but
his rights are clearly not more compelling than hers. To require
mutual consent in the question of abortion is in fact to grant the
right of veto to the male partner, a situation which effectively
denies the right already perceived as primary, namely, the prior
right of the woman *in this time frame* to make the decision as to
whether to continue or terminate her pregnancy.

The italics above would imply that there may be a time
frame when the rights of the woman may not be anywhere near as absolute as those claimed during this period. The Court recognized
this in its provision to allow the states to regulate and even to
prohibit abortions during the third trimester. The Court has been
criticized for making arbitrary distinctions along the line of what
is essentially a biological continuum. The opponents of the Court,
however, are in equal danger of arbitrarily transforming the
changing nature of the developmental process into a static state.

These opponents presume that there are no important differences between a one week embryo and a seven month fetus. It is obvious to
nearly every rational person that there are, beyond genetic con-
stancy, many other differences. The values which are placed on the
aspect of unchangeability (genotype) and the differences (phenotype)
constitute the heart of the controversy.[18] While a person may be
determined by one's genotype in many important ways, the fullness
of human personality is not to be explained by that biological phenomenon alone. To reduce the definition of a human person to a re-
cital of one's biological characteristics is to be unfaithful to
the Genesis insight which affirms that human personality is more
than a biological phenomenon.[19]
        Those who argue that one end of the pregnancy spectrum is
essentially and existentially the same as the other end fall into
two camps. There are those who would argue that since pregnancy is
a medical condition of the woman's body, the right to abort is the
same at eight months as it is at two weeks. Such people are deliberately ignoring the changing reality of the developing life. Paradoxically this position stems from the same methodological mind-
set which argues that the embryo at one day or one week is not to
be distinguished in any important ways from the born child of ten
months. Both approaches attempt to ignore the developmental character of human gestation for the purpose of justifying their own
ideological vested interests.
        If one examines the question of abortion, or induced de-
livery, during the period just prior to the expected date of birth,
the medical, psychic, and social factors are significantly different
from those operating during the first days and weeks of pregnancy.
At birth our society has declared that a born person has rights
which cannot be abrogated by other persons except under extraordinary
circumstances and then only after "due process." In the Christian
community and in the Western world certainly, the state along with
the family are the rightful guardians of the welfare of every born
child.
        The rights of the mother even during this period, however,
remain real. At birth there are rights to life which the state
seeks to guarantee to every born person which may and sometimes do
qualify the rights of the mother. The state, for all the ambiguities
involved, has recently claimed the right to take children away from
their biological parents in situations of gross neglect and incom-
petence.
        The question is frequently asked of those who declare the
humanity of a born child to be nearly inviolable, what about the
status of that same child minutes, hours, days and even weeks prior
to birth? Most thoughtful Christians and Americans would treat the
"about-to-be-born-child" in the same way they would treat a born
child. Few, if any, would say that a seven-month fetus should not
be cared for with the same seriousness one would exercise on behalf
of the new-born at full term.
        This is then to suggest that the pregnant woman toward
the end of her pregnancy and at the time of birth must acknowledge
that her rights of self-determination are increasingly limited by
the claims of "an-about-to-be-born-child." The father, whose

financial resources can be legally attached for the child's support, has an undeniable claim. Likewise the state has an obvious interest in protecting its citizens from those impairments which might affect the new citizen's ability to live as a responsible member of the society and for whose health and maintenance it may be liable if the parents forsake their responsibilities. The hospital and the attending physicians also have obligations to which they must be professionally faithful. For these reasons very few people in the churches or in the society would defend a woman's absolute right to abort anytime she chooses during the pregnancy.

At some point after the fourth month the pregnant woman must come to terms with the reality of otherness which she experiences as the fetal life within her begins to move. Just as the pregnant woman's choices were qualified in the moment she was aware of her pregnancy, now she must acknowledge an even narrower range of options because of the biological process which is rapidly and steadily moving toward the birth of a living human being.

The purpose of this inquiry is to recognize two realities in pregnancy, namely, the nearly absolutely personal nature of the abortion decision in the early weeks of biological development and the increasingly public nature of pregnancy in the closing weeks of gestation. At no time, however, can the pregnant woman's claims to "life, liberty, and the pursuit of happiness" be taken from her, but as the months pass those claims are increasingly limited by the claims of the fetus and of society.

The pregnant woman who has had her values and sensibilities qualified by the Catholic, Protestant, or Jewish communities begins with the assumption that all life is a gift from the Creator. Human life in these traditions is a very special gift in the order of creation, yet most people would not claim that God wills the fusion of any particular ovum and sperm. This does not detract from the very special nature of pregnancy with its sense of wonder and mystery. Because so little has been known about pregnancy, it has been surrounded by superstition, laden with fears, blessed in hope, and - depending upon the situation of the pregnant woman, her family, and the attitudes of society - been celebrated with joy or hidden in fear and shame.

In any case women in our churches and this society have seldom taken the realization of their own pregnancy lightly. With the advances in medical research during the past fifty years, women have been granted increasing control over whether every possible new life would or should be realized. The superabundance of sperm (500,000,000) in each male ejaculation and the life-long release by the female of some 400 ova, suggests to most thoughtful Christians and Jews that God has permitted human planning to determine when and under what conditions new human beings are to be brought into the world.[20]

Persons are more than biological animals. We are creatures not only of our biology, but of our wills, our minds, and our spirits. In Genesis we read that God took the dust of the earth (basar) and breathed into it the breath of life (ruach) and we became living souls (nephesh). Biblically speaking we are not to have our lives shaped by biological necessities, or for that matter by biological accidents, but rather we are to be disciplined and intentional about our lives. In this sense we are to use our minds and hearts to deal responsibly with the biological, emotional, and spiritual possibilities inherent in our sexuality as men and women.

The question then emerges with particular poignancy, what does it mean for human beings to "deal responsibly" with these reproductive possibilities and probabilities inherent in our sexuality? Too often in discussing birth control and abortion, there is an assumption that there is only one moment when we are required to be responsible, and that moment for many people is in the act of coitus. After that moment some protagonists would pretend that human beings and particularly women, have no responsibility other than to let "nature take its course." A sense of human responsibility cannot be anchored to one point in time, rather it is a continuous response to the changing conditions of life. Corrective action is presumed to be required whenever a mistake is made - whether one is driving an automobile on a slippery highway or engaged in scientific experiments. Being responsible is not a once and for all response to life, but rather a continuous response to all of life's changes. Why then do so many people in the discussion about abortion respond to a young woman seeking a termination of her pregnancy, "If she hadn't wanted to get pregnant why did she engage in coitus in the first place!" The hypocrisy is everywhere apparent since most people most of the time enter into sexual intimacies not for procreation but as an expression of love and affection, or, on occasion, for the sheer release of biological passion.

Being responsible morally is trying to respond to all the factors in a given situation, seeking to do the right and the good thing wherever possible under the given circumstances. Sometimes it means taking corrective action; sometimes it means moving along with the action already underway, but in any case human beings are not presumed to be acting responsibly when they arbitrarily say to life, "Let nature take its course." Nature's course may bless or curse life; nature's way is frequently the way of death. The idealization of nature is as unwarranted as its damnation. Not to care about ecology is to be irresponsible with respect to God's creation, but to believe that everything that is natural, biologically and physically, is both right and good - either in terms of the whole creation or for the human enterprise - is naive and in some instances an act of irresponsibility. To whom are we ultimately responsible? The Biblical tradition teaches us that we are ultimately responsible to the One who is nature's creator and our own.

Dealing responsibly with our sexual and reproductive possibilities at the very least presumes that they be consistent with our understanding of what the New Testament calls "the Kingdom of God." The Kingdom of God, for whatever else it may mean, points to a quality of relationships between people in which such words as love, concern, thoughtfulness, tenderness, forgiveness, justice, and helpfulness are not strangers. While this is not the place to set forth a philosophical framework within which to understand human sexuality and reproduction, we can probably agree that they are to be used to enhance our personal and social life.

When both the personal and public aspects of pregnancy are fully appreciated, the abortion debate inevitably moves into a more creative area of discourse where the moral ambiguities facing the pregnant woman and the society can hopefully be dealt with in a legal framework that protects the inalienable constitutional rights of the pregnant woman and the rights of society to care for its born and about-to-be-born children.

It must be granted that in allowing the pregnant woman to decide what to do about her pregnancy during the early weeks of her awareness she may choose a course of action which others would reject. She may act out of too narrow a vision of her self-interest; she may act precipitously out of fear; she may neglect to take into consideration all of the important medical, family, personal, and psychological factors that she ought to. All of this may be true, but she must run the risk, and society can afford to take the risk of her making a mistake.

The clergy, who for many years prior to 1973 were involved in consulting with women about their decisions, soon discovered that an adequate reason to one person frequently seemed inadequate to another. This experience persuaded them that there was no way for an uninvolved party to make the choice for the one who was involved. Questions could be raised, alternatives explored, but finally the responsibility to choose belonged to the pregnant woman herself.

The difficulty of arriving at a good and right decision even in the context of compassionate counseling suggests the nearly impossible probability of arriving at a just and viable decision through the legal process. Laws governing the patterns of sexual intimacy between consenting adults in private have proven to be impossible to enforce and when they are enforced their capricious nature is self-evident.[21] The fact that no society has ever been able to outlaw early abortions because of the private nature of the procedure should suggest that the present effort to overturn the Supreme Court's ruling is futile and unwise. Futile, not because an amendment might not be passed, but because neither the states nor the Federal Government could stop abortions; and unwise because a law prohibiting abortions would result in forcing women to take desperate actions without the assistance of qualified physicians which would be injurious to their health, both physically and psychologically.

If a pregnant woman indeed has an inalienable right to "life, liberty, and the pursuit of happiness," then society cannot be indifferent to the health hazards which would follow if she were denied those rights in matters relating to her own health and welfare.

The group of women who would be most seriously affected, of course, would be the poor. During the 1960's it was estimated that between 200,000 and 1,000,000 abortions were performed annually.[22] In 1974, The United States Center for Disease Control in Atlanta, Georgia declared that there were 763,476 reported abortions performed under medically acceptable circumstances - which is approximately the same number that were performed under highly questionable, illegal medical conditions previously.[23]

While women of means were almost always able to secure safe, though expensive, abortions prior to 1973, the poor were left to their own devices. In Cook County Hospital in Chicago, between 1961 and 1965 there were more than 22,000 women brought into that hospital for emergency treatment because of complications arising from either "spontaneous" or induced abortions. According to Dr. Abraham F. Lash, who was then head of the obstetrical department of the hospital, a conservative estimate would be that at least 75 per cent of those admitted were there because of self-induced or criminally induced abortions.[24]

As a matter of distributive justice such inequities cannot be tolerated if we are really concerned with the welfare of pregnant women. Since 1973, the number of people brought into the emergency rooms of the nation's hospitals for similar complications has dropped dramatically to the point where such injuries no longer constitute a statistically significant health problem.[25]

Toward a Consensus

It is hoped that the primary concern of all parties to this controversy is that persons be free to make moral choices, free from governmental interference, which do not impinge upon the constitutional rights of others. And in the public realm, it is hoped that citizens of the United States shall continue to be guaranteed the constitutional rights to life, liberty, and the pursuit of happiness. Beginning with these fundamental principles, the following are proposed to mitigate, if not resolve, the present controversy over abortion.

First: Because of the highly personal nature of decisions related to human sexuality and reproduction, unless there are consequences of those decisions that impinge upon the rights of others and the good order of society, the state should not intervene.

Second: Since birth control is primarily a personal and familial decision protected by public law and sanctioned by the majority of Jewish and Christian moral theologians, laws that are contrary to such fundamental moral judgments should not be enacted. It must also be recognized that within the concept of birth control there are no longer any easy distinctions between abortion and contraception, though, of course, there are distinctions between surgical abortions and the widely used pharmaceutical and mechanical birth control measures presently available.

Third: Despite the genetic sameness from fertilization through adulthood, the biological development of human life, to say nothing of the psychic and spiritual aspects of life, is dependent upon many other factors if gestation is to produce a functioning human person.

Fourth: The values placed on sameness and differences are highly subjective and because of the developmental nature of human gestation there is no single moment that is quantitatively or qualitatively different from the preceding or following moment. Yet there are broad distinctions that all of us can and do make. Because there is an observable difference between a one-week and

344   BELIEF AND ETHICS

two-month embryo and between a two-month embryo and an eight-month
fetus, we need to shape public policies that recognize these distinctions while at the same time protecting the inalienable rights
of the pregnant woman.
        Fifth: We are dealing with issues of life that are im-
bedded in mystery and meanings that for many people are profoundly
religious. What is often obscured by the rhetoric of controversy
is that the religious dimensions cut both ways. There are those
who conscientiously believe that birth control, including an early
surgical abortion, is morally and medically acceptable and indeed
in many instances imperative, as well as those who believe with
equal ferver that pharmaceutical or mechanical birth control measures, and especially including surgical abortions, are a violation
of God's intention for the human community.
        Recognizing these differences in a free society where,
insofar as possible, the individual conscience should not be coerced,
the wisest and most prudent public policies would seem to be those
that would maximize the rights of the pregnant woman during the
first months of pregnancy and only limit those rights during the
latter weeks of gestation where necessary to protect the welfare
of the about-to-be-born child.
        The Supreme Court essentially took this position in 1973.
However, the Court regarded only the period during the third trimester as the time frame within which the society at large could
claim any compelling interest in the developing life. This position
tended to ignore the biological difficulty of determining the exact
time of viability and underestimated the degree to which this medical imprecision offended the sensibilities of large segments of
the population.
        It is therefore in the interest of seeking a legal con-
sensus despite the unresolved moral differences, that the Supreme
Court's judgment relative to the first trimester ought to be accepted by all as a prudent way of protecting the inalienable rights
of the pregnant woman and the religious liberty of those denominations which believe an early surgical abortion is morally and medically acceptable.[26]
        However, in recognition of the deep cleavages in our
society over the moral appropriateness of abortion at any time, a
viable public policy might well be to permit an abortion after the
first trimester only when there is evidence that it is necessary
for the mental and physical health of the pregnant woman, including
such factors as rape, or when it is ascertained that there is a
serious deformity of the fetus.
        The law should also provide that whenever it becomes
necessary to separate fetal life from maternal life after twenty
weeks of gestation, the procedure, whenever reasonable and possible,
should be undertaken with a view to protecting and sustaining the
life of both the pregnant woman and the fetus. Such a law should
further prescribe that all reasonable medical measures be taken to
insure the continuing life and health of the delivered child consistent with acceptable medical practice.
        Such a compromise would respect the moral indignation of
many citizens who are disturbed by the possibility that now exists

of aborting viable fetuses on or around the twenty-fourth week of
gestation, yet at the same time it would allow women the unlimited
right to decide for or against an abortion during the first trimester.

Such a policy would recognize that since there is no way
to detect an early pregnancy unless the woman herself discloses the
fact voluntarily, and since an induced abortion is a simple procedure during the early weeks, it has the advantage of withdrawing
the law in principle from proscribing what in practice cannot be
prevented. However, since second trimester abortions normally require hospitalization because of the high risks involved, it is
possible and practicable for society to regulate the conditions and
the provisions under which the procedures may be done.[26]

At the present time more than 85 per cent of all intentional abortions are performed before the end of the twelfth week
of gestation, many weeks prior to viability.[27] This suggests that
if the public health agencies, the churches, Planned Parenthood
Associations, and other community agencies would engage in an effective educational campaign to inform people of the medical advis-
ability of early abortions, this percentage could be dramatically
increased, thus effectively eliminating abortions after the first
trimester. Furthermore, if such groups would urge the use of medically effective pharmaceutical and mechanical birth control measures, even early surgical abortions could be substantially eliminated. The paradox is that those religious groups which are most
vehement against surgical abortions are the very groups that have
resisted the public dissemination of other birth control information,
thus aggravating the very problem they themselves apparently abhore.

While most people would agree that early, safe, and effective pharmaceutical measures to prevent pregnancy are to be preferred to those measures of intervention that function only after
pregnancy has begun, such decisions should not be matters of public
law, but rather of moral choice. The 1975 effort to push a Constitutional Amendment through the Congress was worded so that it would
have effectively outlawed provera, stilbesterol, the intra-uterine
devices, and probably the combination pill on the grounds that all
of these were either partially or entirely post-fertilization birth
control measures. The famous Buckley amendment declared that the
states would have the power "to protect human life at all stages
of its biological development." The amendment was carefully and
cleverly worded so as to make it possible to outlaw all post-
fertilization interference in the process of human gestation. Only
by obscuring the real scope of this amendment would it have had any
possibility of passing either the Congress or the state legislatures.

Despite the intensity of the present debate and its chill-
ing effect on ecumenical relationships in the United States, the
basic elements of the popular debate will undoubtedly be altered
within the next decade. Early surgical abortions will be largely
unnecessary as pharmaceutical advances are made to control fertilization and pregnancy.[28] Whether these new medications will be
effective as pre-fertilization or post-fertilization controls will
make little difference to the majority of American women who have
already accepted a number of post-fertilization controls.

It should be noted that those who seek to use the power of government to mandate that every pregnancy be taken to full term need to be aware that governmental action in this area of our personal lives can easily be turned against those who now urge its involvement. If the state and not the person regulates human procreation what is to prevent the state from deciding who shall be sterilized? Insofar as possible and for as long as possible, it would seem that the wisest and most prudent public policy would be to leave questions of birth control and abortion, during the early weeks of pregnancy, to the private conscience of the people rather than permit such matters to be regulated by our state legislatures and courts.

It is with these private and public concerns in mind that the churches and the other institutions of society should reach an accommodation on the abortion issue as speedily as possible. Other problems in the rapidly developing fields of biology and medicine have profound implications for the future of humanity and are being largely neglected because of the continuing polemics surrounding the abortion issue. The nightmare of 1984 can only be avoided if we begin to think now with new seriousness about the meaning and significance of these scientific and technological possibilities. Whether human wisdom can enlist technology in the cause of enriching our life together, or whether technology will embrace all wisdom and values into itself, remains the unanswered question of the twenty-first century.

NOTES AND REFERENCES

1. Supreme Court of the United States, No. 70-18, *Jane Roe et al., Appellants vs. Henry Wade*. On appeal from the United States District Court for the Northern District of Texas. January 22, 1973. (Washington, D.C.: U.S. Government Printing Office). Supreme Court of the United States, No. 70-40, *Mary Doe et al., Appellants vs. Arthur K. Bolton, as Attorney General of the State of Georgia, et al.* On appeal from the United States District Court for the Northern District of Georgia. January 22, 1973. (Washington, D.C.: U.S. Government Printing Office).

2. Arlene Carmen and Howard Moody, *Abortion Counseling and Social Change*, (Valley Forge Pa.: Judson, 1973), p. 72. In April 1970, the New York State Legislature by a margin of one vote passed the Cooke/Leichter Abortion Reform Bill.

3. *Chicago Sun Times*, Wednesday, February 14, 1973; *National Catholic Reporter*, February 16, 1973; "Only a constitutional amendment can stop the flood of abortions," by John T. Noonan, Jr.

4. Testimony of the Roman Catholic Cardinals before the U.S. Subcommittee on constitutional amendments: "We wish to make it clear that we are not seeking to impose the Catholic moral teaching regarding abortion on this country...but a just law cannot be opposed to moral teaching based on God's law."

5. Britannica *Junior Encyclopedia*, Ed. 1963, vol.4, p. 457. Constitution of the United States (December 15, 1791) Amendment 1.

6. Winthrop S. Hudson, *American Protestantism* (Chicago: The University of Chicago Press, 1961), p. 62ff.

7. Pastoral Letter of the Archdiocese of Chicago issued by the Archdiocesan Office for Pro-Life Activities, Chicago, Illinois, September 13, 1976. Press release, March 10, 1976, Religious Coalition for Abortion Rights, citing Bishop James Armstrong, United Methodist Church, and Rabbi Balfour Brickner, Director of the New York Federation of Reform Synagogues in support of the legal option of abortion on grounds of religious liberty and social justice.

8. George Anastaplo, *Human Being and Citizen* (Chicago, Illinois: Swallow Press, 1975), p. 87.

9. H. Richard Niebuhr, *The Responsible Self* (New York: Harper and Row, 1963), p. 44.

10. Bishop Francis J. Mugavero, Brooklyn, New York, Pastoral Letter, published in *Catholic Mind*, May 1976, p. 53-58.

Sexuality is one of God's greatest gifts to man and woman...it is that aspect of personhood which makes us capable of entering into loving relationships with others. Theology teaches that relationship - the gift of oneself to another - is at the very heart of God.

11. *Britannica Junior Encyclopedia*, Ed. 1963, vol. 4, p. 457.Constitution of the United States (December 15, 1791) Amendment 4: "The right of the people to be secure in their persons...shall not be violated."

12. Judith Thomson, "A Defense of Abortion," *Philosophy and Public Affairs*. vol. 1, No. 1 (Fall 1971), 47-66.

13. *Britannica Junior Encyclopedia*, Ed. 1963, vol. 5, p. 43 Declaration of Independence of the United States - In Congress July 4, 1776,

...all men are created equal, that they are endowed by their Creator with certain unalienable Rights, that among these are Life, Liberty, and the pursuit of Happiness.

14. Joseph Swartwout, Director, Out-patient Services, Chicago Lying-In Hospital, University of Chicago (Public Statement).

15. *Ibid*.

16. James Leslie McCary, *Human Sexuality*, 2nd Ed. (New York: D. Van Nostrand Co.), p. 242.

17. Msgr. James McHugh, Secretary for pro-life affairs at the National Conference of Catholic Bishops, Washington, D.C. "Civil Law and Christian Morality, Abortion and the Churches," *Conversations*, Summer 1975; published by Graymoor Ecumenical Institute, Garrison, New York 10524.

18. Paul Ramsey, *The Fabricated Man* (New Haven: Yale University Press, 1970).

19. *Genesis* 1 : 7 (basar + ruach = nephesh).

20. *Op. cit.*, James Leslie McCary, pp. 38 and 79.

21. *Ibid.*, p. 457ff.

22. Daniel Callahan, *Abortion: Law, Choice, and Morality* (New York: The Macmillan Co., 1970), p. 132ff.

23. U.S. Department of Health, Education and Welfare, *Abortion Surveillance 1974*(published by the Center for Disease Control, Atlanta, Georgia: April 1976.)

24. *Transactions of the American Association of Obstetrics and Gynecology*, vol. LXXIX, 1968, p. 110-123. Subsequent interview with Dr. Lash by Dr. Ronald Hammerle, December 5, 1968.

25. Joseph Swartwout, Director of Out-patient Services, Chicago Lying-in Hospital, University of Chicago, Judgment based on public health records: California, New York, and Illinois.

348   BELIEF AND ETHICS

26. *Op. cit.*, Daniel Callahan, p. 32, 33.

27. U.S. Department of Public Health, Education and Welfare, *Abortion Surveillance*, Center for Disease Control, April 1976, p. IV.

28. Frederick Zuspan, formerly Chairman, Department of Obstetrics and Gynecology at Chicago Lying-in Hospital, University of Chicago, presently at Ohio State University. Statement made in connection with a series of seminars at the University of Chicago Medical School analyzing the progress of prostaglandin research at the Karolinska Institute, Stockholm, Sweden.

WHITE BELIEF, MORAL REASONING, SELF-INTEREST AND RACISM

by
Robert W. Terry

Introduction

Alvin Pitcher is a dedicated and practicing anti-racist. His personal odyssey is one that many of us paralleled, as together we sought fresh approaches to combat and limit the dehumanizing effects of white racism on both minorities and whites.

This essay is in honor of Pitcher's quest for racial justice. I hope that it will further that quest through an examination of white self-interest as it is shaped by structures of belief and levels of moral reasoning.

The essay will be divided into six sections: I. A Social Puzzle, II. Focus and Thesis, III. Structures of Belief, IV. Levels of Moral Reasoning, V. Implications for Research and Action, VI. Self-Interest.

I. A Social Puzzle

Over the last two decades, studies of white attitudes toward minorities have shown a dramatic reduction in racial prejudice. Yet analyses of institutional discrimination reveal a significant lag.[1]

Conventional wisdom that suggests white attitudinal changes result in institutional changes appears questionable at best.[2]

What we are experiencing today is a much more complicated and subtle treatment of racial ideas and a possible institutional drift back toward the fifties.[3]

Recent court rulings on "reversed discrimination" cases fuel white male perception that being a white male is now a handicap in employment opportunities. The Supreme Court is retreating from earlier decisions on "proof of intent," versus "proof of effect," in discrimination cases. There is a return to the earlier, less effective proof of intent which, because of the complexity of issues, is almost impossible to prove with certainty.

Added to this litany are the continual controversies about "forced busing," "forced housing," the difficulty in finding and promoting "qualified minorities," fear of street crime gangs, drugs, welfare cheaters and delinquency. Except in the cases of busing and reverse discrimination, color and/or race is rarely mentioned.

349

Yet just below the surface there is the suspicion - are the issues
at bottom racial?
Thus, it seems many whites have retreated to a safer posture, bent on preserving traditional cultural and social institutions
and power arrangements - be they community schools, traditional employment standards, or neighborhood cultural integrity. Confounding
and perhaps even further obscuring the picture is the as yet unknown
impact of the Carter administration on racial progress.
Thus, it appears, to focus an essay on white belief and
moral reasoning and white self-interest in combating racism comes
at a propitious time. White passivity and institutional drift are
dangerous trends. What will it take to mobilize white energy for
anti-racist struggle? That question is one of Pitcher's abiding
concerns,and it is also one for all of us who seek ways to neutralize,
control, and eliminate white racism's effect on all people.

II. Focus and Thesis

No treatment of whites and self-interest can hope to do
justice to the complexities of the subject in one brief essay. Thus
I have narrowed the focus to two cultural dimensions that are crucial
in understanding the social puzzle. One is the *structure of belief*,
the culturally shared mind-sets that orient people to understand
their self-interest; the other is the *stages of moral reasoning*, the
structure and process of moral thinking that is used to justify their
self-interest.
The analysis of structure of belief builds on my own reflections on alternative contemporary theories clarified over the
last eight years working with whites. The analysis of stages of moral
reasoning draws on the pioneering work of Lawrence Kohlberg, Professor
of education and social psychology at Harvard University.
There are many problems with current attitude studies of
whites that a structural analysis of belief can overcome. A critical
one has to do with the type of questions asked. Many of the studies
examine particular responses to particular issues. Angus Campbell's
report on *White Attitudes toward Black People*[4] looks at white views
of interracial contacts, racial discrimination, sympathy with black
protest, and other current social issues. As important as this information is, it does not help us to understand the mind-set or
consciousness that fits the pieces of racial perception together.
Thus, when such studies report progress in white racial attitudes,
they may be measuring a shift from one racist belief to another.
Whites may be developing a more sophisticated means of rationalizing
the racist system. Hence, there exists little new basis to press
for societal anti-racist changes.
When an analysis of the structures of belief is coupled
with an analysis of the structures and processes of moral reasoning,
the picture of whites and self-interest becomes even clearer. Two
whites may agree that housing discrimination is wrong. But they may
do so for very different reasons. These are the reasons that are
important in this essay, not their content *per se*. It is the level
and form of the reasoning process that will directly affect how

whites perceive the moral significance of a given racial situation
and predispose them to act in a particular way.[5]
     In this essay self-interest is being used very broadly to
mean a state of affairs in which the actor, be it a person or key
actors in an organization, decides that short or long term benefits
outweigh the liabilities when pursuing a given course of action.
Self-interest is neither narrow selfishness nor expansive selfless-
ness. To fall into either of those traps is to destroy the appropriate balance between care of self and care for others. Regard for
self and regard for others go hand in hand. To only care about self
is to become disconnected and estranged from a supportive community
and thus lose one's collective bearings. To be concerned only about
others is to be absorbed and assimilated into otherness and thus
lose one's individual bearings.

III. Structures of Belief

     All people are meaning creators. We carry around in our-
selves structures of belief or frameworks that help us interpret
our lives. These perspectives may be only partially explicit, consistent, and developed. Nevertheless, they order our experience
and help us understand our participation in life.

A. Racial Supremist Advocate

     Model -- The root organizing notion, as the title implies,
is superiority/inferiority. A superior race is justified in its
position of dominance because of racial advantages, biologically inherited.
     Key Values -- White supremacy is central. Whites as in-
dividuals and as a racial group are obligated to maximize their inheritance. Whites who do not are sometimes called "poor white
trash."
     Mode of Relationship -- Control is the prized mode of
relationship. Physical force is usually viewed as necessary to enforce obedience to supremist values. Terrorism is a last resort if
legal control is thwarted.
     Threat to Values -- Any resistance or challenge to supremist
authority, whereby minorities behave in such a way as to "get out of
their place," is a threat. The action of a single minority person
may be enough to stimulate a hostile retaliatory action.
     Definition of Racism -- Supremists will often say they are
not racist. To be a racist is to hate another race and practice
genocide. Supremists only want obedience to white authority, not
hatred toward or elimination of a race. Everyone has a "place,"
even if a subordinate place.
     Supremist as Racist -- The supremist becomes a racist on
his or her own terms when threatened. Minority resistance can trig-
ger hatred and genocide in the form of harassment, murder, or burning.
If minorities, as individuals or as groups, are "the problem," then
appropriate controlling and/or perhaps violent action is deemed
necessary.
     Contradiction -- there is little if any contradiction be-
tween racial supremacy and genocidal action. At best there is a

contradiction between control and elimination. For some racial
supremists genocide or terrorism goes too far, and such action
creates a personal moral dilemma. The struggle is over means, not
ends. Everyone is guaranteed a place, but that place is eliminated
for minorities.

   *Positive Whites' Self-Interest to Work for Anti-Racist
Change* -- There is little self-interest to combat white racism except
as one argues that willingness to commit physical genocide reveals a
deep mental illness. Such hatred is destructive to the person doing
the hating. Or that the societal counter-reaction would be to violent
   Anti-Racism Direction -- Personality could be viewed as
being so warped and the hatred so deep that some efforts to constrain
and limit that person's behavior would be justified. There would be
no efforts to resist racial discriminatory practices except to limit
physical genocide.

B. FREE MARKET ADVOCATES

   Model -- The free market advocate pictures life as a
series of exchanges between atomistic individuals. Social activity
is explained as the interaction of these individuals in a free
economic and/or political marketplace. Money and votes are the
currency of exchange.

   Economist Milton Friedman, exponent of this point of view,
elaborates the free market ideal:

> In an ideal free market resting on private property, no individual
> can coerce any other, all cooperation is voluntary, all parties to
> such cooperation benefit as they need to participate.[6]

   Key Values -- Two values get emphasized in this model.
The first is individual freedom, meaning action based on inclination,
taste, reason, or whatever the individual desires so long as that
exercise of freedom coerces no other individual or deprives no other
individual of pursuing his or her own taste or desires. The second
is efficient allocation of resources. The free market is the guar-
antor of the most efficient use of resources because through competition the appropriate balance is found between supply and demand.
   Mode of Relationship -- The mode of relationship that is
prized is *competition*. Competition does not imply using any means
to be a victor, rather it implies working within an agreed social
contract that regulates voluntary participation of all members.
Free market advocates at their best resist price fixing or other
anti-free market activities. When those activities happen, it is
appropriate for government through its anti-trust division to restrict such illegal activity.
   Threat to Values -- The major threat to a free market mode
is any center of coercion or monopoly that permits one individual or
group to act with impunity. Any center of coercion or monopoly that
permits one group unilaterally to set the price or determine the
outcome of a particular exchange violates individual freedom and
becomes inefficient. Free market advocates thus propose a strong
national defense to resist centers of coercion abroad and limited
government at home to preserve individual freedom of the citizenry.

Big government is thus both a protection against international invasion and a threat to domestic individual freedom.

Definition of Racism -- Racism is cast primarily in terms of racial prejudice and racial discrimination. Prejudice is often thought of in terms of hate responses of individuals or groups toward other races, and discrimination is the exclusion of groups from access to the resources of the society.

Free Market Advocate as Racist -- The free market advocate becomes a racist as she/he posits the minority as the center of coercion or the monopoly. The American Indian movement, the Black Panthers, or a Chicano "Militant" group get targeted as that agency that is limiting the rights of whites. As a center of coercion such groups must be controlled, punished, and brought under appropriate legal constraint.

The Contradiction -- Free market advocates say they are for freedom for all; they protect the freedom of whites. By misplacing the problem - shifting the focus from white monopoly to minority monopoly - they rationalize a further concentration of power in the FBI, military, and police. The government they supposedly fear is given further power to control the citizenry. Thus advocates of individual freedom end up supporting state control.

Anti-Racist Solution -- The free market advocate does not have to be a racist. He or she can focus on the white monopoly as the center of coercion and strongly advocate and enforce non-discriminatory legislation which will in effect guarantee a free market.

Self-Interest -- Jeffrey Praeger, a careful student of this theory, identifies the self-interest conclusions that flow from this theory:

> From this argument it follows that white employers (capitalists) lose from discrimination and, therefore, it would be in their economic self-interest to end discrimination. White workers, contrary to white employers, gain from discrimination because of inefficient allocation of resources. It is in the workers' economic self-interest that discrimination persists . . . white employers choose on the basis of "taste;" they discriminate in order to maintain physical distance and, subsequently, lose economically. Implicitly, the major economic obstacle to overcoming discrimination . . . is white workers. As white employers overcome their "taste to discriminate," they will be able to operate more efficiently and, thereby, drive discriminating employers out of business. It will be white workers who resist these changes.[7]

C. OPEN SYSTEMS ADVOCATES

Model -- In contrast to the free market advocates who focused on atomistic individuals and their market relationships, open systems advocates start with questions about the whole society. What holds society together? How do so many interacting parts stabilize and go through orderly changes?

The basic model is one of a *body* as an open system. Society, using this analogy of a body, is viewed as a functionally integrated system held in dynamic equilibrium by a number of

responsive institutionalized processes and legitimated by a shared
cultural history. People are born into this system, raised, educated
(socialized) into it, take on its values and thereby contribute to
its functioning. The body as an integrated whole is more than the
sum of its parts.

      Values -- Two values get highlighted in this model. The
first is personal growth, including increased capacity to trust, be
open, communicate. The second is the development of healthy institutions. A healthy institution exists when institutional policies,
practices, and procedures are responsive to individual and group
needs and adaptable to contingent external circumstances.

      Mode of Relationship -- A *consensual* mode of being is the
prized form of relationship. Barbara Jordan's keynote address to
the National Democratic Convention is an example of consensus in
action. The event will be remembered less for what she said than
for the fact that she as a black woman said it. In fact, what she
talked about was the common beliefs that will form a new consensus
for America. She symbolized the healing of the Democratic Party
family. There is often the assumption, in this model, that most if
not all Americans share in the same values and that conflicts arise
from poor socialization processes or mis-communication.

      Threat -- Personal deviance and rigid, unresponsive in-
stitutions are the major threats to the effective functioning of an
open system. Personal deviance occurs when someone is poorly socialized into the main stream of the society, and inflexible and unresponsive institutions do not permit the system to adapt to changing
conditions.

      Definition of Racism -- Racism is defined as mental illness
and/or social sickness. Sometimes one hears racism described as a
social disease, as a cancer in the body politic that requires radical
surgery. Permitted to spread, it can kill the whole body.

      Systems Advocate as Racist -- As with the free market ad-
vocate, the systems advocate focuses on the victim and the victim's
institutions as the primary arena for change. It is the ghettos,
the barrios, and the reservations that need fundamental restructure.
Worry about the socialization process of minority children activates
systems advocates to suggest remedial action, most likely by the
Federal government.

      Rather than look at the dominant system as a carrier of
racism, systems advocates tend to focus on the recipients of the
racism as the problem. The Kerner Commission report, an expression
of this point of view, illustrates this racist orientation. In education, the Report concluded:

> Education in a democratic society must equip children to develop
> their potential and to participate fully in American life. For the
> community at large schools have discharged this responsibility well,
> but for many minorities, and particularly the children of the ghetto,
> the schools have failed to provide the educational experience which
> could have overcome the effects of discrimination and deprivation.[8]

      Contradiction -- Open systems advocates want positive,
personal growth and healthy institutions for all; they end up

perpetuating sickness for all. How does this happen? When the
ghettoized victims are perceived as the "problem," massive Federal
programs are instituted to help "them." Welfare, Head Start, War
on Poverty are just examples. The programs get entangled in an unresponsive bureaucratic mess, and instead of providing the structures
for liberation they create structures that keep people marginally
related to the dominant society. Furthermore, the focus on victims
takes attention away from the state of the health of the dominant
institutions.
     Is it true that schools have discharged this responsibility
well for the community at large? Does it not make more sense to look
at the dominant institutions, particularly religion, education, and
the family, as three of the main carriers of the social disease?
No matter how broad and aggressive a remedial program might be, if
the dominant institutions are not changed, those remedial programs
will continue to have a negligible positive effect. By focusing on
the victims and the victims' institution, systems advocates end up
recommending programs that perpetuate personal and social sickness.
     Anti-Racist Solution -- Open systems analysts can focus on
the dominant institutions and work for their change. This would involve changing the employment practices, standards used for hiring,
developing aggressive affirmative action programs, eliminating the
discrimination in religion, education, and other dominant institutions
of the society. It would mean attending to everyone's personal
growth - the white as well as the minority person.
     Self-Interest -- A welfare society in which supposedly
"healthy whites" paternalistically help the "culturally deprived
minorities" sets in motion a symbiotic relationship that destroys
both parties. As whites try to rescue minorities they often find
themselves being rejected and feeling victimized by the very "victims"
they supposedly were trying to help. Whites then often strike back
and persecute minorities. This persecution reinforces the minority
perception that the whites really did not care in the first place.
White behavior then becomes indistinguishable from the free market
advocates. In like manner, minorities feel victimized by an oppressive and persecuting system and strike back in hostile self-defense.
The spectre of violence is always close at hand, and the violence
becomes a result of the self-fulfilling paternalism that turns people
into victims.
     On Ethnicity -- Open systems advocates tend to be of two
different orientations within the same broad perspective - assimi-
lationists or pluralists. The above was a description of an assimi-
lationist. In contrast, the ethnic argument stresses pluralism.
Eleven years ago Talcott Parsons succinctly stated the pluralistic
case in an article entitled "Full Citizenship for the Negro American."
In it he concluded:

> Near the beginning of this essay, the distinction between inclusion
> and assimilation was stressed. The purport of this latest phase of
> the analysis suggests that to identify non-discrimination (that is,
> inclusion) too strongly with "color blindness" might be to throw
> away a very precious asset, not only for the Negro, but for American
> society as a whole. My own view is that the healthiest line of

development will be not only the preservation, but the actual building up, of the solidarity of the Negro community and the sense that
the Negro has positive value. In the process there is the danger of
cultivating separatism, as most conspicuously exemplified by the
black Muslims. But the pluralistic solution, which has been stressed
throughout this discussion, is neither one of separatism - with or
without equality - nor of assimilation, but one of full participation
combined with the preservation of identity. The American Jewish and
Catholic groups have, by and large, been able to achieve this goal.[9]

The ethnic model is based on the belief that America is
already a highly differentiated structure dispersing power among a
variety of interest groups. Since there is no ruling class or elite,
ethnic groups have the ability to exert political and economic pressure to secure their rightful place in the society. By using block
voting and political machines, and by dominating particular institutions, racial groups can likewise secure their freedom. All
benefit by this diversity.

D. RADICALS AS CLASS AND/OR COLOR ADVOCATES

Model -- The basic model is one of irreconcilable vested
interests. Groups or societal actors are depicted as powerful agents
who can mold the world to their will. And in that control, they exploit oppressed groups for their own narrow advantage. In the literature and the rhetoric the opposing forces are cast as two hier-
archically positioned groups engaged in perpetual struggle: master/
slave, ruling class/working class, white/minority, colonizer/colonized.

Values -- The freedom of oppressed people to be self-
determining as a people and the redistribution of wealth and power
are the core values of this perspective. Changes which fail to address these values are cosmetic at best.

Mode of Relationship -- *Conflict* and *change* are the basic
modes of relationship in this framework. Because the ruling group
may use power unilaterally and distort supposedly legitimated societal values, the only recourse the oppressed have is struggle through
conflict. The powerful do not give up power without a fight, hence
any peaceful overtures by the ruling group or efforts at democratic
transfer of power from the oppressor to the oppressed is viewed with
great suspicion.

Threat -- The major threat to the values of the oppressed
is the unilateral self-determination of the oppressor. Exploitation
and domination stand in direct contrast to the interest and desires
of those who are relatively powerless and vulnerable.

Definition of Racism -- Racism is almost always cast in
power terms, either as exploitation or domination based on color/race.
The extent to which racism is seen as a basic reality in the analysis
depends on whether the radicals are class advocates or operating out
of an anti-neo-colonial perspective. As we proceed with the outline
we will now distinguish the two dominant orientations within the
radical framework. First, the class advocates.

Class Advocates -- Oliver Cox's classic *Caste, Class, and
Race* makes a strong case for the class perspective.[10]

Radical political economist Howard Sherman, in a more recent treatment of racism and class, argues:

The real causes of racist discrimination do not lie in inherent black inferiority (because that is non-existent), nor even in inherent white racism (since that has changed at different times, and can be changed further in the future). The real causes are the institutional relationships that give racism a useful function for ruling, political and economic interests.[11]

Class Advocates as Racists -- Class advocates become racists when the main thrust of organizing is done in exclusively or primarily white-led revolutionary groups. It is also racist when the assumption is made that all minority interests can be identical with white working class interests. That ethnocentrism on the part of radicals leads class advocates to depreciate and discount Hispanic concerns for bi-lingual, bi-cultural education or native American concerns for tribal identity.

Contradiction -- Class advocates who say they are for the freedom and shared power of all people who are oppressed end up advocating for the white oppressed. Failure to distinguish color from class, and see them as interdependent variables, underplays the importance of racism. Then, because power is not really shared across race/color lines, class advocates' racial action becomes paternalistic. They look and act very similar to systems advocates.

Anti-Racist Solutions -- In working for the liberation of all oppressed people, class advocates can form multi-racial cadres with heavy emphasis on minority leadership. Then their focus on the redistribution of power and resources is more likely to guarantee a redistribution across both class and color lines.

Self-Interest -- Taking just the opposite view from the free market advocate, class advocates believe that white workers can be educated to see that their struggle is parallel and similar to that of their minority brothers and sisters. White workers are in common cause with minorities against the exploitation of the ruling class and monopoly capitalism. It is the ruling class, not the workers, who benefit from racism. Sherman summarizes the overall direction of class advocacy:

> Nothing short of a complete change in the system - the abolition of both poles (wealth, privilege, power - poverty, deprivation, powerlessness) and the substitution of a society in which wealth and power are shared by all - can transform from their condition.[12]

Anti-Neo-Colonialism Advocate -- Operating out of the same basic framework as the class advocates, the anti-neo-colonialists argue that the historical and contemporary experience of oppressed people of color in the United States can best be understood if it is analyzed by using the analogy of international colonialization. Minorities inside the United States suffer similar oppression to that endured and resisted by seized colonies. Race in this model is an interdependent variable; it is not reduced to class but accompanies class struggle.[13]

Robert Blauner, well-known white advocate of this perspective, identifies four characteristics of the process: (1) Colonialization begins with forced, involuntary entry of the racial group into dominant society, (2) the colonizing power carries out an intentional policy of constraint, control, or destruction of the racial group's structure and way of life, (3) the colonized group tends to be administered by representatives of the colonizers, (4) the colonizer uses racism as a principle of social control, stressing the biological superiority of one group and the inferiority of the other.[14]

Self-Interest -- In order to understand the contradictions we must first look at the issue for self-interest for whites. For class advocates white workers had a very positive role to play in the struggle against racism and class oppression. For the anti-neocolonist the role of whites is at best vague. From this perspective *all whites* benefit from racism, not just the white ruling class. The benefits may differ depending upon one's class position, but the benefits are real and cause white resistance to change. Whites are relatively freer to pursue their interests than oppressed people of color. For example, in the economic arena, workers and employers gain from racism. Workers benefit because of their monopoly on the job market (agreement with the free market advocate); employers benefit by having a ready pool of easily identifiable workers available for unskilled labor, especially for jobs undesired by whites (agreement with the class advocates).

James Boggs, in his neo-colonial volume *Racism and the Class Struggle*, states it succinctly:

> Theoretically, the Marxists are worse than the liberals . . . the Negro worker who works in the shop knows that if he (*sic*) is going to depend upon the white worker he (*sic*) will never get anywhere. The average white worker today isn't joining any liberal organization . . . for when the Negro fights he (*sic*) fights not "in the last analysis" - i.e., not according to the thought patterns of the Marxists - but *in reality*. His enemy is not just class . . . his enemy is people, and the people are American whites of all classes, including workers.[15]

Contradiction -- Since all whites benefit from racism, whites cannot be trusted to have the commitment or wisdom to lead American society out of its morass. Third world leadership, domestic and international, is essential. Racism and capitalism have concentrated people of color in ghettos, barrios, reservations and forced them to deepen or create their own cultural values and life styles and, in the process, sensitized them to the inhumanity of the system. Whites caught up in the system have lost the power to see evil in their midst. They are trapped. At best, white revolutionaries become an auxiliary force in the struggle. Any unilateral white action will probably end up perpetuating racism. Whites need constant monitoring or at least periodic supervision.

This suspicion of all whites creates a contradiction. The supposed liberators who are seeking to overthrow the oppressive superiority-inferiority system have created a language and analysis to perpetuate a new one. Now the superior group is the oppressed who because of its new sensitivities is justified in leading the former oppressors. Does greater sensitivity of the oppressed condition

inevitably lead to effective and more humane leadership? Paulo
Freire in *Pedagogy of the Oppressed*[16] worries out loud that the
oppressed will imitate the oppressor unless there is a cultural
transformation of the oppressed mind-set and the oppressive culture.
        Anti-Racist Solution -- A sophisticated interdependent
balance of race and class is crucial for understanding the American racial experience. Coupled with a cultural transformation, an
anti-neo-colonial model becomes one of the most powerful analytic
tools available to understand the impact of and functioning of white
racism.[17] Solutions press toward an international agenda of power
and resource distribution led by Third World countries.[18]

E. NEW CULTURAL ADVOCATES

        Model -- The basic model in this framework builds on
meaning and symbol. The term culture itself, like any fundamental
concept, has been defined in numerous ways. Internationally known
cultural anthropologist Clifford Geertz suggests a definition that
is useful for the purposes of this essay. For him, culture:

> Denotes an historically transmitted pattern of meanings embodied in
> symbols, a system of inherited conceptions expressed in symbolic forms
> by means of which men (*sic*) communicate, perpetuate and develop their
> knowledge about and attitudes toward life.[19]

        Meaning refers to the broad context used to understand one-
self in any given situation. Most people live out of a "taken for
granted" existence. Very little of reality is doubted or questioned.
Patterns of interpretation of the past provide guides to interpret
the present and anticipate the future.
        Meaning is carried through symbols. Again, following
Geertz's lead, symbol will be defined as:

> Any object, act, event, quality or relation which serves as a vehicle
> for a conception - the conception is the symbol's meaning . . . the
> number of "six" written . . . laid out in a row of stones, or even
> punched into the program of a computer is a symbol but so is the
> Cross . . . They're all symbols, or at least symbolic elements, be-
> cause they are tangible formulations of notions, abstractions from
> experience fixed into perceptible forms, concrete embodiments of
> ideas, attitudes, judgments, longings or beliefs.[20]

        Symbols are public and shared. But symbols are not iden-
tical with social events. Reading about skiing is not the same thing
as skiing. Symbols provide cognitive maps both to understand what
is and anticipate and project what might be.
        Key Values -- New culture advocates value a transformation
of contemporary meanings and symbols so that they can provide comprehensive and effective maps for recovering the essential strengths
of the past and coping with the future. Put in other terms, this
perspective values significant directing purpose, purpose that helps
people make sense out of their lives and directs them so that they
can be fully functioning individuals.
        Mode of Relationship -- It is difficult to characterize
the mode of relationship that is prized by culture advocates. How-

ever, I have found a pattern in those people who are redefining significant purpose. It is a *confounding* mode. Just when someone
thinks that he or she has understood a given event, a new cultural
advocate will give a fresh definition and will confound the conversation. There may be a debate around the meaning of oppression
and the struggle of being oppressed. A new culture advocate might
suggest that what needs to be examined is the nature and functioning
of the oppressor. The debate has been confounded. It is through
confounding the old model and maps that one breaks through to new
insight and direction.

   Threat -- Meaninglessness and the breakdown of viable symbols is the major threat to the values of this framework. Meaninglessness occurs when the "recipes of the past," to use Alfred
Schutze's felicitous phrase, no longer order experience so that it
can be grasped, understood, and lived comfortably. One gets dis-
oriented and confused. Meaninglessness usually occurs when the symbols no longer carry the culture's directing purpose. Heroes cease
to provide direction, religious symbols fail to convey an understanding of life, citizens become adrift and rootless.

   Definition of Racism -- Racism is the imposition of one
ethnocentric culture on the culture of a different racial group. It
is crucial to understand another culture. It is just as crucial *not*
to assume the superiority of one's own culture and require people of
other cultures to be absorbed by the imposing group's culture.

   New Culture Advocate as Racist -- New culture advocates
become racist when they ignore or discount the impact of color as
an important ingredient in any new cultural redefinition of the future.
Futurists, for example, who tantalize us with different pictures of
the next decade, often end up perpetuating racial stereotypes.
Through neglect, they fail to propose new symbols to carry new racial
identities and thus end up perpetuating the prevailing culture.
Theodore Roszak's latest book *Where the Wasteland Ends*[21] gives scant
attention to any necessity to wrestle with racism as a fundamental
reality in the culture of post-industrial society.

   Contradiction -- The extent to which new culture advocates
fail to address the impact of white racism on Western and particularly American culture is the extent to which they will most likely
perpetuate their own ethnocentrism. Thus those seeking to find
liberation from ethnocentrism end up captive to a more sophisticated
and subtle cultural prison.

   Anti-Racist Solutions -- A number of new cultural advocates
have taken a color conscious perspective. A few include Winthrop
Jordan, George Fredrickson, Vernon Dixon, Betty Foster, Joel Kovel,
and myself.[22]

   Each author develops two broad lines of argument. First,
no one can be free unless he or she understands the intrinsic character of the meaning of color. Second, no one can be free unless he
or she builds a social and personal identity that is positively color
conscious, a consciousness that transcends past negative definitions
of color and builds an identity that is self-affirming.

   Self-Interest -- Fundamentally, white self-interest in this
perspective is rooted in the personal desire for more complete fulfillment. Some doubt may be raised about the adequacy of a person's

present framework for understanding what is happening in terms of race, and/or some question may arise about one's ability to handle some question of race. Whites often find that, at the cultural level, minority persons have a better grasp of themselves and a clearer sense of their identity than do whites. This challenge might be enough to encourage whites to take a fresh look at white identity.

This quest for a new white identity takes place in the larger quest for a new human identity amidst a high technological order. The coupling of this general quest with a new white quest becomes a powerful tool, a fresh source of energy motivating an increasingly large number of whites to seek new meaning and symbols to carry forward new ways to affirm whiteness that are neither racist nor inhumane.

F. ACTIVE EMERGENT PLURALIST ADVOCATE

Model -- Energy is the root metaphor in this model. Interpersonal, inter-group, and societal relationships are perceived as exchanges of energy. The model draws heavily on the theory development of Amitai Etzioni in his work *The Active Society*. The model seeks to account for the capacity to act. It draws on the language of symbols and objects as these have energy correlates. "Symbols gain a role in social action," writes Etzioni:

> precisely because they are "energized" - commands psychic and social resources, including control of objects. Objects, in turn, can be readily viewed as forms of stored energy which can be released and thus transformed into social action . . . societal units, may be viewed as containing an unprocessed energy; following activation, which entails the transformation of these units, this energy is available for kinetic usages, for social action. The processed energy available to any one unit may be channeled (or committed) to alternative societal usages . . . Cost is used to refer to the loss of kinetic energy, the result of prolonged storage (i.e., inaction), flow to another unit, or consumption by alternative actions of the same units. Both the realization of societal goals and the activation of units consume energy; at the same time, one of the major goals to which the energy can be committed is the attainment of additional resources from which energy can be derived, or to the change of the existing patterns of allocation and thus to the shifting of commitment.[23]

The model then focuses on groups or collectivities as the primary actors in the society which marshal resources by the use of power through structured relationships toward the attainment of long and short term goals.

Key Values -- A key value is *active authenticity*. To be actively authentic requires at least four dimensions of the self to be in place:
1. Adequate resources to move beyond survival existence.
2. Ability to be self-determining and centered for decision-making.
3. Supportive community and institutional support.
4. Positive self-affirming identity.
When any of these four - resources, power, community and identity - become problematic manipulative games quickly take over.[24]

What then would be the characteristics of an authentic society, since a person is only a person in a community of persons? Again, four dimensions: (1) equitable (not necessarily equal) distribution of resources so that differences as well as similarities of needs and wants can be met, (2) shared power so that decision-making is not located in elites, (3) flexible and responsive institutional practices and procedures so that society can support a variety of community interests, (4) cultural pluralism so that the emerging new identities of individuals and groups have room to develop and mature.

Systems advocates suggest minorities can follow ethnic patterns in their own development within the United States. Emergent pluralists disagree. For the latter, white racism is so pervasive that the white ethnic route is not a duplicable route for people of color. A cultural transformation more pervasive than suggested by systems advocates is essential. New identities must be carved out, must emerge, especially for whites if pluralism is to thrive.

Mode of Relation -- The prize mode of relationship is one of *collaboration*. It is through collaboration that energy gets marshalled toward the attainment of goals. In the long term collaboration, in contrast to competition for example, is more likely to bring out the creative resources of the society.

Threat to Values -- The main threat to the value of active authenticity is passive inauthenticity. Passivity de-energizes a system and permits energy to be stored or locked in narrowly defined elites. Such passivity undermines the possibility of authenticity since authenticity requires activation.

The denial of authenticity can take two forms, either alienation or inauthenticity. Alienation exists when the possibility of a group seeking its own direction is sharply denied. The oppressed group experiences direct powerlessness. An example would be the racial condition in the fifties in the South where clearly blacks were oppressed by a dominating system. Inauthenticity exists when there is the appearance of authenticity, but the underlying realities are alienating. This would be more akin to racism in the North where the verbal agreements point toward the possibility of all groups achieving their own self-determination, while the underlying reality perpetuates institutionalized discrimination.

Definition of Racism -- Racism in this model is defined as any activity by one color or race group, intentional or unintentional, that inequitably distributes resources, refuses to share power, maintains unresponsive and inflexible institutional patterns, and practices and imposes an ethnocentric culture on another color/race group, for its "supposed" benefit and rationalizes that process by blaming or ignoring the other group. In short, it is the violation of authenticity for self or others due to color.[25]

The Emergent Pluralist as Racist -- The main racist impulse in this model is to get excited and energized by the language and perspective but fail to translate that excitement into sustained societal change. Thus one becomes a more sophisticated racist by assuming a new language structure without commensurate organizational or societal change of resources, power and structure.

Contradiction -- By being racist in the above manner the emergent pluralist ends up perpetuating passivity and inauthenticity. Playing language games without appropriate organized action gives the illusion of change without the substance of change. The result is a de-energizing of the change process. As whites participate in this inauthenticity it lends credibility to the deep belief held by many minorities that whites cannot be counted on to participate actively in the long term anti-racism struggle.

Anti-Racist Solution -- For whites the anti-racist solution is to work collaboratively with minorities in a common struggle to transform a society from an inauthentic and alienating racist "club" to an authentic society. This entails redistributing the resources and power, making the institutions more flexible and responsive and building a pluralistic culture. Individually for whites it requires the emergence of a self-affirming identity that is highly color conscious. From this perspective whites will realize that efforts to advocate color blindness or common humanity are ruses that have the effect of perpetuating white ethnocentricism. The task is for whites to press their white identity in directions that are humanistic without being color blind.

Self-Interest -- Self-interest in this model is more complicated than in the other four models. Since my own position is the emergent pluralist position, other parts of this paper will spell out in more detail the various types of self-interest in this model.

IV. Levels of Moral Reasoning

For over a decade Lawrence Kohlberg has been investigating the structure of moral reasoning. Building on the work of Jean Piaget, Kohlberg has isolated three distinct levels of moral thinking and sub-divided each level into two related stages. According to Kohlberg "these levels and stages may be considered separate and moral philosophies, distinct views of the social-moral world."[27] What distinguishes the levels and stages are not actions or statements about right or wrong. It is the reasons given why a given activity is wrong. Two whites may not keep a native American from attending a worship service, and both may say that it is wrong to do so. But they give different reasons for their action. One person may not do it for fear of the publicity generated for the church; another because of his or her conviction that everyone has a right to worship wherever he or she pleases. By identifying the different levels and stages Kohlberg can identify the maturity of the moral reasoning process and better understand the dynamics of the movement from one level and stage to another. He also can outline strategies designed to help people move from the lower levels to the higher levels of moral reasoning.

Kohlberg labels the three levels preconventional, conventional and post conventional. In his article "Moral Development and the Education of Adolescence," Kohlberg defines the levels and stages:

I. Preconventional Level
At this level the child is responsive to cultural rules and labels
of good and bad, the right or wrong, but interprets these labels in
terms of either the physical or the hedonistic consequences of action
(punishment, reward, exchange of favors) or in terms of the physical
power of those who enunciate the rules and labels. The level is
divided into the following two stages: *The Punishment and Obedience
Orientation*. The physical consequences of action determine its goodness or badness regardless of the human meaning or value of these
consequences. Avoidance of punishment and unquestioning deference
to power are valued in their own right, not in terms of respect or
an underlined moral order supported by punishment and authority (the
latter being Stage Four). Stage Two: *The Instrumental Relativist
Orientation*. Right action consists of that which instrumentally
satisfies one's own needs and occasionally the needs of others.
Human relations are viewed in terms like those of the marketplace.
Elements of fairness, of reciprocity and equal sharing are present,
but they are always interpreted in a physical pragmatic way. Reciprocity is a matter of "you scratch my back and I'll scratch yours,"
not of loyalty, attitude or justice.

II. Conventional Levels
At this level, maintaining the expectations of the individual's
family, group or nation is perceived as valuable in its own right,
regardless of immediate and obvious consequences. The attitude is
not only one of *conformity* to personal expectations and social order,
but of loyalty to it, of actively *maintaining*, supporting and justifying the order and of identifying with the persons or group involved
in it. At this level, there are the following two stages: Stage
Three: *The Interpersonal Concordance or "Good Boy - Nice Girl"
Orientation*. Good behavior is that which passes or helps others
and is approved by them. There is much conformity to stereotypical
images of what is majority or "natural" behavior. Behavior is frequently judged by intention - "he means well" becomes important for
the first time. One earns approval by being "nice." Stage Four:
"Law and Order" Orientation. There is orientation toward authority,
fixed rules and the maintenance of the social order. Right behavior
consists of doing one's duty, showing respect for authority and
maintaining the given social order for its own sake.

III. Post Conventional, Autonomous, or Principled Levels
At this level, there is a clear effort to define moral values and
principles which have validity and application apart from the authority of the groups or persons holding these principles and apart from
the individual's own identification with these groups. This level
again has two stages: Stage Five: *The Social-Contract Legalistic
Orientation*. Generally has utilitarian overtones. Right action
tends to be defined in terms of general individual rights and in
terms of standards which have been critically examined and agreed
upon by the whole society. There is a clear awareness of the relativism of personal values and opinions and a corresponding emphasis
upon procedural rules for reaching consensus. Aside from what is
constitutionally and democratically agreed upon, the right is a

matter of personal "values" and "opinion." The result is an emphasis
upon the "legal point of view" but with an emphasis upon the possibility of changing law in terms of rational considerations of social
utility. (Rather than freezing it in terms of Stage Four "Law and
Order.") Outside the legal realm, free agreement, and contract is
the binding element of obligation. This is the "official" morality
of the American government and Constitution. Stage Six: *The Universal Ethical Principle Orientation.* Rights are defined by the decision of consciousness in accord with self-chosen *ethical principles*
appealing to logical comprehensiveness, universality and consistency.
These principles are abstract and ethical (The Golden Rule, The
Categorical Imperative); they are not concrete moral rules like the
Ten Commandments. At heart, these are universal principles of *justice,*
of the *reciprocity* and *equality* of the human *rights* and of respect
for the dignity of human beings as individual persons.[28]

In terms of the broad definition of self-interest I'm
using in this essay, Kohlberg distinguishes the stages by motives
given for moral action. Why should I act in a certain way? Controlling for motive, the six stages look like this: (1) obey rules
to avoid punishment, (2) conform to obtain rewards, have favors returned, etc., (3) conform to avoid disapproval, dislike by others,
(4) conform to avoid censure by legitimate authorities and result
in guilt, (5) conform to maintain the respect of the impartial
spectator judging in terms of community welfare, (6) conform to
avoid self-condemnation.[29] Kohlberg is also exploring the possibility of there being a stage seven which goes beyond universal ethical
principles.[30] Duska and Whelan[31] have identified four qualities of stage
development in Kohlberg's theory that have important implications
for white belief and self-interest. First, stage development is
invariant; one does not skip stages but goes through each one in
turn, from lower to higher. Second, people cannot comprehend moral
reasoning at a stage more than one level beyond their own. Third,
there is a cognitive attraction to one level above a person's predominant level of moral reasoning. And fourth, movement through
the stages is affected when cognitive dis-equilibrium is created,
when a person's "cognitive outlook is not adequate to cope with a
given moral dilemma."[32] Thus, moral development, like other natural
growth processes, follows a predictable pattern.

V. Implications for Research and Action

A. Research
This paper opened with a social puzzle. Why the dis-
parity between relatively rapid attitude changes in whites and slow
commensurate institutional change? One hypothesis, worthy of serious investigation, is that *white structures of belief are developmental,* in Kohlberg's sense, and *what we are witnessing today is a
shift from one racist consciousness to another.* We see this particularly in the shift from supremist to free market advocate to systems
advocate. And, furthermore when threatened, for whatever reason,

or when passivity or inattention takes over, whites revert to a
lower level of reasoning and belief. Systems advocates revert to
and act like free market advocates; free market advocates become
supremists,and supremists are willing to commit racial genocide.
Each group contradicts its own values and behaves like the group
just below it. However, in keeping with Kohlberg, whites can also be challenged to move up a level when their current level has
proven to be ineffective in coping with the current situation.
      To get an overview of the structures of belief and levels
of moral reasoning, let us put this in chart form.
      Do the levels of moral reasoning correspond with the
structures of belief? The supremist is clearly into punishment and
obedience, given her/his authority orientation. Not only are supremists willing to punish disobedience of minorities; that same
energy can be directed to whites, including each other, who vacillate
on white supremacy. External authority is the key to unlocking this
orientation.
      The Free Market Advocate commitments tie closely with an
instrumental relativist mode of reasoning. Working for one's
narrow self-interest, within broad social restraints but without
monopolistic competition,brings the greatest good to the greatest
number. Open exchange in a free market is crucial.
      Open Systems Advocates, especially assimilationists, with
their concern for consensus and institutional support, fit nicely
with interpersonal conformity. Family and peers are pivotal in the
socialization process.
      The ethnic orientation breaks new ground by pressing the
conformity to a designated ethnic group rather than American society
as a whole. But it fails to break totally with that structure of
belief. There is still the contention that America is a pluralistic
society and that racial development will follow white ethnic development. Thus, this ethnic view becomes a bridge between open systems
advocates and radicals.
      The match between radicals, especially class advocates,
and law and order moral reasoning is more difficult to discern. In
fact, there may not be a clear match. However, I began to make connections between the law and order form of moral reasoning and radicals when, in the presence of radicals, I continually heard them
use a very tightly controlled jargon and witnessed a studied obedience to "the correct analysis." Whereas Kohlberg's theory ties to
people being obedient to the current social order, class advocates
exhibit a similar law and order orientation to a *new* social order.
The new social order is intrinsically good and requires obedience
to that order to bring it to fruition.
      Anti-neo-colonists, a second bridge group, move beyond
a class analysis and are forced to deal with cultural issues of
racial identity. They are attracted by new cultural meanings and
symbols of color but remain within the irreconcilable interest model.
The initiation of change is essentially restricted to minorities;
whites will resist changes.
      The new culture advocate examines white identity for util-
itarian purposes - it is necessary to cope with the changing racial
times. Laws, whether in the new or old social order, get challenged

Structures of Belief

Dimensions

	Model	Key Values	Mode of Relationship	Threat
Emergent Pluralist Advocates	Energy	Authenticity, resources, power, support, identity	Collaboration	Passivity and inauthenticity
New Culture Advocates	Meaning and symbol	Significant directing purpose	Confounding	Meaninglessness, loss of symbols
Radicals as Class and/or Color Advocates	Irreconcilable vested interests	Oppressed group's freedom, redistribution of power	Conflict	Oppressive group
Open Systems Advocates	Body as open system	Personal growth, organizational flexibility and adaptability	Consensus	Personal deviance and unresponsive institutions
Free Market Advocates	Atomistic individuals in free market exchange	Individual freedom, efficient allocation of resources	Competition	Centers of coercion or monopoly
Racial Supremist	Superiority/ inferiority	White supremacy	Control	Individual or group challenge to authority

Structures of Belief (Continued)

	Definition of Racism	As Racist	Contradiction	Positive Self-Interest
Emergent Pluralist Advocates	Violation of authenticity	Use language but no societal or organizational change	Say for authenticity yet end up being inauthentic	Different strokes for different folks - see last column
New Culture Advocates	Ethnocentrism	Ignore or discount importance of color	Say for new meaning yet perpetuate old meaning	Whites seeking more fulfillment or problem coping
Radicals as Class and/or Color Advocates	Domination and exploitation of one race/color group by another	Revolution, white led, assume all class interests same	Say freedom for all oppressed yet defend white oppressed	White workers
Open Systems Advocates	Mental illness/ social sickness	Minorities are sick, need to be helped	Say support health yet create sick institutions that supposedly help	All as members of body
Free Market Advocates	Racial prejudice and racial discrimination as exclusion	Minorities are center of coercion, need to be controlled if violate law/order	Say freedom for all yet defend freedom for whites	Managers of society and organizations
Racial Supremist Advocates	Hatred of individual groups, genocide of group by race	Hate and willing to commit genocide	Say everyone has place yet eliminate place for some	Very little, limit mentally ill person

	Anti-Racist Direction	Bridges	Levels of Moral Reasoning	Types of Self-Interest
Emergent Pluralist Advocates	Build authentic society, long term change effort		Universal principle	To gain integrity by acting on transcendent principle
New Culture Advocates	Build new positive white identity		Social contract	To transform oneself and culture to better cope with changes
Radicals as Class and/or Color Advocates	Organize the oppressed	*Anti-neo-colonialism*, race/class interdependent, no white self-interest to change	Law and order	To avoid trouble by conforming with the law, new or old
Open Systems Advocates	Affirmative action in all major institutions, affirm personal identity	*Ethnic* U.S. already pluralistic all benefit by diversity	Interpersonal conformity	To secure traditional approval of significant others
Free Market Advocates	Non-discrimination legislation and enforcement		Instrumental relativist	To benefit personally from trade-off
Racial Supremist Advocates	Some control over genocidal tendencies		Punishment and obedience	To avoid threat of punishment

as a new social contract, nurtured by deeply humane historical antecedents, is affirmed. A social contract is open to a confounding interpretation as new insights about the past, present, or future call for a new definition of the purpose of the social contract.

The active emergent pluralist operates from a universal ethical principle - authenticity - and willingly acts on ideas of justice, equality and equity. It is a color conscious and humane orientation, addressing societal as well as cultural changes.

If there is a match between Kohlberg's levels and the structures of belief, then do the other four aspects of development also apply? Is the developmental sequence invariant? As far as I know this has never been empirically researched. However, anecdotal data and personal familiarity with many whites over time, suggests the strong possibility of a developmental sequence. The pattern is most clear in the movement from supremist to free market advocate to open systems advocate. Then there may be a branching to either class or anti-neo-colonial advocates and on to culturalist and emergent pluralist.

However, in contrast to Kohlberg, one may not have to start at the bottom. But probably one's parents are the next step below where one starts.

What about only being able to deal with one level above your present level of thinking? Again, research is lacking. But I have been struck repeatedly, when explaining this chart to colleagues and teaching it in courses, how often the phenomenon occurs. Open systems advocates, for example, have no difficulty grasping the two lower levels, have some insight to the one above, usually say they are at *level six*, yet continually argue from a level three. That phenomenon has repeated itself enough times to suggest a developmental process is at work.

What about the cognitive attractiveness of the next level up? In training with whites over the last ten years, I have found but never really understood the cognitive lure for whites to change orientations. Yet I have seen it happen repeatedly. Supremists become free market advocates, free market advocates become open systems advocates and so on up the chart. The next level is close enough to one's orientation to make sense but not so distant as to be threatening.

Confusion sometimes arises when the active emergent pluralist position is laid out in training. Often many people find it intellectually attractive, no matter what level they are at. That may be because it is the position I advocate and hence takes on disproportionate energy in a group. It may be because the position is a unification of the other levels. Nevertheless, for whatever reason, I still find that the initial attraction of level six has limited staying power until the other more proximate steps have been mastered.

Finally, what about cognitive dis-equilibrium as the impetus for change? The Human Relations Department of St. Cloud State University self-consciously uses this method of change, with good success. Douglas Risberg employs cognitive dissonance as a key to bring about the change.

I have used three methods to encourage dis-equilibrium: force contradictions of values to the surface; demonstrate the consequences of a given structure of belief for self and organization; and confound the definition of the issue. Using the first method, the basic message to participants is to be authentic to what you say you are - if free market, be an authentic one; eliminate the contradiction and affirm the freedom for all, not just freedom for whites.

Second, see the personal and organizational consequences of a given structure of belief. Know what the impact will be if you act as a free market advocate or as a culturalist. Understand that there are alternative structures of belief and modes of action and see how those alternatives are available to you.

And third, examine the problem in a confounded way. For example, focus on white racism, not the victims of white racism. See strengths in the oppressed, not just weaknesses. See that to be tender and caring is powerful. See that no one is free until all are free. Each of these methods points toward the inadequacy of one's current structure of belief and encourages one to move to resolution at a higher level.

One aspect of the developmental process not explicitly identified by Duska and Whelan but implied is the process of regression.[33] If someone is threatened at one level or is indifferent or passive at that level, she/he will regress to the next lower level. Minorities often tell whites that racism dehumanizes them. One way to see this in action or to experience it in oneself is to be aware of threat situations or situations where action has been required and/or one has acted "without thinking." Regression often occurs.

The latent desire to punish minorities, the inadvertent "slip of the tongue,"the tendencies toward paternalism all dehumanize us in the process of dehumanizing others. If developmentally we become less than who we currently are, we are part of the losers. If we continue to be less than we might be, we are part of the losers. If we become passive, we are part of the losers.

B. ACTION IMPLICATIONS

As was stated earlier, structures of belief and moral reasoning do not by themselves determine action. However, they are predisposers to new action and as such are crucial in the change process.

If what has been presented so far has merit and can be shown to be empirically accurate, then action implications follow. To cite a few:
   - careful diagnosis of whites in critical power positions in organizations would be crucial in identifying their structures of belief and the organizational policy implications.
   - anti-racism training would be developmental and would need to start from where people are and move them along stage by stage.
   - self-interest would be different for different people.
   - research would move from attitude studies to the studies of the structures of belief.
   - racial progress would be more complexly discussed and evaluated.

VI. Self-Interest

In the light of the preceding analysis it is possible to identify six broad types of self-interest.
Why be anti-racist?
Level Six - to gain integrity by acting on a transcendent principle.
Level Five - to transform oneself and one's culture to better cope with changing racial times.
Level Four - to be a good citizen by conforming with the law.
Level Three - to secure the approval of significant others.
Level Two - to benefit personally from a trade-off.
Level One - to avoid threat of punishment.
It is a mistake to assume that all whites, or anyone for that matter, is at any one level on every issue concerned with racism. It is also a mistake to assume that everyone is consistent or that anyone is necessarily unwilling to change. What we have to remember about ourselves as well as others is our complexity. At times the confusion may be overwhelming. We hope we can move from our confusion, through the complexity, to profound simplicity. In studying whites, the movement is slow, arduous yet very necessary. It is also deeply satisfying.[34]

Concluding Note

The lack of careful research on white belief, moral reasoning, self-interest and racism is not surprising. The oppressors and the oppressive system are usually the last to be studied and understood. I hope this essay has contributed to that understanding and as such contributed to the struggle for liberation to which Alvin Pitcher and many of us are totally committed.

Notes and References

1. See Paul Sheatsley, "White Attitudes toward the Negro," in *The Negro American*, edited by Talcott Parsons and Kenneth Clark, (Boston: Houghton-Mifflin, 1965), pp. 303-324; Herbert Hyman and Paul Sheatsley, "Attitudes toward Desegregation," *Scientific American*, 211 (July, 1964), pp. 16-23; Andrew Greeley and Paul Sheatsley, "Attitudes toward Racial Integration," *Scientific American*, 225 (December, 1971), pp. 14ff; Angus Campbell, *White Attitudes toward Black People*, (Ann Arbor, Michigan: ISR, 1971).
2. Joe Fagin, *Institutional Discrimination: A Working Paper*, U.S. Commission on Civil Rights, August 1975, pp. 3-4.
3. See Edward Banfield, "The Unheavenly City Revisited," (Boston: Little, Brown, and Company, 1974) and Nathan Glazer, *Affirmative Discrimination*, (New York: Basic Books, Inc., 1975).
4. *Op. cit.*, Campbell.

5. The cultural factors mentioned above are only two of a number of aspects of life that have direct influence on white self-interest.

6. Milton Friedman, "The Social Responsibility of Business," *The New York Times Magazine*, September 13, 1970, p. 126.

7. Jeffrey Praeger, "White Racial Privilege and Social Change: An Examination of the Theories of Racism," Mimeo. See also Gary S. Becker, *The Economics of Discrimination*, second edition, (Chicago: University of Chicago Press, 1971).

8. *Report of the National Advisory Commission on Civil Disorders*, (Bantam Books, 1968), pp. 424-25.

9. Talcott Parsons, "Full Citizenship for the Negro American?," *Daedalus*, Volume 94, Number 4, Fall 1965, p. 1050. The ethnic model was astutely criticized by Raymond Franklin and Solomon Resnik in *The Political Economy of Racism*, (New York: Holt,Rinehart, Winston, 1973).

10. Oliver Cox, *Caste, Class,and Race*, (New York: Modern Reader Paperbacks, 1948), p. 532.

11. Howard Sherman, *Radical Political Economy*, (New York: Basic Books, 1972), p. 180. Sherman lists three functions that racism serves for the ruling class:

First, racism justifies economic exploitation. "Inferior" identifiable people can be used. Second, people of color are convenient scapegoats for problems. They can be blamed and take the pressure off the system as a whole. Third, racism makes it possible for the ruling class to divide the working class and control it. On this last point, most class advocates resist color conscious organizing. Racially conscious nationalistic movements are perceived to be counter-revolutionary. Color consciousness sets false antagonisms between the same class. From this class advocate point of view, nothing should separate the working class; nothing should be able to be used by the ruling class to separate that class from itself.

12. *Ibid.*, p. 181.

13. The beginning of this fast-rising theory goes back at least to 1950 when Harold Cruise characterized relations in the United States as "domestic colonialism." See also Cruise, *The Crisis of the Negro Intellectual*, (New York: Morrow and Company, 1967). The framework gained wide-spread popularity with the publication of *Black Power* (1967) by Stoklely Hamilton and Charles Carmichael. Today it is used extensively by Hispanic, Asian and native American groups. See Joan Moore, "Colonialism: The Case of the Mexican Americans," *Social Problems*, Volume 17, Number 4, (Spring, 1970), pp. 463-472.

14. Race prejudice can exist without colonization but racism as a system of domination is a part of the colonizing process. See Robert Blauner, ed., *Racial Conflict*, (Boston: Little, Brown, and Company, 1971), p. 54. Also see Moore, *op. cit.*, pp. 463-472.

15. James Boggs, *Racism and Class Struggle*, (New York: Modern Reader, 1970), p. 30.

16. Paulo Freire, *Pedagogy of the Oppressed*, (New York: Seabury Press, 1974).

17. See Raymond Franklin and Solomon Reisnik, *The Political Economy of Racism, op. cit.*, for a sophisticated analysis using an anti-neo-colonial model.

18. See James and Grace Boggs, *Evolution and Revolution in Twentieth Century America*, (New York: Modern Reader, 1975) for a neo-colonial model leading

toward new cultural advocacy. It's a bridge volume that's very important in the transition process.

19. Clifford Geertz, "Religion as a Cultural System," in *Religious Situation, 1968*, Donald R. Cutler, ed.,(Boston: Deacon Press, 1968), p. 475.

20. *Ibid.*, p. 479.

21. Theodore Roszak, *Where the Wasteland Ends*, (New York: Anchor Books, 1973).

22. See Winthrop Jordan, *White over Black*, (Baltimore: Penguin Books, 1968); George Fredrickson, *The Black Image in the White Mind*, (New York: Harper and Row, 1971); Vernon Dixon and Betty Foster, *Beyond Black or White*, (New York: Little, Brown, and Company, 1971); Joel Kovel, *White Racism: A Psycho History*, (New York: Pantheon Books, 1970); Robert W. Terry, *For Whites Only*, (Grand Rapids, Michigan: Eerdmans, 1970).

23. Amitai Etzioni, *The Active Society*, (New York: The Free Press, 1968), p. 35-36. See also Warren Breed, *The Self-Guiding Society*, (New York: The Free Press, 1971).

24. See Claude Steiner, *Scripts People Live*, (New York: Bantam Books, 1974).

25. See Robert W. Terry, "Racism Isn't Just," *Life and Work*, Volume 13, Number 2, (Summer, 1971), pp. 1-3.

26. My special thanks to Jean Alvarez for introducing me to Lawrence Kohlberg's important work and challenging me to apply it to the area of racism.

27. Quoted in Ronald Duska and Mariellen Whelan, *A Guide to Piaget and Kohlberg*, (New York: Paulist Press, 1975), p. 43.

28. Lawrence Kohlberg, "Moral Development and the Education of Adolescence," reprinted in Duska and Whelan, *op. cit.*, p. 45-47.

29. Kohlberg, *Continuities in Childhood and Adult Moral Development Revisited*, quoted in Duska and Whelan, *op. cit.*, p. 48.

30. In essence, what Kohlberg is grappling with is what Paul Tillich calls theonomy. Although Kohlberg outlines more refined steps, the movement to a full and mature moral reasoning follows the same basic outline articulated by Tillich in his distinctions between heteronomy, autonomy and theonomy.

31. Duska and Whelan, *op. cit.*, pp. 47-50.

32. *Ibid.*, p. 49.

33. Elizabeth Simpson, "A Holistic Approach to Moral Development and Behavior," in Thomas Lickona, ed., *Moral Development & Behavior*, (New York: Holt, Rinehart, Winston, 1976).

34. See Mark Chesler "Contemporary Sociological Theories of Racism," in Phyllis Katz, ed., *Toward the Elimination of Racism*, (New York: Pergamon Press, 1976) and Glenn Buchner, ed., *Straight/White/Male*, (Philadelphia: Fortress Press, 1976).

A PERSONAL ESSAY: PUBLIC MINISTRIES IN MEMORY AND HOPE — CLARIFYING THE LEGACY

by
Peggy Way

The personal flavor of this essay has as its integrity the quality of relationship I shared with Al Pitcher during a part of the time reflected upon here. But it also demonstrates my commitment to autobiography as a part of the methodologies by which we seek to discern truth.

Essays written by others are now defining as an historical period years and events that shaped my life and ministry. Yet I carry the sixties and my associations with the public ministries of those years within me, and represent some of those who seek to continue their legacies. Before the experiences slip away forever, formalized in others' images and concepts, I would simply remember those particular times and name them for myself. Where were you then, my brothers, and where are you now? What were we about in our "sixties style," and what understandings of it become our ongoing legacy...in memory and in hope?

An Invitation to Remember

I remember a very lonely time as a woman-in-the-church, never quite knowing whether I was welcome to join the all male groups gathered in the hall or bar or, even though I had equivalent portfolio, meeting in offices, still, in those days, wearing suits. But what I remember best was a pride of being included and a puzzlement of listening to what seemed to be self-evident to the others, a pain of being afraid to speak out at the same time as being caught up in the unutterably exquisite illusion of being in control of history. Continually propelled beyond my energy resources, caught up in time demands to which no one ever said "no," participant and shaper of the future with funds to be spent to make a difference and power to be called forth and utilized for Good... I was intoxicated for years.

Perhaps some flavored sentences will recall your own particularities of this very special historical time, when I was fortunate enough to be on the Chicago scene. I remember:

...the time that we divided Chicago into neighborhood sections and talked the denominational leaders into assigning two staff to each sector to organize and empower a coherent policy to

make Chicago human. Few noticed (I did) that none of us were
freed from other portfolios to undertake this Gargantuan task.
No one heard (see the minutes which still exist somewhere)
when I tenuously suggested that we begin with one sector instead of all of them. Did anyone notice when we stopped
meeting?

...the time that a Famous Foundation was rumored to be "about
ready" to invest "several millions" thru church structures to
renew the metropolis (Chicago, of course). I have in my files
products of the brainstorming sessions where we, the elite
leadership, put our dreams on paper under the stimulus of
money-about-to-be-in-hand. None ever came.

...the years that we at the Urban Training Center received and
re-educated hundreds of men (and a handful of women) to be the
avant-garde leadership in urban and public ministries; the
situation analyses on which they worked and toward which we
directed our strategies; the guests (highly paid) that came
in and out and variously lectured to us about Commonsteal
Edison and how to take over Cook County Hospital, how to turn
a ghetto into an extended family, how to destroy the public
welfare system and replace it with our own vision, how to turn
a parish into an arena of public issues concerns. Can anyone
forget The Plunge and how we sent those soldiers home to be
about our tasks? (Am I responsible for some who left any form
of ministry to undertake a search for where their expectations,
stimulated by us, *could* be fulfilled?)

...the strategies that we formulated to get funds from the War on
Poverty and our early failures to take seriously alternative
vehicles to control this funding, i.e., Mayor Daley.

...the one morning a week that we got up early and arrived at our
offices or store fronts scattered all over the city and spoke
with one another--and the emerging "indigenous groups" that
we were funding--on a Conference Call. Did anyone ever work
on agenda? I don't remember; I think it was supposed to emerge.
Perhaps I would remember if anyone had...

...the ways that we found to "discover" the "indigenous" and give
them funds...the subpoenas to our Board when we were successful, and the evaluations that I did to convince our Board to
continue the funding...the busses that I could buy for SDS
(pre-Weathermen) when they were developing Jobs Or Income Now
with alcoholic men on Skid Rows, and the marvelous welfare
mothers who nurtured me and whom I transported to share their
stories in suburban churches...

...the marches and the glory, the huge staffs and the volunteers
who came to us to learn how to help Chicago from locations in
Wilmette and Hinsdale, and never forgetting those meetings in

inner city restaurants, carefully checking the cleanliness of the silverware...

...getting a student the first field education credit for work in a community organization and, later, arranging the substitution of working on political organization for a black candidate and organizing for racial justice in a white suburb for CPE credit, and, even later, placing the first field ed student in a homophile organization...

...and all of the rest, day by day, night by night, how gloriously alive, in charge, new idea following new idea, no time for marriages or families...

...how the days, the ways, the conversations died, the funds diminished, we left for other places (many in the institutions we had so devastatingly critiqued), the music ended, we were sent home to work on white racism, some of us no longer had homes...

...the marvelous self-evidents, uncritiqued, by which we lived...

The feelings of memory, for me, are those of being propelled by a history that I could find the ways to grasp, followed by its growing elusiveness, if not in rhetoric, at least in reality. I presided not only at program birth, but also at program burial. Most of my major psychological and denomination/ecumenical investments no longer exist, and some that do take shapes I cannot claim. Some died too late and others too soon. And I remember best, sometimes, the neat sociological analyses written on the boards from which we derived our strategies. At worst I remember the Hot Summers when we junior staff persons looked around and saw our leaders at their summer homes.

I claim a full complicity--of pride and power, of having grasped history and tried to run with it, of my trust in analysis and propulsion to move from theological vision and sociological principle to practice. Too many non-participants are now writing my history. Too quickly skimmed over, the wrong phrases will be created to explain us, and our legacies will not be enriched by our learnings. How did we go on, and learn to hope again--and find a more ongoing center for our just concerns, passions and participations in public ministries? I must make my own statement.

Analyzing the Analytic

Only last week I met a fellow traveler of those years. We shared some memories and, at the end, he expressed his surprise as I shared my feelings of not-belonging. "But I remember you as at the center..."

And in one of those glorious accidents of history I was-- but I never belonged. I understood the analyses, implemented the strategies, interpreted directions in which we must move and, as I

could not march, paid the way for others to go. I was, above all,
an excellent broker. But a part of me--shared only at home--never
belonged. I agonized over what was wrong with me: at times, I
laid it to a faulty intellect in the presence of great minds; at
others, to my process-oriented social work education and my un-
familiarity with power due to too much past experience in a therapeutic orientation; sometimes the schedule seemed impossible for
one who was a wife and mother, but I coped well and *always* kept up.
I wrote my first tentative article on women during this time, in
that glorious *Renewal* magazine ("Women in the Church: Comic Strip?
Society Section? Front Page?") but, generally, when I thought of
myself as woman at all, experienced it as a puzzlement, an outsider
status. I let my own puzzlements go in order to enter in, and
wouldn't have known where to begin anyway to raise the questions
that I couldn't phrase. It took a further pilgrimage to phrase
what it was then that I couldn't say. For it wasn't MY center that
was out of place; the center itself was faulty and ultimately could
not hold. What was our center?
        I remember those days now as exquisitely Western and
masculine. We took for granted we could solve the problems of metropolis thru application of secular theory and technique, and our
primarily sociological analyses were the self-evidents by which we
could name the problems. Then, utilizing an analysis that almost
always went from principle to practice--or what SHOULD be to how
to get it there--we could develop strategies to call forth the Good.
Such a vision completely engaged our energies and occupied our
meetings. I think of us now as magnificent Visionaries, ill-equipped
to implement, with the hope of the Vision ever seductive and filter-
ing out the growing data that might have suggested cautions. I can
describe myself as a Listener to Great Ideas, from minds unfettered
with the ordinary, and as participant in a massive Arrogance of
Goodness that could tolerate neither the everyday nor the complex.
I do not remember playing with my colleagues, or praying with them,
or touching them. Nor do I remember, to my present dismay, ever
seriously critiquing what we were about.
        We were, of course, ourselves the victims of a rapidly
changing world and of our own past histories. I remember us best
as proud and arrogant, certain that we were Right about History,
filled with visions to be announced as possible realities, one
dimensional thinkers whom only the failure of history to shape itself to our perspectives could touch. And we saw that only after
the fact, if at all.
        For, since we were on the right historical track, we lived
out of an analytic of enemies who, at best, did not understand and,
at worst, refused to see the truth. We were marvelous at an analysis of blame which, when located, could be fought and eliminated.
Only the descent of white racism upon us moved us closer toward our
own complicity--and even that we viewed as problem-to-be-solved,
analyzed in terms of principle, as we devoted ourselves to eliminating it, not only in opportunity but also in result. "After"
racism, sexism came in at the tag end of our heyday of sixties-
style public ministries to further name our own complicities, but
I do not recall that it was ever in serious contention for our

energies during this period, just as we had no time to invest in
developing an early Chicago center for Religion and the Homophile.
        At the tag end of Our Days, my memories are more diffuse
and personally psychological. I thought I was going crazy. I sat
and heard some of our paid speakers talk about killing and burning
and watched us clap. I participated in paying street gang members
to take our UTC students into the ghettos and "understood" when
they purposefully lost them there and delighted in having ripped
us off--again. I watched an English gentleman train roomfulls of
white people in how to build a ghetto community in Chicago, and
heard him say he could not work with me because I stood too tall
as a woman. I developed strategies to eliminate racism in other
institutions than those in which I lived (which had no more minority
staff than the ones we were analyzing and where the Board of the
one that had employed me consistently voted down the development
of scholarships for the training of women), and grew progressively
more detached and confused. I felt no permission to raise my concerns, yet take full responsibility for not having done so. The
time was out of joint; o blessed spite that ever I was born to set
it right...
        For I couldn't do it any longer. Later I experienced a
profound sense of guilt for the dynamic that created the Symbianese
Liberation Army and felt that I knew well each of its participants.
Were they my legacy? For, in pain, I saw few places anywhere where
our legacy seemed to have ongoing vitality...
        Yet, more importantly, I couldn't go home again! This
period inevitably shaped my life and ministry. I knew that its
rightness and passions and visions must not be lost in my own ongoingness. I sensed, even then, that it was somehow the analytic--
the center--that was wrong and undertook, self-consciously, leaving
these people, my brothers, behind,to undertake my own pilgrimage
toward hope and toward a center, an analytic that might better root
the truths that we were about and have the capacity to sustain us
in a more human wholeness.
        Where are you now, my brothers? I have watched you read
Heidegger or go to Esalen, leave the sociological analytic and,
to my despair, appear to choose an existentialism that is without
a sociology. Actually, I now believe, our analytic itself did not
take seriously even then a concept of an embedded self, living inevitably within a complex of determinisms, institutions and cultural
forms, and positively structured and nurtured by them as well as
oppressed. The movement beyond us but made this evident--as did
our rampant individualism, without community and touch, show up in
different forms in our later pilgrimages to find our selves thru
body and touch and the search after relationships to enhance our
own growth. If they did not, "It can't be helped." At a profoundly deep level and, again, with pain, as with the SLA, I wonder
if this may be our legacy.
        For I find, today, that the apparent shift in analytics
is a deceptive one. Back of the sociological analytic of my Chicago
days lay the self-evident of the possibility of grasping control of
history, utilizing principles derived from Western visions of the
Good, and of growth without limits, and following a principled use

of power and of technologically based strategies to bring about
changes that would be inevitable were it not for some recalcitrant
enemy, a somehow impersonal force to be encountered and conquered.
We assumed our own basic goodness and, implicitly, set about to
change history as ahistorical creatures not ourselves bound by
personal or social histories, sub- or major cultural embeddedness.
I was only recently struck by an embarrassingly simple realization:
we were ourselves a subculture, affirming and sustaining one
another with the proper rhetorics and positions in battle. The
use of language marked us--erudite and principled, turning into
slogans that sustained us by the rightness of their identifications.
We were our own dynamic. No wonder it took so long for other voices
to be heard. If one of Ours supported ghetto gangs, we could not
hear the voices of minorities who were oppressed by them! We were
all basically white, and male, and middle class, and gradually everyone had to go off from us. Are the liberation movements, then, our
legacy?

    But back of all those that may seem to be our ongoing
legacies appear to lie some of the same limitations of our own prevailing analytic. The shifts appear to me to be deceptive, and the
learnings from our failures not yet incorporated. At a recent conference of Roman Catholic campus ministers, out of seventy in atten-
dance approximately ten signed up for workshops on social justice
ministries and sixty for workshops on relationship and encounter.
But this latter analytic, too, is a puzzlement to me. It is déjà
vu, I am there again, in the sixties, assuming the possibility of
grasping control--of Self, this time, before Society or History; of
discovering a basic growth orientation and uncovering a wealth of
unlimited potentialities which some enemy (parent, spouse, church,
culture) has kept us from achieving; of affirming the ahistorical,
and celebrating Selves who, when they declare their maturity, their
Coming of Age, can stand apart from psychological past and cultural
present; moving from victim to victor thru psychosynthesis and
fantasy; assuming the negativity of institution and culture viewed
primarily as repressive force; another subculture, touching this
time, and sometimes worshipping together, but yet without a disciplined critique of the self-evidents. IS the "new analytic" that
much new? Is Carl Rogers' announcement of "the new political
figure," who sounds suspiciously like a composite of Reich and the
regulars of encounter group weekends, even one whit touched by what
happened to us?

    It is true, I am afraid, that the base of public minis-
tries appears to be gone, at least as I knew them and continue to
hold a high valuation on our sense of social responsibility and
participation in the public sectors. For responsibility for society
and others becomes an ex post facto consideration to the primary
responsibility to realize the Self or to find identity in cultural
subgroupings that will somehow in and of themselves provide--or be
identical with--an implicit economic, political, sociological analysis. No one is left for "public" concern, which, indeed, becomes
positively disvalued. I have come to the conclusion that there is
finally nowhere else to go with an analytic rooted in ontological
anxiety and angst--nowhere but to an isolated Self, responsible for

its own being, subsuming Otherness in itself and thus having no
concern for otherness apart from the achievement of the Self--and
the identity of One's Own Group. In that sense, I much prefer our
days, but the responsibility part of our legacy has fallen on hard
times. For I fail to find a base for *public* ministry in this new
analytic.

Nor in either analytic does there appear to be a base for
negotiation, so crucial for public participation. Both rely too
heavily upon an analytic of enemy and blame. In both, a sense of
complicity is hard to come by, whether in the assumed Goodness of
those of us working for justice in the sixties, or in the assumed
Rightness of those about their own liberation. For how, after all,
can one critique an oppressed people? Or expect them to demonstrate concern for the bodies (personal and corporate) which have
oppressed? One about identity cannot, perhaps, allow external
critique, nor yet, on the other hand, afford even internal criticism.

In other words, I recognize myself all over again, and
the puzzlement is as profound as before, heightened, probably, by
the assumption that it is a different analytic. But what has happened, really? I suggest that we have lost the base for public
ministry in a sense of responsibility that lies prior to self, and
replaced it by growing numbers who, in various ways, refuse responsibility prior to the establishment of their own Identity or
Self, which seems to me to be a Vision as impossible of achievement
as those we held and thereby, of course, removes any dynamic of
public concern. A dynamic for a public ministry must perforce
embody a valuation upon "public" that, if not preceding, must at
least be correlative with the private self. And it must perforce
place a valuation upon the worth of institutions or some of the
most creative will live in social isolation out of the illusions
that occur when one lives only with one's own. For example, an
understanding of marriage which places a prior if not sole valuation
upon the end of stimulating the personal growth of each partner,
and with children raised to be their "own people" without a sense
of family responsibility, does not bode well for the future of
public responsibility. Nor does the high valuation placed upon the
meanings found in transient encounter groups offer promise to the
type of investment over time, continuity through history, and stick-
ing by thru difficulty that is more frequently than not the base
for social change. A rhetoric of beautiful words--such as we used
in the sixties--cannot hide for long the emptiness and superficiality
of the view of history expressed in Carl Rogers' most recent book,
On Personal Power. Rogers is describing what he calls "a new political figure."

These persons are seeking new forms of community, of closeness, of
intimacy, of shared purpose. He and she are seeking new forms of
communication in such a community--verbal and nonverbal, feelingful
as well as intellectual. There is a recognition that personal life
will be transient, mostly in temporary relationships, and that they
must be able to establish closeness quickly. In this mobile world
persons do not live long in one community. These individuals are
not surrounded by family or relatives. They are a part of the

temporary society. There is a realization that if they are to live
in a human context, there must be an ability to establish intimate,
communicative, personal bonds with others in a very short space of
time. They must be able to leave these close relationships behind,
without excessive conflict or mourning.[1]

A profound sadness engulfs me. I am no more at home in the seventies than I was in the sixties. Once again we celebrate the
possibilities of grasping control of history and shaping it to our
own ends. We live out of subcultures and do not move beyond them
long enough to experience the pluralisms that we conceptualize--and
hence to truly take on critique of our own self-evidents. We do
not embed self, institution, or culture in history, give credit for
the power of determinisms or even note the possibility of institutional and cultural forces as providing necessary structural and
nurturing support for the emergence of self and society, along with
their more rapidly recognized oppressive role. And where, at depth,
do either of us negotiate, for analyses of enemy and blame, with
self as victim, make any "Other" unworthy of negotiation, the enemy
other look different, somehow, from ourselves and, once again, we
let go our own complicity.
     What was most at fault in our analytic continues un-
touched in those that appear to have replaced it, and this is what
I fear the most about the future of our own legacy. For that which
was of highest value in our own, the assumption of public responsibility in an arena of valuation, and of having a public as well
as a private self, and even, however one dimensional, embodying a
passion for public participation, has been subsumed, transmuted, by
an analytic of anxiety that appears to lead inevitably toward the
isolated, if not narcissistic, Self. And the Self seems always to
be in preparation, or engaged in a dynamic of achieving Identity in
relation to one's own, with ever lessening sense of the public. No
one is left for the whole. It is no wonder that we are left without a base for public ministries somewhere in between subcultural
groupings such as the SLA or FANON, on the one hand, the liberation
movements, or the evangelicals, on the other.
     Let me repeat myself. What I have learned from an anal-
ysis of the original public ministries analytic and its apparent
legacies is:

1.   that public ministries must be rooted in an ontology of
     responsibility that is at least correlative with an ontology
     of anxiety;

2.   that public ministries must be rooted in an analysis of
     history that views justice as an ongoing activity rather
     than a series of victories and accomplishments...that
     being about justice is being in there for the long haul;

3.   that public ministries must have the capacity to analyze
     the structuring, nurturing and other positive qualities of
     institutions and cultures, or there is no positive evalu-
     ation of the "public" that makes public activities of

"worth;" or include friendly if regretful recognition of
the various determinisms and embeddednesses that affect
all strategies for change;

4. that public ministries must transcend an analysis of enemy
   or blame, claim always one's own complicity, and hence be
   always open to processes of negotiation, for the public is,
   at least, a pluralism; OR a more profound recognition of
   what it means to choose martyrdom, letting go the romantic
   notion of having/being both;

5. that alternatives to our analytic have not yet incorporated
   the primary failures of our own, and seem destined to move
   us farther away from public participation in any continuous
   sense, becoming instead a very strange inversion of ourselves into isolation and removal from the public scene
   except on our own terms or in sudden "explosions" into it.

     In other words, to finally confess openly my basic old-
fashionedness, we lack, and have lacked for several generations now,
a theology that clarifies the questions and offers a systematic base
of critique. I recognize, of course, that this is no great discovery, but I have come to believe that the future of public ministries will be one with the future of theology itself. I confess my
own despair in being left bereft by theology in all of my ministries,
and while I sympathize with the situation of a theology-in-search-
of-its-own-soul, can no longer rest assured that theology will "one
day" (like the Self will one day be ready again for responsibility
and self-giving) make "public" again meaningful, and "ministry,"
rooted in faith perspectives that allow for the integrity of justice
and care, offer a base of critique and of ongoingness, and remind
us of the worth of who we are in the particularities and history of
our magnificent tradition. What better place than to raise up

An Invitation To Hope

     I went on, from the sixties, tapping into this and that.
To what did you go on? What shaped you next, so that our legacy
might at least partake of how we understand our own histories in
public ministries and their aftermaths?
     As I now understand my presence in the center of the
public ministries arena of the sixties as a gift that has been an
ongoing part of me, so do I now understand my interim pilgrimages
as gifts offered to me, urging me toward an analytic of ministry
where "public" and "private" have common roots, where personal and
social transformation arise from and are critiqued by a common base,
where we dare confrontation with our most cherished self-evidents
and formulate once again and anew the theological foundations for
our styles and commitments of living in the world.
     My ongoing pilgrimage led from public ministries and
power to sexuality, spirituality, and personal transformation and
growth--but as always having been previously shaped by the sense

and spirit of public ministries. Yet just as my earlier role as
woman, and training in pastoral counseling and sensitivity to the
absence of prayer amongst us kept me from full belonging in public
ministry days, so did the depth of my participation there keep me
from a full celebration of the "new" analytics. Once again at the
center, and with the base of my ministries preceding the gay liberation movement, I found myself caught up in gay liberation, first
as therapist who did not work for a change in orientation as prior
to humanness or full Christian participation, and always as full
advocate for civil and clerical rights. Here I experienced a sense
of the integrity of my caring and justice perspectives that had
been missing from the sixties.
     At center again, in my own liberation movement with its
agonies and joys, I found emerging clarification of some of the
things that had happened to me and within me in that exquisitely
masculine period of public ministries. I found not only caring and
justice perspectives coming together, but also a passionate need
for principles that could critique and transcend even the orientations of my emerging self and identity as woman. I found myself
watching carefully for my own movement's self-evidents, one dimensional analytics, too easy definitions of enemy and blame, too
ready identification as The new dynamic of history--and related
hesitancies to let in alternative data that might not fit.
     Corollary were four years with the Jesuits, and fasci-
nation with a history of spirituality and spiritual formation.
Here I came closest to at-homeness, as kind of a final irony of my
own history, for spirituality alternated with integrity, with justice concerns, and with commitments for personal and group caring.
Moreover, my preliminary graspings for common commitments to be
about care *and* justice found a base of recognition and support. To
my amazement, I found here as well openness to gay and women's perspectives, and experienced for the first time with my brothers full
permission not to withhold any dimensions of who I am.
     I rapidly accumulated a whole new set of memories to add
to those of public ministry days--and just as rapidly discovered
that they couldn't simply be *added* one to another. ALL of the
memories needed new dimensions of understanding. This insight was
not easily achieved. I suffered three crises: first, did I have
no center? Was I but a reflection of events around me, fitting in
wherever I turned up, a mirror of my surroundings? I moved at ease
between personal and social transformation perspectives, raised
justice concerns with my pastoral counseling colleagues and urged
my justice-oriented students toward awareness of their own and their
group's internal needs and dynamics. No, I decided; I experienced
myself as strange but not centerless. I found myself saying the
same things in different groupings, pushing always toward a base
that began to explain what I had experienced as their integrity,
although from admittedly different perspectives or beginning points.
     Second, was there, then, no center? Better that I finally
pick and choose, find a home; join in developing a center of training
in growth groups; become a full-time therapist with the casualties
of a changing world, especially those worn out, eroded, burned out,
in justice pursuits; focus on My Own, women's issues, and be a woman

theologian, woman pastor, woman pastoral counselor; stand by a/or
one secular analytic, pursue it where it goes, follow one set of
organized principles, a female Norman Thomas in three decades, a
Marxist theorist, a career in politics, competence in economics.
No, none of these was right--and whole--for me. It was too late.
         Third, was it just that I had seen too much, been in too
many places, incorporated so many perspectives that I was confused
and had best step back and simplify? Care for myself and family,
live on the farm forever rather than as an interim, forget what I
had seen, where I had been? With my sisters, I sang with unusual
poignancy: Oh, how I wish my eyes hadn't been opened...
         But they had been. What does one do with such a pilgrimage?
Was it that I was confused and had that worst of all horrors to my
academic colleagues, an undisciplined, undifferentiating mind? Or
was it that I was perceptive in finding most of the books and articles that I read sounding just alike at the crucial point of their
central analytic, however disparate they appeared at first glance?
         I found that what I actually did was to live with the
particular, as I had done in public ministries days, for I was still
broker and implementer and hence always in touch with the people
living behind the visions and the concepts. The complexities of the
people kept spoiling the certainties which others seemed, more easily,
to find. I kept raising questions of care with the justice folk
and questions of justice with the care colleagues. When I found *no*
theology in places in my field of pastoral counseling where others
were celebrating the *new* theology, I said so. I spoke of humanness as a prior category to homosexuality with straights and reminded gays that genital sexual freedom may be illusory or an insufficient base of final identification for living in the world.
I tried to embody with the brothers who the sisters are, and to be
with the sisters who we might be that fulfilled us but did not
oppress others. I counseled with the fatigued activist and urged
the charismatic not to forget the world outside the circle, all of
the ones untouched by our kisses of peace. In all of these people-
places I found hope, and I gradually understood myself to be an
interim legacy from the sixties, an ongoing heritage from the Urban
Training Center, a living reminder of one touched deeply by Chicago
of the sixties, a vulnerable embodiment of a vision.
         But in what did I stand? What was the source of the felt
integrity and the experienced hope? To my dismay, I did not find
the liberation theologians and theologians of hope particularly
helpful, nor the more specialized, if intriguing, theological discourse to which I turned. Everything was moving so fast, again,
what was to protect me (us) from new faddisms? Again the same
sense of grasping for control of history, the fitting of it into
one dimensional principles of analysis, the same lack of critique
of one's own base and assumptions of one's own rightness, a variety
of enemy or blame analyses, assumptions that structures always stood
in the way of the emergence of the Self--or that we could create
structures that would not. That for which I stood, that one must
have a self to lose it, seemed forever inverted into the continuing
postponement of the giving of the self to or for the other, the continuing erosion of the basis for a proud involvement in public

ministries and an ongoing caring in particularity about the public
structures that shape us all.

I felt ever more bereft of a comprehensive base that took
seriously a variety of perspectives, that was sophisticated in the
workings of modernity and the analytic of power politics, that could
deal with structures and with individuals, that would incorporate
the complex without becoming one dimensional, obscurantist or wishy-
washy, and that rested on Christian foundations and embodied theological visions for continuity and sustenance, offering ways of
seeing that could center, that could hold. Can there be public or
private ministries without such a base? Can there be continuity,
ongoingness, a sense of being signed up for the long haul--whether
doing public or private ministries, justice or care--without such
an undergirding?

I think not. In my old age, without competence or cre-
dential, I become a theologian, offering only a lengthy and exhaustive, painful and exhilarating pilgrimage thru ministries. I
am convinced that the legacy of public ministry lies in its finding
a conceptual and theological base that is congruent with the other
ministries and they with it. So, just as the case study method--
which I have used for years--becomes self-evident, I affirm the need
for a constructive theology that performs the old-fashioned tasks of
clarifying the questions and continually critiquing the answers. I
am, as always, out of tune, but this time trusting my own religious
musicality, for me necessarily in ongoing congruence with my caring
and justice ministries. Confused or perceptive? Probably both.
But it is the conceptual task which intrigues and in which I place
a vulnerable hope. Where do you place yours?

A Peculiar Sensitivity Toward Finitude

In my own ways, I have been faithful to the sixties and
to my brothers, colleagues, of public ministries past. I offer up
my ongoingness, in principle and concept. I learn that I must be
responsible regardless of the state of my own identity, self or
state of anxiety, and whether or not I am ready. Ultimately, the
autobiography shapes and, for me, the autobiography is one with
twenty years of pilgrimage in ministry. I find that I keep correcting the analytic of public ministry so that our legacy of public
responsibility and participation might go on; and that it is necessary in the process to suggest correctives of all those that appear
to be our legacy but have incorporated the basic faultiness of our
analytic. As of today, it takes a threefold affirmation.

POST-SELF-CONSCIOUS FINITUDE.

I can now remember my public ministries days as an expression of my concern for the *pre*-self-conscious finitude of others
those whose identities and social roles are imposed upon them and my
commitment that they find self and their group's own consciousness.
I found this continuity in the liberation movements: a movement
always toward intrinsic rather than derivative identity, and in my
therapeutic endeavors: that *this* self find its own source and being
Here I could experience an integrity between my caring and my justic

ministries. My anger arises when "others" seek to establish the limits, boundaries, allowed experiences of a person or a group. I rage at injustice and prophetically lift up its many instances; I live in pain and mutual lack of freedom with those who are oppressed.

ALL of my ministries are rooted in a stance that opposes pre-self-conscious finitude. As self- and group-consciousness occurs, I celebrate; mine occurs, too; we share the joys and pains for the boundaries that had defined us no longer hold; even, sometimes, the centers themselves shake. And yet, beyond the points of celebration, can readily occur a new emergent, a post-self-conscious arrogance or new alienation from any sense of whole. We move so easily from being too tightly bound and rooted by another's definition to the exultation of being rooted only in our own, insulation from any broader sense of the human. From having no control, there comes the delicate moment when one takes control of oneself. The Self becomes norm in its unfettered potentiality; "man" comes Of Age; groups of selves with varying likenesses view themselves or are viewed by others as The New Liberators; "the other" (and The Other) exist only for me and mine, are to blame for my continuing oppression, are to be viewed as enemy; all structuring, other than my own, is denied. And this, too, commonly roots my therapies and liberation endeavors. Post-self-conscious arrogance needs no "other," persons, institution, culture, god. Illusions of control abound, exhilaration of boundless energies, yes, alternating with depths of despair. For the individual, the isolation of unmet expectation may be transmuted into a series of therapeutic communities, instantly attained, left without "excessive mourning." For groups, there may occur explosions into the public arena on behalf of My People. Only.

I find another integrity: I do battle against post-self-conscious arrogance precisely as against pre-self-conscious finitude. I find that I possess a critical principle that cuts thru the multiplicity of my ministries. And, in my search for clarifying principles, I find that I stand for post-self-conscious finitude: the historic Faith that affirms the self and its emergence within only the limits of its recognition that it (I, We) is (am, are) not God.

I remember my public ministries days as a series of Palm Sundays, riding in glory on our asses, totally unprepared for what followed. The dynamic seems so right to me:

First, You (you) are God (god); I grovel before you for I am nobody. You (you) tell me my identity; I will not question, however deep the suffering.

Second, NO! I am Somebody. Edging easily into: I am God; We are God; There is no Other.

Third, YES! We are Selves, Rich Groupings. But we live in a complex history which we do not control. I (We) are not God. You are.

The classically simple Christian affirmation, I am not God, arises from my ministries, even as it finds me ongoingly embedded

within them. For as I battle for self-consciousness, so, too, do
I do battle for the self-consciousness of finitude, for a view of
the world that gives up illusions of control, holds onto wonder,
mystery and a sense of the holy, and in that spirit welcomes the
world and is *always* about the tasks of embodying care and justice
amongst it. On the one hand, how is one to bow down if one has not
already stood up? But, on the other, what does history say to those
who try to stand with eyes unfocused except upon the Self?
        The critical issue, then, is the delicacy of the defini-
tions of those points where post-self-consciousness slips into
arrogance and needs critique...a task of therapist and organizer
alike. The critique, offered prematurely, or from the outside, remains oppressive; the principles of its use must at least include
a sense of timing and of mutuality/participation over time. But not
raised up, and only self or group defined, the illusion remains un-
clarified and the analytic of the sixties has not yet found its
critique.
        Along with such a critical delicacy emerge some tonal
qualities, a sense of the holy or religious musicality, perhaps, or
"second naivete," or even "wisdom." We may not be as far removed
from them as we think.
        And we find, perhaps, a shift in the dynamics of anger,
leading to cynicism, arrogance, inevitable disappointment and with-
drawal or explosions, into some profoundly human experiences of
sadness, perhaps, or humility. But we are not talking about an
Eastern orientation. Post-self-consciousness is inevitably Western.
We affirm the valuation of self- and group-consciousness, of the
insights of modernity, certainly, as we will see, of history. But
we seek to repossess, as right for us, that crucial and perceptive
historic and religious insight of our Faith: I (We) am not God;
You are. I am willing to try out this tonal quality as an alternative in which to root our ongoing work, our forever continuity,
of being about public ministries. We may not, then, burn out so
fast and go away, accuse one another of "copping out," withdraw and
explode, live cynically and in a continual state of transitoriness.
We look again to see the slow and complex movements of history and
society, and offer respect for the Gargantuan tasks of shaping the
human self who can never be announced, whether by foe or friend.

A PECULIAR SENSIBILITY TO DETERMINISMS.
        My deepest regret of the sixties remains the ease with
which I let go my experiential and substantive knowledge about the
complex dynamics of change. I forgot to expect to find *at least* my
own intransigence in others and in what I envisioned for them,
whether "enemy" or friend. I forgot my own peculiarity of having
generally friendly relationships with the given, to be taken seriously even as they are moved through. I forgot that meaning, change,
possibility, limits--all occur in an undulating context of personal
and cultural history which provides structural realities not easily
transgressed. I forgot that my Faith was also about this; indeed
was centered in a classical perception that God's choice of human
history and human form gave shape to this complex of determinisms
about which we can be "appreciatively aware" and respectful even as
the human spirit struggles forever with their interrelated boundaries

and gifts. This, too, has come to root my caring and my justice
ministries. For example:

1. The processes of actualizing choice carry a No with every
    Yes, and responsibility goes with each. Our sensitivity
    to the Nos was transmuted in our Western, masculine anal-
    ytic.

2. The tenaciousness of resistance to change is a part of
    givenness, intrinsic in the complexities of history and
    not accidental. Victories are always occasions for further
    working through; implementation may require a different
    sensibility and set of skills than the stimulation of
    awareness.

3. A respect for human limitation is correlative with an
    affirmation of human dignity. Without that, we cannot
    care for the neutrality or intransigence of biology or be
    just ourselves with those who refuse change. The classical
    affirmation of God's unconditioned love and forgiveness
    cannot enter into our own practicalities of ministry.

4. We easily remain unaware of the shaping of our own Nos and
    hence resistant to critique of our most cherished self-
    evidents. I wonder, sometimes, what are the analogues of
    cure by bleeding that affect my own strategies of being
    about care and justice. Perhaps it is the assumption that
    words and emotional expression cure, and my related dis-
    respect for the determinisms of body chemistry and the
    workings of the human brain about which we appear to remain
    in almost total ignorance.

        Does this perspective immobilize, remove one from the
scenes of action? Not at all--and certainly not when viewed in relation to what happened to us of the sixties when we did not get our
own ways; or in relation to the dynamic toward narcissism that
seems to pervade the workings out of the anxiety ontology. I find
that this peculiar sensibility keeps me hanging in there: a humble
perspective on givenness that frees my aspirations and roots my
ministries. Here, here, o my people, I am present with you, even
as You are Present with us.

A Peculiar Avoidance of Blame.

        If one is to be in control of history, the tendency is to
blame all who resist one's dynamic and the fulfillment of one's own
vision. Jew or male, white or corporate structure, mother or spouse
--all, in our subtle or gross analyses separate us from our own responsibility and complicity. Our very analyses separate us, for I
may be aware of your role in my life but you have not been a part
of my process of understanding and you leave when I lay it upon you.
Yet you and I, ultimately, have no choice but to work it out together.
Our analytics do not prepare leadership or conceptualization for
these social roles. We denegrate those few who continue to affirm

them. Our analytic affirms separation toward the end of "later" integration; does history validate such a perspective?
   Ironically, I find that I give up too much for the luxury of having you as my enemy; that it so diminishes me that I may not be ready for you even when you are. Without such a perspective, I fear for "the public" and "the human" (even as concept; I recognize their insubstantiality as substance) in a pluralistic world. Which, of course, it has always been. Only our rampant ahistoricism, which appears to free us to be in control of history, would view this as a new insight into the workings of the social order. Again, our history of public participation without such a base is spotty at best. And with it I have continued to do my battles: with straights, on behalf of gays; with men, on behalf of women; with whites, on behalf of ourselves as well as the minorities of our Western cultures and the majorities of peoples of the world. But I do battle in love and a profound sense of mutuality, of knowing my own complicity; and why, after all, should I expect others to be less intransigent, more open to change, more self-giving, less bound or more hopeful than myself?
   For it is always in the midst of finitude, determinisms, complicity that the Christian affirms, lives, goes about ministries. Herein our Psalms of joy arise, our miracles of meeting with the Stranger, our claiming of the Cross as way of life and experiences of Resurrection as within the histories of our own lives. And so we are strengthened to take the hands of strangers and walk with them and stand there, not in arrogance, when they go away. And we are sustained both to proclaim and to work out the visions--as our forever ministries.

We Are Simply Asked

   Peter Bryne is a Jesuit who invited Us to his ordination with these words:

> We are simply asked
> to make gentle our bruised world
> to be compassionate of all
> including oneself
> then, in the time left over
> to repeat the ancient tale
> and go the way
> of God's foolish ones.

   I accept the invitation, in memory...and hope.

NOTES AND REFERENCES

1. Carl Rogers, *On Personal Power* (New York: Delacourt Press: 1977), pp. 270-71.

NOTES ABOUT THE CONTRIBUTORS

JAMES LUTHER ADAMS is Professor Emeritus of Divinity, Harvard University. He was previously a member of the Ethics and Society field in the Divinity School of the University of Chicago. In addition to his authorship of many articles and contributions to books, he is the author of *Taking Time Seriously* (1957), *Paul Tillich's Philosophy of Culture, Science, and Religion* (1965), *On Being Human Religiously* (1976), and co-editor of *Pastoral Care in the Liberal Churches* (1970).

ALAN B. ANDERSON is Professor of Interdisciplinary Studies at Wilberforce University. He was previously a member of the Ethics and Society field in the Divinity School of the University of Chicago. He is co-author of *Pastoral Ministry and the Life of the Priest: A Research Report* (1969) and editor of *Desegregation and Chicago Public Schools: Issues and Options* (1976).

ROBERT BENNE is Professor of Church and Society at the Lutheran School of Theology at Chicago. He is author of *Wandering in the Wilderness* (1972), co-author of *Defining America: A Christian Critique of the American Dream* (1974), and a contributor to several volumes.

BERNARD OWEN BROWN is Coordinator of Ministerial Studies and Assistant Professor of Ethics and Society in the Divinity School of the University of Chicago. He also serves as Associate Dean of Rockefeller Memorial Chapel. He is the author of *Ideology and Community Action: The West Side Organization of Chicago, 1964-67* (1978).

DON S. BROWNING is Professor of Religion and Psychological Studies in the Divinity School and Dean of Disciples Divinity House of the University of Chicago. He is the author of *Atonement and Psychotherapy* (1966), *Generative Man* (1973), *The Moral Context of Pastoral Care* (1976), and numerous papers in the field of religion and the psychological studies.

J. RONALD ENGEL is Associate Professor of Social Ethics at Meadville/Lombard Theological School. He contributed an essay to *Belonging and Alienation* (1976). His "Sydney E. Mead's Tragic Theology of the Republic" was published in the *Journal of the American Academy of Religion* in 1976.

JOHN HALL FISH is a member of the faculty of the Urban Studies Program of the Associated Colleges of the Midwest. He is author of *Black Power/White Control* (1973) and co-author of *The Edge of the Ghetto* (1968). He has also contributed an essay to *Belonging and Alienation* (1976) and has published several papers.

FRANKLIN I. GAMWELL is Philanthropic Associate with Rockefeller Family and Associates. His "Reinhold Niebuhr's Theistic Ethic" was published in the *Journal of Religion* in 1974.

PHILIP HEFNER is Professor of Systematic Theology at the Lutheran School of Theology at Chicago. He is author of *Faith and the Vitalities of History* (1966) and *The Promise of Teilhard* (1970), co-author of *Defining America: A Christian Critique of the American Dream* (1974), editor and translator of *Three Essays by Albrecht Ritschl* (1972), co-editor of *Belonging and Alienation: Religious Foundations for the Human Future* (1976), contributor to several volumes, and author of numerous papers.

PAUL HEYNE is Lecturer in Economics, University of Washington and Adjunct Faculty Member, Center for Urban Studies of Fairhaven, College, Western Washington State. He is author of *The Christian Encounters the World of Economics* (1965),

Private Keepers of the Public Interest (1968), *The Economic Way of Thinking* (1973, 2nd edition, 1976) and co-author of *Toward Economic Understanding* (1976).

JOSEPH M. KITAGAWA is Dean and Professor of History of Religions, the University of Chicago Divinity School. He is author of *Religions of the East* (1960), *Gibt es ein Verstehen fremder Religionen?* (1963) and *Religion in Japanese History* (1965), co-editor of *The History of Religions: Essays in Methodology* (1959), and author of numerous papers in the area of the history of religions.

CLARK KUCHEMAN is Professor of Christian Ethics at Claremont Men's College and Claremont Graduate School. He was previously a member of the faculty of the Ethics and Society field in the Divinity School of the University of Chicago. He is a contributor to *Social Ethics: Issues in Ethics and Society* (1968) and the author of several papers.

LOWELL LIVEZEY is the Executive Vice-President of the World Without War Council.

BERNARD M. LOOMER is Professor of Philosophical Theology at the Graduate Theological Union. He was Dean of the Federated Theological Faculty of the University of Chicago at the time the Ethics and Society field was constituted. He is a contributor to *Process Theology* (1971), *Religious Experience and Process Theology* (1976), and author of numerous papers published in both theological and philosophical journals.

PETER PARIS is Associate Professor of Ethics and Society in the Divinity School of Vanderbilt University. He is the author of *Black Leaders in Conflict* (1978).

E. SPENCER PARSONS is Dean of Rockefeller Chapel, the University of Chicago, and Associate Professor of Church and Society in the Divinity School of the University of Chicago. He is author of *Christian Yes -- Or No* (1963) and of numerous papers.

GEORGE W. PICKERING is Associate Professor of Social Ethics at the University of Detroit. He is a contributor to *Technology, Values and Education* (1971) and *Desegregation and Chicago Public Schools* (1976) and has published numerous papers.

W. WIDICK SCHROEDER is Professor of Religion and Society at the Chicago Theological Seminary. In earlier time he was a member of the Ethics and Society field of the Federated Theological Faculty of the University of Chicago, and in recent years has frequently served as Visiting Lecturer in the Divinity School. He is author of *Cognitive Structure and Religious Research* (1970), co-author of *Religion in American Culture: Unity and Diversity in a Midwestern County* (1964), *Where Do I Stand? Living Theological Options for Contemporary Christians* (1973) and *Suburban Religion: Churches and Synagogues in the American Experience* (1974), co-editor of *Belonging and Alienation: Religious Foundations for the Human Future* (1976), a contributor to several volumes, and author of numerous papers in both theological and social scientific journals.

DOUGLAS STURM is Presidential Professor of Political Science and Religion at Bucknell University. He is a contributor to *Law and Philosophy: Readings in Legal Philosophy* (1970) and to *Theology and the Church in a Time of Change* (1970) and the author of several papers published in both theological and legal journals.

ROBERT TERRY is a partner in the consulting firm, Organizational Leadership, Inc. He is the author of *For Whites Only* (1970) and several papers. He also has contributed papers for the in-service training program of the Madison Public Schools.

PEGGY ANN WAY is a member of the faculty in the area of pastoral theology and counseling in the Divinity School of Vanderbilt University. She is the author of several papers.

GIBSON WINTER is Professor of Christianity and Society at Princeton Theological Seminary. From 1956 through 1975 he was a member of the Ethics and Society field of the Divinity School of the University of Chicago. He is the author of *Love and Conflict: New Patterns in Family Life* (1958), *The Suburban Captivity of the Churches* (1961), *The New Creation as Metropolis* (1963), *Elements for a Social Ethic* (1966), *Religious Identity* (1968), and *Being Free: Reflections on America's Cultural Revolution* (1970), editor of *Social Ethics: Issues in Ethics and Society* (1968), contributor to several volumes, and author of many papers.

STUDIES IN RELIGION AND SOCIETY

edited by

Thomas C. Campbell, W. Alvin Pitcher,
W. Widick Schroeder and Gibson Winter

Other CSSR Publications in the Series:

Bernard O. Brown, *Ideology and Community Action:
The West Side Organization of Chicago, 1964-67* (1978)

Philip Hefner and W. Widick Schroeder, eds., *Belonging and Alienation:
Religious Foundations for the Human Future* (1976)

Paul E. Kraemer, *Awakening from the American Dream: The Human Rights
Movement in the United States Assessed during a
Crucial Decade, 1960-1970* (1973)

William C. Martin, *Christians in Conflict* (1972)

Victor Obenhaus, *And See the People* (1968)

W. Widick Schroeder, Victor Obenhaus, Larry A. Jones, and
Thomas Sweetser, SJ, *Suburban Religion: Churches
and Synagogues in the American Experience* (1974)

Walter M. Stuhr, Jr., *The Public Style: A Study
of the Community Participation of Protestant Ministers* (1972)

Thomas P. Sweetser, SJ, *The Catholic Parish: Shifting
Membership in a Changing Church* (1974)

Lawrence Witmer, ed., *Issues in Community Organization* (1972)

Order from your bookstore or the Center for the Scientific Study of Religion

Other Books in the Series:

Thomas C. Campbell and Yoshio Fukuyama, *The Fragmented
Layman* (1970)

John Fish, *Black Power/White Control: The Struggle
of the Woodlawn Organization in Chicago* (1973)

John Fish, Gordon Nelson, Walter M. Stuhr, Jr., and Lawrence Witmer
The Edge of the Ghetto (1968)

W. Widick Schroeder and Victor Obenhaus,
Religion in American Culture (1964)

Gibson Winter, *Religious Identity* (1968)

Order from your bookstore